A Spirituality that Secularizes

Volume 1

Discerning the Trajectory of the Spirit In the Old Testament

Emerito P. Nacpil

Edited by Florita V. Miranda

Abingdon Press
Nashville

A SPIRITUALITY THAT SECULARIZES

VOLUME I
DISCERNING THE TRAJECTORY OF THE SPIRIT
IN THE OLD TESTAMENT

This edition published by Abingdon Press 2015

ISBN 978-16308-8837-4

Library of Congress Cataloging-in-Publication Data has been requested.

15 16 17 18 19 20 21 22 23 24 – 10 9 8 7 6 5 4 3 2 1
MANUFACTURED IN THE UNITED STATES OF AMERICA

To
Wesleyan College of Manila
for uniting piety and learning

Contents

Editor's Note . . . vii
Foreword: Chief Justice Reynato Puno (retired) . . . ix
Preface . . . xiii
Chapter I: In Search of a Spirituality That Secularizes . . . 1
1. Living in an Intolerably Complicated World . . . 1
2. The Need for a New Vision for Life . . . 7
3. The Secularizing Movement . . . 10
Chapter II: The Spirit in Creation as Secular . . . 20
1. The Sweep and Depth of the Spirit's Work . . . 20
2. The Creation of Possibility out of Non-Possibility . . . 25
3. Actualizing the Possible by the Word . . . 27
4. The Sovereignty of God in Creation . . . 30
5. The Emergence of Life as Gift . . . 32
6. Creation by "Letting Be" . . . 34
7. Creation Is Good . . . 37
Chapter III: Life in the Spirit as Secular . . . 42
1. The Life-Giving Spirit . . . 43
2. The Spirit and the Human Form . . . 46
3. The Spirit and Human Life . . . 50
4. The Distinctively Human Features . . . 53
5. Nature and the Human in the Spirit . . . 57
Chapter IV: Life-Together in the Spirit . . . 67
1. The Issue of Life-Together . . . 67
2. The Making of a People . . . 69
3. The Spirit and Crisis . . . 73
4. The Spirit and Law . . . 82

Chapter V: Judgment and Secularization 97
1. The Awareness of Good and Evil 98
2. This, but Not That: Between Permission and Prohibition 100
Chapter VI: Covenant and Judgment 121
1. *Religare* and Covenant 121
2. Covenant as Criterion for Confession and Judgment 125
3. Yahweh or Baal? 131
4. Prophetic Judgment 137
5. The Judgment of God 143
Chapter VII: Renewal: Between Creation and Salvation 158
1. The Possibility of Renewal 159
2. The Act of Renewal and Salvation 168
Chapter VIII: Wisdom as a Form of Secularity 182
1. A New Challenge to Israel's Faith 182
2. Wisdom Is Fear of the Lord 183
3. Secular Features of Wisdom 185
4. Wisdom and the Moral Order 187
5. The Underside of Wisdom: Job 192
6. Wisdom and the Search for God 197
7. Revelation in Dialogue 199
8. Revelation by Interrogation 201
9. Creation and the Moral Issue 211
10. Wisdom in Cul-de-Sac: Qoheleth 214
Chapter IX: The Secular Dimensions of Israel's Hope
I—Apocalyptic Hope 226
1. Setting Up the Issue 226
2. Apocalypticism as a Literary Genre 229
3. Historical Apocalyptic 234
4. Heavenly Apocalyptic 251
Chapter X: The Secular Dimensions of Israel's Hope
II—Messianic Hope 261
1. The Problem 261
2. The Beginning of a Solution 264
3. Israel's Experience of Kingship 266
4. God Himself Shall Be the Good Shepherd 277
5. Prophetic Messianic Hope 284
6. Hope: Between Promise and Fulfillment 288
Epilogue 291
Bibliography 296

Editor's Note

In my early days as a Christian I realized that when faith moves mountains one has to deal with the rubble. Bishop Nacpil's book *A Spirituality That Secularizes* challenged me to wrestle with my own questions of faith, eventually moving mountains of doubts and ultimately clearing away the rubble of sheer credulity.

Back then, I was taught the divine can never be secular, and treating the secular as divine is outright profanity. My conviction was firmly grounded in the belief that the secular and spiritual are by no means foundationally or otherwise relational, bonded, and united. And I unreservedly embraced this belief. Religion widened the breach between the spiritual and the secular into a gaping chasm.

My "eureka" moment came when the task of editing Bishop Nacpil's book was given to me. The inherent connectedness between creator and creation is made more concrete and decipherable. As the bishop and I discussed each word, each sentence, in each and every page of his book, it dawned on me that this book is about you and me!

We are all longing for that elusive and unfathomable something that strengthens our relationship with our Creator. This book delves into the nature of our relationship with God. God, as our God, and we, as his people, have an unbreakable bond—the religaric bond as Bishop Nacpil aptly calls it, the Spirit that secularizes. For the first time, I see how the Spirit at work empowers us from within for us to make choices that promote, preserve, and enrich the good of God's creation. This is exactly how God wants us to live! Devoid of the Spirit, we end up energetically floating above our vessel of clay rather than fully living in it, overwhelmed, oversaturated, and robotic in our mania to succeed—lost in a limbo leading to chronic drain.

A Spirituality That Secularizes emanates wholeness in an erratic frenzy of vibes and movements we call daily living. It makes meaningful the otherwise tireless and ceaseless to-and-fro of mindless survival and meaningless existence.

Bishop Nacpil's book is an affirmation of God's faithfulness to himself and to his creation in the adamantine and unbreakable bond—the religaric bond, the Spirit that secularizes. Bishop Nacpil's profound and exceptional insights (although very cerebral) transformed my understanding of Christianity!

How amazing and uplifting it is to know and embrace the fact that all the good of what we are doing in the secular world is our active participation in the work of the Spirit. In Bishop Nacpil's words, "creating, sustaining, and flourishing life" as a community of believers! Even the bad that we do comes under the judging and "winnowing" of the Spirit. Just as I thought that the social fabric holding individuals together is vanishing, this book gives me the complete turnaround—a validation of being connected to one another and to our Creator in a very concrete and visible level that we humans understand and can relate to. Now the chasm has been bridged! Truly the spiritual and the secular are inseparable! The Spirit is the ground of meaning that permeates and completes everything, working from within and allowing us to accept the degree of vulnerability and uncertainty that describes the gift of freedom through God's unconditional love! God's faithfulness is amazing!

I am deeply grateful to Bishop Nacpil for the privilege of editing this book. His palpable wisdom paved the way for a perfect union of opposing minds in *coincidentia oppositorum*! It is not about our imperfections, it is about God's work in us and our participation in God's work. Nacpil, the intellectual giant, philosopher, and theologian, writes with logical clarity and explicitness aiming at genuine change of view coming from within, enabling readers to be believers through the workings of their own intellect!

Florita V. Miranda

Foreword

I have just bought Prof. Luc Ferry's book titled *A Brief History of Thought*, touted as "the phenomenal international bestseller." The French professor was lucidly explaining in his slim book the essence of the teachings of the major philosophies from the Greeks, Christianity, Enlightenment, existentialism and postmodernism. Like other chronicles of philosophy, Ferry's book discomfited me for as I reached its end, the impression I got is that Christianity is losing its grip as the better worldview to postmodernism.

For centuries, the foundation of Christianity has been subjected to bashing by such gigantic thinkers like Plato, Aristotle, Kant, Rousseau, Descartes, Marx, and Nietzsche who takes pride in proclaiming himself as the "anti-Christ" and as "immoralist par excellence." The velocity and vigor of these blows are growing with the entry into center stage of outstanding biologists, anthropologists, mathematicians, physicists, and other scientists led by Richard Dawkins, all redefining the meaning of being human, all rethinking the idea of salvation, all pushing for a world without cosmos, all purveying a universe without divinity, all proclaiming salvation without a Savior. To say the least, these are devastating ideas to Christians, especially to Christians unfamiliar with the esoterics of theology. I am certain that believers crave a refutation of all anti-Christian philosophies but they are terrorized by the fear, that personally tangling with these titans in a debate is like engaging them in an intellectual jujitsu with an amputated arm. Christians need a white knight, somebody with similar eyes but who sees differently, possessed with the same brain but who thinks differently, equipped with more than the five senses, one with a firm traction on theology that will allow him to negotiate its slippery slopes and smash the seductions of wayward philosophies. Amid God's troublemakers, enter God's troubleshooter, Bishop Emerito P. Nacpil.

Bishop Nacpil is coming out with a three-volume magnum opus, titled *A Spirituality That Secularizes.* Its volume 1 is all about "Discerning the Trajectory of the Spirit iIn the Old Testament." Volumes 2 and 3 are still in the writing stage. In the preface to the first volume of his book, Bishop Nacpil revealed the reason that induced him to come out with his "claims." The reason resonates to many Christians who are bothered by a perspective, both religious and nonreligious, that is increasingly out of sync with the God of grace, love, peace, mercy—the God of creation and the creature.

Bishop Nacpil expressed the fear of every believer: "The flow in the tide of secularization unleashed by the Enlightenment and the rise of modern science and technology shows no sign of ebbing or slowing down. In fact, it is gaining more strength and momentum by the so-called postmodern developments." Vis-á-vis the threat of these tsunamis, Bishop Nacpil then observed that "this tide of secularization" cannot be made to ebb by opposing it with a "traditional Christian spirituality that seems determined to fossilize." He submits that Christianity has to reinvent itself "in a way that it can become much bigger and deeper and more pervasive than the secularization and the civilization that it spawns." As he sees it, the problem with this torrent of secularization is how "to respect it, permeate it, embrace and value it as it truly is, and make it part of its inclusiveness, integrity and truth!" Significantly, this spiritual vision from Bishop Nacpil is punctuated by an exclamation point. The exclamation point captures the brilliance of Bishop Nacpil's thesis that further postulates a perspective on spirituality that is "a necessary corrective to traditional spirituality." To be sure, his thesis will shock the traditional doorkeepers of our faith. He forewarns: "Its impact would be like new wine tearing apart old wineskin."

Bishop Nacpil has never been easy to understand by believers with a Pepe and Pilar comprehension of the Scriptures. But what will compel the reader of his book to hang on to every syllable and polysyllable of his thesis is its fresh originality, its boldness to traverse the boundaries of old religion, its cutting critique of some doctrines of religion that reason and common sense can no longer defend, and its dismissal of some too-far-out musings of postmodernism while generously conceding to both protagonists their contribution to the difficult and endless effort to explain God, creation, creature, life herein, and life hereafter. Bishop Nacpil discusses many of their thesis and antithesis and comes out with a synthesis that is comforting to Christians. His new submissions cannot but strengthen their flabby and flagging faith undergoing heavy battering in a world getting to idolize technology without theology. He achieves his objective by positing what he humbly calls "claims" as he explains the hitherto unexamined role of the Spirit in "creation, judgment, in blessing and in the promise of salvation, all of which has a secular thrust," hence, the book's title, the *A Spirituality That Secularizes*. In this monumental effort, Bishop Nacpil has to excise from our subconscious centuries of religious thought whose effect is "to reduce the work of the Spirit to the narrow confines of personal piety, religious communities, and institutional religion" which "would leave large tracts of reality and human experiences outside of the realm of the Spirit." Bishop Nacpil condemns the error "as an insult, a grievous sin, against the Spirit that cannot be forgiven."

But even while Bishop Nacpil appears to be overwhelming in his submissions about the Spirit, especially about its function as the "religaric" bond between God and his creation, he announces that he is not yet done in awakening us out of our spiritual stupor. He has just started "discerning the trajectory of the Spirit in the Old Testament." He then warned: "It is obvious that my treatment of this kind of spirituality is still incomplete. When we come to the New Testament—which is the subject of the next volume—what we discover here is more radical and far-reaching than we have so far envisioned. Without the New Testament thrust, our treatment of the subject would be at best only a half truth."

And so hold your breath. The best of Bishop Nacpil is yet to come. His book *A Spirituality That Secularizes* is a must read for believers whose faith is falling apart. I said before that Bishop Nacpil is God's gift to the Filipino people. I say that again.

Chief Justice Reynato S. Puno *(retired)*

Preface

For as long as I can remember I have felt uncomfortable about preaching and practicing a spirituality that seemed opposed to the secular and its stuff of the material, the natural, the earthly, the biological, the this-worldly, the human, and the social and cultural. I was raised as a Christian in an atmosphere in which any obvious tendency to appreciate the this-worldly was considered unchristian and was therefore proscribed. This unease intensified as I began my calling as a pastor and as a teacher of Christianity. I began to appreciate more keenly the toil, the struggle, the intelligence, and the energy (even the pain) that church people put in making a worthwhile life in this world (which is their world) when there is no other life and there is no other world than the ones that are given! Moreover, the spirituality that they are inwardly constrained to appreciate and practice does not seem to lend them foundational support and vital inspiration since, on supposedly biblical and Christian grounds, it normatively opposes their effort to live an earthly but worthy human life with an anti-worldly perspective and a decidedly pro-heavenly religiosity!

Moreover, the flow in the tide of secularization unleashed by the Enlightenment and the rise of modern science and technology shows no sign of ebbing or slowing down. In fact, it is gaining more strength and momentum because of the so-called postmodern developments. These postmodern features include the deconstruction and relativization of thinking, thought, and action; the pluralization and multiculturalization of social relations; the truncation and fragmentation of language and communication into bits and pieces that can be flashed momentarily on the tube, or abbreviated into ciphers that can be squeezed into a cell phone and its many variants, thus preventing the grasp of things and events and trends in the form of full and grammatical sentences in which reality and its truth can be understood with some clarity and so be the basis for responsible action; the algorithmic but dynamic complexification of life and its stuff and conditions as they evolve into a multi-diversity one cannot predict or plan for in the long term; the inescapable technologization of the human life-world in which technique, tools, gadgets procedures, chemicals and drugs—with their rapid obsolescence and turnover—determine the way we live and work and celebrate, including what is enjoyed in the bed in one's own private bedroom! All these are being spread and shared on a global scale radically affecting all peoples and wreaking havoc on their traditions and habits without a global vision that could steer them forward except what seems right in their own light!

It is this complicated secular milieu that is now the unavoidable environment of contemporary life. Could this tide of secularization be made to ebb by opposing it with a spirituality that retreats into its own hardened shell like a turtle that is contented to swim in the safety of the shoreline instead of launching out into the dangerous deep with its wild currents? To do so would surely be self-defeating for a traditional Christian spirituality that seems determined to fossilize! There are sectors of Christianity that are dead set in fighting secularity as "an enemy." In my considered judgment they will be killed by the "enemy" instead of killing the enemy. Unless, of course, Christianity can reinvent itself more as a vital spirituality than as an institutional religion in a way that it can become much bigger and deeper and more pervasive than the secularization movement and the civilization that it spawns, and be able to respect it, permeate it, embrace it, and value it as it truly is, and make it an essential part of its inclusiveness, integrity, and truth! Moreover, to reduce the work of the Spirit to the narrow confines of personal piety, religious communities, and institutional religion would leave large tracts of reality and human experience outside of the realm of the Spirit. That seems to me an insult, a grievous sin, against the Spirit that cannot be forgiven.

When I mention such a possibility of discerning a bigger and deeper and more pervasive spiritual vision in sermons, lectures, and Bible studies to laypeople actively engaged with the world, they raise their eyebrows in quizzical doubt. After all, what they hear is different from what they habitually expect from a preacher, let alone a bishop! And what has to be changed is so deeply entrenched as a spiritual habit in the culture that it seems impossible to make a dent in it. And for so long they seemed to be on track in their doubt; they still are. I dared not challenge them, for I had nothing with which to challenge them. I had no handle on the issue at the time and did not know what would work, although I never gave up thinking about it!

What eventually quickened me to plunge into doing something about the issue, with the thought that one does not really get to know what to do unless one simply goes about doing something about it, is the poignant plea of so many of the present generation—mostly young people and young professionals—that they want to be spiritual without being religious, that they want to be human without necessarily believing in a god or God or being members of a religious group or institution. But I asked myself the question: Does that also mean that they can be spiritual without being secular? I do not think so! What I hear in their plea is that they want a spirituality that would enable them to remain being genuinely secular and be clear in conscience about it! Certainly they have no wish of reducing spirituality to secularity or vice versa. That raised the issue of whether it is possible to discern a vision of spirituality large enough to respect, permeate, affirm, and embrace the secular as a blessing to humankind.

The following pages are an initial attempt to discern such a spiritual vision along the lines indicated by a reading of Holy Scriptures. Not being a biblical scholar, I have availed myself of the expertise of biblical interpreters. My debt to them is so much greater than the acknowledgment made in the footnotes. But my theological musings—especially when they seem biblically out of sync—are to be attributed to my failure or fault. This volume traces the trajectory of the Spirit in the Old Testament. A second volume will do the same with the New Testament. A final volume will deal with the practice of a spirituality that secularizes.

I discussed some earlier versions of the manuscript with my Monday morning Bible study class of pastors and with my students in the doctor of ministry program of Wesley Divinity School. The purpose was to gauge whether the viewpoint of the book would resonate with them and the congregations they serve. The response was that the perspective on spirituality represented here is a necessary corrective to traditional spirituality, but that it would be difficult to share it with their people because its impact would be like new wine tearing apart old wineskins. The Reverend Dr. Jeremias Resus, who has served congregations in the United States and is now a retired minister of the Presbyterian Church U.S.A. has read the whole manuscript in its final version while on vacation in the Philippines. His suggestions for improving the manuscript have been incorporated. His verdict is more or less the same as that of my Bible study class of pastors and graduate students. Their evaluation may in fact be on target, and I am deeply grateful to them for sharing it with me. But that would all the more encourage me to share with a wider public my view of a spirituality that secularizes for whatever worth it may have. The retired chief justice of the Supreme Court of the Philippines, Justice Reynato Puno, a devout Christian and a layleader in The United Methodist Church, has done the author the honor not only of reading the manuscript but of writing a foreword to the book. I am deeply grateful to him. Another lay leader of The United Methodist Church, Judge Benjamin Turgano, read the manuscript.

For his encouragement and comments I am deeply grateful. It is not for the author to say that he has succeeded in accomplishing the task he has set for himself. But if this initial effort can inspire others to take some steps along the same direction, that would already be a blessing to be grateful for!

Writing and preparing the manuscript for publication were greatly assisted and facilitated by the competent editorial work of Dr. Florita V. Miranda, president of Wesleyan College of Manila who has specialized in English. More than merely doing the editing, she gently and patiently pushed me into clarifying my own obscure musings and made me express them in readable and comprehensible English. She fulfilled the role of an incisive, probing partner in intellectual dialogue. Whatever obscurity in thought and infelicity of language remain are certainly due to my stubbornness. To her I owe a depth of gratitude that is more than words can express. I also want to thank Ms. Analyn S. Burgos, who was assigned by the college to encode in her computer several handwritten drafts of the manuscript and get it ready for publication. I am also deeply grateful to my wife, Angelina, and daughter, Cynthia, for understanding that I could not join them in vacations and other occasions where I should have been present because of the need to finish the manuscript on schedule under the pressure of old age!

Emerito P. Nacpil
Wesleyan College of Manila

CHAPTER I

In Search of a Spirituality That Secularizes

1. Living in an Intolerably Complicated World

Many people around the world are finding that living in today's world is becoming more and more intolerably difficult. The difficulty comes not only from problems themselves that are increasingly hard to sort out and find a solution to, but also from the deeply felt inability to deal successfully with them. This sense of inability generates paralyzing anxiety, and thus makes the problems more threatening and harder to deal with. The threats to life in today's world are more alarmingly ominous than ever before.

Some of the threatening problems are chronic and endemic, and so are perennial. But they have become global as well, requiring global understanding, global effort in dealing with them, and global solutions that have to be thought out globally but enacted and applied locally. The problem of poverty, for example, is chronic, endemic, perennial, and has become global. None of the solutions appear to make a dent in dealing with it. The enormous increase in population and the corresponding increase of consumption of goods and services have brought the demand and supply levels beyond the carrying capacity of the earth and its environmental resources.

Moreover, the carrying capacity of the earth is being irreplenishably diminished by the deleterious human impact upon it. And so the scarcity of resources will continue to increase, and any herculean effort to overcome this deterioration and depletion through development and technology to increase production and make distribution more even can take place only within the parameters of scarcity and eventual exhaustibility, if nothing is done adequately to stem this slide toward inevitable destruction.

These parameters are further problematized by injustice and greed and corruption in the social systems that are severely parochial and ideological. They do not have the wherewithal to deal with social and economic injustice on a global scale. The destructive impact upon local economies of global economic meltdowns precipitate a chain of dislocation and enormous loss, wreaking havoc to whatever development gains have been achieved. This havoc on economies exacerbates further the pain and suffering that poverty and injustice necessarily entail. This dislocation inevitably results in the increase of violence and crime whose threat to life and limb and property are locally faced at home, in the streets, in the workplace, in the marketplace, and in the nation as a whole, which even the police power of the state is unable to contain, let alone prevent and eliminate. These are not the only the age-old problems that people face today and there are many more of the same magnitude. Add to them and further complicate them a new set of problems that have been inevitably spawned by so-called postmodernizing developments in today's world.[1] They have to be added simply because these postmodern issues are simply a given facet of life today and therefore inescapable factors and features of today's world and they have to be faced unavoidably.

Adding these new postmodernizing developments renders life in today's world more complicated. New difficulties will be added to the old ones that have remained unsolved. This will make the resulting problems more intricate, complex and intractable. Finding solutions to them will be doubly difficult, making living in today's world harder, more difficult and troublesome. It would intensify one's feeling of anxiety and the threat to life more frightening.

One postmodernizing feature in today's world is the sharpened awareness of difference and the variety of differences. What is new here is not the fact of difference nor its variety. There is gender difference—a fact we take for granted. But our sharpened awareness of it and the depth of the difference between male and female have become an indelible part of our consciousness only recently. More-

1. The word *postmodern* is used here as a cultural term to describe developments in today's world that indicate how the contemporary world is somewhat different from the world of modernity. It is double-edged in its thrust. On the one hand it points to aspects of modernity that seem out of place in today's world. On the other hand, it points to trends that are continuous with modernity but have attained some degree of essentiality as to characterize what appears to be distinctive in today's world.

over, the entailments that this awareness reveals are only now beginning to be seen and appreciated. Only recently have we come to realize that the woman is a human being who has inherent rights as a human being. Moreover she is a woman, a female, and as such she has rights as a woman that are additional to her rights as a human being. Gender difference is of the same magnitude and equality in dignity as the creation of the human being. "Male and female he created them" (Gen. 1:27). Moreover, within the gender of being female, there are as well differences in facial forms, body built, height, skin color, and so on. And the same is true of the male gender. Thus there is profound difference between male and female, and variety of differences within each gender. The entailments of all these differences in the labor industry, in the beauty industry, in the fashion industry, in inheritance laws, and in the mores and customs of culture, to mention only a few, are surfacing only recently and pressing for appreciation and for dealing with the problems arising from them.

Our awareness of how persons and peoples are different from one another in their personality makeup, in character, in interests, in habits, in patterns of behavior, in relationships and view points and life orientations, formed and normed by their differing cultures and careers as a result of the interaction of cultures in today's world, has only recently been seen in bold relief. The sympathetic understanding and mutual appreciation that this awareness entails are only now pressing themselves upon people of today's world.

We have also come to see more clearly if not yet appreciatively that cultures differ greatly in their basic beliefs and ideas, in their values and norms, in the relationships they forge, and in their ways of doing things. Cultures have their own gods and idols, heroes and sages, models of life, convictions on what life is all about, and they all come into close encounter in today's world. The fact of multiculturalism and its many implications for life in today's world are a characteristic feature of today's postmodernizing world.

What would be some consequences of this sharpened awareness of difference and the variety of differences? Without the prior background of familiarity, the sudden close encounter of forms of differences with their characteristic features would give rise to a sense of strangeness and the mutual reaction of inhospitality, if not outright intolerance and conflict. Another result is that differences mutually relativize one another. Any claim to universalize and to standardize on the basis of what is seen as common to all would be eschewed. The further result of this differentiation and relativization is pluralization. In a multidifferentiated, multicultural, relativizing and pluralizing world, there cannot be a centering power in which things may cohere. Seeking unity in diversity and diversity in unity is an impossible dream. This complication, this profusion of differences, this strong disposition to relativize, this inevitable pluralization of things are a defining characteristic of today's postmodernizing world. What Shakespeare's Hamlet says—that "the time is out of joint"—or what Yeats laments—that "things fall apart; the centre cannot hold"—describes aptly the milieu of life in today's world. The conclusion to the book of Judges (21:25), describing the condition of Israel at that time, speaks of the same situation today. "In those days there was no king in Israel; all the people did what was right in their own eyes."

This situation breeds deepened insecurity and uncertainty. This would further intensify anxiety in the face of threats. The abyss of nihilism is what awaits life at the end of the precipice. Would not daily life in such a milieu be a lot more negotiable if things lend themselves to sorting out against the background of stability and similarity, if differences are lighted up in their sharpness against the backdrop of commonalities that run across the variety and so enable the human mind to take in all this complicated plurality and make sense out of it all? This is a big conditional "if." What seems to be actually happening is that this complicating variety of differences comes upon the human mind profusely and torrentially as a confusing mixture that seems impossible to sort out and make some sense of.

One would have thought that the appropriate response to this giddying abyss of nihilistic threat is one of angry passionate protest and stark unremitting opposition. How can life be negotiated in this terrifying condition? But no! This is not the response. Indeed, the response is one of rising up to the challenge and of appreciating the new situation, of finding resources in it to deal with it in its own terms. The postmodernizing response is to accept this situation as distinctively ours and we must simply find our way through it by dint of patient struggle and muddling through. Why? What value is there to this complex confusing mixture of things? Why celebrate the mixture of differences? We have already noted that the close encounter of things in mixture has the effect of relativizing one another. This relativizing not only shows up the limits of things in their discrete identities, it also opens them up in their relation to other things. This mutual opening up in relationship has the effect of loosening up the fixities of things and shattering their patterns of configurations, and thus making them open-ended and receptive to new possibilities of becoming. It is this relativizing mixture and mutual interaction and interfacing that is the arena of change. Where change is possible or is already occurring, there emerges a clearing in the forest for new horizons of possibilities to appear. To be in such a clearing space where new horizons of possibilities show up is precisely to be free. To be free is to be liberated from limiting fixities that stunt and stifle becoming. But it is also liberation for new possibilities. The exercise of this liberated freedom is by free choice, which is always a choice *from* and a choice *for* in a clearing space that is its *conditio sine qua non*! Making a choice is a decision for something that is a not-yet, a possibility that can be. The initial act for it to be is precisely the choice for it. And so the mixture of difference as the clearing space for the liberation of freedom is the arena of possibility for new things to happen, for creativity, innovation, production, revolution, for the making of the new, for altering the way things are. This liberation of freedom from limiting and oppressive fixities and releasing its creative power for new possibilities of life is a defining feature of the postmodernizing world. This is precisely the reason for valuing the mixture of things that precipitate their relativization and so liberates freedom for its creative power.

From this relativizing factor and the liberation of freedom for creativity also springs another defining feature of this new postmodernizing world we now live in. This feature has to do with the rejection of any totalizing, universalizing, and standardizing point of view or system that organizes or configures in a fixing way any portion of reality. These attempts at systemic and total organization and explanation, whether in philosophy (in the grand manner), in science, in ideology, or in religion, are an exercise in power arbitrarily imposed as order on the way things are. They serve only the interest of those who wield such power. We normally think of violence through physical means. But the victimizing impact of violence through totalizing systems that organize life into fixed configurations and so limit the creativity of freedom is only now being consciously felt and known for the havoc that it inflicts and the pain that it causes. The strong resistance to all kinds of "isms" and the passion for free choice and creative activity is a characteristic feature of today's world.

Daily life in such a world would be more of an excitement than a stultifying bore if one knew exactly what choice was best for the flourishing of life. That one must make a choice is a gift one cannot refuse. We have now entered into and participate in a global mind-set that makes everything a matter of free choice. And in a way we are condemned to celebrate the freedom that makes the exercise of free choice possible. But making the best choice for the flourishing of life is anything but easy. For there is no more best that bests all the best. The best has been relativized and pluralized into fragments. A best is only best for the one who takes it as best! One must be content in choosing only the relative best.

But choices are nothing unless they translate into action and activity. Thinking without doing does not fully change the way things are. True knowledge is not only propositional but performative. Decisions that do not issue into action are powerless and useless. It is by thinking and deciding and doing—and all three presuppose freedom and are an exercise of it in terms of choice—that any change happens in the human world of culture and in the interaction of the human with the natural environment, in addition to changes that are naturally autonomic.

Human activity that is the exercise of creative freedom requires some form and measure of management. It calls for some degree of visioning, planning, organizing, harnessing of resources, implementing, and evaluating that ends in achievement. And achievement is always localized. Global thought that does not succeed in local action is futile. Today's mantra is "think globally and act locally."

Managed activity, however, is deliberate movement toward a purpose, a goal, a vision for life—no matter how relative and localized—that inspires and enables the movement toward the realization of its purpose, or goal, or vision. Such a beckoning, challenging vision makes the movement unstoppable and progressive and so lends hope and aspiration and motivates action. One may ask, should not such a purpose, goal, or vision have some quality of ultimacy in value, such as the true, the right, the just, the beautiful, the noble, the good, the virtuous? And should not the measure of ultimacy be such that it brings some sense of unity to the plurality of things, and provides some orientation to the dynamism of change by gathering up the elements of broken time and scattered space into a manageable activity *in* and *as* here and now in one's life world? This frenzy of activity, this irrepressible drive to manage human doings, this strong constraint to orient and direct the dynamism of change, this harnessing of knowledge and energy into tools and gadgets for significant change—these too are characteristics of today's world. But while the postmodernizing movement would concede the need for purpose, goal, and vision in any managed activity, it would not lend any measure or degree of ultimacy in value to any such visioning. The relativization of ultimacy into relative fragments is a characteristic feature of today's world.

Would not daily life in such a flattened and fragmented world be a more exhilarating journey in adventure and discovery if one were lured by a vision of a fullness of life instead of being holed up in the potholes of a life-road that has become rutted by the so many who travel on it and finally ends up in the routine of everywhere and nowhere? Unfortunately, in a relativized and pluralized world, there could not be any such vision that can beckon, unify, inspire, energize, orient, guide, and destine with some measure of ultimacy. Such a vision need not adopt a negative and pessimistic attitude toward the world. It need not give in to the anxiety provoked by the uncertainty and insecurity that characterize contemporary life. It need not be giddily intimidated and paralyzed by the threat of the abyss of nihilism. Indeed it can adopt a perspective on the world that affirms, values, promotes, and develops the world in all its aspects, including the whole of nature and the cosmos, life and human life, society and culture, and all the good that it envisions, seeks, and hopes to realize. Such a visionary perspective may even acknowledge and attempt an account of the underside of such a world: its distortions, perversions, conflicts, its wrongheadedness, and its destructive tendencies. Accompanying such an accounting may be a way of finding a solution that would at least mitigate its ills and its pains and provide a breathing space for some measure of relief to regain strength and courage to get on with the journey.

Combining the old and new problems that one has to face in today's world only complicates them further. The irony here is that we have hardly completed our transition from the premodern world to the "modern world" as such, with its values and problems, and suddenly we now find ourselves in the midst of new issues to contend with arising out of a postmodernizing world. This mixing of traditional, modern, and postmodernizing challenges breeds a very complicated situation that is difficult to handle. And that makes any hope for easing the suffering recede into darkness. Is this all there is to life? A life of compounded, insurmountable, and intolerable difficulties? Martin Heidegger's thought has made death somewhat into a virtue. His philosophy is about being in the world and being with others as inexorably being-unto-death. But in his walks together with his friend, Max Müller, while passing by a chapel, it is said that he always "dipped his finger in the stoup and genuflected." Müller asked him on one occasion whether this was not inconsistent with his philosophy that tended to question the reality of the God of theism without falling outright into atheism, Heidegger replied: "One must think historically. And where there has been so much praying, there the divine is present in a very special way."[2] It is also reported that in an interview shortly before he died, he said, "only a god can save us."[3] The big question that has to be faced is that at this juncture of history, is it still possible to do much praying, and in much praying be assured that the divine or a god is present in a special way?

2. The Need for a New Vision for Life

We have hinted in the sort of problems we have summarily described that perhaps negotiating life in today's world would be greatly helped if it were constrained and moved and oriented toward a vision that pictures some fullness of meaning or well-being that makes life worth living and its life-world worth affirming and valuing. A vision is about a future that is hoped for, and it is a hope that

---

2. Rudiger Safranski, *Martin Heidegger, Between Good and Evil*, trans. Ewald Osevs (Cambridge, MA: Harvard University Press, 1998), 32–433.

3. John Macquarrie, *Heidegger and Christianity* (New York: Continuum, 1994), 94–108.

has a future. It is about the not-yet that comes and seeks to be. It is about a promise that awaits fulfillment. It is about the desired destiny of things to which they aspire. It arises partly out of the deficiencies and distortions and confusions of life and its "life-world." And so a vision is seen as having a significant word to say about filling up those deficiencies and correcting those distortions and clearing up those confusions. Further, it lights up what in life and its life-world are already there that can be affirmed, appreciated, and promoted because they have been proven by hard lessons learned through actual living that they contain resources for help in life and in forming a life-world that is friendly to it.

Furthermore, a vision opens up a clearing from all the clutter and slag heaps of failures and dead ends that lead into vistas of new possibilities only dimly seen before, but now boldly etched out for discerning and grasping and actualizing. Moreover, a vision releases new energies that it harnesses into new dynamisms that are creative, and so empower the struggle to bring flexible parameters, direction, and guidance.

It frames *loosely* because the act of creation is by the freedom of choice among options. Creation comes by "letting be." It comes by luring and being lured. It comes by summoning and being summoned at the same time. And so a vision may be seen as outside and beyond things as they are. That is why it can lure and challenge and beckon and orient. But it also evokes and constrains and releases from within. It has manuietic power. It has this birthing power because it is both within and beyond things as they are. A genuine vision has the quality of being other than, and as such is yet significantly related to, things as they are. It is both being other than, and yet being involved deeply in, the way things are and so in some measure is a part of them. By being a part of, and so being in the world, it can affirm, value, and promote the existence and well-being of the world and all that is properly and fittingly in it. There is an inescapable secular dimension to it, if by "secular" is meant the "this-worldly" reality and value of the world as such. (The term "secular" as used in this essay is further described below.)

A genuine vision is double-edged. On the one hand, a genuine vision has the quality of being in, for, and with the world as such, and to the extent that this is the case, it can be said to be involved in the world and so a part of it. On the other hand, it is outside and beyond and transcends the world by being other than it. This otherness from the world is both for itself to be itself, and, at the same time, also for the world as such. Its being for the world is a dimension of its otherness. To the extent that this is the case, it can be said that it is not of this world. A vision is thus both in, for, and with the world but at the same time is not of the world.

And yet this quality of not being of the world is precisely what makes it relate to, and be a part of, the world.

The world in turn is constituted by this relation. The world as world— things as they are—can, as it were, see and feel and know and embrace this vision as being for itself. The world cannot feel and know and do without this vision. But the world also feels and knows that it is critically judged by this vision and in the light of this critique, the world can discern new possibilities that are not yet actualized in it and so is not yet a part of it. When these visions occur in the world they appear as new and they reconstitute the world. A new configuration and orientation of things take place. A genuine vision is capable of doing this precisely by being other than, and yet involved in, the world.

Because a genuine vision has this double quality, there is a basis for grounding, justifying, and appreciating the world not only in its being and existence but also for all the differences and variety of difference that make the world what it is. The secularity of the world, that is, the world as it is and what it is and what it can yet be as world, is affirmed, secured, valued, appreciated, and promoted as such. This securing and affirming and valuing include the relativizing and pluralizing and complexifying power that is latent in difference and its variety. This power is released actively in their coming together confusingly in close encounter and interaction.

Moreover, a genuine vision reconciles. Reconciliation consists of two movements: it both restores and unifies. It restores things in their genuine relations and identities. The restoring includes a critical and judging thrust that exposes and removes the movements' distortions and straightens out their perversions and so restores them to their proper form and order. Reconciliation is returning things to their truthful differentiated identities and proper relations and ordering and so to their authentic existence.

Reconciliation unifies at the same time as it restores. It restores things into what unifies them in their genuine differentiations. It is not a discerning enough vision to see what is common in things in their difference. This move will not yield what truly unifies. It will only see the one thing common to them all, namely, that they commonly exist in differentiation. What is common is different from difference. What has to be clearly discerned is what unifies this commonality with differentiation and vice versa. And this is not found in either the common or the different. What is it that unifyingly grounds unity in diversity and diversity in unity in which commonality and difference coincide? Is there a point in which the opposites coincide in unity? Is there such a thing that Nicholas of Cusa called a *coincidentia oppositorum*? Is there such a unity? This is what a genuine vision that reconciles sees. But may it be seen? Like all things seen, it may be seen only if it appears as being there to be seen in its own light. A genuine vision is seen in its own light. Is there a vision that lights itself in its own light?

But there is more to a genuine vision than we have already pointed out. Does a genuine vision do only what we have said above, namely, it sees and reveals things as they truly are? Or in so doing, does it also transform and destine these things? To transform is to actualize the potential of a thing that cannot happen when it is distorted and perverted and so is stifled and stunted. The potential of a thing is what it can truly be, which it is not-yet. Transformation is the inner process of a thing that makes it become what it truly can be. But this process is not a movement in circles that spirals into nowhere except into its own circularity. It is a movement that orients and destines, a movement that leads to the fulfillment of the destiny of things, namely their fullness, but not merely their fullness in their different identities, but their fullness together in unity as a whole.

A vision not only sees thing as they are but also transforms them to fulfill the fullness of their respective destinies in one whole. In transforming them, a vision moves and takes them beyond themselves into something that is more ultimate than they are in their respective relative differences and unity. Such a vision can only be a *spiritual vision*. It cannot be merely physical, or biological, or psychological, or cultural, or social, and human because it is all these that it affirms, unites, transforms, destines, and takes into an ultimacy that fulfills each and integrates them into a whole. A spirituality that does all these can only be described as a *spirituality that secularizes.*

3. The Secularizing Movement

The coupling of these words *spiritual* and *secular* and their relationship in the phrase "spirituality that secularizes," which appears as rather unorthodox in today's cultural and spiritual landscape, need further explanation. The concept "secular" combines two notions from Latin. One is the idea of *saecularis*, which means "worldly," or "of or pertaining to worldly things or to things that are not regarded as religious, spiritual, or sacred." The other Latin word is *saeculum*, which means a "long period of time," an age or era that is temporal, as contrasted with "eternal."[4] The secular then has to do with the world in time. It has to do with what is of the world and of its time; it is about the worldly and the temporal.

4. From Webster's *Encyclopedic Unabridged Dictionary of the English Language*, sv "spiritual" and "secular."

Both conceptually and historically, the secular has been considered in relation to the "religious," which pertains to gods whose order of existence is other than that of the world, but includes the world as the domain of their sovereignty and to which the world must pay obeisance, obedience, and worship. For that to happen requires that the order and operation of the world must represent and reflect the order—or disorder—of the gods. That presupposes a bond that binds (*religare,* to bind, to tie) the order of the gods superiority in being, power, and value of the gods over that of the world and all that is in it and pertains to it.

The gods represent themselves in the affairs of the world through heroes and rulers who attribute their exploits and successes to the power of a divinity to which they pay obeisance. These heroes and rulers in turn eventually represent themselves as gods.

The story of this interfacing relationship between gods and the world is what is told in myths, legends, rituals, and rites, and together they enshrine beliefs, values, and practices. These stories, beliefs, and practices have been thematized and institutionalized in various religious traditions and cultural forms that have shaped many parts of the world. To tell their story is also to tell the story of the cultures they have spawned. This kind of storytelling continues to re-create the world of the gods. It tells the story of the world as being also the story of the gods. The story of the world cannot be properly told except as a religious story. Of course, there have been varying episodes in this story—some more religious than others, some more worldly than others. But the red thread that runs through all of them—the plot that holds the episodes together—is still the religious plot, until recently.

With the rise of the religious mind-set and the traditions that form and normalize it, there has been a countermovement that sought to break the bond between the religious and the worldly, between the story of the gods and the story of the world. It started slowly at first and as it steadily continued, it has gained more momentum and strength. In the last four centuries it has become more rapid, more radical and penetrating, more militant, and more far-reaching in scope. This historical movement is what is referred to by the term "secularization." It is not within my competence to tell the story of this historical process. Charles Taylor, the British philosopher and historian of culture, tells it better than anyone I know of in his magisterial opus, *A Secular Age* (Harvard University Press, 2007). What I can do—for the purposes of this essay—is to indicate its character and direction and highlight some of the decisive moves that steered and strengthened it and made it stay its course in spite of the obstacles it had to overcome.

The first characteristic of this secularizing movement was to emancipate the world from the domination of the world of the gods and of institutional religion.

To do this, it had to break the domination of the religious upon the world. But the bond was strong in its religious domination. It operated as an unquestioned assumption. It was presuppositional to all else that was thought and said and done. Events happen because of the will of the gods, permitted or forbidden by the authority of religion and its institutions and guardians. Not only was it a bond that operated as an unquestioned axiom but also as a frame that supplied both the parameters and structures of whatever order was found in the world. But since the gods were sovereign in power and value, they also were the powers that operated in things and gave the energy and the direction in which things moved. Any stepping beyond these boundaries and any challenge against the dynamism at work in the world was met unavoidably with vengeful religious sanctions that disrupt the order of things, interrupt the regularity of the seasons, and wreak havoc to the routine, stability, and certainty of negotiating life. The world must be set free from the stranglehold of institutional religion. This emancipating character of secularization continues unabated to this day. But how to break this religious bond in its dominant prevailing form? Indeed, is it breakable?

The second characteristic of this secularizing process is the use of the powers of reason and the value of the benefits that derive from it. Reason is nothing if it does not ask questions of what is given at hand. It inquires into why things are and what they are. It searches and investigates. And in this process it sifts what is real from what is not, what is true from false, what is useful from harmful, what is right from wrong, what is dependable from what is not. This rational process also brings into some coherent relationship what it finds true, right, just, beneficial, beautiful, and good, and develops these into some system that then presents itself as an alternative to the way things are as seen religiously. It is what gave rise to philosophy in the grand manner in which various aspects of reality are seen in their differences and relates them together to form a holistic picture of the way things are. This rational way of viewing things in contrast to the religious mindset is a decisive step in the secularizing process. It undergirded and strengthened this process. This rational element will eventually constitute itself as essential to this process.

Reason through the knowledge that it generates emancipates from authority, especially religious authority. It is what liberates freedom from captivity and secures its dignity and essential status in the way things are. But freedom wedded to rational knowledge is not yet strong enough to break the strong grip of religion upon the affairs of the world. Rational knowledge combined with the power of freedom needs another ally, namely, political will, which is the exercise of implementing and achieving what is desired and preferred over the prevailing order of things. This is a *third* element of the secular process. Political will is usually wielded by a ruler who is advocate, legislator, judge, and executive all rolled into one role as ruler or prince or king or emperor. An early example of a ruler who favors rational order over that of the religious is the fourteenth-century B.C. Egyptian pharaoh who by decree (that its, exercise of political power and authority) abolished the divinities and cults of his kingdom in favor of a social order more consonant with rational knowledge available at the time. Another example is Plato's deliberately considered opinion that those who rule must be rationally wise. And rational wisdom is the knowledge of the good that unites the true, the just, and the beautiful. This gave birth to the idea of the philosopher-king who rules wisely and thus secures what is just in the way things are. Needless to say, the use of political will with rational wisdom is a further decisive step in the secularizing process. It will remain as an essential component of this historical process.

This combining of rational knowledge, the exercise of freedom of choice, and the implementing power of political will has succeeded in breaking the bond between the order of the gods and the order of the world up to a point. It did not, however, eliminate religion and its form of life and mind-set. What it produced is the juxtaposition of two orders, namely, the religious and the secular. Augustine's two contrasting loves, the love of the City of God and the love of the City of Man, and Thomas Aquinas's order of grace and order of nature are good examples of this juxtaposition.

However, this juxtaposition, though running parallel, was anything but peaceful coexistence. New factors were unleashed that powered the secularizing movement into new successes and accelerated its unstoppable ascendancy, while institutional religion was forced to go on retreat and to cede territory after territory, which originally were its domains, to the expansive thrust of secularization. For example, secularization was used as term to refer to the forcible takeover by the state of properties of the church for worldly use, mostly against the vehement objection of the church. This act is symbolic of the many inroads made by secularization into affairs that originally belonged to institutional religion but now have been taken over by the secular. This taking over of spheres that originally were religious by the worldly for secular benefits through secular means is an essential feature of the secularizing movement.

One factor that propelled secularization in its ascendant movement over the institutionally religious is its humanistic thrust. This thrust originated in the Grecian emphasis on the virtues as uniquely characteristic of what is excellent in human behavior. It was later picked up by a new rising social class in Italy—the manufacturers, the merchants, the bankers, the artists, expert artisans—to refine manners and civilize behavior. This emphasis on virtue and the refinement of behavior was then applied to education and scholarship. Its aim was to cultivate what is truly human in mind, in behavior, in what is best for human perfection. This is done no longer on the basis of divine will but on the sheer capabilities of the human. This spirit of cultivating the human for its perfection—the humanistic spirit—has become an essential feature of the secularizing process. One can be good without God. That is the humanistic mantra.

Besides the discovery of the human and its dignity and placing it at center stage is the new secularizing interest in nature, to know it as it is, and to make of it a resource for human benefit, not simply as a finished divine artifact and a theater of divine activity and glory. This gave rise to the scientific method, to scientific knowledge, to scientific technology for human benefit, and to the scientific explanation and understanding of things, the scientific mind-set. The scientific movement has disenchanted nature; it seeks to displace God as an explanation for the origin of the universe and the behavior of nature. The benefits of technology and a scientific technological culture have displaced the religious view of salvation as leaving earth and going to heaven with living a good life on earth as it might be in heaven. University education, which started as education for the clergy and sponsored by the church, was taken over by a new academic program the core of which are the humanities and the sciences. This scientific thrust has decisively become an essential component of the secularizing process.

We now have to ask where this historical process is leading up to. We have at least indicated the basic components of this process. We have also pointed out that it is a movement away from the dominance of the order of the gods, the religious order of things. And all the elements we have described are attacks on this order—some hostile and vicious, some kind and diplomatic, but decisive, nevertheless. But where does it all end? Quite simply but profoundly, *it is to establish secularity*. And by secularity is meant the following: the right of the world to be an existent in itself, together with all its support systems; to possess its own intrinsic value that merits appropriate appreciation; to acknowledge its inner impetus to develop its potentialities and potencies to their maximum fullness; to let it generate its own creative and complexifying dynamism; to accord it the freedom to operate according to its own laws without undue interference; to respect its own interconnectedness and order and not impose some contrived order or arbitrary configuration upon it. Such arbitrary imposition serves only the interest of the powers that be and not its intrinsic interest; to allow it to make critical assessment of itself and rid itself of the distortions that pervert insofar as this can be done by worldly ability, both natural and human. To put the matter in a nutshell, secularization aims at establishing and making the world quite simply world through what makes it world!

We have described secularization as a process of change. It includes cosmic, natural, human, and cultural change insofar as this change contributes to the founding and making of the world as such. So far we have pointed to its unstoppable ascendancy. The question to ask now is, should it stop? From the secular perspective, there should be nothing that is exempt from change. The cosmic, the natural, the historical, the cultural, the human all undergo change. Even God is seen as subject to change. Is it in the nature of secularization as change to stop change and no longer be open to further change? The temptation to do so is strong. The process of change can be made to stop and the reality and value of what has thus been achieved may be regarded as all there is to it. In a word, secularization may become no more than secularistic, and the secular may become secularism. In which case secularization as a process is no longer open to new possibilities. Its capacity to transcend itself and be transcended is now finally ended and there is no more to it than simply and only it. However, it may be that this is not yet the case. It is quite possible to consider the postmodernizing movement as a continuation of the secularizing process. But this would entail a more positive understanding of some of the negative aspects of postmodernization as contributory to what makes world truly world. Some of the negative features of postmodernization such as the rejection of the so-called Enlightenment project, its penchant for deconstruction, and its antimetaphysical bent may in fact be seen as stripping the world of its unnecessary accretions and thus open it to be what it truly is as world. The postmodernizing process may thus be regarded as a contemporary expression of the kind of change that secularization provokes and sustains.

Meanwhile, we may well ask how traditional and institutional religion and its agencies, especially the church and religious communities, have been impacted by the secularization process.

There is no doubt that the attack of secularization against the order of the gods has a profaning thrust. It tends to bring down the religious from its lofty place to the gutter of the world. It uses language that is discourteous and impolite. It has a desecrating attitude toward the order of the gods. What it seeks to achieve is often counter to the interest of religious communities and institutions. It has eliminated some of the "bulwarks of belief"[5] and this has weakened the hold of the religious upon its devotees.

---

5. Charles Taylor, *A Secular Age* (Cambridge, MA: Harvard University Press, 2007), 25–89.

The religious in turn has understandably recoiled from these attacks and this has had some salutary effects on its communities and institutions. For one thing, it has removed from its belief and value systems some of the more magical and superstitious elements that cannot stand up to rational and scientific criticism.

For another thing, it has divested itself of the more worldly trappings that do not seem to be appropriate to its character as a spiritual icon through which the divine becomes transparent. Furthermore, secularization has forced the religious to come to terms with its own relevance to the secular by being precisely spiritual. But this spirituality has a built-in hostility toward the world. The "spiritual" and the "secular" have always been seen historically as opposed to each other.

There is a long tradition in Western Christianity as a religion that comes from the pervasive influence on it of Greco-Roman culture, which holds that spirit is opposed to matter, that the spiritual is against the material, that the religious is against the worldly, that the sacred is against the secular, that the holy is against the profane. This mutual hostility continues up to the present, and it is now regarded as the defining relationship between the order of the gods and the order of the world. In short, the spiritual as spiritual conflicts with the secular. It is anti-worldly. This conflict is at the heart of traditional Christian spirituality.

What is the position of Christian faith on the secularization process and on what seems to be the defining relation between the secular and the spiritual? The answer as indicated by the phase "a spirituality that secularizes" is to claim that the secularization process is a work of the Spirit understood in the full range and depth of its biblical provenance. It is the Spirit that secularizes.

And because of this, the relation of the Spirit to the world is unmistakably positive, supportive, and fulfilling, and also critical and transformative. The world is best comprehended within the horizon of the Spirit. A helpful definition of spirituality is given by Geoffrey Wainwright: "spirituality is the combining of prayer and daily life."

The key word in this definition is *combining*. Praying without living is not spirituality. Living without praying is not spirituality either. But what is it that combines prayer and daily life? Obviously it is neither praying nor living, but something else: it is the spirit of God. Spirituality can only be the ongoing activity of God through his Spirit. But the ongoing activity of God the Spirit is precisely in the world and life in the world in its day-to-day affairs. It is in fact a secularizing activity. Its direction is this-worldly!

The question to be asked at this point is, can the tie that binds the spiritual and the secular really be broken? Can it be snapped out by secularization unilaterally? I do not think so! Perhaps what can be broken is the dominance of one over the other. The *way* the tie binds can be broken, but not the *bonding tie* itself. Another aspect of the way the tie binds that needs breaking is its expression historically and institutionally in the form of creeds, confessions, dogmas, theological systems, and ethical norms and practices that are merely self-serving to the religious community and its traditions. Together with the metaphysical perspectives that undergird these creedal and theological systems, they need to be shattered to make room for deeper understanding of what they sought to express, which is seeking new ways of self-expression and self-definition. Another feature of the way the tie that binds needs breaking is the opposition to scientific knowledge to the extent that it threatens the order of the gods. This view—allegedly based on the religious order of things that promote this conflict—must be rejected, for it does not help the combining of prayer and living.

What is needed more deeply perhaps is to reconceive the bond, not in terms of power, thought, and practice but as an enduring relation—a covenant relation—that critically expresses itself in contingent historical and relative forms of power, thought, and practice. This covenant binding relation—as the work of the Spirit—is what makes world as such. And so one can be spiritual without necessarily being religious. But one cannot be spiritual without necessarily being secular and secularizing. That is because from a biblical/ Christian perspective it is the Spirit that constitutes and sustains the bond that ties the one with the other. From here on, I will use the term *religare* to refer to this bonding of the Spirit and to claim that the secular can only be properly established and its reality affirmed and appreciated within this bonding.

There seem to be four major strands of Christian spirituality that are emerging in our time. They seem to be developing in their own separate ways. One is what Matthew Fox calls the "Fall/Redemption"-centered spirituality. This emphasizes the sin/salvation strand of biblical thought and Christian theology. It is the burden of Christian preaching, teaching, and practice. And so it operates largely within the confines of Christian communities, especially of the fundamentalist or conservative variety. Fox wants to replace this spirituality with what he calls "creation spirituality" that is centered in a new appreciation of creation in all its processes, relations, complexity, and variety. This second type yields an almost mystical relation to nature and care for its integrity. This type of spirituality goes beyond the confines of the churches to embrace all of creation and is friendly to all efforts that seek to care for the environment. There is a third type of spirituality that has been in place following the Enlightenment. This type may be called liberal spirituality. It seeks to correlate the religious as a category in itself to the secular. It seeks to show the relevance of the religious to the concerns of the worldly, sometimes even to the point of adapting itself to the worldly. This relevance is often configured in terms of the moral and the ethical, which are implicit in the religious. But the worldly does not seem to adopt what the religious seeks to offer because it can avail of these by its own means and its own terms. Then there is a fourth emerging type, namely the one exhibited by charismatic and Pentecostal communities. Here, the emphasis is not on traditional doctrine, nor on the embrace of creation and its care, nor in relating the relevance of the religious to the secular, but in so-called manifestations of the Spirit, which are celebrated as being born again, speaking in tongues, the gifts of the Spirit, and a form of worship that is emotion-centered and so aims at evoking the feelings of praise, joy, gratitude, and a sense of well-being. Bits of Christian doctrine and theology are invoked not as ascriptions to the nature and glory of God but as evocative of emotional well-being in the presence of God. I may be wrong, but my view is that all these strands are elements of genuine Christian spirituality.

The Fall/Redemption spirituality emphasis is an essential element of the Christian gospel, which judges and strips away the idolatrous, the perverted, and the evil elements in the world and in human life and seeks not only to restore the world to its genuine integrity but also set it on course toward its true destiny. To the extent that this is the case, it is an expression of a spirituality that secularizes.

The creation spirituality proposed by Fox and practiced by communities that advocate the care of nature by respecting its right; by appreciating the order of its laws as known in science; by bringing life and all its concerns in line with what is sustainable by nature and its resources; and by celebrating its grandeur, its complexity and variety, its multifaceted beauty, especially as this is expressed and enshrined in art and culture—this is all part of a spirituality that secularizes. There is indeed a moral and ethical dimension in the religious. But this-worldly thought believes it can avail of this without religious underpinning or warrants. It can legislate for itself what *ought* or what *should* without the sanctions of religion. The spirituality promoted by charismatics and Pentecostals, which emphasizes the spontaneous irruption of the Spirit in its power to transform, to bring forth a new birth, and to celebrate with joyful exuberance the life-nourishing presence of the Spirit in its directness and immediacy can be regarded as the energizing power at work in the secularization process as the power of change and of transformation. All these forms of spirituality in the author's opinion presuppose or assume a relation between the religious and the secular. That relation is a reality deeper and broader than any of its manifestations in the religious forms mentioned above. If so, is it possible to bring them together into a larger relational and paradigmatic vision of spirituality in which these elements mutually enrich one another, and are also taken up into the larger thrust and horizon of biblical/Christian spirituality, which is a profound relational reality that secularizes?

The following chapters are a modest effort to establish the claim for a spirituality that secularizes.

CHAPTER II

The Spirit in Creation as Secular

1. The Sweep and Depth of the Spirit's Work

It may be recalled from the previous chapter that the goal of the secularization movement is to establish secularity. A fundamental meaning of secularization is establishing the world—"the heavens and the earth," the universe, all that there is—as an existent in itself, together with all its support systems, which is to be affirmed, to have its own rights that have to be respected, and to possess its own intrinsic value that merits its distinct appreciation. To do this the world has to detach itself somehow from the dominance of the institutionally and historically religious upon it. We have in the previous chapter highlighted some of the decisive steps in this secularizing movement.

The aim of this chapter is to consider the way biblical/Christian faith goes about in establishing the world as an existent in itself. To do this, it seems necessary to expand and to deepen the traditional understanding of the Spirit to include God's work of creation through the agency of the Spirit and the Word, and to see the world and understand it as an existent within the horizon of the Spirit. This would constitute a fundamental and decisive step in developing theologically a spirituality that is secularizing.

The work of the Spirit has been traditionally connected with the grace of salvation and the existence and activities of the church as signifying and mediating that grace. This is correct as far as it goes. The grace of salvation and the being and work of the church are indeed the work of the Spirit. However, this has had the historical effect of confining the agency of the Spirit to the parameters of the church. The result is to leave out much of the world and what happens in it and to it outside of the agency of the Spirit. This neglect has also tended to foster the view that the standard attitude of the Spirit to the world is one of hostility to it, and so provoking from the world a similar reaction of hostility that profanes the Spirit. This development does not do justice to the depth and scope of the scriptural understanding of the agency of the Spirit.

The secularization process that has spawned the search for a spirituality that secularizes seeks to overcome this interfacing of hostility by enlarging and deepening the understanding of the agency of the Spirit and incorporating the secular into its horizon by doing justice—as far as possible—to what Scriptures say about this issue.

The best way to proceed is to begin with creation and to reopen the scriptural texts dealing with it for some measure of reconsideration. But why begin with creation and not with the big bang theory which is now the standard theory that science has developed to explain the origin of the world. The author is not a scientist and he is not competent to deal with the details and complexities of the big bang theory. My layman's view is that the big bang theory is a scientific theory that is warranted by a great deal of scientific evidence and formulated in mathematical terms. Scientists call the big bang theory of the origin of the universe a "Singularity." The reason is because the laws, procedures, and formulations of physics cannot and do not penetrate deep enough to this point of primal beginning. That is because the laws of physics are given with the existence of the universe. The big bang theory is the product of the application of the laws, procedures, and formulations of physics that already assume the existence of the universe and can thus only go so far as this existence allows. It is a theory that already presupposes the actual physical existence of the universe. It does not go deep and far enough to consider the *possibility* of the universe at all, for to do so would make its considerations no longer science but most likely philosophical, and at worst theological. It would not be able to consider the tie that binds the secular and the spiritual—the relational reality to which *religare* points, and of which the religious seek to make sense. As indicated in the previous chapter, I will use the term *religare* to refer to the relational bond that ties the spiritual to the secular and establish it with the claim that the binding bond is the Spirit. But the theory itself, as are the other scientific theories, such as evolution, may well be affirmed—to the extent that they are an essential aspect of the secularity of the world—as being within the matrix of the Spirit's agency. The big bang is the result of a method that infers from scientific evidence to the best possible explanation.[1]

It is an inference that best explains as warranted by evidence. But science also assumes that not all the evidence for a theory are at hand at any given time and circumstance, and so the theory is tentative in its inferential status and partial in its explanatory power. For example: Scientists are still looking with the aid of sophisticated scientific tools for Higgs boson, dabbed "the God particle" because if found it would decisively contribute to the formulation of a grand theory of everything (TOE), which would unite the atomic and cosmic forces in the universe, the force of gravity, electromagnetism, the strong and weak forms of nuclear energy, and who knows what else. The evidence so far gathered is not yet conclusive.

The Heisenberg uncertainty principle states that the measurements of physics as far as they go presently cannot measure both the position and speed of an atomic particle. One can measure the speed but not position at the same time. The result is the view that there is an essential indeterminacy in the measurement of the composition of reality at the quantum level. Moreover, mathematics that is alleged to be the most exact form of thinking and configuring in mathematical patterns has problems of its own that remain unsolved, as for instance the theorem of Kurt Gödel (1906–78).[2]

All this implies that a theory can be changed in part or in whole depending on new evidence and new procedures that justify the change. And so this scientific process is an aspect of secularizing change that has to be seen within the matrix of the Spirit's agency.

In reopening the scriptural texts on creation that testify to the creative work of the Spirit, we are to some extent employing the method of making an inference from the text to the best possible explanation in understanding what it may yield. The text is once a piece of living tissue of experience that enshrines a significant live-experience that is now frozen in the form of a text. As a text it embodies a significant meaning that has a background, an inner ground, and a foreground. The text has a context. The range and depth of its meaning depends upon how far back, how deep down, and how far forward are the limits of this context. To reopen a text is to reinterpret its meaning in the light of the extent and depth of its context. We use the word *reinterpretation* to include the various interpretations

---

1. For what this method entails, see Arthur Peacocke, *Paths from Science Toward God* (Oxford: Oneworld Publications, 2002), 26–30.
2. For a discussion of the above example, see Hans Küng, *The Beginning of All Things* (Grand Rapids: Eerdmans, 2007), and the various works cited.

already made of the text and its context. There is thus a history of interpretation in the understanding of a text, which itself may need interpretation.

That reinterpretation may warrant philosophical, theological, and even scientific considerations that may be necessary to unfold the explanatory power of the text. The reinterpretation may thus have the character of an inference warranted by evidence to the best explanation possible.

It is the contention of the writer that it is not enough theoretically to simply presuppose or assume the existence of the universe and explain such existence by a theory, such as the big bang. One has also to consider the *possibility* of the universe—the why of it and the conditions for it—as part of the explanation required for understanding it. To establish the universe as existent one must consider its possibility and, of course, its actuality.

To consider the possibility of the universe at all seems to be an impossible intellectual task. The frame in which it is considered in the Genesis texts has two poles; both make the possibility of the existence of the universe seemingly impossible. On the one hand there is "God" who creates the beginning and so is not part of it. The time of beginning cannot be applied to God. His being is his own being. The being of creation or any creaturely part of it cannot be applied to God. His necessity to be God is his own necessity. We cannot apply creaturely necessity to him. His existence is his own as God. We cannot apply creaturely existence to him. If we say "God exists," and we mean by "exist" creaturely existing, then he does not exist in the creaturely sense. He is therefore not a part at all of the world that has a beginning. The self-naming of God in Exodus 3:14: "I AM WHO I AM," or "I will be what I will be" means that God constitutes himself as God. His becoming as God is his own becoming. We cannot apply creaturely becoming to him. He does not "become" the way creatures become. It is he—and he alone—who makes himself God. So he alone can name himself, if "naming" designates "existence" or being as such and its essential character. This means that for God to be God he need not create a world, a universe, since he is already God by himself and can continue to be God by his own becoming without a world. The word *create* as applied to the world cannot be applied to God except negatively and in quotation marks: God is "uncreated." And so as God he is other than the world, and this otherness is unique, a class by itself. He alone is God, and there is none like him. The word *being* insofar as this refers to the being of the world as created, that is, as creaturely being, cannot be applied to God since God's being is uncreated; it is his own "being" as God. So the possibility of the world cannot arise from God's self-constitution because God is already God without the world.

The other pole in the text in Genesis "describes" a pre-creation condition. The language is obviously narrative. In narrating something, story language tends to invest what it describes with some semblance of intelligible or historical "reality." Moreover, the language is metaphorical in that it intends something else that has the character of a more significant "reality." In my opinion, the text seeks to describe "something" that is real neither in the "God" sense that we described above, nor in the "created" sense of reality that will be described below. What other sense of reality is there? The language used is difficult to ascertain in its meaning. The pre-creation condition is "formless void." Both terms—formlessness and voidness—denote what is impossible to perceive, let alone to conceive. Voidness denotes Nothing, in the sense of nothing being there and so is empty and has no form, and therefore cannot be perceived. And because it is a "formless void," it may be interpreted as the "*nihilo*," the Nothing, in *creatio nihilo*. As primal Nothing, it cannot give rise by itself to something or anything. Nothing can come out of Nothing except nothing. Being cannot arise by itself from nonbeing. Possibility cannot arise by itself from non-possibility. And so the possibility of the world from the non-possibility of the Nothing cannot arise at all.

Moreover, the other metaphor of "the deep" and the "darkness that covered it" more or less denote practically the same thing. "The deep" refers to the primal waters of chaos that cover the earth. Primal chaos cannot by itself produce cosmos, that is, a world established and structured by order that subsists in order. And "darkness" refers to the absence of light, life, and intelligibility. One cannot see anything in the dark. There is nothing worth seeing in the dark. My honest opinion is that the language used here intends to point to Nothing. And "Nothing" is to be understood as the impossibility of anything. The text also is not interested in asking about the "origin" of this pre-creation condition. That would be pointless, would it not? Simply because nothing points to nothing, to the non-possibility of anything, including that of "origin." And so there is no possibility of the world to arise at all either from its nonnecessity in God or from the non-possibility of the Nothing. Given these factors, how then may the possibility of the world emerge at all?

What emerges in this primal dilemma is, as it were, God facing the Nothing. What happens in this primal facing? Is God intimidated by the Nothing? Is the Nothing a condition for his self-constitution? Is his own becoming limited at all by this Nothing? Is God's posture in the face of the Nothing one of passivity because he is unable to deal with it in some creative way? Or does he react to it as though it were a force contrary to and were in active opposition to his powers? And the best that he can do is to contain it? Or is the Nothing the breeding ground of all the evils that oppose God and God has no choice but to destroy "it." But what is "there" to destroy? And into what is it to be destroyed? To destroy it into Nothing and so return it into Nothing? To destroy nonreality to unreality? To destroy chaos into chaos? To destroy darkness into darkness? This would surely be empty talk. The text on the contrary points to the way God deals with the Nothing that expresses his utter sovereignty over "it."

2. The Creation of Possibility out of Non-Possibility

Now, the text goes on to say that all the while that there "is" this pre- creation condition, already "a wind from God" has been sweeping over the face of the waters (v. 2). This "wind" can be translated "Spirit," and so the phrase can be read "a Spirit from God." This Spirit is from and so is of God. This Spirit is God reaching out to the formless void, the deep covered with darkness, the Nothing that "is" the impossibility of anything! This reaching out of the Spirit that is of God and from God is what establishes the *religare*, the binding bond, between God and the heavens and the earth, a relational bond that no one and no force can break. Only God can break it. But will he?

The "wind" has certain characteristics that are universally experienced. Wind is real; one hears its sound although it is invisible. Wind can be felt by our sense of touch; its reality is felt. Wind is free; it blows where it wills, and one cannot tell where it comes from or where it goes. Wind is power; it can sweep, it can penetrate, it can encompass; it can transform, it can destroy. It can also be the breath of life, the life-giving Spirit. These are properties that can be applied metaphorically to God as Spirit. The Spirit is God reaching out in freedom and power to be present to and active upon the pre-creation condition! God is sovereign over chaos, over impossibility, over the formless void through the Spirit. And so the relation of bonding by the Spirit is "real" in God's sense as being of God and from God, and made real to us also in our sense of "real" through the sensible experience of the characteristics of the Spirit. The Spirit that is this bonding relation is both of God and from God and is in, and with, and for the world. The Spirit has a worldly dimension; it has a secular thrust, a worldly reality.

Verse 1 speaks of God creating the heavens and the earth. Verse 2 speaks of the Spirit from God sweeping over the face of the waters. Is not the "sweeping" related to the "creating"? Moreover, verse 1 points to "the beginning" when God created the heavens and the earth. This means that the Spirit sweeping over the face of the waters has something to do with "the beginning" of creation. Is not "the sweeping over" the pre-creation condition precisely "the beginning" of creation?

And what would constitute "the beginning" of creation? Is it not the making of its possibility out of its non-possibility? The Spirit of God "sweeping over the face of the deep" means making creation possible out of its non-possibility in pre-creation condition, which is the Nothing. Transforming pre-creation conditions into conditions for the possibility of creation—that is the work of the Spirit of God. That is the beginning of creation. That is also the beginning of the secular since creation is the making of the world—the heavens and the earth, the universe, all that there is! The secular is established by creation, which is the primal work of God the Spirit.

Scholars tell us that the verb "to create" has God alone for its subject, although the idea of creating is derived from human experience. If so, then we can say from the foregoing that it is God as Spirit who is the subject active in creating the possibility of creation out of its non-possibility. No one else is able to do this. And since God is the sole subject of creation, then creation is dependent solely upon God the Spirit for its possibility. Moreover, the adverb "when" implies that God as Spirit acting to begin to create is a free decision on the part of God. God need not create a world to be God. Even "before" creation, God already is God. But God did decide to create and so creation is entirely contingent upon this free decision of God.

The free decision of God to create is, as it were, a new turn in God's self-constitution. In "addition" to being in himself, by himself, and for himself, he decided to be in, with, and for *another*, one that is other than him, and also other than the Nothing. This "being for another" is an aspect of God's becoming, of God's self-constitution; it is God becoming himself for another that is not God. This free decision of being for another is God's self-determination as grace and so of being gracious, of determining himself as love, and therefore loving. The same God who self-constitutes himself for himself is the same God who turns to self-constitute himself for another; and so he remains other than this another, and this another is other than him, and yet he is fully God for this another. He is grace and love and care for this another. And so God's relation to this another is a relation of grace and love and care in the Spirit. The beneficiary of this gracious, loving, and caring relation is the world, that is, the secular. And since the world in its secularity is grounded in this relation bindingly, it cannot unbind itself from it because it is what constitutes it; and so it has to participate actively in it in such ways that witness to this relational reality.

Moreover, since only God as Spirit is the subject of the beginning of creation, that is, its possibility, and since he freely decided to create, then the possibility of creation is unique. There is no other possibility like it; it is *sui generis*. It is not a possibility that is necessary in, and generically derivable from, God. It is not a possibility that is of God. Nor is it a possibility that is potentially latent in pre-creation condition that is precisely the non- possibility of possibility. It is a possibility solely by the decision and action of God. It is a possibility of a unique kind! Because of this, it is a possibility that cannot be either this or that; it can only be this one thing— as the possibility of creation itself. No other! Even at the level of the possibility of creation the term used by scientists to describe the big bang applies: It is a singularity.

The possibility of creation in its utter contingency and uniqueness and singularity makes of creation a primal miracle. Equally fundamental, it is this possibility—created by the Spirit—that is the ground of miracle! In this connection, miracle has nothing to do with a breaking of known laws of nature by divine intervention in an already existing universe. Pre-creation condition is chaos; there are no laws of nature that structure it with rational order. Talk of miracle as the breaking of the laws of nature in this context is meaningless. The Spirit's intervention upon pre-creation chaos to create the possibility of creation is a primal miracle! This follows from the fact that the possibility that is created is not the possibility of some part or aspect or dimension of creation, but of the *whole of creation itself*. What is created by the Spirit is the primal possibility of "the heavens and the earth" and all that is in them. To use modern language, it is the possibility *of all that there is and is yet to be* that is created by the Spirit! The possibility of novelty within the universe is ultimately grounded in the same source as the possibility of the whole creation itself, namely, in God the Spirit.

3. Actualizing the Possible by the Word

A second point in the creation narrative in Genesis worth noting is this: the possibility created by the Spirit is the condition and basis of the actuality of creation that comes about by God speaking. Verse 3 carries the work of creation one step further: from possibility into actuality. The activity of actualizing creation from its possibility is attributed to God speaking: "And God said." Here it is God in his self-constitution and self-existence who speaks. What he says comes from him as God. And since it is he who says it, it is his Word, and so it is of him as God. And so the word spoken is by God, of God, and from God. But now, he speaks his word not to himself but to the formless void and to the darkness upon which the Spirit has already been at work to make possible what is not possible. It is the speaking that translates the possible into actuality. This speaking by God is again a free act. It is a free decision he makes. It is a free response to the work of the Spirit in making possible what is impossible. It is a responsive and most appropriate act. Its thrust is to actualize creation as made possible by the Spirit. And so the intention and direction of God speaking is to establish the actuality of creation as such, the universe as such, the world as such, all that there is as such. And so we can say, God speaking is what gives creation its existent reality, its reality as world, its character as secular.

We should note here the relationship between the Spirit from God sweeping over the face of the deep and of God speaking to the possibility that the Spirit has brought about from the condition of non-possibility in pre-creation. Both come from God. Both are of God. Both have the same intention and thrust. It is the making of creation from its possibility through the Spirit to its actuality by the Word. What is created as possible by the Spirit is made actual by the Word, and what is actualized by the Word is what has been determined as possible by the Spirit. In Wisdom thought in the Old Testament, what God planned as possible is what God implemented. The planning is the work of the Spirit. The executing and implementing and the achieving in actuality are the work of the Word. Spirit and Word that are of God and from God are what created "the heavens and the earth" and gifted them their creaturely secularity. In dealing with the Nothing and the Chaos, God is exercising his sovereignty over this condition and over the result of this exercise, which is the actuality of creation. That sovereignty is exercised by God in the making of the possible and in actualizing it into reality. The creaturely secularity of the world is wholly established, sustained, respected, and valued by God through his Spirit and by his Word.

There is a close relation between God speaking and "And it was so." What is so cannot be so, that is, it cannot happen without God speaking. It is entirely contingent upon God speaking. Moreover, God's speaking makes what it says happen. The speaking itself—the act of speaking—is the power that makes what it says happen. There is no gap or contradiction whatsoever between the act of speaking and the event of happening, so that God's speaking never fails to bring about what it says. God's Word, which is both the speaking and what is said, is creative. The inner relation between the speaking and the happening may be discerned as an interpenetrating, a co-inhering and interfacing between them. This, however, can only occur in the power of the Spirit who energizes the "possibilizing" (that is, making possible), the speaking, and the happening. In the power of the Spirit all these occur as a unitary event, a single happening. The speaking is an event, a linguistic event. It happens as it is spoken. The "And it was so," the being so, the being of being and of existence in the variety of its forms, the sheer occurrence of facticity, simply happens. It happens as creative event. Happening is event; event is happening. So creation is Speech/Event. The "And it was so" happens by the speaking that happens and makes happen what it says.

This sheer happening is unique: Only God and none other makes it happen. It is contingent: It is contingent only in God making it happen. It happens as new, as a novelty. It is new generally in that it is different from God since it is not of God; and it is different from the Nothing since it is already a possibility that is being actualized. It is already a Something. It is also new in its definiteness and particularity. A thing as something is different from any other something. It is new in its difference from them. There is therefore diversity and variety. Their configuration and ordering is also dependent upon the Speech/Event. Thus, the interconnectedness of things in their variety and diversity is dependent upon their happening at all in, through, and by the Speech/Event. Does not all this warrant the inference, the conclusion, that the creaturely secularity of "And it was so" that covers "all that there is" cannot and should never be absolutized, or sacralized, or idolized, let alone divinized or deified, because it is utterly contingent upon the Speech/Event that can only happen through the Spirit by the Word? Does that not mean that the secular cannot and should not be made into secularism? If this were done, there is likely to occur a movement that strips, deconstructs, redresses, retrieves, and restores the secular to its genuine secularity. This process could be understood as protecting the secular in its creaturely dignity, and so affirming it as an existent, respecting its rights, and appreciating its value.

We may ask at this point, what is it that comes to be from what may come to be that is not-yet? What is it that has become actual from its possibility?

The first that makes its appearance in the Genesis narrative is that of light: "Then God said, 'Let there be light,' and there was light" (1:3). The fact that light appears first is given its priority over everything else that follows. And that means it is absolutely necessary for everything else that follows. While its priority may appear temporally (as it may be in any narrative or storytelling) its temporal priority signifies its priority in order and dignity and so is axiomatic and presuppositional to all else—to being, existence, variety and diversity, to life and the processes of life, to consciousness and intelligibility, and so on. Moreover, its appearance does not come from the formless void and the darkness that covers it. Its emergence is not a possibility from non-possibility, from the Nothing and the Chaos. Given these considerations, we may ask: Where did it come from? The most appropriate answer, it seems, is to say that it comes from the Spirit hovering and sweeping over the formless void and its darkness. Light is light of the Spirit. It is this light that shines upon the darkness of the formless void in order to differentiate darkness from it and to make something possible out of the Nothing of the formless void. Light, however, does not eliminate darkness; otherwise there is nothing for light to shine upon. Light does not eliminate the nonpossible; otherwise there is none from which to create. However, the darkness cannot overcome the light; it has no power over it. The formless void cannot overcome the possibility-making power of the Spirit, let alone resist and defeat the actualizing power of Spirit/Word.

So then what does God do with the darkness from which light has shown to be different but does not erase? What does he do with the formless void that is empty of everything? What does he do with the unruly and disorderly waters of chaos that flood the surface of the deep?

4. The Sovereignty of God in Creation

The answer: He makes creative use of them! In so doing he exercises sovereign authority over them. He incorporates them into his creative work. He endows them with potentials that when realized turn out to their own benefit. When they are allowed to participate in his creative activity they become, in their own measure and degree, self-creative themselves and co-creators with God in the continuing enrichment of creation as such. In so doing, he lays down the basic constitutive and general lines and parameters of creaturely reality and so of secularity. What follows sketches these universal features of created reality.

By distinguishing light from darkness he separates them into day and night, respectively, which then gives rise to evening and morning. At the same time, he brings together the day and night into a single unit called the first Day. In effect, God through Spirit and Word constitutes the beginning of time and sets its linear movement, its *chronos* character (Gen. 1:14). And since the succeeding creation events now happen in time, linear time is now invested with its opportune sense. Each day in *chronos* time becomes a time, an occasion, of creative happening; it becomes timely time for something to happen, *kairos* time. Each creative happening has a time in which it is to occur. And so everything has a time of its own (Eccles. 3:1-8). Thus, things and events are timed: They happen in time and in their own time. This combining of *chronos* time and *kairos* time transforms the linear character of time into a direction toward the fulfillment of time—the fullness of time, the end-time, the *eschaton*. What would this be? (More of this below.) This temporality of all things and events is an inescapable feature of the creatureliness of secular reality. It is what constitutes the *saeculum* feature of the secular world. This essential temporality cannot be transformed into timelessness or to endlessness or into the so-called "eternal." To do so in any way would violate and distort the creaturely temporality of secular reality. It is God who creates time, and so only he can change time. Time cannot change itself by itself into something else. If time changes, it cannot change changing, for to do so would still be change. Any change in it or upon it that is not from God and of God would distort and pervert it and it would then require restoring it to its genuine character. What does it take to restore perverted time to its genuine creaturely, secular temporality? Is time transformable by God into something else?

What does God do with the formless void and the unruly chaos? He creates a dome and puts the unruly waters in their proper places in relation to the dome. The dome separated the waters above it and the waters below it. God called the dome Sky. He also gathered the unruly waters under the sky and let the dry land appear. God called the dry land Earth and the gathered waters Sea. So the waters have their own placing as does the earth and both have their own places in relation to each other.

What does this narrative of creating primal places and at the same time putting primal things in their proper places in relation to one another signify? He is creating space out of the formless void and putting primal things such as water and earth in their proper order. Space is not an empty container into which things are put. Space is the placing of things in their proper relations and order; or to use a modern term, space is creating an ecosystem in which things, non-alive and alive, are ordered together for their own benefit. In this perspective, one can hardly distinguish what is placed in their ordered relations and into that in which they are placed. In short, space is the ordering of things in their appropriate and complex relations. Space is in, out, above, below, from, to, beyond, for, against, with. All these words are relational. They are what create space. In short, space is the ordered relations of things. The world of things now has its own space in proper relation. There is now a *saecularis*—a world in its own space!

From formless void, God creates space. From unruly chaos, he creates order by putting things in their proper places in ordered relation to each other. All this, God does in and through the Spirit and by the Word and actualizes them by speaking that makes happen what he says: Both time and space are contingent upon God and they exist creaturely in this relation. It is in this primal relation that they have their existent status and right. It is their creaturely being and thus their secular existence. But about what happens in this relation, what processes take place within it, how things behave in detail in this relation, the text is silent. What does this silence mean? Might not this silence mean the making of a clearing for science to have its own workshop in which to do its work? After all, does not science presuppose a world already there to know and assumes a light already there that makes knowing possible? And should the primal relation of *religare* prevent science from doing its job? Is not that job an essential feature of the secularity of creaturely existence and should it not therefore be affirmed, protected, promoted, and valued?

5. The Emergence of Life as Gift

With verses 3 and 20 in the Genesis narrative, we encounter another decisive turn in the story of creation, namely, the emergence of life in its various forms. The first thing to note is that it is the earth that brings forth the first form of life: vegetation. But the earth is described as dry. That means it is lifeless. (cf. Gen. 2:5) It cannot possibly yield life. How can nonlife bring forth life? Again we return to what is said of the Spirit earlier. It is the Spirit that creates the possibility of life out of nonlife. And this possibility is brought forth into actuality by God speaking the word that summons the possibility into actuality. "Then God said: 'Let the earth put forth vegetation.'. . . And it was so. The earth brought forth vegetation" (1:11, 12). Again we note that there is no contradiction between the possibility created by the Spirit and the actuality brought forth by the Word. The text does not say how long in time the actualizing process takes place. The text simply connects the happening with time, *chronos* time, linear time—*a third day*. But the actualizing takes place in *chronos* time, thus transforming *chronos* time into *kairos* time by the event happening in it. *Chronos* time and *kairos* time are the times ordained by God for creation time, including the emergence of life on earth as created life.

The text on life in the Genesis narrative when reopened for further understanding has a context whose background stretches back to the possibility-making work of the Spirit, the actualizing process summoned by the Word; and for its foreground, what further diverse forms it may take in the course of its development in participation in the continuing creative process. And so the temporal continuum of life stretches backward to its possibility, inward to its development, in diversity and complexity, and forward to its transformation and fullness. Life is in time and so is timed. That its emergence happens on "the third day" is a temporal metaphor for the whole time of creation and for the time of each specific life-form.

What the components of life are and their details are not mentioned. That leaves ample room for scientific investigation. Now I do not wish to enter into a discussion on life (biology) in the light of evolution. The geneticist Theodosius

Dobzhansky has said, "Nothing in biology makes sense except in the light of evolution." Insofar as the theory of evolution and the understanding of life in the light of it are aspects of the secularity of the world there is in principle no critical objection to it. The interest of this writer, as has already been shown above, is to affirm secularization as a process of appreciating the integrity of the world, and to place this affirmation within the horizon of the Spirit in view of a binding bond *religare* established by the same Spirit. I leave the details to biology in the light of evolution.[3] We may only take note of those aspects of life mentioned in the Genesis texts and say more in the next chapter:

- the emergence of life from nonlife
- the self-perpetuation of life through "seed"
- the appearance of different and various forms or species of life
- their appearance from lower to higher: plants, fish, birds, animals
- the fecundity of life and the multiplication of species (1:22)

The universal and cosmic aspects of creation that are the structural conditions and support systems for everything that exists and lives—light and darkness, day and night, land and water, firmament and earth—all these aspects of life and its conditions and more are left open in their details and processes. They have become the subject of scientific study and science has learned much about the. They may all be seen from evidence as falling under the light of evolution.

To the extent that the study of evolution and its findings may be regarded as confirming the secularity of life in an evolving universe, they are to be appreciated and valued. But the fact that life and all its aspects are placed within the parameters of the creation story puts them within the dynamic sphere of the Spirit/Word as the agency of God's creative activity. The findings of the science of biology in the light of evolution may indeed redound to the enrichment and deepening of the appreciation for the secularizing dynamism of the Spirit.

What would be the most theologically reasonable inference to the best possible explanation from what has been said so far? Must we not claim that the possibility of all cosmic things—existences, definiteness, distinction (or differentiation), separation, and ordering—is indeed the work of the Spirit? Must not the Spirit then be seen as effectively creating the possibility of anything that has come to actuality by the Word? Moreover, what comes into actuality as a specific thing—whether alive or not—takes on physical or material form in any of the states in which "matter"

3. Kenneth R. Miller, *Finding Darwin's God* (New York: Cliff Street Books, 1999), xi, quoted in John F. Haught, *Making Sense of Evolution* (Louisville: John Knox, 2010), xv.

exists (more of this process below). If this is so, must we not also include in the work of the Spirit the creation of such a possibility? The possibility of matter taking on in actuality a specific form—whether a physical thing or a species of life or a temporal event entailing some configuration of matter—is a function of the Spirit, is it not? If these claims are anywhere near the truth, is there any possibility at all that has been actualized that is outside the realm of the Spirit in its creative power?

My view of the open-endedness of life and its diverse forms to scientific study excludes me from the company of those who reduce the texts on creation to literalism and do not appreciate the understanding of life and its processes yielded by evolution. They reject evolution in favor of a creationism based on a literal understanding of the Scriptures. I value their theological concern and their effort to protect biblical faith. I have tried to incorporate their concern into my view of the Spirit as the horizon of secularity. Alternatively, I also do not go so far as to join the company of the likes of Richard Dawkins and Daniel C. Dennett, who reduce secularity to materialistic secularism and regard the secularizing process as leading inevitably to materialistic atheism. Their science may be on target. I do not have the competence to judge it. But it seems to me that the conclusions they derive from it are a bit too far out and are not warranted by the evidence seen in a wider context. They do not justify the inference to atheism as the best possible explanation.[4]

6. Creation by "Letting Be"

There is another point worth noting that runs through what has been said so far and merits highlighting: The process of transformation from possibility to actuality, not only from non-possibility to possibility, is energized, sustained, and accompanied by the Spirit. The potency of the Word in making happen what it says derives from the power of the Spirit. The effectiveness of the Word in achieving what it aims is effected by the power of the Spirit. The pointedness of the Word in expressing and accomplishing God's will in creation is shaped and sharpened by the cutting edge of the Spirit. But the way the Spirit accompanies in effective power and pointed thrust the transition from possibility to actuality is such that it makes room for spontaneity and freedom and participation to appear as elements in the creative process. (Since the power of the Spirit is the same power of the Word, I will use the term "the Spirit" to include the Word.)

---

4. Richard Dawkins, *The God Delusion* (Boston: Houghton Mifflin, 2006); Daniel C. Dennett, *Darwin's Dangerous Idea* (New York: Touchtone, 1995).

Consider the following: God creates by "letting be" (Gen. 1:3, 6). God's speaking in creating has the sense of "summoning" or a calling forth of something specific that has been formed from what has been made possible (cf. Rom. 4:17). Creation is not an act of inducement, or manipulation, or coercion, or violence that forces something to come to be. Rather, God lets be what he creates by summoning it. This can only mean that he creates in the power of grace, not in the force of violence. He makes room for what he creates. He does this by giving his creation its own space and time in which it becomes actual and develops. And that room for actuality and development is within his Spirit. In letting be, he permits what he creates to arise out of nothing. Does not this arising come from the possibility created by the Spirit? He confers upon what arises its own spontaneity, freedom, and power to be. Is not this conferring done in the power of God as Spirit? His letting be is precisely the conferring of the freedom and power to be out of the possibility as already determined by the Spirit, and so it is a summons to arise in concrete being, in a specific form of existence, in a definite species of life. In letting be, God also respects, affirms, and values the actuality of what he creates—in its freedom, dignity, existence, and life.

The activity of creation appears to have a threefold dimension: an inner dimension that has to do with possibilities, a process dimension that has to do with actualizing what has been possibilized, and a summoning dimension that has to do with specific forming into particular types of existences and discrete forms of life. This threefold dimension of its process is inspired, enabled, sustained, and accompanied by the Spirit. What would be the best theological inference from all these? Is it not to say that the secular reality of the world and all that there is take place within the power and horizon of the Spirit?

What God says that it be is definite in its particularity. Let there be *light*; let there be a *dome*; let the *earth put forth vegetation*. This "let there be" is followed by "and it was so." It comes to be. But God does not stop there. He goes on to call the name of what he lets be and thus comes to be. What does this mean? Giving the name of something means being identified as such by that name. When one's given name is called, one responds to the calling of one's name. This means naming a thing is defining the correct form and nature of a specific existing thing. It is this naming that identifies the discrete particularity of a thing in its existence, form, essence, or nature. This naming confers to what is named the integrity and dignity of its existence in the form that it is. And so it establishes its difference from all others. It accords to it its right to be and to be different from all others.

The "naming" is coupled with the "separating": "Let there be a dome in the midst of the waters, and let it separate the waters from the waters. . . . God called the dome Sky" (Gen. 1:6, 8, 14). This "separating" activity of God of what has come to be is an act acknowledging and respecting the distinctiveness and difference of each entity that has come to be and named. The "separating" is based on difference and distinctiveness. The separating is also an act of placing each entity in its own "space" in which it can be "at home" as its own ecosystem. In this eco-habitat it can thrive and develop and so it can carve out a life-space of its own in relation to the other things that are also assigned their specific space by the act of separation. Together with the assigning of space for each entity goes the act of separation that divides time into days, and seasons, and years, and gives time to each entity its own time. In its own time and through its own time-process, the entity can carve out from time its own life-time. With its own life-space and life-time, the named entity can make its own life-world, which has its own life-story! One's own life-world with its own life-story in one's own life-time and life-space, one secures one's own *saeculum* and *saecularis* that defines one's individual and personal secularity—and this applies universally to the this-worldly character of all life!

God's activity of letting be, of naming, and of separating goes on to the extent of assigning the specific functions of each created entity. The dome is given the task of "separating the waters from the waters." The earth is given the task of bringing forth vegetation. The lights in the dome are tasked to separate the day from the night and be signs for seasons, days, and years, and for them to be lights in the dome of the sky to give light upon the earth. God made the two great lights, the greater light (the sun) to rule the day, and the lesser light (the moon) to rule the night (Gen. 1:6, 9, 11, 14-18). With the function or task given to each named and separated entity go the capacity and the authority to do the task, or carry out the function, and so to achieve it in coordination with one another, which also are doing their tasks for the good of the whole of creation. That they do their functions and behave in a way that enables them to do their work properly goes without saying. Their behavior is assumed to be in accordance with the laws that derive from their form of existence, characteristic features, and their relations with one another. This assigning of functions with corresponding capacities and carried out properly in coordination with others for mutual benefit when fulfilled is what gives usefulness, meaning, worth, and a sense of profound satisfaction to their existence. These are secular benefits that are distributed universally and so are common to all and enjoyed by all.

God not only creates but allows what he has already created to participate in its own self-creation and self-perpetuation: "Then God said, 'Let the earth put forth vegetation: plants yielding seed, and fruit trees of every kind on earth that bear fruit with the seed in it.' And it was so"(Gen. 1:11). The "earth" here is the "dry land" that has already been rendered dry by God separating the waters and gathering them into seas. And it is this dry earth that is summoned to "put forth vegetation." This earth is summoned to give birth, not to more earth, but to something different, namely, vegetation. Earth itself has become creative of something new; it now has been allowed to participate in the creative process. Moreover, it does this from within itself, from possibilities generated within it, by whom? By the Spirit, of course. Creativity from within, made possible and accompanied by the Spirit, has now become part of the creative process set in motion by God! Furthermore, the vegetation put forth by earth includes within it its own seed, the potentiality of its own self-perpetuation and self-creation. Again this is a potency exercised from within, and so it is a potency for self-participation in the creative process in the form of self-creation and self-perpetuation! This leaves the future of creation open, not only to new possibilities that the Spirit will create but also because of the contribution of creation itself to its own self-creation and self-perpetuation.

How should we take theologically this activity of naming things that have come to be, separating them from one another in their proper and coordinated relationships, and assigning them with functions with corresponding capacities enabling them to participate, in the measure proper to them, in God's creative activity? Would it be too far-fetched to conclude that this is God's way of creatively bringing order and life out of primal chaos and thus making a living cosmos, an ordered living world? And since the ordering is of the world, does not that ordering belong to the world and is for the world as such? If so, then this order is a this-worldly order; it is a secular order. But if all this-worldly ordering is done and accomplished in and through the power of the Spirit and by the Word in its wisdom, must it not be seen as within the agency and horizon of Spirit and Word? That could only mean that it is God that secularizes. And what is secularized bears the seal of the Spirit/Word and is open, receptive, and transparent to, and influenced by, the agency of Spirit and Word. And for this reason the secularity of the ordered life of the world is not merely secular as such, as though that can be by itself and for itself. It is a spiritual secularity because it is the Spirit that secularizes!

7. Creation Is Good

We suggest a final point to be noted in the Genesis text on creation. This has to do with the Spirit's role in God's evaluation of what is created as good. The text is worded as follows: "And God saw that it was good" (see 1:4; 1:10, 12, 18, 21, 25).

One may imagine God as somewhat withdrawing to some distance from what he created in order to look at it a little bit more intently. This seeing is at the same time an evaluating of what is seen. It is a seeing that looks at every part of creation and judges it. Lo and behold, the seeing and the judging are unmistakably appreciative: "And God *saw* that it was *good*." What is it in what God has created that God sees as good? What he sees and declares good are not just specific things but those that are presuppositional to all things. He sees light, and declares it good. He sees the dry land, which he called earth—the habitat of land life—and he declares it good. He sees vegetation as alive and self-creating and self-perpetuating in its life-form. He declares it good. He sees the order that results from separating and the giving of functions to light, time, space, and he declares it good. He sees the waters bringing forth marine life in its diversity and the birds flying freely in the sky, and God declares it all good. He sees the earth bringing forth living creatures of every kind: cattle, and creeping things and wild animals of every kind and he declares it good. In all these, there is existence in all its diverse forms common to all. This is good. There is life in all its forms common to all. This is good. There is diversity and difference and yet there is order. This is good. There is a variety of functions and different ways of functioning and doing. This is good. There is fecundity through which life participates in God's creativity. This is good. There is not only structuring order but dynamic development and the emergence of the new. This is good. There is the inner underlying possibility-making work of the Spirit and the actualizing power of God's Word—and this is undeniably good, for without this there won't be creation itself. There would simply be Nothing; there would simply be Chaos. But fundamental to all this is God's *turn* in his self-becoming to be God of another, namely his creation! It is this turning to another in God's self-definition of himself that is the ground of the creative secularity of all that there is! It is this turn that binds God to the creaturely reality of the secular. It is this seeing and evaluating as good that sustains creatively secular reality in its possibility, its actuality, its diversity, its order, its self-creation and perpetuation, and in all the processes that these entail. God's withdrawal of his presence and of his "seeing" inevitably leads to the collapse and destruction of his creation. Moreover, it is this being present to and seeing creation that provides God the vantage point for making an evaluation of what he has done in creation. It is this face-to-face and intimate involvement in his creation that enables him to experience it and know it and be able to pass judgment upon it. And how else is God present to and indeed sees his creation in face-to-face relation and intimacy except as Spirit and in the light of the Spirit?

Alternatively, the normative posture of creation in relation to God is being "before him" (*coram deo*), being in his presence and in his sight! Creation is creation precisely by being open to God's presence and to his sight. The loss of this openness so that creation or any of its parts or relations is no longer transparent to God would mean the diminution of light and the onset of darkness and the eventual loss of existence and of life! It would mean the return of primal darkness. This transparency to God is celebrated in Psalm 139. How else may creation remain open and transparent to God except by the light of the Spirit?

God sees creation as good. This means that goodness is built into creation. St. Augustine formulated this truth with unsurpassed terseness: "To be is to be good." The word translated "saw" has the double meaning of perception and evaluation. Goodness is objective to and is in what God creates. Because goodness is built into creation, it can be perceived. It is not something merely subjective to the perceiver, nor merely conferred by the valuer. God's primal deed not merely put goodness in creation; rather, God sees creation itself as good. One can take this a step further and say that it is God seeing as good that makes a thing good. What God sees as good is thereby affirmed as good. It is as God affirms what is good that it is good. What is good of creation is what is good in God's sight. Any good that is not perceived and affirmed as good by God in his sight is no good at all, even if it is good to somebody else. God is the true judge of what is good and so also of what is evil. This is a prerogative only God rightfully possesses and exercises.

Finally, what is said above implies that what is truly good is what can stand in the presence or sight of God, that is, in his Spirit. Goodness does not simply inhere in being and existence, or in actuality. What St. Augustine said about being as in itself good is only a half-truth. Good is being and existence and actuality in the sight of God, *coram Deo*, in his presence, in his Spirit. In the sight of God means being before him, being seen, affirmed, enjoyed, celebrated by God. This is why a truly good life is one that is lived in the worship of God. Life is lived inescapably in God's sight, and so it is best lived acceptably to him as worship of God. *The transparency of creation to the sight of God is what makes it good.* It is transparent because it is in right relation to God as a whole and in its parts. What is rightly related to God is what God loves to see and so is transparent to him. This he affirms and values. It is good because it is righteous, that is, in right relation with him. What is distortedly or wrongly related to him and to others he does not want to see; he hides his face from it. This he banishes from his sight. It is evil because it is unrighteous. In short, righteousness—being in right relation to God and to one another within the whole and so transparent to him—is what makes creation good.

But now the goodness of creation is secured only because it happens in the Spirit through the Word. It is by being in the Spirit through the Word that creation is given its transparency in God's sight. It is in the Spirit through the Word that creation is rightly ordered. In short, it is by being in the Spirit through the Word that creation is righteous and so is good in God's sight (cf. Ps. 33:6).

What further take may we make theologically from what has been said of the goodness of creation? *The goodness that God sees and declares good is of the world and belongs to the world.* It is a this-worldly goodness. It is the goodness of creaturely secularity. And since it is a goodness seen by God as having come to be in and through his Spirit and by his Word and is declared as good in the light of the Spirit, this goodness of creaturely secularity, this this-worldly goodness is utterly contingent on God's seeing it and declaring it good. Thus, whatever good there is in this world, in however form this goodness may take—whether that of virtue, or happiness, or well-being, or truth, beauty, justice, or peace—insofar as it remains contingent on God's turn to it in perception and evaluation, it is the goodness of the world. It is secular goodness so long as it exists, sustained and prospered in this relation. Cutting off that contingent relationship by absolutizing and idolizing whatever that good is perverts the good into evil.

To conclude this chapter, it may well be asked, and rightly so, how trustworthy and enduring is the binding relationship, the *religare*, on which utterly depends the creaturely contingency of creation in its secular existence, life, and goodness? The answer is perhaps God's covenant relationship with creation that he established through Noah as testified in Scripture (Gen. 9: 8-17; cf. Ps. 104).

> Then God said to Noah and to his sons with him. "As for me, I am establishing my covenant with you and your descendants after you, and with every living creature that is with you, the birds, the domestic animals, and every animal of the earth with you, as many as came out of the ark. I establish my covenant with you, that never again shall all flesh be cut off by the waters of a flood, and never again shall there be a flood to destroy the earth." God said, "This is the sign of the covenant that I make between me and you and every living creature that is with you, for all future generations: I have set my bow in the clouds, and it shall be a sign of the covenant between me and the earth. When I bring clouds over the earth and the bow is seen in the clouds, I will remember my covenant that is between me and you and every living creature of all flesh; and the waters shall never again become a flood to destroy all flesh. When the bow is in the clouds, I will see it and remember the everlasting covenant between God and every living creature of all flesh that is on the earth." God said to Noah, "This is the sign of the covenant that I have established between me and all flesh that is on the earth."

We may note the following in the text.

- God's establishing a covenant with Noah and with all creation is a turn in God's self-constitution to be himself for all creation.

- He binds himself as God in covenant with his creation.
- His making and keeping this covenant is an aspect of his self- constitution. And so in keeping his covenant he is being faithful to himself as God for his creation.
- The covenant is inclusive of all creation, including its possibility, its actuality, its order, its goodness, its future and destiny. All this is in and through the Spirit and by the Word and both are of God and from God by which he constitutes himself in his turning to creative activity.
- While the covenant is also in the form of a promise, God has given an enduring sign that he will and he can fulfill his promise.
- The promise and its sign, however, are possibilized by the Spirit and implemented by the actualizing word. In God both the promising and the fulfilling go hand and hand in his faithfulness to the covenant. What he says he does and it happens. Must we not therefore conclude that even now God continues his creative activity not only to preserve it but to bring it to its fulfillment and destiny?

The covenant is "everlasting" because God has taken up creation in its secularity into his self-constitution for it and so in being faithful to himself he is at the same time being faithful to his covenant with creation, and in being faithful to his covenant, he is being faithful to himself as God.

But can creation as such break the covenant, the *religare*? Not creation as such! But maybe a participant in the creative process, namely, humankind? Not even humankind can cut off the primal umbilical relation, *the religare*. Humankind can only pervert and distort it and corrupt it into a devilish power that harms and destroys and imperils creation. And it can happen! Creation can be destroyed. That is the meaning of the Great Flood! It can be destroyed by God because of human sin (Gen. 6:5-7, 11-13). But this is another story that will be told in another chapter in this book.

CHAPTER III

LIFE IN THE SPIRIT AS SECULAR

In this essay we are exploring the breadth and depth of the presence and activity of God the Spirit. Our aim is to see the this-worldly character of this world—its secularity—within this horizon of the Spirit and discern the affirmation and appreciation of this secularity as a work of the Spirit. The claim that we are making is that it is the Spirit that secularizes. A genuine spirituality is one that secularizes; and a genuine secularity is open to, and receptive of, the Spirit.

So far we have pointed to the Spirit's role in making creation possible, thereby determining what becomes actual through God speaking the creative word. We have suggested that in letting creation be, God the Spirit makes room within himself for what he creates. He places it within his sight so that it is transparent to him and he can evaluate it as good. In this evaluation, it is also he who can see and judge the evil that befalls it. We have sought to encompass within the widest possible frame (as suggested by the text) the matrix of the most basic, differentiated, universal, and cosmic elements that go into the making of creation. And, of course, the all-encompassing frame and matrix is nothing less than God the Spirit who is both other than, and yet present to and active in, his creation as a whole and in all its parts and processes. Because God the Spirit encompasses his creation in his presence and power, creation must be seen as being within and transparent to the Spirit of God. Discerning God the Spirit at work at the depth levels of creation and viewing all of creation as encompassed within, and penetrated by, the Spirit of God would seem to be basic to a spirituality that secularizes and is able to take into account the findings of science and the plurality and richness of secular experience.

Although we have touched the issue of life in the previous chapter, we have not, however, given it the kind of reflection that it deserves as equally basic and important to what was considered in that chapter. The issue about the emergence of life and of the human being in its form, life, vocation, and destiny are matters that will occupy us in this chapter.

1. The Life-Giving Spirit

The main thing that has to be said about life is that its possibility and emergence must also be seen as the work and gift of the Spirit. The Spirit is not only presence and power but also life and life-giving.

To appreciate this, we must see the emergence of life against the background of "what went on before" it has appeared. Every aspect of creation that God the Spirit through the Word has put in place (what the text calls "Let there be . . . and it was so," and which we have termed as "actualization")—such as light (Gen. 3), time (day and night, evening and morning, seasons and years: vv. 5, 8, 13, 14, 19, and so on), the firmament of space (vv. 6-8), the seas and the earth (vv. 9-10), the sun and the stars (v. 16)—has its own distinctive nature, status, identity, relationships, and processes. All these are in direct relation to God within his Spirit and power. God's judgment and appreciation that each is good in its own right, integrity, and relationships must be affirmed, appreciated, and celebrated (vv. 4, 10, 12, 18, 21, 25). This it seems is the foundation for affirming, respecting, and protecting what today is called in secular language "the rights of nature."

Moreover, their actualization and ordering took "some time." Although it is true that time began *with* creation (St. Augustine), it is also true that as creation "began" with time (linear time, *chronos* time), it has taken place *in* time (*kairos* time, eventful time). Creation, therefore, has a history. Or to use the language of biology, there is an "evolving" that took time in the actualization of creation. And both evolution and history require historical time (significant time, which is both linear and *kairos* time).

To regard creation as having a history is, of course, suggested by the narrative character of the text. Narration tells the story of what happens in time. The story happens in time and so takes time. The story line has a plot that unfolds, and the unfolding takes time. But while the story is told in literal terms, its intention is to point to a deeper, larger, and universal reality. So the literal must be understood metaphorically. The reality to which the metaphor points is the story of God's creation of the "heavens and the earth." The time of "six days" metaphorically refers to the time it took for God to create the universe. And births are the births of lifetimes, and so "generations" and "genealogies" are the successions of lifetimes. Additionally, Genesis 2:4 speaks of creation as "the generations of the heavens and the earth when they were created." The word *generation* means birth or a succession of births. And that takes time.

Moreover, the idea of generation is associated with the idea of "genealogy," which is a central theme in the account of primeval history in Genesis. A genealogy is an account of succession of births or of generations of lifetimes. Thus, one may interpret Genesis 1 as an "account" of a genealogy of the heavens and the earth, or of creation. And both generation and genealogy require time, succession of lifetimes, for their taking place, which therefore makes them historical in character.

The view that creation is historical and its process as in some sense an "evolving" that takes some time is important for a vision of spirituality that secularizes. It allows us to take into account the history of the universe and the earth as happening in its own time as allotted to it. It makes us appreciate the "emergent" character of life. It enables us to view creation from the perspective of eschatology, and so to regard it as still "unfinished" and as having a "future" that is yet to be fulfilled, hence a destiny of its own. This makes room for evolution as the history of earth and of life.

It is extremely appropriate and important to affirm and appreciate the integrity and history of the basic elements of creation in their relationship to God within his Spirit. It is equally important that their significance in relation to the appearance of life must also be affirmed and appreciated. That significance consists in the fact that they are the universal conditions that are essential for the emergence of life. The text acknowledges that life appears on "the dry land Earth" (vv. 11-12) and in the "waters" that form part of the Earth (v. 20). But this happens only after "the dry land" has appeared and "waters" have been gathered into seas (vv. 9-10). Only after the earth has become "land" by being dry and only after the waters have been "gathered" so that they don't flood and overwhelm the earth does life appear. This earth as land and the waters as seas become one of the universal conditions for life to appear. Moreover, God did this only after he has let light, time, space, and so on, to appear. All these—and others—constitute the essential conditions for the appearance of life, and all these have been put in place by God as Spirit through his Word. Precisely because they constitute the essential conditions of life on earth, it is critically important to respect and protect "the rights of nature." These rights belong to nature as nature because God has given them to nature as nature and so are bound to, and contingent upon, God's covenanting himself with nature. These rights belong to the secularity of nature as such.

Having acknowledged the pre-history of life and its significance, we must nevertheless go on and say that none of these elements separately or together can make life possible, produce it, cause it to appear on earth, and actualize it. The "dry land" cannot of itself generate vegetation. One may interpret Genesis 1:10-11 in the light of Genesis 2:5-6. Here "the earth" is without any sign of life. There are no plants, no herbs, no rain to wet the dry ground so that it can generate and nourish plant life, and there is no one to till the ground (v. 5). The earth already exists as land but it is completely lifeless, and so it cannot of itself produce life and cause it to appear. Life is not at all possible from lifeless earth. But how long it took for life to emerge from nonlife, this text does not say. Might the information on this be supplied by science? Some eleven billion years?

There is a parallel to this in modern physics. The atoms, the molecules, the elements, the forces, the planets, the stars, the galaxies, while they provide the cosmic conditions for the possibility of life on earth, nevertheless, cannot separately nor together originate life. The best that they can do together, so far, is to provide for the emergence of complexity and organization, that is, of cosmic order. Life appears at a very high level of complexity and organization from quantum disorder. But pinpointing "the threshold" at which disordered lifelessness crosses into ordered life, that is still unknown. One physicist states: "The origin of life remains a mystery, and contentious even among scientists. . . . Let us regard life, not as an isolated miracle in an otherwise clockwork universe, but as an integral part of the cosmic miracle."[1]

For the earth to generate life from itself, it is absolutely necessary for life to be made possible from its non-possibility, and this we have said earlier is the function of the Spirit. And for life to appear actually on earth and assume its creaturely form it is equally necessary for God to speak his creative word: "Let the earth put forth vegetation. . . . And it was so. . . . And God saw that it was good" (vv. 11, 12). And what God says happens because it has been made possible in the Spirit and placed in a position within his presence to which it is bound by the Spirit, and so is transparent to him in the light of the same Spirit. The next form of life—higher than plants and trees—are "swarms of living creatures" brought forth by the waters, "birds [that] fly above the earth across the dome of the sky," and then "cattle and creeping things and wild animals of the earth of every kind" (vv. 20-23). Though imprecise in method and limited in scope compared with the methods and findings of modern science, there is here a classification of levels and kinds of life. Not scientific in the modern sense, but nevertheless on target.

1. Paul Davies, *The Fifth Miracle* (New York: Simon and Schuster, 2000).

Furthermore, God gives the life he originates with the potentiality to reproduce itself: the plants yielding seed, trees bearing fruit with seed in it (vv. 11-12). It is through the seed breaking through the sod that life generates itself and so perpetuates itself. In the case of the higher forms of life—fish, birds, animals—he gave the same capacity by "blessing them," saying, "Be fruitful and multiply." That blessing is in the form of the sexual reproduction of life. Gender sexuality, being male and female, is a blessing God gives to life as a gift. One of its purposes is for it to participate in the creation and continuation of life at its creaturely, secular level and form. That participation can only take place in and through the Spirit. And so it is included within the everlasting covenant of God with creation and is contingent upon that covenant. This is established by the fact that life and its capacity to reproduce itself are both characterized as having "the breath of life" (v. 30). And this "breath of life" is possible only as a gift of the Spirit (cf. 2:7). With the capacity to reproduce itself, life is thus given the potentiality to participate in the creative process through its self-creation, self-formation, and self-perpetuation. Thus life is made to share in the power of God to create and preserve and perpetuate life. This self-creating and self-perpetuating power of life is the basis of "generations" and "genealogies" (so prominent in Genesis 1–11) that express the unbroken continuity and complex interrelatedness of all life, from the beginning until now! Life itself is historical. And this happens in the Spirit through the blessing of the spoken Word! Life in its various levels, forms, dynamic processes, and history has all these as dimensions of its secularity, its this-worldliness.

The texts we are considering are silent about the emergence of consciousness in life. But could we not suppose that "being alive" can at least include "a feeling for life" that is undeniably present in the lower forms of life, and is the initial manifestation of the emergence of consciousness?

2. The Spirit and the Human Form

We now come to a most decisive turn in the story of creation, namely, the creation of the human! The text is "Let us make humankind" (Gen. 1:26; cf. 2:7). The first thing to be said here is that this is a most significant move on the part of God. It represents a new decisive turn in his self-constitution as God, namely his self-determination to be God for a new "entity" that he decides to create, the human. He is not just God in himself and for himself and by himself, but now he is all this also for and with and in the human. Being God for the human is a new turn in the self-becoming of God. He embraces the human in his reality as God. He involves himself as God the Spirit in the human and so he "experiences" as

God the Spirit the manifold richness of the drama of human life in its twists and turns. There is thus in God's becoming (this turning to the human, in the self-constitution of God) a human and humanizing dimension. It is this "humanity" in God (Karl Barth) that is the seedbed of genuine humanity. It is what makes for the truly and fully human. God is unquestionably for the human. And so there is nothing in genuine humanity that is not grounded in, and embraced by, God's humanity in the Spirit. And to the extent that the human is "this-worldly"—and this is essentially so, and is therefore secular—it is affirmed and appreciated as good, in the Spirit of God. And so, the mantra of this essay is worth repeating: it is God the Spirit that makes the human secular. A genuine spirituality includes the secularity of the human.

The second thing to be said is that the distinctively human form is a work of God the Spirit. The form comes from God the Spirit and is impressed upon the dust of the ground by God. The creation of the human being is part of a "series" of creative acts of God, with each part of the series introducing something new and different (light, sky, night and day, dry land and seas, vegetation, animals, and so on). There is continuity and difference in this series. There is continuity in terms of being and life, but also difference in terms of forms of existence and species of life. The same pattern is seen in the creation of the human being. The words *Let there be* introduce the series of creative activity before the making of the human. Here it seems God creates by allowing indirectly the appearance of existence and its distinctive forms. This "indirect creation" appears more emphasized in the appearance of life, since God summons "earth to put forth vegetation," and "the waters bring forth swarms of living creatures" (vv. 11, 20; see also v. 24) than in the other parts in the series of creative activity. This "indirect creation" emphasizes, it seems to me, the continuity and interrelatedness of life in both its non-human and human forms. All life shares the common coming forth from the earth as made possible by the Spirit through the Word. But now a more radical novelty and of far-reaching difference is introduced. The creation of the human is done in a new way. This is introduced by the words *Let us make* (v. 26). It seems that this new formulation emphasizes God's direct hand in the creation of the human. The word *us* in this phase may refer to the divine beings who compose the court or "cabinet" of God (1 Kings 22:19 ff.; Job.1:6), certainly not to a trinitarian godhead.

In Genesis 2:7 God is portrayed as directly forming the human without a mediating agent. The "dust of the ground" is unformed. In itself it is not the form of the human. It is just dust. It represents the non-possibility of the human form. God has to shape the dust into a distinctively human form. The form does not and cannot derive from the "dust" material. It is rather impressed upon it—from the outside, as it were. The form comes from elsewhere—from God's mind, from God's wisdom—and by his Spirit shapes the dust into the form he wants, the human form. This "dustness" of the human form as part of the "ground" is a graphic and palpable "this-worldliness" of the human form, its secularity. And precisely as this-worldly— as dust of the ground—it is open to a possibility that God makes of it. It is thus receptive to that possibility. This, too, is an aspect of its this-worldliness, its secularity. That it is open and receptive to God's creative activity makes it possible for it to be taken up into God's covenanting and binding relation. The forming is at the same time a binding, and so a bond, a *religare*, is established between God and the human in its form shaped from the "dust of the ground." The "forming," which is also the binding, is done in and through the Spirit. It is the Spirit that shapes the human in its secular form and binds it to himself and also binds himself as Spirit as being for this secular human form. God as creator is here pictured as a potter working upon clay, molding it into a form, a pattern, "he has in mind" (see Jer. 18.6). Alternatively, the clay is malleable and tenderly soft to the touch of the shaping hand and moldable to a form into which the potter makes it.

Why does the text picture God as being more directly involved in the shaping of the human than in his other creating activities? The Genesis 2:17 text does not describe the form of the human specifically. But Genesis 1:26-27 does so. Here the form of the human is specified as "in the image of God," and "in the likeness of God" (cf. Gen. 5:1). The God who is to be "imaged" by the form of the human is not described and specified. It is not possible to do that, for God's form is his alone; it is part of his self constituting power as God. But he decides to make an "image" of himself that mirrors his "likeness." This turn on the part of God to make an image of himself in the form of the human out of the dust of the ground—what could it possibly mean? It profoundly means, does it not, that God turns to make himself known. But to make himself known, he has to reveal himself. In order to reveal himself in a manner that he can be known, he must do so in the way the knower knows. It is God who shapes the form by which he is known in the way the knower knows. And that form is the form of the human. The human form is "the image of God," "the likeness of God." The form of the human fits its function. As form, it yields an image, and so it can image. As image, it yields itself to perception. As perception, it yields itself to conceptualization. As such it yields itself for knowing.

One may denigrate the human form as only an image of God, a likeness of God, as formed from the dust of the earth. But that is precisely what it is—an image formed from the dust. That is exactly its this-worldly reality, its creaturely secularity. That is also precisely its dignity and its worth: It images God; it is the likeness of God. It is the way God has chosen to reveal himself and make himself known. It is also the way a knower may know God as he makes himself known. God has chosen a way to make himself known in the manner the knower knows. And in that way what God makes known is precisely what is known by the knower in the way he knows. The truth of what is made known by the revealer is the truth of what is known by the knower.

There is a correspondence between what is made known and what is known. But here a caveat must be strongly made and absolutely observed: The image and the likeness must not be turned into what is imaged and likened. It is simply an image of a mystery that in itself cannot be known. It is simply a likeness of a reality that is absolutely *sui generis*. If the image becomes a substitute for what is imaged, and it has happened again and again, the image becomes an idol, the likeness becomes a surrogate. And image that has become an idol is false; a likeness that has become a surrogate is a lie. The image as idol no longer mediates the truth of God. A likeness that has become a surrogate no longer mirrors the mysterious reality of God. God disappears from the secular, and the secular is detached from the Spirit and so it becomes secularistic; it becomes its own idol.

If the form of the human images God in his likeness, may we not interpret "the image of God" as the etching boldly of his presence as Spirit—and so also as power, the power to make the human in its proper form? And is not Spirit as power sensed and felt deeply and directly in its immediacy in all dimensions of the human form—physically, feelingly, consciously, mentally, and actively? And does not this sensing and feeling mean the porousness of the dust to the pouring and penetrating presence of God's power into forming the human humanly? God has to be present to what images him, otherwise the image cannot image him. God has to be present to what can liken him, otherwise the likeness may not mirror him. And is not his presence also sensed and felt as power—the power to mold, to penetrate, to make alive, and to energize? Presence and power always go together. Presence without power can be fixed, petrified, and fossilized. Power, without presence cannot be what it can be as actual presence. Power without presence is wild, unformed, unstructured, unordered, chaotic. It cannot be sensed as a stabilizing and trustworthy presence. God as Spirit is both presence and power. And so God as Spirit is palpably and elementally experienced in this world as both presence and power. Presence and power are the this-worldly forms of God as Spirit in the world of dust. They are the secular forms of the spiritual.

But this secular form is precisely the form of the human molded from the dust of the ground. To the question asked earlier, why would God be so interested in taking a direct hand in the creation of the human? The answer is given here: He wants to be sure that the form of the human is in his image, in his likeness. He wants to be sure that the image mediates and radiates his truth. He wills that his likeness may mirror his presence. For that to happen the image must simply be an image and not the reality it images; the likeness must simply be a likeness and not a surrogate of what it likens. The human form is what God has chosen and made to image and liken him. It is the form that reflects God the Spirit in his presence and power. It is the form that is uniquely distinctive of the human. This form is not given to any other aspect of creation.

3. The Spirit and Human Life

The image of God includes not only the human form but also the life that is appropriate to it: life as human. And so it must also be said that God the Spirit creates and gives the life that is appropriate to the distinctive form of the human. Life in human form is not any mere life. It is specifically human life. As human life it is different from the other forms of created life: It is not the life of vegetation, of marine creatures, of fowls, and of animals. Insofar as it is life generally, the human shares in this life that which is common to all and shared by all. But insofar as it is human life, it is this particular life of and for the human only. It is the life proper to the human form: It is the life-form of the human. One elemental feature of the form of the human is what we have already noted above: Though of dust and from the ground it is nevertheless porously open and transparent to the Spirit. This is appropriately and picturesquely symbolized in Genesis 2:7 by "the nostrils" of the human form. Nostrils are designated for a very specific function: to receive or inhale air and to exhale it. The nostrils are specifically for breathing. And "breathing" is an unmistakable sign of life. "Breath," however, is another name for the Spirit of God. And so "breath" is the sign of the life of God, that God is alive. When, therefore, "the breath of life" is breathed into the lifeless human form it imparts life appropriate to it and so makes it come alive as human life.

We may note, before going further, that this breathing of life to the human form is a direct action of God. It is unlike the way vegetation life emerges from the dry land. God lets the earth bring forth vegetation life. It is unlike the way marine life appears! God directs the waters "to bring forth swarms of living creatures" (Gen. 1:20). This is some sort of indirect creation, but creation, nevertheless. In the case of the human form, the Spirit of life breathes directly into the human form through its "nostrils."

But now we must also note that the act of breathing is at the same time the act of creating the life that is appropriate to the human form. The Spirit as the life of God belongs to God, and to God alone. The life imparted to the human form is for this human form only. It is not an extension of the life of God in the human. Human life is not a human version of the life of God; it is not continuous with the life of God. The breathing of life, the giving of life, is at the same time the creation of the life appropriate to the human form. It is created by the Spirit. The human form is thus specially formed to receive the Spirit who gives it the measure and kind of life that is appropriate to it. It is creaturely life. Alternatively, the Spirit as life freely reaches out to the lifeless form of the human to share generously its life- giving powers with it in a way that both respects and sustains the human. This means that both the human form and the life proper to it are created by God, they are creaturely. Both the form and its life are for the this-worldly human. They belong essentially to the creaturely secularity of the human.

Furthermore, this breathing and creating and life-giving act is also at the same time a mutual interpenetrating and interfacing of life and lifeless dust. They become united by and in the same Spirit. The result of all this is tersely stated: "and the man became a living being" (2:7).

This is a most important statement: that the image of God and his likeness in all creation is that of a living human being. The living human being is precisely this because he is created in God's image and likeness. This little word, *in* is a relational word. It indicates that the living human being exists and lives and moves and has its being in God and God in him; that the human being is alive in its distinctive form, that his life-time and his life-space and his life-world, that his becoming into all the possibilities of being human, his life-story in "this world," this secular world, are all embedded in, and contingent upon, the human being in God. He has to be in God to be the image and likeness of God, otherwise there is nothing to image and to liken. To be in God is to be in the Spirit of God, to be encompassed by the Spirit of God. It is the Spirit of God who does the imaging and likening of God through the human. It is the Spirit that makes the human reflect and mirror God in all of creation. It is to "this world," this secular world, that the human is to image God, to point to the reality of God as such, and to testify that it is this God who is the creator of this world and all that there is in it. Because this world is created, it is creaturely, it is secular. But precisely by being created by God and existing in the Spirit of God, the human images and mirrors being in God in a creaturely and secular way. It is in this way that the secular world comes to know that its secularity is firmly bound to and contingent upon God the Spirit. The living human being as the image of God is the incontrovertible testimony to that truth.

In making the statement that the human now has become a living being, the text seems to underscore—does it not?—the fact that with the human form now becoming alive in and through the Spirit, there has now emerged a new and unique reality, or a new form of existence and life. This new reality is neither merely physical, nor merely organic, nor merely animal, but incorporates all these into a new unified entity, namely, the human. This means—does it not? —that the human possesses complexity, organization, unity, characteristics, and potentialities that make it a fit image of God in this world. And so we ask: What is so special about the human being as alive?

In answering this question, we are not to lose sight of the fact that whatever these distinctive qualities are, the human is still deeply connected with, and embedded in, the pre-creation and pre-human conditions described earlier. The "living being" that results from the infusion of life into the human form shaped from the dust of the ground by God the Spirit includes precisely this "dust of the ground." With the "breathing of life" by the Spirit of God, this "dust" of the ground astonishingly becomes alive as flesh. In the form of the human as dust, this dust becomes human flesh by the breathing of life into it. Dust becoming flesh is a work of the Spirit. "Flesh" is dust of the ground incorporated into and infused with life by the Spirit. It is not so much matter being animated as matter being incorporated into and thus given life by the Spirit. It is not so much the Spirit being embodied in flesh as the flesh being bodied with life by the Spirit. As flesh made alive from dust, from lifelessness, it partakes of "the way of all flesh," the law of atrophy and inevitable entropy. It is weak in that it is needy and has to renew its strength by meeting its needs from what would satisfy them. We may ask, Would other forms of "flesh" ultimately satisfy the one need of flesh, namely to stay in the Spirit who makes the dust alive as flesh? Flesh is *finite*. Being bodied with created life, it is a body with bodied limits and limits others that are also bodied and is in turn limited by them. Flesh is *perishable*. It wanes and decays and dies. To dust it returns as dust. But surprisingly it is precisely as flesh—as dust formed into the human and made creaturely alive by the Spirit, and maintained as such—that it is the image of God on earth and in all creation. It is precisely as flesh that it is open to, and dependent upon, the Spirit of God. Its weakness can be made strong by the Spirit. (2 Cor. 12:9-10). From finitude, perishability, and mortality arise the longing and hope for the infinite, the imperishable, the immortal (cf. 1 Cor. 15:42 ff.). The Spirit is "poured upon all flesh" (see Joel 2:28-32). To use postmodern language, flesh is "Spirit-friendly" and "Spirit is flesh-friendly." This is the Spirit that secularizes. This is secularization formed and moved by the Spirit.

It seems to me one can go so far as to say that this mutual openness between the human form and its life, on the one hand, and of the Spirit of God reaching out in presence and power to the human, on the other hand, is the fundamental relation (the *religare*) between God and the human and also between God and all of his creatures, each in the form appropriate to its respective level of being and life. This is the basic and universal relation. This being the case, it is also the basis for creaturely, and also of human, response to God's presence and activity. Responding to God's Spirit out of and as an expression of mutual openness is also a universal possibility, and in the sphere of the human it is an inescapable responsibility. From this, it follows that this basic relation of openness is the fertile soil from which a variety of ways and forms of responding may arise, as indeed they have. There are examples of these responses.

These examples may be classified depending on their evaluation of this primal openness. The various religious faiths may be viewed as positive responses to this openness. Various philosophical systems orient themselves to this openness. Other responses exhibit a negative attitude. They are the agnostic, the naturalistic, the humanistic, the secularistic, and the atheistic. And so we find here also the basic problem we are seeking to address: What is the style of life that best celebrates and nurtures the mutual openness between human life and its forms and God the Spirit in his presence and power? What are those attitudes, sensibilities, and habits of life expressed in the form of basic life-orientation, behavior, and practice that celebrate human life as creaturely and dependent upon God? It is not easy to discover and "practice the presence of God" especially when one takes into account the other characteristics of life in its human form and possibilities.

While we have pointed to the fact that human life is connected with and shares in the characteristics common to all forms of earthly life, it has, nevertheless, features that are distinctive to itself. To these we now turn.

4. The Distinctively Human Features

The first thing to note about what is distinctively human is gender difference, the fact that the human is male and female. This statement refers to the difference between being male and being female, to their being for each other in this difference, to their common relation of being "in" the image of God, and so to their common vocation of imaging God in his likeness through both their difference and commonality.

Gender difference, being male and being female, takes place at the level of creation: "So God created humankind in his image, in the image of God he created them; male and female he created them (Gen. 1:27). The word *created* appears in all three lines describing the act of creation. We may take it that gender difference is created difference, and as created it is an act of God. There should be no human playing around with it because it is an essential difference that cannot be undone without ceasing to be human. While it cannot be undone, it can nevertheless be perverted with disastrous consequences. To acknowledge this gender difference and all its implications for human relations entail respecting and observing the equality, integrity, dignity, and value of the difference. Only in recent times are we beginning to appreciate this created difference.

Moreover, this gender difference is difference between equals. The word *and* in "male and female he created them" is a conjunction, not a preposition: It connects but does not specify the relation in the connection. Any attempt to specify the kind of relation in the connection in any direction will likely distort and pervert the equal dignity and integrity indicated by the connection. This has happened in the gender relations characteristic in various cultures. Some are patriarchal. Others matriarchal. Some chauvinistic, some seeking to correct the inequalities and injustices in their social systems that arose out of distortions in gender relations. There is still a long way to go in gender relation reforms. Gender difference is only now being appreciated and the distortions in gender relations are only now being seriously addressed.

Gender difference though deep and dispositional is not however an end in itself and for itself. The human is created male for the female and female for the male. The one is not completely itself without the other. For to be for the female, the male must be fully male. For the female to be for the male, the female must be fully female. Each completes the other in its gender. And so it is by being for the other that the other one is fully himself or herself. Moreover, this mutuality of being for each other is not merely a structural form that is simply given. It is also a disposition that has to be exercised in terms of attitudes and activities that are definitely for the other as another. This disposition aims at securing, promoting, and appreciating the good of the other and that includes the other's being for itself in its difference. There is thus a mutual building up of each other's selfhood that is the self-determining exercise of being in itself and for the other at the same time. This mutual building up of selves may entail one to make sacrifices for the good of the other. But for as long as this is freely done and has the motive of securing the good of the other he or she is being fully himself or herself for the other. And so being actively for the other is no diminution of selfhood but actually a building up of the self.

But gender relation is not only being oneself for the other, it is also structurally and dispositionally and actively being *with* the other, it is being with each other. One cannot do what is entailed by being mutually for each other except by being *with* the other. Of course this being-with may entail distance. It may mean far, far away; or it may mean close, too close; indifferent or intimate. But these are measures of distances in being-with. All entails some form of presence, and absence is a form of presence. The mode of presence, of being-with, may entail behavior or activity that takes into account such a presence in its mode. But whatever mode is the presence, being-with takes the other into account. This taking into account may express itself in terms of sympathy, concern, care, help, or self-giving and self-sacrifice; or in terms of distancing, ignoring, disliking, hating, or harming. There is no escaping this matter of taking account of the other because being male and female is precisely and essentially being with the other. One brings into being with the other his being himself/herself and his/her being for the other. The one relation brings into play all the others.

There is another primal significance of being male and female. It is the structural process of the self-creation and self-perpetuation and self- development of human life. This has reference to the sexual act. And in this process all that has been said about the structural form, disposition, and activity of being male and female, of each being male or female in oneself, of being for each other mutually, and of being with each other, and of taking account of each other, are deeply and inescapably involved in this process of self-creation and self-development of human life.

So far, we have, as best as we could, described in foundational and general terms the phenomenon of gender difference—of being male and female. From an observer's point of view, this is merely an ordinary secular reality of our everyday life that we simply take for granted. It is in fact a this-worldly reality that we take as a matter of course. Later in the next chapter of this book, we will consider another aspect of gender difference as a foundational aspect of human community life. But given all that has been said so far, is this our only take of this phenomenon, that it is palpably a this-worldly or secular reality and an essential feature of being human?

The text seems to say something deeper and more far-reaching in importance. The text says "in the image of God he created them; male and female he created them" (Gen. 1:27). The text is saying unmistakably that it is in the image of God that the human is created male and female. That little word *in* indicates the relational positioning of the human as male and female. The human is created in God's image. Since this relational positioning is an act of the creating God, it cannot be undone by the created human. Not even his given capacity of self-creation and self-development can undo it because that capacity presupposes this primal positioning of the human. Of course, the human can distort and pervert it, but he/she cannot break and undo it. Moreover, it is precisely in this primal relation that the human is positioned to image God and reflect his likeness and radiate this imaging and likening to the world. Apart from this relational positioning the human is diminished in his humanity and lives it distortedly. Whatever he does to image and reflect God in religion, in philosophy, in art, and in the rest of culture becomes merely an idol that has lost its luminosity as an icon. But it cannot be overemphasized that it is in and through the human form made alive by the Spirit that God is imaged and likened. This is a this-worldly human form and life. Further, it is all that is entailed for God to image himself in the world. This is a this-worldly secular reality of our everyday life. And finally it is in and through the self-creation and self-development of human life—which we also take for granted as a this-worldly reality of ordinary life and experience—that God images and reflects his creative activity in the world.

Seeing all that he has created so far, he declares it all as good: "God saw everything that he had made, and indeed it was very good" (Gen. 1:31). With that declaration that all creation is good he now blesses life in its prehuman and human forms: "God blessed them, saying 'Be fruitful and multiply and fill the waters in the seas and let birds multiply on the earth'" (Gen. 1:22; see also v. 28). This relational positioning of the human in the image of God—of being in and before God, including his participation in the creative activity of God through his self-creation and self-development—are indeed a blessing, a gift, and so a benefit. Creation is blessing. It is benefit. But this is only real and true and of value in and through the Spirit. This blessing is all done by God the Spirit to creaturely reality, which is this-worldly. This creaturely reality is secular. The Spirit benefits creaturely secular reality with secular benefits through palpably secular means! But it is God the Spirit who thus endows this reality with benefit and value. And what he does cannot be undone. Moreover, he does all this for his own purpose. That purpose is for him to have a form and a life and an agent that reflects and mirrors him in the world. But this purpose can only be fulfilled by and through a creaturely secular agent, the human, in a creaturely this-worldly reality, the secular world.

This activity of the Spirit is a form of spirituality that secularizes. But secularization cannot de-spiritualize the Spirit. If that happens, it exists as a perverted relation to the Spirit. That perverted relation is mere secularism, which can have many features that are all secularistic. The features are aspects of creaturely reality that have been singled out and reduced to their barest proportion, and then made to represent the whole. Creation is reduced to nature and the natural to naturalistic. The human is reduced to humanism and humanism becomes humanistic. Gender difference is reduced to sexuality and sexuality then becomes sexism. Reason is reduced to the rational and the rational becomes rationalistic. The making of the secular results in secularity and then everything else becomes secularistic. This is perversion by reduction and the feature to which the whole is reduced is then represented as the whole. The biblical term for this is idolatry.

There are other general characteristics that are distinctively human that emerge from the bio-historical development of the primal form, life, gender difference, and relational positioning of the human in the Spirit. They are known to us from our experience and reflection of them and through the findings and refinements of modern science. While they are generally common to all humans, they are embodied and expressed and developed in each human being, by both the male as male and the female as female and in their being in, for, and with each other. I will simply mention them and will not detail their development and characteristic features. These distinctively human features include self-consciousness, which is always intentional as consciousness of something, including consciousness of consciousness; self-hood, which includes self-centering, self-will, self-determination, and self-identity in its social, cultural, and historical expressions and development; rationality, knowledge, language, and symbolization; aesthetic and moral sense; the capacity to transcend inwardly and outwardly; and to sense that there is more to life beyond its secular limits in its depth and in its reach.

The human is to make use of all these in fulfilling its vocation and destiny of being the image and likeness of God in the world. Of course, the Spirit enhances the development of these human capacities and inspires and enables their use by the human to image God. The Spirit works with and through them, not against them. Any alleged action of the Spirit that would suspend them, render them passive, or bypass them is a form of what Geoffrey Lampe calls "pneumatological docetism," which is anti-human, anti–this-worldly, and anti-secular. Surely these capacities and their transparency to the action of the Spirit provide the conditions and possibilities for the rich variety, depth, range, and value of human experience. And when put in the service of imaging and mirroring God in the world in human life as an act of worship celebrating the reality of God, they become luminous icons of the divine precisely in their secular forms!

5. Nature and the Human in the Spirit

There is another primal relation stated in the Genesis text (1:28-29; 2:8-9, 15) in which the human is to image and liken God, namely as steward of creation. As a task and a responsibility given by God, it falls clearly under the primal vocation given to the human. There is no doubt at all that the human being is to image God in his form, his life, in his relations, and in all his responsibilities and tasks. The development in the history of Christian thought of seeking what special aspect of the human that sets him out as distinct from the rest of creation and single this aspect and give it the status of bearing the image of God is misleading. This search has identified various special aspects of the human as the bearer of God's image. As examples, one can cite the following. Human rationality is distinctive of the human and so it is this special feature that bears the image of God, and by being rational the human images God. The same is true of conscience, the human sense of right and wrong, of good and bad, the obligation that one should do the right and the good, and the accompanying feeling of guilt if one does not do what is right and good. Conscience is the image of God in the human. By following it one images God. Another example is the addressability of the human and his capacity to respond and to dialogue. The fact that the human can be talked to and respond and that his life is thus dialogically structured is the image of God in the human and so it is what images God.

The reason all these attempts are misleading is that it is the human as a whole, and not some distinctive feature or aspect of him, that is in God's image and likeness. It is not what is in the human, no matter how distinctive, that is the image of God. Rather it is the human as a whole that distinguishes him from all creation. It is his whole humanity, including its distinctive features, that is in God's image. And this means it is the whole human being that must image God. And, of course, that includes all of his human properties, altogether and not singly and separately. And that includes the relation of the human to the rest of creation.

Genesis 2:8-15 speaks of a garden. A garden is a piece of nature that has been carved from it artistically. A garden is a work of art. The root meaning of "Eden" in Hebrew is "delight." And so the garden of Eden may be translated "garden of Delight." This garden was planted by God as an artist whose artistry is unsurpassed. It is he who designed it in art form and put in it what makes of it into an art form: a garden of delight. Ezekiel calls the garden of Eden the garden of God (Ezek. 28:13; 31:9, 16, 18; cf. Isa. 51:3; Joel 2:3). It is not too far-fetched to say that the garden of Eden is a symbol of God's creation. One meaning of God's seeing his creation and declaring all of it good is that it is beautiful, "it is a thing of beauty," it is a work of art and so it is delightful. But what is delightful about it is not only its art form but also its serving as a resource for life. In it are plants for food. And food is delightful. Through it rivers of waters, waters flow to water the garden and make it lush and make of it a resource for the nourishing and flourishing of life. And life in a garden full of food is delightful. In the garden are precious metals like gold, and stones like beryl and onyx, that can be made into jewels and other artifacts that beautify and delight. In the garden are also placed two trees, one the tree of life, and the other the tree of the knowledge of good and evil. That there are two trees means there are two options that evoke freedom and its exercise in terms of making a choice. The choice is between two ways of life: the way of living or the way of dying; a way that leads to life, and a way that makes one know good and evil but ends in death (Gen. 2:15-17). But what is good is not only delightful but also desirable. This was how what was in the garden was seen by the woman! "So when the woman saw that the tree was good for food, and that it was a delight to the eyes, and the tree was to be desired to make one wise, she took of its fruit and ate" (Gen. 3:6). It is clear that the human has the capacity to appreciate beauty, to value what is good, and to desire what makes for wisdom. These are capacities essential to being human. And the woman exercised this capacity of treasuring and valuing. What happened after that fateful deed of exercising this capacity by eating of the fruit of the tree of good and evil is another story to be told in chapter 5 of the book.

So God put the human that he had formed into the garden that he made (2:8, 15). This putting in of what he had formed in his image into what he had made as a garden to mirror his goodness, his beauty, and his delightfulness establishes the primal relation between God the Spirit and the human and the garden. In that relation, it also establishes the relation between the human and the garden. Both relations are also positioning relations: it places the human in and before God; it places the human in the garden and makes the garden a place of delight for the human. Thus, the garden of Eden and the human in it, being both in God, symbolize the primal unbroken binding relation (the *religare*); between God and his creation and between God and the human.

But this relational positioning of the human in the garden means that he is placed in his habitat where he is to feel at home by enjoying its delights and be himself/herself. The earth as a garden is the human home. Here is where the human is to live, nourish, and flourish. This is also the place where he will flounder. But this entails not only his being at home in the garden and delighting in its beauty but also entails a primal responsibility for the garden. God gives the human a task that he must carry out as his proper grateful response to God's putting him in the garden as his home and to enjoy its delights. That task is "to till and keep it": "The Lord God took the man and put him in the garden of Eden to *till it and keep it*." The human is given the task of *gardener*—a tiller and keeper of the garden; a steward of creation. That means he is given some measure of freedom of control over the garden, some degree of "dominion." That freedom of control is for fulfilling a threefold purpose: to till the garden, to keep the garden, and to maintain the delicate balance between tilling and keeping. The text does not say specifically how the human is to carry out this threefold task. The human himself has to decide freely what to do and how to do what he decides to do. In that way he is given a measure of "dominion," that is, of control, in carrying out his task (Gen.1:26b). The exercise of freedom in carrying out the threefold task mentioned above means that the human is given the honor and dignity of participating in the activity of God the Spirit to perpetuate and develop his garden, his creation. The task is a secular one to be carried out in a secular way in order to develop and preserve a secular reality by a human secular agent so that it may become a secular home.

What does it mean "to till" the garden? Those two little words are put together so simply that one is likely to miss the profound and far-reaching meaning that they entail. To till means to break ground, to cultivate it, to prepare it for planting and so to make it productive for human good. To break and cultivate ground for planting means to make it generative of life, to produce food that will nourish and flourish life of all kinds, especially the human kind of life. To till therefore means to make the earth productive of all that nourishes and flourishes life.

As this "tilling" activity developed in the history of civilization, we can now see what it has entailed. It moved from gathering food to its agricultural production and distribution and to all the economic processes, industries, and the politico-economic systems that were consequently generated. It gave rise to forms of human settlements, from nomadic, to tribal, to town, to city, to highly urban centers of population with all the social and cultural opportunities, problems, and prospects that they produce in their wake. It prompted the making of simple tools to a complicated and sophisticated culture of technology that the human can no longer do without. It has spawned new types of leadership with their attendant qualifications, performance, and expertise. From all these emerged all sorts of work and labor and subsidiary services and employment that have to be distinguished, organized into a system of division of labor, and managed with the most efficiency for the purpose of the greatest production with the view to making the biggest profit possible. An agricultural, industrial, commercial, technological civilization has arisen from those two little words *to till*.

Moreover, in order for the human to do what is entailed by this little word *till* to participate in the continued development of the garden of Creation for human habitat and delight, the human must know the earth as to what it is, how it behaves, why it behaves in a particular way, and how it may be put to good use as a human habitat and delight. He also must know what life is, its many forms and levels, where it can exist, nourished and made to flourish, how it develops and what conditions are necessary to sustain and develop it as a life at home on earth, and takes delight in it. He must know what he can do and what means and ways of doing are necessary in order to till the earth properly.

From all this, one can only be astonished to realize how that little word *till* can give rise to science and technology and a whole culture and civilization shaped and pervaded by it. Science is a reliable method of knowing that establishes the truth about things in nature. It is an assured way of predicting and explaining the behavior of nature according to its own laws and processes. It is a body of knowledge that can be learned and used as a reliable basis for human action. Its findings have practical significance that can be put to good use. It has produced tools, goods, and services that have altered the way things are and changed the courses and ways for negotiating life on earth. It has produced a point of view, a perspective or a way of seeing things, that has broadened the human understanding of the overwhelming vastness of God's creation and of the intricacies and complexities of the universe from subatomic particles to billions of galaxies and the cosmic forces that hold them in place and in their movements. Surely, God cannot be less than the awe-inspiring, mind- boggling, and mystery-pervaded world or universe that he has created. And what is more sobering is that the responsibility for having all these happen is placed upon the shoulders of the human who has been given the task of "tilling" the earth as God's garden of Delight.

It is clear that this human activity of "tilling" is profoundly significant and has enormous implications and far-reaching consequences. One motive of the secularizing process is for it to win what it must do through the means it deems necessary and appropriate. Religion is one cultural authority from which this right has to be won. The emphasis of religion on a spirituality that is anti-materialistic and anti-this-worldly has been an obstacle that the secularizing process has had to overcome to win for tilling its right to be itself and to do what it is supposed to do. And so to a certain extent, how "tilling" has developed historically is a product of the secularizing process and is a part of that process. But how far it can be taken theologically as an expression of the human vocation to image God has to wait until its twin activity, which is "to keep" the garden of Delight has also been considered. Since the two activities are essentially related, it can be asked whether the "tilling" has helped the "keeping," and whether the "keeping" has helped the "tilling." To this we now turn.

It seems that "keeping" has its own meaning and dynamics quite distinct from "tilling." Keeping entails *preserving*, and that means protecting against defacing, deforming, deterioration, and decay; and causing destruction. It means maintaining something as it is. It also means *celebrating*, and that means appreciating the value of something and taking delight in it, which in turn is a reason for preserving it. It also means saving it for the future, and that means rescuing it from what would distort or pervert it and providing for the development of its potencies and potentialities.

Taken in the above senses, "keeping" has certain aspects that appear to conflict with some aspects of "tilling." For example, keeping as protecting and maintaining seems to conflict with breaking up, opening up, working on, and so to some extent, manipulating. All these entail changing something from what it is to something else. Moreover, keeping as celebrating the intrinsic value of something is transformed into another value by "tilling," with the new value considered as more valuable than the original one. Furthermore, "tilling" may unleash a process of diminution and extinction in the process of tilling change. This process may be irreversible and may lead to destruction. There may not be a counter-process of rescuing, redeeming, restoring, and saving that are all entailed by "keeping." Thus, "to keep" has its own aim, its own activity, its own dynamism, its own right to be itself and do what is necessary and appropriate accordingly. "To keep" is part of the human vocation to bear the image of God and so to image him in the world of creaturely reality.

What then are some of the elements entailed in this human vocation? The first that may be said because it is elemental is the binding relation (the *religare*) between God the creator as Spirit and all of creation. That relation, we have claimed, is spiritual. It is that to which religion as a historical reality in its various institutional forms point. So it is spiritual in prior order and dignity to historical and institutional religion. It is also as spiritual that it secularizes. It has a this-worldly trajectory in its creative movement. Because it is elemental and constitutive of the creaturely secular, it must be kept: preserved, celebrated, and saved!

To do this one must see theologically the "heavens and the earth," that is, the whole universe, all that there is, as *creation rather than nature*. To see "the heavens and the earth," this whole cosmic yet secular reality, is to see it as the theater of the glory of God. That maybe expressed in considering creation as the dwelling place of God the Spirit in presence, power, and blessing. To put it bluntly: The whole universe—heaven and earth—is the Temple of God. And so it is the place for celebrating in adoration, praise, and gratitude the benefit of creation itself and all the gifts for the nourishing, satisfying, and flourishing of all of life and its many forms, including human life.

And that means the worship of God! For worship is the human act that celebrates the *religare*, the binding relation of God as Spirit and the Universe as his creation. Worship is what preserves and celebrates creation as the garden of Delight. It focuses on the beauty of the earth, which makes for delight and enjoyment. It witnesses to the artistic dimension of creation in its order, proportion, variety, and the mutual fitness of all things in their complexity and intricacy. Worship preserves and celebrates creation as creaturely reality. It has a secularizing impact.

It does this for the human task of "tilling." But tilling is another way of considering and handling creation. It turns creation into nature. For example, to till is to choose what soil to break up for cultivation. It selects what plant life it grows as fit for growing in the soil it breaks up for cultivation and planting. Selecting what soil to cultivate and choosing what form of plant life to farm and make productive in such a cultivated land is a form of domestication. To domesticate is to turn something into home and family use. This meaning can be extended to mean turning plant life into human benefit in terms of the many ways and uses it can be made or produced. Agriculture is a form of domestication. The food that it produces for consumption is what determines, sustains, and promotes the kind of life-form in its self-maintenance and self-perpetuation. And so to the extent that agriculture does this, it also domesticates life by the way and kind of food it selects and produces to feed such a life. We hope, but not always genuinely, although ostensibly, it domesticates life for life on earth. What we eat is what we are!

The same may be said of animal life. From the many forms of animal life, some forms are chosen, tamed, nurtured, and raised for home use and benefit, whether as pet or as food, and so domesticated. Human life is versatile in doing this for it selects from a wide variety of both vegetative and animal life what it can domesticate for its benefit and delight. However, many plants and animal life are not so versatile. They eat only what is by nature fit for them. And this is found only in specific forms and particular places. They have no way of varying the kinds of food and changing the places where they are found and raise them for present and future consumption. When the particular place where the food fit for them to eat is changed and the food diminishes or disappears, they too as species of life become extinct. This seems to be an inevitable consequence of "tilling." Are there forms of life that are also to be protected and celebrated precisely as forms of creaturely life that are covered by the binding relation of *religare*? Human selection, domestication, production, and consumption are an instance of manipulation. This can only be done by turning creation into nature. What is to be celebrated here is that creation yields to becoming nature for and by human tilling.

But as we indicated earlier, this yielding of creation into nature for tilling also means that creation can be the object of studying, knowing, being acted upon, and being put into use. That would entail not merely the ordinary experience of creation as nature by means of observation and practical daily use, but more important, the scientific study of it and putting its uses into technological gadgets and products. Science transforms creation into nature. In this way it manipulates and domesticates creation into nature. This process may also be understood as a dimension of secularization because it is a this-worldly process. To the extent that science enables the "tilling" that is an essential aspect of the human vocation to image God in a secular world, it is an elemental feature of a spirituality that secularizes.

But these processes and the tasks they do and the uses and benefits they produce are to be affirmed and valued within the *religare*, the binding relation that is also "keeping," preserving, celebrating, and rescuing. These two aspects of the human vocation of bearing the image of God and mirroring it in a this-worldly world have to be done together and must mutually help each other. The human vocation is "to till and keep." There is an essential connection between them that cannot and must not be cut. Moreover, the connection is a balancing between them. This balancing, because delicate, must not be disturbed. It should not be made to tip in favor of the one against the other. Furthermore, the connecting and the balancing are meant to interpenetrate and interface each other so that the tilling helps the keeping and the keeping helps the tilling to be and so both do what needs doing. And so the question has to be asked, Has this happened actually?

In recent decades, the awareness and acceptance of the connection between tilling and keeping has steadily increased. Moreover, the human as the primary agent of both tilling and keeping is also seen as an essential component of what is being tilled and kept. He is part of nature. What he does in knowing and acting upon it affects him decisively for ill or good. His survival and well-being depend on what he does as he transforms creation into nature. The fact that the binding connection between God the Spirit and his creation is affirmed despite its transformation into nature by tilling and keeping by human agency is to be appreciated. This recognition and affirmation augurs well for the future of nature and humankind in it.

There is, however, a fundamental issue, and that is finding the right balance between tilling and keeping. This is not an easy task. One cannot readily and accurately determine by any of the means available when the tilling affects the keeping in a harmful way. It is also true to say that the keeping does not know when it can say to the tilling to stop as it is preventing the keeping. The result is that an imbalance occurs with disastrous consequences both to nature and to the human agent. Recent developments, in the opinion of many analysts, is that the balance has tipped undoubtedly in the direction of the tilling. The human manipulation of creation into nature, its interference with its processes to sustain life in its biodiversity, has precipitated an inevitable ecological crisis of ominous proportions. If nothing is done to heal the crisis and avert its disastrous consequences it may well ring the death knell of the earth and its inhabitants. The crisis is often detailed as the following.

- Pollution, which poisons the soil, the water, and the air, and precipitates global warming and the destruction of the ozone layer. All these elements are essential to sustain the self-replenishing and life-sustaining capacity of planet earth.
- Diminution and exhaustion of the carrying and sustaining capacity of the earth. The earth is finite in its resources and capacity. All the life forms, including the human, depend upon planet earth for their survival and well-being. And they compete with one another for the earth's resources. If the demand upon the resources of the earth exceeds what it can supply, and its processes are manipulated in a way that distorts them, then it may be inevitable that both the earth and the life that depends on it will find themselves on the way to extinction. It is the opinion of ecological experts that we may have crossed the threshold irreversibly toward extinction.
- Population explosion and the maldistribution of the earth's resources. The increase in human population has accelerated in exponential rates. Inevitably the demand upon planet earth to sustain this dramatic increase with life-giving resources has also increased. The demand may be greater than the supply of resources to meet it.

Even with the use of science and technology the supply may not be enough to meet the demand. The problem is exacerbated by the unequal distribution of these resources and the wasteful consumption of the rich and affluent. It is estimated that 20 percent of the world's population consume 80 percent of the earth's resources, while the majority population of 80 percent are left to compete for the remaining 20 percent of the world's resources.

The above points are not exhaustive but only illustrative of the ecological crisis.[2] They are here mentioned summarily merely to underscore the judgment of many analysts that the ecological balance has tipped in favor of the tilling process with disastrous effects both upon the garden of Delight and the gardener. Of course, there are policies and efforts on the part of the keeping activity. The question remains, however: Are they being implemented by all concerned, and is what is being done effective enough to stem the tide toward destruction? The current

2. See Andrew Goudie, *The Human Impact on the Natural Environment* (Cambridge, MA: MIT Press, 2000).

opinion of many is that both policy and action are not enough and effective. And so the keeping process seems to be failing in its task of preserving, celebrating, and saving planet earth as nature.

How does one take this crisis theologically? Might it not be the case that the appearance of the ecological crisis and the recognition that the human efforts to deal with it, which are in fact a part of the crisis, is a work of the secularizing process? The crisis is opening up a crack through which one may discern that the binding relation, the *religare*, remains intact. Might it not be also the case that it is in the light of the *religare* remaining intact and unbroken that the imbalances in the connection have been seen for what they are—a distorting and perverting of the connection with disastrous consequences. The tilling appears aggressively excessive and the keeping appears passively recessive. And the agent is caught in a dilemma he cannot resolve. Any effort he makes to resolve the dilemma becomes part of the dilemma. Might it not be the case that since the crisis is brought into the open by the secularizing process, it is a dimension of the work of God as Spirit? And since the primal work of the Spirit is to create possibility where there appears to be none, is not the crisis precisely the moment of *kairos* of new possibilities? We will return to this issue in later chapters.

To conclude this chapter, at every decisive point in the discussion we have consistently claimed that the creative activity of God the Spirit is a secularizing process. The thrust of the Spirit as presence, power, and blessing is to establish the this-worldly character of his creation. The spirituality that pervades this process is a secularizing thrust, even when it reveals a crisis that endangers the secularity of creation. Whether we have succeeded is for the reader to say.

CHAPTER IV

Life-Together in the Spirit

1. The Issue of Life-Together

Our aim in this book is to deepen and broaden our understanding of God the Spirit. To do that we have been discerning the trajectory of the Spirit's movement to cover all of creation. We have described this movement as a secularizing process. Historically this process sought to establish the this-worldly character of reality by weaning it from the dominant influence of institutional religion. In this chapter we take up life in community. We will seek the role that the Spirit plays in community life.

To some extent we have already touched on some of the more basic elements that are presuppositional to community life and the Spirit's role in them. We have indicated the possibility-creating work of the Spirit out of non-possibility. We have pointed to the energizing power of the Spirit in conjunction with God speaking, which actualizes the possibility created by the Spirit. We have alluded to the ordering work of the Spirit together with the Word in transforming chaos into cosmos. We have indicated the life-giving power of the Spirit in both the emergence of life and in creating the conditions for its appearance and continuance. At the level of human life, we have also indicated the distinctive life-form and capacities of the human that make him/her bear the image of God and to mirror God in the form of his existence and life, in all his relations, and as steward of creation. Through all this we staked out the claim that the Spirit is the presence, power, and blessing that establishes the world as a creaturely earthly secular reality. There is a *religare*, a binding tie, which is the Spirit himself that binds God to his creation and creation to him, which God has sealed in an everlasting covenant that cannot be broken. We claim that the secularization process takes place within the sphere of this binding tie. And since that binding is the Spirit, it is the Spirit that secularizes.

The reason for taking life in community and the role of the Spirit in it is because community, or life-together, is basic to being human. As we have seen, human life is structured sexually for community, not solely for procreation. Procreation itself presupposes and is an exercise of community. It may happen when male and female come together in the intimacy of community. Neither being merely male nor being merely female completes the human being. Each requires the other in community, in life-together, for the fullness of being human. No human life is lived apart from community because becoming a personal self that is integral to the human is not possible except in life-together.

Community, however, is not simply the aggregate of selves, persons, and people. There are basic ties—gender, marriage, family, clan, tribal, racial, national, linguistic, cultural, social, political, and economic factors—that bind people together. Does the Spirit have any role to play in all these? What could that role be? Moreover, these ties meld into a social ethos that through institutions, traditions, and socialization form, orient, and norm people into a community with a measure of cohesion and furnish them their cultural identity. Unless we can see the Spirit being present to, and playing a significant role in, the formation and building-up of human community, we leave out a large and significant aspect of human reality and experience from the Spirit's reach and influence.

Moreover, the community historically and sociologically antedates the individual human who joins it. A human being is born into a community that already exists and is organized in some specific ways. Its social ethos and its cultural forms are already operational formatively and normatively in most forms of the social ethos and its cultural expressions such as its language, its customs, its laws, and so on, and are pervaded and shaped by a religion that provides a dominant unifying vision. The spirituality that results from this blending and which in turn blends them is, as it were, the pervasive air that the human being breathes for his life, the deep water in which he swims his life. In short the way life-together is structured, the processes that make it work, the life-orientation it provides, and the mold into which it shapes people and their lives, are already there, pre-existing the generations born into it. Furthermore, the way all these factors are woven together into a kind of social and cultural tapestry, together with the tensions and problems precipitated by their interaction, produces a lifestyle and a worldview that determines what is and what is not, what is possible and what is not, what is right and what is not, what is good and what is not. We may well ask in the light of our purposes, can all this be taken as being in the sphere of the Spirit? These are all earthly, secular activities. To that extent they may be claimed as aspects of the secularizing work of the Spirit. If so, may they be evaluated also in the light of whether they keep the bind, the *religare*, of the Spirit?

Furthermore, although the human is structured for community, the ways and forms of life-together are not thereby prescribed specifically. They are left to human creativity; they are to be constructed by human ability. And this, the human has done. We have also seen that the human vocation of tilling and keeping creation transforms it into nature. But this process goes further. The human interaction and interfacing with nature results in culture and its forms and even in whole civilizations. This has also happened. The historical movement from creation to nature and from nature to culture may be claimed as a secularizing process. But since the making of culture from human interaction with and manipulation of nature is a human construct, then the culture that shapes the human being in community and the forms that community take are also by human construction. And so while it is culture that shapes the human in community, it is also the human who constructs culture and its social forms. The human creates the community that shapes him. One may claim this secularizing activity as taking place within the sphere of the Spirit. If so, may it also be assessed as to whether it keeps the bind of the Spirit?

The entry of the human into the secularizing process as organizer of community and as maker of culture and so, into his own self-creation, is a major factor in the process. Up to this point the previous discussion has centered in God the Spirit playing the dominant role in the dynamics of the *religare*. However, with the entry of the human and its activities, a complicating factor makes its appearance in the overall scene. The move from creation to nature and from nature to culture is a secularizing process. But this is partly carried by human activity that to a certain degree is manipulative. This manipulation is likely to result in some measure of distortion and perversion in the relation of the human to the *religare*. These distortions and perversions are yet to be dealt with in the next chapter. And so the entry of the human factor in the secularization process decisively makes a lot of difference. That difference has to be theologically assessed in the light of the *religare*, the binding bond of the Spirit. It is for all these reasons mentioned above that we take up the issue of life-together in the Spirit.

2. The Making of a People

The book of Judges tells the dramatic story of seminomadic tribal clans, just emerging from slavery in Egypt, seeking to form a nation-community on a promised land not yet fully their own and without a central authority and leadership. To appreciate this difficult transition from being a slave-people to becoming a nation-people, we need to be taken back to when Israel was not yet, when it was not even possible to imagine its possibility at all. This transition may be construed as a purely secular struggle, and there are many such in history. But that would be a mistake. For even in this secular struggle there was already a kind of spiritual bond that held the tribal clans together. That bond was celebrated in a central shrine at feast days to which all the clans sent representatives. Where did this bond come from and how did it function?

Israel was born in a divine resolve when God decided to create a people for himself and establish a covenant of promise with it. In Genesis 12:1-3 there is an unmistakable abruptness in the placing and content of the phrase "Now the Lord said." Genesis 10–11 tells of the spread of the descendants of Noah and his sons to people and inhabit the earth. Then suddenly, a new story begins, and the characters are only two, God and a person called Abram. The plot of the story is about a journey into promise—the promise of a land yet to be shown, the promise of a people yet to be created, and the promise of a blessing to be bestowed upon all peoples through this people yet to be formed. The promise was sealed in a covenant initiated by this God with Abram and his yet-to-be descendants (Gen. 17:1-22). The covenant is established as "an everlasting covenant" in which God promises "to be God to you and to your offspring after you" (v. 7). With the establishment of the covenant of promise, Abram's name was changed to Abraham to signify a new relationship and a new reality.

It may not be far from the truth to say that God's resolve to create a people for himself and to covenant everlastingly with it is a theological datum that we need to take seriously as saying something about God. May we not infer from it that there is here a new turn on the part of God in his self-constitution and self-becoming by making himself in an everlasting covenant the God of this new people he is about to create and through which he turns also to all peoples to bless them? God would still be God without creating a new people, as he would still have been the same God without creating the heavens and the earth. Here the creation of a new people may be regarded as of the same magnitude as the creation of the universe: from chaos to cosmos, from no people to being a people of God! The first turn is the creation of the universe. The second turn is the creation of a people for himself. Each creative act is a new turn in God's self-constitution and becoming. And the direction of his turning is to a reality other than him. It is to a reality whose otherness is this-worldly, earthy life in the flesh, and to the creation of the human—male and female—to image him in creation. The third turn is to create a new people with which he covenants and so binds himself to be God as God, in the fullness of being God for this people, he will be fully and intimately engaged in the history of this people. And that history is a secular one. It would entail a people enslaved in Egypt, a difficult journey through the wilderness, the giving of a Torah to guide them in their life-together, the military conquest and defense of the land and its distribution for the habitation of the tribal clans, and eventually their effort of becoming a national community with a national order and leadership. These are patently secular affairs done as secular activities by secular agents. And God would be intimately and fully engaged in this secularity as a dimension of his everlasting covenant.

Not only was Israel born in God's resolve but also the historical and secular process of implementing it by the human party in the covenant is borne out of faith in the God who made the promise, and trust that the promise would be fulfilled, even though the odds against its fulfillment seem insurmountable. For Abraham was old and without a son when the promise came to him that he would be the father of many nations. He was without a son also because his wife, Sarai, was barren. How could an old man with a barren wife produce an heir? (Gen. 17:17). Impossible! When Abraham was told by God that he would bless Sarai, his wife, and she would bear a son, Abraham fell on his face and laughed and said to himself, "Can a child be born to a man who is a hundred years old? Can Sarah, who is ninety years old, bear a child?" (Gen. 17:17). When Sarah overheard the conversation between Abraham and one of three guests who visited Abraham by the Oaks of Mamre who said that Sarah would bear a son, she also laughed, probably because what was said that would happen to her was utterly impossible. And when God asked Abraham why Sarah laughed, knowing the incongruity between what was promised and her barrenness, God asked, "Is anything too difficult for the LORD?" (Gen. 18:14 CEB). How can non-possibility yield possibility? How can barrenness give rise to fertility? How can cosmos come out of chaos? How can national community be forged from tribalism and clannishness? We return to an earlier claim in connection with the possibility of creation. It is God the Spirit that makes the possible out of the impossible, from non-people to being a people. It is possibility becoming actual when God speaks "Let there be," which makes happen actually what he says. "The Lord said to Abram: 'Go from your country and your kindred and your father's house to the land that I will show you. . . . So Abram went, as the LORD had told him" (Gen. 12:1, 4).

And so the story of making a people begins! It begins in a resolve of God and is carried out in faith and obedience by a man. The story is told as a secular story within an everlasting covenant, a *religare*. Further details of the covenant are mentioned in Genesis 15 and 17. The covenant was then reaffirmed by God and passed on to Isaac, Abraham's heir (Gen. 26:2-4), and to Isaac's son Jacob (Gen. 28:10-17). It was reaffirmed by God and ratified by the people on Sinai (Exodus 19–20). It was passed on to David and his heirs (2 Sam. 7:1-16). The story tells of God's election of a ragtag people whom he was liberating from oppression and are now journeying in the wilderness. God speaks to them through Moses: "You have seen what I did to the Egyptians, and how I bore you on eagles' wings and brought you to myself. Now therefore, if you obey my voice and keep my covenant, you shall be my treasured possession out of all peoples. Indeed, the whole earth is mine, but you shall be for me a priestly kingdom and a holy nation" (Exod. 19:4-6; cf. Deut. 7:6-11). And in Joshua 21:43 God fulfills his promise of giving the land that he swore to the ancestors of Israel. Joshua 21:45 then concludes: "Not one of all the good promises that the Lord had made to the house of Israel had failed; all came to pass." Those promises include God's turning as God to be God to his people whom he elects in love to be his covenant people, and through whom he will bless the peoples of the earth. He gives them the promised land on which to settle as God's own people. As God's people they are to be a "priestly kingdom," which mediates and celebrates in worship God's covenanting presence and life-giving power. To be able to do this, they are to be holy as God is holy, i.e. to be his alone, to be his treasured possession (Lev. 19:2) They are not to be just a kingdom, a secular entity like other kingdoms, but a priestly one, with a vocation to celebrate God's covenanting and life- giving presence. They are not to be just a nation like any other nation, but a holy nation, one consecrated to and sanctified by God. The fusing of priestly with kingdom and of holy with nation in a binding bond results in a spirituality that embraces the secular and in a secularity that receives the Spirit. It is this fusing that makes for and pervades a truly covenant community in which God is for the community and the community is for God: "I will be your God and you will be my people" (Lev. 26:12 CEB). Joshua was correct: All the good promises that God made to the house of Israel were fulfilled. But did Israel fulfill her side of the covenant? Did she succeed in being a priestly kingdom and a holy nation, a covenant community, God's treasured possession?

The book of Judges allows one to peek into the chaotic conditions of Israel during the period between the Exodus and the monarchy. For Israel it was a difficult transition period from being a tribal slave-people to becoming a nation-people settling in a land of their own. Many of the difficult problems in forming a viable national community life based on something more than tribal cohesion, a shared social status (of being slaves), and a miraculous deliverance from an oppressor (Exodus and wilderness experience), though these were foundational, had to be faced by Israel during this period. Israel was seeking to settle into a land that it had yet to acquire from peoples who had been there ahead of it (Judges 1). It had to justify its claims over the land it had occupied already (Judg. 11:12-28). It was threatened by armed might by its neighbors and had to go to war to defend itself and ensure its survival. It was a wandering desert people seeking to live among an agricultural and settled people whose culture centered around the celebration of nature fertility. That culture was ready to ensnare and absorb Israel into extinction. Israel had to struggle hard to preserve its core identity. Since it rejected the form of rule prevailing among its neighbors, which led to oppression and slavery (from which Israel had just been delivered), it had yet to develop a form of governance and leadership that would forge it into a community of free people, enjoying not only security and freedom but justice and prosperity and peace. A viable community requires homeland, security of survival, cultural identity and social cohesion, and a form of political authority at the very least. And Israel to be a viable community had yet to acquire them! Meanwhile, "all the people did what was right in their own eyes" (Judg. 17:6; 21:1-25), a formula for social anarchy. What was the role of the Spirit in forging Israel into a new community? To answer this question we will consider three formative factors: first, the role of the Spirit in forging community around charismatic leaders; second, the formation of a central political authority in terms of the monarchy; and third, in developing community on the basis of common social and ethical standards. In considering the first, we will study some text taken from the book of Judges: 3:7-11; 6:33-35; 11:14, 27-29. In dealing with the second factor, we turn to the story of David, and for the third, we will turn to the early collection of Laws, the Covenant Code: Exodus 20:22–23:19.

3. The Spirit and Crisis

Reflection on the texts in the book of Judges yields some basic observations about the role of the Spirit in the formation and building up of community. The first observation is: the occasion that brings the Spirit into action is one of profound collective crisis that shows in human helplessness when merely secular efforts are detached from their moorings in *religare*. This is the case in each of the texts we are considering where the phrase "the Spirit of the Lord came upon" appears (Judg. 3:10, 6:34; 11:29, and so on), as well as in those cases where the phrase does not appear. The significance of the coming of the Spirit is that it exposes the failure of a people to live up to the more obvious demands essential for community, reveals the lack of other elements necessary for community, and shows in the conditions that urgently demand community. These threefold features may be regarded as the *underside* of the coming of the Spirit. The coming of the Spirit in itself already is an unmistakable sign that a crisis beyond secular and human ability to deal with has occurred. Without the coming of the Spirit, the crisis and its gravity would not have been exposed. Secularity when uprooted from the soil that makes it grow will not be aware of this because it believes it can do things on its own, and has no measuring standard to plumb its limits. The coming of the Spirit is the plumb line that does the measuring. This is the underside of the secularizing effect of the coming of the Spirit. In the case of the Israelites, according to the testimony of the book of Judges, the crisis has several dimensions.

For one thing, there is the immediate threat to Israel's survival that comes from its "enemies": the Canaanites in whose lands the Israelites sought to settle, and their neighbors, such as the Philistines, who threatened them with war and superior military strength. The Israelites were tribal minorities and foreigners in the communities where they began to settle. They were often oppressed and marginalized (3:8; 4:3). Some of the tribes were conquered and subjugated and their lands taken (3:13-14). Some of them were threatened with war and superior military strength. And there appeared no way they could muster enough military capability either to defend themselves or overthrow the threat of the enemy (4:3, etc.). Some tribes tried to settle disputes through diplomacy and negotiation in order to avoid war. But that didn't work either (11:12-28). Their economic resources and means of livelihood were often plundered, severely impoverishing the people: "They [the Midianites[destroy the produce of the land . . . and leave no sustenance in Israel, and no sheep or ox or donkey . . . they waste the land . . . thus Israel was greatly impoverished" (6:4-6). When one adds up all these—superior military strength, war, subjugation and oppression, marginalization and impoverishment— and consider their cumulative impact upon a divided people with mainly tribal loyalties, is it at all surprising that Israel felt threatened in its very survival as a people? In the face of such a threat, Israel felt helpless and hopeless: "They could no longer withstand their enemies. Whenever they marched out, the hand of the Lord was against them to bring misfortune . . . and they were in great distress" (2:14-15).

Another aspect of the crisis derives from Israel's inability to act together and rise up to the occasion. Usually such a situation of grave crisis would galvanize a people into decisive and concerted action. It seems that this did not happen in Israel. Instead, the crisis served only to show that the people were not united enough to act together, and there was no established and continuing leadership structure that could pull them together into decisive and common action. As the book of Judges itself puts it: "In those days there was no king in Israel; all the people did what was right in their own eyes" (17:6; 21:1-25). Not only did Israel see the situation hopeless it also felt helpless and distressed. When objective hopelessness and subjective helplessness combine, the result is inner panic and disintegration, paralysis and the loss of the capacity to decide and act. "Things fall apart; the centre cannot hold" (Yeats). Community disintegrates. And when failure to act cancels out the chance for survival, the result is desperation. Is it not the case that Israel's "cry unto the Lord" is partly prompted by panic, paralysis, distress, and desperation? Does a people that cannot act for the sake of its own survival still have what it takes for it to understand itself as a community?

A third aspect of Israel's crisis is its honest belief that it is by its own doing that Israel has been handed over to its ruinous and deplorable fate in the hands of its enemies. It had been repeatedly told that it was to live "in the sight of God," that it is to be a "priestly kingdom and a holy nation" (Exod. 19:6). It is in this "sight," in this priestliness and holiness, that is the life-nourishing source of its existence. These are the reasons for its being. Israel is to be priestly and so live as a kingdom community. Israel is to be a holy nation, consecrated to what is the sole property of God, his holiness, and this holiness will sanctify Israel and enable her to be and do what is holy and so live as a nation-community. All this meant that Israel is to celebrate God's covenanting and life-giving presence in the Spirit. This is to be done in the worship of this God and none other. Worship issues forth in doing what serves the honor and glory of this God. And that means obeying his commandments. The command is that Israel is not to look for other gods and follow them. There were these other gods around—the gods of fertility who were believed to replenish the earth seasonally and so nourish its life-sustaining capacity. This would mean idolizing an aspect of creation—its blessing to multiply—instead of worshiping the Giver of this blessing. The temptation to idolize the gift instead of worshiping the Giver and valuing the Giving is a powerfully seductive attraction. And Israel fell for it. In so doing, Israel violated the absolute condition for its survival and its unity and identity as a people. All these are elements of community. Israel knew that it "did what was evil in the sight of the Lord."

And so Israel felt in its guts that the Lord's anger had been kindled and that the Lord had given Israel over to its plunderers (2:11-15; 10:6-9). And because its sin was so grave since it uprooted itself from the soil of its life, Israel believed that God would no longer deliver her and would abandon her to her extinction: "Yet you have abandoned me and worshiped other gods; therefore I will deliver you no more" (10:13). This was an aspect of the crisis more profound and serious and far from Israel's ability to deal with than those previously mentioned because it struck at the very basis of Israel's existence and reason for being. In fact, this element in the crisis is the root and cause of the other features of the crisis. Israel seemed to have lost its sense of what constituted it as a people. It had been "handed over" to its dissolution as a people. Given that loss, can such a people still recover its sense of what it takes to be a community?

Is this crisis situation a theological datum? Or is it merely a military one, or a social anomie, or simply a failure of nerve that can be handled with more military strength, or political acumen, or a stronger sense of ethnocentrism or nationalism that would inspire a people to rise up to the occasion? But what if the occasion is seen as beyond the ken of military, political, economic, and social ingenuity—and so of merely human and secular provenance? In theology, this situation would be called a divine judgment. Seen in this light, judgment is the exposure of the truth of one's being and doing and living in relation to the primal moorings of reality and life. It is judgment that acts as plumb line in measuring accurately one's loss of anchor and how far one has sailed away with one's sails, assuming that the winds will always blow in one's set direction. But what if the winds of the Spirit blow strongly and irresistibly against one's sails, and the waters of chaos become uncontrollably unruly and deeply unstable and the waves overwhelming? Then what?

If this is indeed judgment showing how one has lost anchor and set adrift in uncharted and stormy waters, whose work could this measuring process be? The author's take on this is that this is also the work of the Spirit. In embracing the secular into itself, the Spirit establishes and affirms its this-worldliness by rooting it in the *religare*, the binding relationship that the Spirit is. That is the soil where community in its secular dimensions grows and flourishes. And a secularity that receives the Spirit into itself and binds itself to the Spirit discovers the creativity in which as secular it participates. And so one can say that the spirituality, which is the practice of this mutual binding, is a spirituality that secularizes, and the secularity that participates in the Spirit is a secularity that is spiritual. It is this kind of spirituality that founds and nourishes community. It is also what gives community its reason for being; its mission is to be this kind of community. Israel is to be a kingdom by being priestly. It is to be a nation by being holy. The two must always go together—the spiritual and the secular—otherwise, there cannot be community. Moreover, it is this kind of spirituality that makes a people cohere. It binds them together with an ethos that provides them with spiritual resources for decisively acting together. When a people has become so tribal and ethnocentric in its constituencies, so parochial in its loyalties, so plural in its commitments, so relativistic in its standards, and so divided within itself and alienated from one another that they can hardly put their act together around a common cause in face of a crisis, what has it become? Certainly, not a community. That is because it no longer has a vital spirituality that unites, identifies, and energizes it.

Finally, is it not the case that a spirituality enables a people to live with its neighbors—now in a global village—by providing it with a frame of meaning large enough to include the best and most meaningful experiences of itself and its neighbors, and still transcend them toward a larger and fuller vision of what life can yet be not only for itself but for all of humankind? Should not such a frame of meaning—"the big picture," so-called—be as wide and as deep as one's understanding of the Spirit and the *religare* that it is as embracive of all the good of the secular? When a people becomes severely limited in its imagination of reality, when it becomes in-grown in its sense of belonging, narrowly culture-bound in its spirituality, and even exclusively confessional in articulating its prime beliefs, that people has lost its capacity to be a part of a larger community called the community of humankind. The question we must put is, how big is our God? Is God big not only for ourselves but also for all of humankind and for all the universe?

What does the Spirit do when it comes to a situation of crisis? The second observation we can make on the basis of the texts from the book of Judges is this: Out of compassion and mercy, the Spirit responds to the cry of the people in distress by sending a deliverer (2:16; 18:3-9, 15; etc.). This is the positive side of the coming of the Spirit.

Israel, out of desperation, cries out to the Lord. This is a plea for help. It comes out of the deepest of need—the need for survival, for continued existence and life, for the restoration of a reason for being, for a new beginning and for renewal of community. It is a plea for help that is not humanly available because it is not humanly possible. The reason for this is that it is precisely the human in the form of a specific community as such that needs help as deliverance for itself. This kind of help it cannot give to itself because it is precisely itself and what it does with itself that need saving. And so whatever it does for itself out of itself needs deliverance and saving too. And therefore the plea for help can only be formed into a cry—a cry out of the deep. The cry cannot be self-addressed. It can only be addressed to the one who can provide the help that is really needed—the help of deliverance and salvation! It can only be a cry to God who is not only creator but redeemer as well.

The question to ask is, what makes such a cry for help possible? Surely, it is not merely the crisis and the desperation out of which it is made. One can stoically or cynically bear the suffering born out of the crisis and not flinch or whimper for help! And many have done this as a way of life, as a form of spirituality! Take what is dished out by fate. Don't whine! "Be a hero in the strife" (Longfellow, "A

Psalm of Life"). Have "the courage to be" (Tillich). For some, hope for help may even be regarded as a form of self-deception because hope is an illusion that prevents one from facing one's real predicament, namely, existential hopelessness! And many regard hope in this way. When Pandora's box is opened, hope is the last form of evil that goes out to seduce the human, for it blinds him to his miserable condition and so prevents him from accepting it and so deal with it in quiet courage (Kafka, Camus, et al.). What makes the cry to the Lord for help possible? Again we are back to the primal function of the Spirit, to create possibility where there is none!

The texts speak of God responding out of compassion and mercy: "For the Lord would be moved to pity by their groaning because of those who persecuted and oppressed them" (2:18). "And he [the Lord] could no longer bear to see Israel suffer" (10:16). These texts say very deep things about God, about Israel, and about violence. About God, they say that God, in turning to Israel to be God for her, opens up himself, makes himself vulnerable to, and sympathetic with, human suffering, and thus suffer the suffering of Israel and so of the human. There is in God in himself and in his turning to an other and being for the other, a capacity to suffer, a deep pathos, as only he can feel in his own way—the pain of the human in his suffering. This is an expression of his self-determination to be God for his people. And he expresses this pathos by compassion and mercy to those whose suffering he bears. This pathos is therefore of his becoming as God. And since it is out of love that he chose Israel to be his people for whom he self-constituted himself as God, it is this love that radiates itself forcefully and irresistibly in compassion and mercy toward the one whose suffering he bears. It is by bearing the suffering of his beloved that God becomes truly God to his beloved Israel and so to all humankind. Because he is love and so he loves, he can be "moved to pity" and "he could no longer bear to see Israel suffer."

Although Israel has repeatedly abandoned God in favor of other gods, this God has not abandoned Israel. He faithfully keeps Israel within his sight, and continued to be present to and engaged with Israel, all the way to the point of bearing Israel's suffering. In what mode does God do this? Is it not as Spirit? It is as Spirit that he reaches out in sympathy and pathos to the one who suffers. And in so doing, is he not doing his primal work, namely, creating hope where there is only hopelessness, making available help where there is only helplessness, offering salvation where there is only destruction? The Lord does this out of compassion, out of his inner being as compassionate. The Lord does this out of pathos, out of his inner character as sensitive to the pain of human suffering and so bears it with the sufferer. And because he walks with the sufferer, he can lead to where help may surely be found. It is the Spirit that makes possible the cry for help (cf. Rom. 8:26-27).

The texts also say something about what makes Israel suffer. It is the persecution and oppression (that is, the violence) inflicted upon Israel before which Israel is hopelessly helpless. Israel's condition testifies to the fact that there are forces abroad in the world that are opposed to God and his beloved and inimical to their purpose. (We shall deal with this issue in more detail in the next chapter.) But the important point is that Israel believes, and rightly so, that she brought this violence upon herself. The guilt and suffering that this violence brought in its train are justly deserved by Israel. The pain of being responsible for one's pain is indeed painful.

Finally, the texts say something also about Israel. Although Israel has sinned greatly against God, and felt that the suffering she bears is one that she deserved and knew that there was nothing she could do in her helplessness, still she cried to the Lord. That cry has an element of defiance against all odds in it. Its logic is not "Because this is the case, therefore this is the thing to do." This is normal and commonsense reasoning. But the logic of faith is quite the opposite. It reasons thus: "In spite of the fact that this is the case, nevertheless, this is what is to be done." Job expressed the logic of faith succinctly when he exclaimed, "though he slay me, yet will I trust him" (Job 13:15 KJV). "In spite of . . . nevertheless," that is the reasoning of faith. It is a complete trust in the power of the Spirit to make possibility out of non-possibility. And so with this trust and its logic, Israel would not let go of God. Israel would not let God off the hook with which she bound herself with God in the *religare*. This trust with its logic is also what prompts Israel to appeal to the pathos of God and his sympathy for the sufferer. Since God has a soft heart for one in pain and suffers with him, one can invoke his pity and his mercy, but leave it to him how he would take pity and be merciful. He would know what to do. He would respond as he deems wise in his own way and in his own time. He sees the situation and he would know how to deal with it.

The texts indicate that God responds to the cry for help by sending the help that is really needed in the crisis, namely, deliverance and salvation. God is not only creator; he is redeemer and savior also. And since he is both in himself for the other, his creating is also a saving and his saving is also a creating. He saves by creating: He calls into being the things that are not, and so he saves from the nothing, from non-possibility. He saves by giving life to the dead, and so he saves from nonlife by creating life and giving it to the dead. He makes a people out of a non-people. But as we shall see in due course, he does more than restore what he creates to its genuine form and status, which is a secularizing act, he also transforms it for something greater. He gives not only life but "abundant life."

In the case of Israel's situation, God does the work of deliverance by raising up "judges," who delivered them out of the power of those who plundered them (2:16; 3:9). Whatever else "judge" might mean here, he or she is more than an adjudicator of disputes. What appears dominant in his or her work is that of a deliverer, a redeemer. The "judges" come into the scene of crisis from among their own people in crisis, and so they are part of the crisis. But the Spirit "raised" them up from among them. This was so with Othniel (3:10), Ehud son of Gera (3:15), Barak and Deborah (4:4-6), Gideon son of Joash the Abiezrite (6:11ff.) and so on. They are "raised up" by the Spirit coming to them. Raising up includes summoning, commissioning, empowering, and sending them to carry out a dangerous task. Some doubted their call and were afraid to carry out the task given them (see Gideon in chap. 6). Some had to devise devious means to do what they had to do (so Ehud, 3:15-30). All this is done by the Spirit who comes upon them! This simply but profoundly means that the Spirit of the Lord does not work deliverance directly. Rather, he makes it possible out of what seems impossible by raising up and anointing and sending and empowering and appointing "deliverers" who by themselves actually do and achieve the task of deliverance. The Spirit uses human agency—human capacity, leadership, and activity—to achieve a divine task for human benefit! In itself and by itself, being part of what is to be redeemed, the human cannot do this. So the human reluctance is well placed. But with the Spirit raising up what is down, nothing is out. Anything is possible!

And who were these people whom the Spirit of the Lord enlisted to achieve the divine work of redemption and salvation? For the most part, they were a motley crowd of ordinary people. Some had special skills. Gideon was a farmer-warrior. He was a doubter who demanded signs to confirm that he had indeed found favor with God and was being sent to deliver his people (6:13, 15, 17-18, 36-40). He was a very cautious person who did at night what the Lord had asked him to do because he was "afraid" of what his family and the townsfolk would say (6:25-27). Jephthah was a bastard, son of a prostitute, who was rejected by his family and became an outlaw (11:1-3). Samson was a Nazirite who broke all his vows and was an inveterate womanizer. As for the rest, nothing more is mentioned about them except their names, those whom they succeeded as judge, how long they served as judge, how large a family they each had, and that each died! (12:8-15). It was these ordinary people whom the Spirit turned into extraordinary leaders through whom God responded to the anguished cry of his people for liberation! The extraordinary comes from the ordinary! The one down is the one raised up! This is another version of the Spirit creating possibility out of the impossible.

And what exactly did these ordinary people do to accomplish a divine task? Their methods varied but they were all ordinary human methods that in the hand of the Spirit produced the divinely intended result: liberation from injustice and oppression and impoverishment. Their methods had some common features. Unlike the leaders of their enemies, these "deliverers" did not inflict injustice on their own people. They were not homegrown tyrants and oppressors. They led by securing the consent of the people who willingly rallied behind their leadership (3:26-30; 4:10; 6:34-35; 7:23-25; etc.). They renewed communal loyalty and commitment among the people as a whole, thus restoring community solidarity among them as a whole. As a result, they restored to the people their capacity to act together decisively and doggedly pursue a common cause. From tribal groups torn to pieces by fear and distress and paralysis, they became again a community solidly mobilized to overcome the threat to their survival as a people. And so the leaders persuaded the people to resist the enemy, go to war against their oppressors knowing they were fighting a superior force, and march on to overpower and vanquish their enemy. The leaders succeeded in enabling the people to liberate themselves. The people's sense of being forgiven, of making a new beginning, of being restored to the sight of God, and being at peace among themselves and with their neighbors, was assured for as long as the judge was alive: "Whenever the LORD raised up judges for them, the LORD was with the judge, and he delivered them from the hand of their enemies all the days of the judge" (2:18; cf. 3:11; 3:30; 5:31; 8:28; etc.). Where does one put the emphasis here? On God as warrior or as deliverer? Can one be a deliverer without being a warrior in the face of an enemy? Where does the motive to redeem come from? From love, compassion, and mercy or from hatred, vengeance, and anger?

What is our take on all of this? Israel's sense of community at the early formative stage was loose, episodic, and centered around a charismatic leader whose tenure lasted only for an emergency situation and was therefore limited and temporary. Theologically this means community is contingent upon the work of the Spirit. It is he who provides ways to secure the land, protect the people, and mobilize them for concerted action against threats to their survival, raise up leaders from among them, deliver them from oppression for freedom and peace, and make them stay the course in *religare*. The Spirit does this to a people who repeatedly stray away from the *religare* by their idolatry and unfaithfulness. The work of the Spirit in making community contingent upon him and using human agency to create it is a dimension of the secularizing activity of the Spirit. But the Spirit also pushes Israel to move into a further form of community beyond what has already been achieved. The last verse of the book of Judges shows the way, and it proposes a twofold solution: Israel is to have a king, a central political authority, and it should develop common standards for community life.

But these have to be built upon a primal element and cornerstone of community life, namely, freedom—freedom from threat and oppression, and freedom for becoming a people, to be God's people, to be the people of this God. This is secured only through compassion, mercy, and forgiveness. It is premised upon staying the course in the Spirit who is the covenanting bond between God and his people, the *religare*. Staying the course in that bond is by trust whose logic and practice is defiance against any status quo in the light of new possibilities created by the Spirit out of the impossible. Securing freedom for community is what is achieved by Exodus and Judges. Indeed, this is the basic message of biblical and Christian faith: "For freedom, Christ has set us free." Without this there is no community. But how is freedom to be expressed and practiced through a central political authority and through common social and moral standards?

4. The Spirit and Law

We will deal with the latter theme first. The reason is that even the monarchy, the central political authority, is subject to the same common social and moral standards for making community. It is set up precisely to execute and enforce these standards. Monarchy is for the making and building-up of community. This is its reason for being. Although the fortunes of the community partly depend upon political leadership, one cannot say flatly that community is for monarchy, that a people exists primarily to serve its political authority. In this connection, we make our second claim, namely, the formation of social and moral standards for community life in the form of justice through ethos and law is also the work of the Spirit. The reason we frame the claim in this particular way is because we have to see the interplay between freedom and justice in the form of law in community life. Freedom without justice in the form of ethos and law is license, and justice as law without freedom is oppression. And neither license nor oppression makes for a viable and valid community life. Freedom, justice, and law are dimensions of community life. Their interplay that generates an ethos is a dimension of the spirituality of a community. And so they and their interplay are secular dimensions of spirituality. To treat them as purely secular realities, apart from their spiritual moorings—which is the predominant disposition of the modern world—is to rob them of their community-forming power and place them outside the sphere of the Spirit. This is not a direction in which we are to move. We have to stay on course within the *religare* within which they are best secured in their respective integrity and in their appropriate interplay.

The Spirit not only liberates from injustice and oppression to secure freedom for the community, it also gives freedom a direction in which to move, which is justice. It also provides justice a public face in the form of law that regulates freedom and releases its creative power toward the just ordering and building up of community life.

The law that constitutes, forms, and norms Israel as the people of God is Torah given by God through Moses as expressing his will in the making of a people for himself and with which he covenants. It is given as command. It is not derived from any prior axiom or ethical principle, although its content may have some measure of similarity with the laws of other people who are neighbors of Israel. It is God the Lord himself who issues, proclaims, and promulgates the Torah. It is by his authority as God—and there is no other God but him—that the Torah comes to be as constituting, forming, and norming Israel as a people for him. The Torah has no other source but God. Without this promulgation by his authority as God, there is no Torah, and without the Torah there is no Israel.

As God's command, the Torah has several essential characteristics. For one, it is God's will in that it comes from the heart and mind of God; it reveals that will, which would otherwise be hidden; it is revealed to Moses for the people, for their good and for their life and for remaining as God's people. The Torah is from God for the people. For another thing, because it is command, it is mandatory. It calls for an obligatory response. It is to be obeyed, to be executed, to be done. Only this obedient response is appropriate to it. Furthermore, it is universal. It intends to lay out all the essential features or issues to be covered in making a people for God. There may be other issues that might be uncovered in the course of obeying or applying it. They are to be seen as arising from and covered by the scope of the Torah. And finally, because the Torah has all three features mentioned above, it is pertinent and applicable to all issues that have to do with the ordering and building up of community life. The Torah was promulgated by God to the assembly of all Israel and the whole assembly heard God speak. What they heard they pledged to do. And so the Covenant and its Torah were ratified by Israel (Exod.19–20; cf. Deut. 5–6). Thus, Covenant and Torah have come to exist to make history. In existing historically and making their way through history and shaping that history, they have become and are a secular reality.

A look at the Torah shows that it has two parts. The first part has four commands: you shall have no other gods before me; you shall not make for yourself an idol; you shall not use the name of God wrongfully; you shall keep the Sabbath holy. All these pertain to God as God. It is through these four prohibitions that God as God is to be acknowledged and honored. Whatever else the worship of God may be, it has to be based upon and must express this fourfold command of God. But although these commands are of God and for God, they are put as prohibitions. How they are to be done positively is left unsaid. But who should do them is clear: The people must obey. It is the people who must do what they decide to do in the way that would carry out the prohibition. What is of God is to be done by a people for their own good, for their life and peace and prosperity, as a people of God. And in this way who God is in his will for a people becomes a secular reality in the midst of secular reality.

The second part of the Torah has six provisions. The first is an injunction, expressed positively, not prohibitively: you shall honor your father and mother. The rest are all in the form of prohibitions. You shall not commit murder; you shall not commit adultery; you shall not steal; you shall not bear false witness against your neighbor; you shall not covet your neighbor's house, your neighbor's wife, male or female slave, or ox, or donkey, or anything that belongs to your neighbor. All these are matters of the community and its various relationships—parents and family, male and female relationship, life and its value, the use of language, and property issues. Again what to do positively and how to do them in interaction with others who are also enjoined to observe them is not mentioned. This is left to the people to decide and do. Although they are yet to be broken down to specific ordinances covering specific cases later, the obedience is still the people's responsibility for which they are to be held accountable. As one may readily notice these issues are matters that members of a community face every day in their ordinary lives. They provide the context, the issues, and the obligations of secular living.

But what is intriguing in the structure of the Torah is the question of what unites and energizes the two parts—the one dealing with what is of God, and the other pertaining to the people, to the human community. There is a big gap between these two parts, a gap of otherness; God is other than the human and the human is other than God. This gap cannot be bridged from the human side. It can only be bridged by the initiative and the action of the divine side. Who and by what is the gap bridged? The same question may be asked of the covenant formula: I will be your God and you shall be my people. The first part deals with what is of God, and the other deals with what is of people, of community, of the human. The two parts belong to two different orders of being; there is an abyss between them. To whom and by what are they conjoined? What connects them? What brings them into interaction and into interfacing so that the other is in the one and the one is in the other? Would it be too far from the truth and outrageous to infer that perhaps there is a *religare* here, a bonding, a covenanting that is a function of the Spirit, which in fact is the Spirit? May it not be the Spirit who brings the holy into the midst of the secular and the secular taken up into and sanctified by the Spirit? Is it not the Spirit that sanctifies by secularizing? And so one cannot be spiritual without being secular? And one cannot be genuinely secular without being spiritual?

It could be said that the Torah needs to be broken down into specific laws that apply the Torah upon particular cases that require resolution. These laws are termed "ordinances" and not "commandment" because they derive their authority from human decisions that have legal validity. This validity is based, on the one hand, upon the Torah, and, on the other hand, in effectively resolving the particular case in dispute. And because of this applicability and validity they are then coded as precedents and guides in resolving issues of a similar nature. In legal parlance, the Torah is apodictic as a command because of its derivation from God and promulgated by him and so is foundational, mandatory, universal, and applicable, and so demands obligatory obedience. The ordinances are termed "casuistic" because they are particular legal formulations that seek to apply the Torah to specific cases, thus establishing their effectiveness as well as the validity of the Torah as command. When laws are coded—they carry a mandatory authority as a coded whole, but the individual ordinances or particular laws they code consist of carrying the authority of validity and effectiveness in resolving specific cases. But the distinction between mandatory authority and valid authority is difficult to carry out in practice. The two types of authority meld into each other and they reinforce each other. And so the obedience they require becomes absolute and is then the basis for judgment. This is both beneficial and dangerous. It is beneficial because the Torah is fulfilled through obedience to the ordinances. It is dangerous because the ordinances may be substituted for the Torah. But who fulfills both? The people in covenant, of course. But did they? As the book of Job generally asks: Who is innocent in the sight of the Lord?

The Pentateuch presents three codes: the Covenant Code in Exodus 20–23, the legal code in Deuteronomy (12–26), and the Priestly Code in Leviticus (17–26).

Historically, the earliest of these three is the Covenant Code. The laws coded here represent Israel's earliest attempts at ordering community life on the basis of communal standards. The historical period that is most likely reflected in the Covenant Code is between Exodus and the Monarchy of Israel. It could be regarded as the earliest "commentary" on the Torah.[1] Because of this, the Covenant Code

1. See J. Davies Pleins, *The Social Vision of the Hebrew Bible* (Louisville: Westminster John Knox, 2001), 50–54.

is important not only for legal history but also foundationally for society because it exhibits what is distinctive about Israel's view about ordering community life. This view has remained both materially and structurally influential in later developments. The Deuteronomic Code that came later reflects the conditions of urban society and the requirements of centralized rule in the monarchy. It can also be construed to be a "commentary" on the Covenant Code. Structurally and materially it embodies the essential elements of both Torah and the Covenant Code, as will be indicated shortly.[2] There are other legal issues it deals with and so it is a further development and enrichment of the growing tradition of legal ethics in Israel. The Priestly or Holiness Code has its provenance originating from the Exile, and so historically is much later than the former two but is canonically the first as it appears in Genesis 1. It has some elements distinctive to itself, although in itself as a whole it constitutes a fundamental element in the social constitution of Israel.

The author of this book will not deal with the legal details and the technicalities in the transmission of legal traditions as this is beyond his competence. But a summary indication in general of the basic legal lines in the codes may be helpful for the purposes of this book.

A cursory analysis of the material content of the codes reveals four types of legal ethos. One type of material deals with the worship of Israel, or what Michael Welker calls "the public, regulated, and accessible relation to God."[3] I would call this the secular practice of the presence of God in the midst of Israel, or simply the public practice of knowing God. The Holiness Code puts special emphasis on this. This type seeks to implement in Israel's community life in its very public face the first four provisions in the Torah about God. Another type of material, in form and content showing that some of it is borrowed from the surrounding culture, involves laws dealing with specific cases with the view to dispensing justice. What is important here is that the primary aim of law is to dispense justice. The legal regulation of life-together aims at developing and cultivating a just society. A justly ordered society is what life-together means. But what is such a society in the face of the poor, the deprived, the marginalized in its midst? A third type of material gives special consideration to this issue. The codes have special provisions dealing with the protection of the rights and welfare of the vulnerable members of society: the slave, the stranger, the widow, the orphan, the poor, and those without social influence and power. I would call this "the secularization of grace."[4] A fourth type of material

2. Ibid., 54–61.

3. See Michael Welker, *God the Spirit* (Minneapolis: Fortress, 1994).

4. Compare this term with Michael Welker's term, "the routinization of Mercy."

deals with the protection and care of creation, a responsibility given over to the human in terms of the mandate to have "dominion" over the "works" of God's hands. Along with the emphasis on temple and liturgical worship this is an emphasis of the Priestly Code. It reflects the inclusion in Israel's confession of faith that God is the creator of all things and so is Lord of all and there is none like him. This confession reached its peak of development during the Exile and through the exilic prophets Isaiah, Jeremiah, and Ezekiel.

What is distinctive about Israel's ordering of community life? For one thing, the worship and praise of God provides the framework for the whole Code (Exod. 20:21-26; 23:19). What regulates the community is its character as a people responding in gratitude and praise to God for having redeemed it, covenanted with it, and promised to bless it and be present to it. Worship shapes and norms the whole community and thereby celebrates its standing as being open to and in the sight of God. The knowledge and praise of God are not relegated to the private sphere nor is the cult separated from public life. Worship and cult permeate the whole private and public life of the community because they celebrate Israel as a people of God, which is its basic self-definition.

For another thing, from the character of God who in mercy liberated an enslaved and oppressed people, Israel derived laws that acknowledged the rights, secured the welfare, and protected the dignity of the vulnerable members of society: the slave, the alien, the widow, and the orphan, the poor, and the marginalized. The ordinances with respect to this segment of society are part of the whole law. These laws exemplify and operationalize the mercy and compassion of God in society. As legally established, mercy is "routinized" (Welker). It is thereby removed from the whim and caprice of human beings. It is established normatively and made available and accessible by law. It is something one can expect with some degree of certainty, and not pleaded for uncertainly "for humanitarian reasons." It has to become a norm of society and a pattern of behavior! In short, mercy is apportioned grace and so made available secularly by law! Moreover, by advocating the rights, protection, and welfare of the vulnerable members of society, the law treats them not as passive objects, but as active subjects and participants of the community. This means the law must be merciful and saving, not by setting aside justice, but making justice compassionate. Alternatively, mercy must become just not by setting aside the law but by making it become liberating and redeeming!

Furthermore, the laws that stipulate the care of creation as an elemental part of the responsibility of the human community in creating a just, peaceful, and prosperous world signify that the intention of the creator of all things is to bring the order of the community in line with the order of the cosmos. This means, finally, that worship as the secular celebration of God's public presence, and the establishment of justice as the secularization of grace, are to be interrelated and interfaced into one dynamic encompassing norm for the whole society. The harmonious co-inhering of these primal elements, not in the abstract, but in the actual shaping, norming, and functioning of community, is what makes for "righteousness." Righteousness is not mere moral rectitude, though it includes it. It is not mere conformity to a law, although it includes what is legally right. It is not mere natural law embodied in legal constructs, although this, too, is included. Righteousness in community is justice as the creative interaction of the worship of God and the saving grace of God in life-together in the world. It is not an entity separate from any one of the features mentioned above but the lively and creative practice of the covenant relation between God and his people and among his people in community. Righteousness is the secular practice and the public face of *religare*. Righteousness is justice as the ethos of society, permeating, forming, and norming it!

Can righteousness in this pervasive and comprehensive sense be even humanly approximated, let alone attained? At the community level, some modern and contemporary societies find it easier to tone down the demand by separating law and justice from mercy and compassion and vice versa. They publicly institutionalize law and justice, but privatize mercy and compassion and consign them to private choice and exercise. They find it more convenient to relegate the public worship of God away from the public realm and confine it to the private, inner, and esoteric sphere, and leave the public sphere entirely to the dominion of the so-called "secular." By doing this—either by deliberate action or passive acquiescence—they turn their backs to the creative interaction of these elements of community life. They intentionally repudiate "righteousness." But must they not rather seek righteousness publicly and privately under the quiet and imperceptible prompting and inspiring of the Spirit and receive it gratefully by working for it with the enabling of the Spirit? Is not the secular where the Spirit is quietly but effectively at work? If the Spirit is creatively life-giving and if life is life in community, is not the work of the Spirit in life-togethering, life-giving, and life-flourishing? The reason the law was given for Israel to obey is clear: "Then the Lord commanded us to observe all these statutes, to fear the Lord our God, for our lasting good, so as to keep us alive" (Deut. 6:24).

We now take up the contribution of the central political authority—the Monarchy—to the building up of life-together of the covenant community. As indicated in the concluding verse of the book of Judges, there was an urgent need for common standards for the conduct of community life. (21:25). The Hebrew tribes are now free. They have began to take possession of the land promised to them through their ancestors from the original inhabitants (the Canaanites who of course opposed the invasion) and against neighbors who wanted them out (the Philistines). In spite of their fierce tribal independence and rivalry, they now sought to become a nation by having a king "like other nations" (1 Sam. 8). This was a radical move. It indicated a deep dissatisfaction with the inadequacy of the amphictyony, their loosely organized tribal community life with no central political authority (1 Sam. 8:1-3). What somehow "governed" them was the Spirit of the Lord. But the coming of the Spirit was episodic and only in response to the cry of the people out of deep need for survival. The Spirit appeared through "judges" whose tenure, though redeeming, was temporary and thus could not provide stability to community life. Samuel also was a "judge," although a priest-judge, not a warrior-judge as the others. He mediated between God and the people on a covenantal basis. But his ministry was coterminus with his life, like the other judges. And it was about to end. These factors clearly indicated that Israel had no experience of being ruled by a king; there was no precedent for it. The only model they could choose from was the practice of other nations who were governed by a king. Because of this, Samuel was reluctant to agree with the people's request for a king. But they replied to him: "No! but we are determined to have a king over us, so that we also maybe like other nations, and that our king may govern us, and go out before us and fight our battles" (1 Sam. 8:19-20).

Following the Lord's advice, Samuel had to warn them about what it means to have a king: The king would have power and authority to govern all the tribes; he would build a military machine out of their sons; he would put their daughters into the service of his court; he would tax their properties and their products; he would exact labor from them to serve his needs and his projects. He would demand obedience from them, and this would mean a loss of their tribal freedom. In the end Samuel gave in to their demand, with the Lord's consent (1 Sam. 9:22).

The move toward establishing a monarchy for Israel may be seen as a further step toward secularizing community life. This may be gathered from 1 Samuel 8:7-9: "The Lord said to Samuel. 'Listen to the voice of the people in all that they say; for they have not rejected you, but they have rejected me from being king over them. Just as they have done to me, from the day I brought them out of Egypt to this day, forsaking me and serving other gods, so also they are doing to you. Now then, listen to their voice; only you shall solemnly warn them, and show them the ways of the king who shall reign over them.'" It may be worth noting the following secularizing moves: (1) It is the people in one voice making the demand for a king; (2) in doing so, they were rejecting God's kingship over them; (3) they were in effect also rejecting the mediation of God's rule through the priest-judge represented by Samuel and his ministry. These are all secularizing moves. But one ironic feature that overarches them all: They are authorized by the Lord (1 Sam. 8:22). It is the Lord who chose Saul, the first king of Israel, anointed him, and set him up as king to rule over his people (1 Sam.10). And so it is the Lord the Spirit who allowed these secularizing moves that established the monarchy. Is it not the Spirit that makes political authority secular?

Although the king can now do what he pleases to do as king because the Spirit is with him (1 Sam. 10:7), the very presence of the Spirit provides basic limitations to what he can do as king. Fundamental is the fact that he, together with his people, shall be absolutely loyal to the Lord and him only, and no other shall they serve wholeheartedly. In serving the Lord, the king can do no less and no better than simply obey the Torah and its ordinances and keep the covenant and therefore secure the land, protect and promote freedom, rule according to law and thus secure justice and righteousness, and achieve order and peace and prosperity for the people. In Deuteronomy 17:14-20, where there is a parallel passage establishing the monarchy and its limitations, it is explicitly stated: "When he [the king] has taken the throne and his kingdom, he shall have a copy of this law [the Torah and the Mosaic law] written for him in the presence of the levitical priests. It shall remain with him and he shall read in it all the days of his life, so that he may learn to fear the Lord his God, diligently observing all the words of this law and those statutes, neither exalting himself above other members of the community nor turning aside from the commandment, either to the right or to the left, so that he and his descendants may reign long over his kingdom in Israel" (vv. 18-20). It is clear from the above that it is not from the king that the law comes. Nor is he the law. The Law comes from God for his people. The king is to rule according to this law. He is not above the law but under the law. And if he violates the law, he is to be judged according to the same law. And what he does under the law is ultimately to be measured by the standard of the law in seeking to achieve justice and righteousness. It is the law that rules the king, not the king ruling over the law.

Saul was judged by the Law although he was anointed by the Spirit (1 Sam. 13:1-14; 15:1-24). This means the Spirit rules through the law by what his agent does in obedience to the law. The Spirit is not at the beck and call of the king. Saul violated the law when he sought to secure the loyalty of the people to himself by doing what would please them rather than God, whose people they are (1 Sam. 13:1-14). He kept the spoils of war with the pretense that they will be used as sacrifice to the Lord, a clear case of using the name of the Lord wrongly, or justifying a wrong deed by a religious reason (1 Sam. 15:1-24). In both cases, Saul was "setting up a monument for himself" (1 Sam. 15:12). And a third violation of the law was Saul's persistent pursuit of David to kill him out of jealously over David's popularity among the people and the perceived threat that David might succeed him to his throne. (1 Sam. 18:6-9; 19:1-7; 24:1-15). In fact, David had done Saul no wrong and was loyal to Saul. And Saul was judged for being unjust to an innocent member of God's people who only sought to serve the Lord by dutifully serving the king whom God has anointed. Because of this failure to abide by the law, Saul was deposed as king and the Spirit withdrew from him (1 Sam. 13:13-14, 22-23; 16:1, 14).

And so enters David and succeeds to the throne. It is God who chooses him, anoints him, and installs him as king over his people. "The Spirit of the LORD came mightily upon David from that day forward" (16:1-13). And David goes forth to do what a king is obliged to do: to secure the land and extend it and protect it against those who would take it from God's people; put down rebellion; professionalize the army; ensure justice and righteousness by the proper administration of law, especially the rights and well-being of the poor, the stranger, the widow, the orphan, and the disenfranchised; set up a bureaucracy for running the government; establish diplomatic relations with neighboring nations; set up his own capital city acceptable to all the tribes by conquering the city of the Jebusites with his own army without the help of the armies of the other tribes—Jerusalem, and naming it "the city of David"—and made it the seat of his throne and the center of his governance over and above the tribes and their rivalries (see 2 Sam. 5:6-9). He not only established his throne in his capital city, he also brought the ark of the covenant from where it lay nearly forgotten in Kirjath-jearim (1 Sam. 6:21) and brought it with great cultic fanfare to Jerusalem. A tent-shrine was specially set up and the ark was placed in it, pending the building of a temple for its permanent residence, which David intended to undertake (2 Sam. 6). But David was forbidden to build the Temple. That task was given to Solomon, David's son and successor. David also established the priesthood by appointing Abiathar and Zadok to ensure the worship of the Lord and "institutionalize" his presence among his people through the tent-shrine, and eventually the Temple. Thus, in addition to the law, three more institutions were added to the community build-up of Israel: a capital city, a throne, and the Temple.

But what is unusual or unique about the kingship of David is that the Lord made a covenant with David that with him a house of royalty, a dynasty, shall be established. Like the Abrahamic covenant, the covenant is upon the initiative of

God and will be maintained by God as "an everlasting covenant" (2 Sam. 7:4-29). There will be a succession of kings in this one Davidic dynasty until it ends with the exile in Babylon. Is this then the final end of the covenant of the Lord with the royal house of David? Not quite so! For out of this dynasty will arise a messianic hope that is to be fulfilled by his anointed agent, the Messiah, who shall spring from the root of David (Isa. 6:13; 7:13-17; 9:1-7; 11:1-9). In the messianic texts in Isaiah we are permitted to catch a vision of Israel as a righteous community. In this vision all the elemental factors of community life are present. They are embodied in the servant community. They are all rightly related to one another. Justice is merciful. Compassion is just. The knowledge of God makes justice merciful and compassion just. And justice and mercy make the knowledge of God effectively at work in social life. But all this happens because the Spirit has rested upon the messianic community and is making it visibly and publicly righteous. But, of course, the vision is messianic: It is the future anticipated in the present! Precisely because it is messianic, should it not therefore be sought now because it is anticipated as coming? Today, peoples are overthrowing structures of oppression. They seek liberation, they want freedom. This is their dignity and their right to it is a global phenomenon. Must not this be construed as a secular work of the Spirit? Is not this deep aspiration of the human spirit a secular sign of the presence and activity of God the Spirit? Today, societies that have become free are looking for the public face of freedom. Can this not be embodied and expressed in secular standards of community life that seek to attain justice, lift the lowly, secure peace, and make life flourish? Giving freedom a secular public face in terms of norms and values for life in community is also a secular work of the Spirit. Political will and power for good governance to achieve the common good are lacking in many societies. Is this because they have stepped out of the *religare*?

Yet one senses that this urgent need (and the awareness that if it is not responsibly addressed) will loom ominously as a threat that could be fatal to the survival of the world community. Is not this sense and awareness a secular prompting of the Spirit and a secular sign that the Spirit is already at work to inspire the rise of new leadership committed to achieving the common good? Stripped of its historical conditionedness, may not the messianic vision of the house of David serve as an inspiring model in the search for a public face of freedom?

It may also be asked: Is the historical end of the Davidic dynasty also the end of Temple worship? May it also be claimed, as so many do, that worship is useless and futile in today's world? Is not worship an antisecular, antiworldly, antihuman, antinatural, and antimaterial activity? At best it draws attention away from the nitty-gritty problems of daily life. It points to "heaven," away from the earth.

And so it devalues the earthly. Worship is a waste of time and a useless activity. Places of worship such as cathedrals and church buildings are better emptied of worshipers and replaced with tourists. What is important about these buildings is their art—the architectural design, the stained glass images, the paintings, the statuary—not the faith and the cult they stand for, and most certainly not the so-called divine presence in the midst of a people, which after all is merely a projection of human values and aspirations, at best, or an illusion created by the imagination as a way of escape from the messiness of daily life, at worst. This may be a "modern" view with which a secularistic, antispiritual mind may regard religion.

But this is not the way Temple worship is understood and practiced at its best. The primal beginnings of Temple worship are found in the Sinai wilderness through which the Israelites led by Moses journeyed from being slaves in Egypt to become a people of God. As a part of God's self-disclosure to this people through Moses, they were told: "And have them make me a sanctuary [tabernacle] so I may dwell among them" (Exod. 25:8). Some essential details are added to this bare statement in Exodus 29:42-46. At the "tent of meeting . . . where I will meet with you, to speak to you there. I will meet with the Israelites there, and it shall be sanctified by my glory. I will consecrate the tent of meeting and the altar; Aaron also and his sons I will consecrate, to serve me as priests. I will dwell among the Israelites, and I will be their God. And they shall know that I am the LORD their God, who brought them out of the land of Egypt that I might dwell among them; I am the LORD their God." In addition to the "sanctuary" or "tent of meeting," an "ark" made of "acacia wood" is to be made with specific measurements (45 × 27 × 27 inches, Exod. 25:10). The ark symbolized the Lord's presence with the people as they journeyed in the wilderness to the Promised Land, to be ahead of them and so to guide them (Num. 10:33), to help them in overcoming obstacles in their journey, as in war (Num. 10:35-36), and to be a place where God, seated on a throne, as it were, would give instructions to Moses and to the people (1 Sam. 3). As a "portable wooden chest" the ark can be carried in the journey and thus be part of it (2 Sam. 7:5-11). Inside the ark is to be placed "the covenant," that is, the Tablets of Stone on which the Torah is written (24:12; 25:16, 21). And so the ark is called "the Ark of the Covenant." The covering of the ark is the "mercy seat," symbolizing an empty seat on which God the Lord sits as in a throne (25:17, 21) to judge in mercy and hear the prayers of his people. The whole unit—tent of meeting, the ark, the tablets of Torah, the covenant, the mercy seat, the priesthood, the "glory that fills the place"—symbolizes one thing: God dwelling in the midst of his people so that he shall be their God and they shall be his people. The tent of meeting, the ark, the mercy seat are all made of material things—of metal, stone, wood, and cloth. They are all made by human hands gifted by God with artistic skills (Exod. 31:1-11). The ark of the covenant is the itinerant presence of God that accompanied the people in their journey across the wilderness. Later, the Tabernacle, the tent of meeting, was replaced by the Temple built by Solomon, and the ark of the covenant placed in it in the capital city where the throne is also located. But the meaning of the Temple is the same as the tent of meeting: it is the dwelling place of God to be with and in the midst of his people so that he shall be their God and they shall be his people (1 Kings 8). Moreover, worship was the way to keep the Sabbath of the Lord. The Sabbath was set aside from all time as a time consecrated to, and sanctified by, the Lord. It is he who gave it its meaning: "This is a sign between me and you throughout your generations, given in order that you may know that I, the Lord, sanctify you. . . . It is a sign forever between me and the people of Israel that in six days the Lord made heaven and earth, and on the seventh day he rested, and was refreshed" (Exod. 31:12-13, 17). The "six days" of creation, that is, all creation time, are taken into and sanctified by Sabbath time.

We may ask, What is the relation between Temple worship and Sabbath? Temple worship is celebration of God's dwelling with his people so that they may know he is their God and they are his people. The cultic acts in worship celebrate the deliverance from Egypt, the possession of the Promised Land, the giving of the Law, the amphictyonic community, the monarchy, and the covenants that run through them, holding them together. Sabbath celebrates the creation of Israel as God's people, the creation of heaven and earth, everything that is. Temple and Sabbath are linked together. God's covenants with Abraham and Moses and David are linked indissolubly with the covenant with Noah. God's binding himself with his people links with his binding himself with creation. The order of community as a people of God is linked with the order of the cosmos. Heaven and earth are linked together by the Spirit, by the *religare*. To both God makes a turn in himself to constitute himself for and with his people and to be for and with his creation. God's turning in covenant is done with a sign, a public, visible, natural, cultural—in short, a secular—sign. God's sign for his covenant with creation is the Sabbath and the rainbow. God's sign for his covenant with his people is Temple worship and all that pertains to it.

As God's signs he wills to be known in the way the natural and the human know, and that is to be a natural, human, public, secular icon through which his glory radiates for public and community beholding!

This raises a very important question: What links God and his public signs? Is it not the Spirit, God's Spirit, the binding bond, the *religare*? But the signs remain as signs. They are made to remain as such, otherwise they lose their transparency, their translucency, to the God whose signs they are. They lose their iconic character when they are detached from their mooring in the Spirit, and in their self-regard and self-pointing or self-witness, they become idols. They become sacral instead of secular. As secular they are open to the Spirit who transcends them and so leads then to ever-new possibilities of public meaning. In the hands of the Spirit signs are polyvalent in their meaning-possibilities without losing their literal sense and their secular character. Are not all these the work of the Spirit that secularizes?

But the signs are not only what the Lord has chosen to be the vessels of his presence among his people. The signs are also what his people do in worship in the shrines, in the tent of meeting, and in the Temple. We cannot give here a detailed consideration of Temple worship as described in the priestly tradition of Israel's faith. For our purposes, it may suffice to consider some essential elements of worship. The Hebrew word translated as "worship" means "serve." Services of worship are called *leitourgia* in Greek, and the word means public service. To serve God is to worship him privately and publicly. Temple worship is public worship of God. The public worship of God includes many things, such as prayer, the reading of the Law, the offer of sacrifices, the ascription of praises to God, and expressions of gratitude for his benefits. The Psalms are the book of hymns of Israel. They include praise, prayer, gratitude, lament, petition, and protest, which are acts of the people in worship. The horizon of worship is not only the story of God's making a people for himself, but the story of his creation activity and all its benefits. In the Psalms (106, 107, 135, 136, 146, 147, 148) we are taken in, through worship, to participate not only in praising God for what he has done for his people, but also—and usually in the same psalm—are brought into the wider horizon of God's creational activity. Redemption/Salvation and Creation are linked together, and they are linked in God as Creator and Savior and Lord of all things. The question may be asked, What is the link between "the redeemed of the Lord" and the rest of creation? May it not be the Spirit? What is the link between the order of life-together and the order of the cosmos? May it not be the Spirit? What is the link in God's turn to create the heavens and the earth and to make a people for himself? May it not be the Spirit? And may not the praise of Israel in worship be a sign of this linkage?

Today, there is talk of "the rights of nature." This implies that nature is to be treated and appreciated according to its own being, character, and behavior. It has its own laws that make it behave as it does. It has a right to be respected and treated as it is. This right belongs to it by simply being what it is. They are not conferred by human being. The State can only acknowledge them. Is it too far-fetched to suggest that one of those rights is the right of nature to praise its creator and express its gratitude for being a part of the whole creation? May not nature declare with the psalmist, "The heavens are telling the glory of God; and the firmament proclaims his handiwork" (Ps. 19:1). Or "All the earth worships you; they sing praises to you, sing praises to your name" (Ps. 66:4). May not creation acknowledge that it belongs to no one but God: "The heavens are yours, the earth also is yours; the world and all that is in it—you have founded them"? (Ps. 89:16; 24:1-2). Because of this, may not creation be accorded the right to rejoice in its creator: "Let the heavens be glad, and let the earth rejoice; let the sea roar, and all that fills it; let the fields exult, and everything in it. Then shall all the trees of the forest sing for joy before the Lord" (Pss. 96:11-12; cf. 97:1; 98:4-8).

Today there are efforts to identify so-called "endangered species" and take measures to save them. They are endangered not because they are prey to other nonhuman living creatures, but because of human vanity, sport, cruelty, and the devastation of their natural habitat. The real problem is bigger and more intractable and more dangerous than this. It is the whole earth now that is the endangered species. It is threatened with destruction not by another planet, nor by other space entities like asteroids or comets, but by human earthlings who are part of it and will perish with it. And since it appears that what humans can do to save it is not good enough, may not the earth cry for help and salvation to its creator who is also its savior? He creates by saving and he saves by creating. "These all look to you to give them their food in due season; when you give to them, they gather it up; when you open your hand, they are filled with good things. When you hide your face, they are dismayed; when you take their breath, they die away and return to their dust. When you send forth your spirit, they are created; and you renew the face of the ground" (Ps. 104:27-30).

Today, there is a global awareness of the ecological crisis. There is a pressing need to link policies and activities of government, industry, development, population growth, and technology to Mother Nature and its resources. The survival of life, including human life, is indissolubly linked with the resources of the earth. Might not this awareness and the activities that it entails be a sign that the Spirit is already at work to bring into interplay for their mutual benefit the order of community life and the order of creation, the order of society and the order of the cosmos? Would it be too much to suggest that this linkage and its signs be celebrated in the worship of God in whose covenanting turn this linkage is founded and sustained? That linkage by and in the Spirit has a secular dimension as indicated by secular signs. These signs must be taken urgently and seriously. It is the Spirit that secularizes through signs. To ignore them would be disastrous!

CHAPTER V

JUDGMENT AND SECULARIZATION

Up to this point we have sought to indicate the role of the Spirit in the secularizing process. We have done this by showing that it is the Spirit who establishes the this-worldly and creaturely character of all that there is. This has been done in at least three features of reality: in creation, in life, and in community. We have tried to do this within the framework of *religare*, the binding bond between God and all that there is, who is himself the Spirit. The overall evaluation of all this is that it is good. God is good in himself because he turns to constitute himself as a creating and blessing God. Creation itself is good—"to be is to be good"—because it comes from non-possibility by the possibilizing activity of the Spirit and the actualizing power of the Word. Life in all its forms and dynamisms is good because it is given by God the Spirit as blessing and benefit and as a way of participating in God's creative activity. Being human is good because one becomes deeply and indelibly aware of the glory and goodness of God, because one has been called and destined to be the creaturely and worldly image of God in his creation, because of being given the honor and dignity of being God's gardener and steward of all the works of his hands, and because of being with the other human is so much joy and so self-fulfilling. Being human is good because the appreciation of the good goes with being human. This appreciation of the good leads to valuing the truly and really valuable, namely, God himself in his holiness and glory. This valuing of God is precisely the worship of God. We have staked out the claim that the this-worldly creaturely character of all this is the work of the Spirit within the bond of the *religare* who is himself that bond.

But now and strangely enough and with deep puzzlement, it is not only the good of creation and the good of the creator and the good of being human that one is keenly and indelibly aware of. There is also the awareness, equally deep and inextinguishable and spread out throughout all humanity, that something bad has happened to God's creation. Something is thwarting the work of the Spirit, disrupting the *religare*, distorting the good, and threatening secular reality with destruction. More strangely, this sense of something bad happening to the good is given together with the awareness of the good. One cannot be aware of the good without at the same time being aware of the bad and its threat. To be aware of good is to be aware of the bad and to be aware of the bad is to be aware of the good. Why is this? Is there a way of understanding this very disturbing puzzle? It is this puzzling matter that this chapter seeks to consider.

1. The Awareness of Good and Evil

This issue of what has gone wrong with the good has bothered humankind to no end for as long as humans can remember. It has been considered in connection with the beginning of things. And if beginning is viewed in terms of a primal creative act or event as in the Bible, it is logical to consider it at that primal level. But if it is taken up at that level, at the level of "in the beginning" and of beginning as creation, then we cannot avoid the conclusion that it affects all that is in creation. That means that it is a possibility in creation. That something bad can happen in and to creation is possible. As a possibility, it is a universal condition in creation. We can ask, why is it at all possible? If the possibility has been actualized in a specific way—as an act or an event, as it is claimed in Scripture—we have to ask by whom, why, and how. And if it has consequences for ill or good, we have also to ask what these are and how effective they are. And in all this, we need to consider the burden of this book, namely, the role of the Spirit. Considering the role of the Spirit in relation to what has gone wrong with creation is on the face of it odd, very odd indeed. It could be regarded as an oxymoron. But still we have to ask the question and seek the answer, if there is one.

For the sake of consideration at the level of "beginnings," we may distinguish four levels of this issue. Level one would be the primal deed or act as a possibility in creation and affecting all creation and all that is in it. Level two would be the act done within the covenant that created Israel as God's people, which act has the consequence of distorting the covenanting relation and of perverting life within it. Level three would be the cumulative activity of both personal and social participation in community life brought in turn by the effect of the two previous levels.

And finally, level four, the level at which all creation is now "subjected to futility" by "this evil age."

While we distinguish these levels for the sake of gaining some measure of clarity in discussion, they are in reality interwoven and co-inhering in and affecting one another; and not only with one another but also with the good of creation and the good of all there is in it. The inevitable result is that there is some measure of good in the bad, and some sort of bad in the good. To say that the bad is "objective," that it is independent by itself and quite apart from the good would be misleading, for the bad is only seen in the light of the good. But, on the other hand, one can say that there is good as seen by God in what he has created, which cannot be said of the bad in creation. It is in the light of the good that God sees and declares, and in the light of what measure of good that is seen humanly, which provide the standard for measuring in some way the bad that has happened to the good. But the bad that is measured does not have the same status and dignity that the good possesses in the sight of God. Still there is the mixture that is inescapably real. Why does this mixture of the good and the bad exist? How did it come about?

There is another factor that intrudes itself into this complex mixture. If the experience and knowledge of good are always intertwined with the bad or the wrong, why is it that the human inevitably feels responsible and accountable for this unavoidable mixture? Since this mixture is not of his own making and he is in fact messed into it as a situation already there and for which he cannot avoid, why should he be held responsible and accountable for it? And yet this feeling of being held responsible and accountable for the mixture of good and in one's deed or action, is a phenomenon that appears rooted in the human psyche and seems obvious as a universal element in humankind. Does this mean that there is a moral structure built into creation and in the human as such? What gives to creation this moral order? Is it of God for God? If so, why should the human be responsible for it? Or could it be of God for the human? If so, what does this mean for the human? Would it be right for the human to seek it for himself?

Moreover, this sense of good and bad, right and wrong, in their intertwining and mixture is also accompanied by a deep sense of anxiety, of the threat to, and precariousness of, existence, of the uncertainty and instability of things as they are, of the utter fragility of life, of disease, pain, aging, disability, suffering, and death. Why is this the case? What is the relation of this experience of the negativities of existence and life to the experience of good and bad, of right and wrong? And what is the relation of this twofold experience to the goodness, blessing, and benefit of God? These are very complicated issues quite obviously. They are raised out of a salvific concern. Is there a "balm in Gilead" that heals and saves?

They should be dealt with from this perspective, and rightly so. They also include, however, an etiological concern, asking for illumination in terms of origin and causes if only for the sake of understanding. Salvation and explanation are both asked for in the raising of these questions, and for that reason they call for dealing with them at the levels we have indicated above. Of course, we cannot do justice to them in terms of what can be done in this book. The best we can do is to indicate the general lines in dealing with them as indicated by the Scriptures. This may be all that can be done in this book.

2. This, But Not That: Between Permission and Prohibition

The section considers the primal conditions from which could arise the creaturely possibility of being tempted and of succumbing to temptation, thus violating and distorting the primal human relation with God and with the other nonhuman creatures. The *locus classicus* for reflection on this issue is to be found in the texts in Genesis: 2:4-9, 15-17; 3:1-24. We leave to the experts the detailed exegesis of these texts. It is available in standard commentaries. Our interest is mainly in the structural lines and dynamics brought into play that condition the human to temptation.

The creaturely situation partly assumed by Genesis 3:1-7 may be summarized as follows. The human, male and female understood in the text generically and representing all humankind, are already created and alive. They already exist out of the Nothing. They are already alive out of the dust of nonlife. This, by the activity of the Spirit. The garden of God, creation itself, is already made but needs cultivation to bring out its potential as the source for the nourishing and flourishing of life. God puts the human in the Garden and gives him "dominion" over it by "tilling and keeping it." He is thus placed within God's life-giving and life-sustaining presence. Being in God in God's creation, the human may thus fulfill his vocation to image God in God's world. The human is to mirror God in all that he is, does, relates, and becomes, in God's world. He is blessed by God "to multiply and subdue" the earth. The human is thus given the unique privilege to participate generatively in God's creative activity in perpetuating the continuity and developing the potentialities of life. The primal relation established in creation between God and the human is religaric and therefore dialogic: God addresses the human; he talks to the human, and the human listens and responds freely in talk and in deed. God can and does "command" the human, and the human "may" obey (2:15) and he does so. The subject of the conversation that God initiates is God's purpose for the human in creation, the place and role of the human in creation, and his life and destiny in creation. God's word in this dialogue is spoken as a command. God's word is command; it cannot be otherwise. What he says must happen and it does happen. But as command, it has two parts or dimensions. It is both permissive and prohibitive: "You may freely eat of every tree of the garden" [permissive]; but of the tree of the knowledge of good and evil you shall not eat, for in the day that you eat of it you shall die" [prohibitive] (Gen. 2:16-17). The command of God as both permissive and prohibitive is what structures the human, its nature, and its life morally. It is the moral order of human reality. It is also what confers to the human the blessing and dignity of human freedom its moral quality. In freedom the human may freely respond to God. In freedom he may determine how he may respond, and he does. He may exercise his freedom, and he does. He may exercise his freedom by making a choice, and he does. He can freely make a choice, because there are options from which to choose, and he does make a choice. The options are given in the command: permission or prohibition. Both options are possibilities not of the human's own making. They are given to the human by God. And so a choice made in freedom between options is a choice made by the human in God. The consequences and the possibility of their happening are also in God's hands. He can let the consequences happen, or he can withhold them, or temper them, or make them a teaching opportunity, or make them a means for renewal and growth, or all of these! The human chooses; God disposes.

Thus, freedom and its exercise are fraught with immense and profound possibilities and consequences. To stay within the permission and its possibilities is life nourished and flourished and fulfilled by God's blessings and benefits. To go beyond the permission and step into what is prohibited is to flounder and die. Where else may one go in stepping beyond life and crossing its limits? Is it not to plunge back into nonlife, "into dust" from which the human came? Is it not from the non-possibility of being and existence, that is from the Nothing, that from which being and existence were created? Is it not from nonlife, from the dry dust of the earth, that the human was formed and given life by the Spirit? If one freely opts to cross the blessing and limit of life, is it not into death that one is helplessly plunged? Death is given as a possibility of life by the exercise of freedom, and it is precipitated factually by the exercise of freedom by crossing the limits of life!

This is the case universally because creaturely existence is a combination, made by God alone, of both being and nonbeing, of both life and nonlife. The fact of being and existence is the result of God creating out of nonbeing and nonexistence. It is the creaturely product of God self-constituting himself as Creator. The fact of life in all its variety of forms and possibilities is the creaturely result of God self-constituting himself as living and so is life-giving as Creator. Both are God's exercise of his sovereignty over the Nothing and the Nonlife. But it is worthwhile to realize that human freedom is wedged within this combination of being and nonbeing and of life and nonlife. It is fraught with the possibilities of being, existence, and life on the one hand, and on the other hand, with the possibilities nonbeing, nonexistence, and nonlife, and ultimately of death and extinction. Freedom to make a choice that is its proper exercise is the freedom to be or not to be, to be alive or to die! But this freedom and its exercise, the options given to it, and the consequences a choice may result in are all within God's sovereignty. They are established by God for the human. And so they are all contingent upon God, upon his grace as creator and life-giver. The exercise of freedom in making a choice is made in God and is directed to God both immediately and ultimately. And since the relation of God to the human is religaric and dialogic, God may respond freely in accordance to his self-constitution: "I am who I am" (Exod. 3:14). It is existence and life in-between the command of permission and prohibition, and in the combination created by God of being and nonbeing, of existence and nonexistence, of life and nonlife, of possibilities and limits, of life and death, that is the ground and condition of human vulnerability to temptation. Freedom is precisely what makes the human vulnerable to temptation.

So now enters temptation. It is important to note that temptation enters the scene in the form of a dialogue. This is the way it comes in a primal way. The tempter may appear as coming from outside of the self but addresses the self and the self responds. It may be a dialogue with oneself, with the self as another. In Genesis 3:1-7 the primal dialogue is given a narrative form. It is between the serpent and the woman, with the man as a silent partner. The serpent is God's creature, a form of animal life, a part of creation. It is from creation and within creation that temptation comes. The serpent is "wild" in that it can use any means to sneak up on someone unsuspectingly. Temptation knows and follows no rules. It is "crafty" because, as the text shows, it can question any claim to truth and cast doubt on it and unsettle one's confidence in it. Temptation is the advocacy of opposition. There is room for doubting truth—even the truth of God, especially if God's truth comes as command that includes both permission and prohibition. Truth can be doubted in terms of what may contradict it or falsify it. The truth that is doubted is the truth of God's Word. The serpent said to the woman: "Did God say, 'You shall not eat from any tree in the garden'?" (3:1). This query contradicts God's word spoken in 2:16 to the man: "You may freely eat of every tree of the garden." The woman replies to the serpent: "We may eat of the fruit of the trees in the garden" (3:2). Note that the eating of fruit in the garden is stated by the serpent in the form of a question, thus casting doubt on the truth of what God said:

"Did God say, 'you shall not eat from tree in the garden'?" (3:1b). The woman correctly replies by saying that the command is permissive: "We may eat." The woman, however, adds to her reply something that the serpent did not ask for: "But God said, 'You shall not eat of the fruit of the tree that is in the middle of the garden, nor shall you touch it, or you shall die'" (3:3). The woman includes the prohibition with a consequence. She even adds that the fruit in question is not to be "touched," for to touch it is already for the purpose of taking it to be eaten.

The reply of the serpent is twofold. First, he denies the consequence of eating the fruit in question: "You will not die." This again casts doubt on the truth of God's word by denying its consequence if disobeyed. The ground for this denial is that because the fruit has not yet been eaten, therefore its consequence cannot yet happen. There is yet no palpable evidence to confirm the claim: "You shall not die." So the doubting is also a challenge to dare! But the serpent goes beyond this. He informs the woman of something the woman did not know, but which the serpent knows. The serpent knows what God knows, which the woman did not know. What God knows is that when one eats of the prohibited fruit, "your eyes will be opened, and you will be like God, knowing good and evil" (3:4-5). Since the serpent knows what God knows about the eating of the forbidden fruit, he tells it to the woman in the hearing of the man for both of them to know! But by what means can she know? If by means of authority, whose authority will she take for knowing? God did not include in his word about the forbidden truth the various possibilities for the human that are opened up by eating it, only the final consequence, which is death. So there is no word from God about it, and so there is no word of authority from God as a basis for knowing. Should she take the authority of the serpent? What the serpent said about the forbidden fruit is so enticingly good that it is difficult to resist the urgent desire to claim and possess the good for oneself: You will not die, your eyes will be opened, you will know good and evil, and you will be like God, you will be wise. The serpent tells the woman that all this is about the good of the human; they are possibilities of good that belong to the human and it is open to the human to take them and realize and possess them. God knows that these are possibilities of the human for the human. But he forbids the human from taking possession of them. And that is odd. The serpent knows that those possibilities are not for itself, but for the human; they are also not possibilities for God but for the human; and they are for the taking by the human. Now, the serpent subtly entices the woman. To doubting, daring, he now adds enticing. He appeals not to any bad that may result from the eating of the forbidden fruit, but only to the good that it will give to the woman! This is temptation of the first order.

Consider the "good" that the eating of the fruit will bring. Your eyes will be opened. The woman and man already have eyes. But they only see the fruit of the tree as "good for food" and that the tree was "a delight to the eyes" (3:6). But is this all that the eyes are for? If they were fully opened would they not see more? They would see each other nakedly in their difference and mutuality and enjoy each other's company and not be embarrassed. They would see the world—and there is a lot of such a world to see. But seeing is also observing, identifying, analyzing, classifying, synthesizing, interpreting, and understanding. To see is to know things as they are. To know is also to think at the same time. One can do knowing by thinking; thinking is the activity of knowing. Thinking is knowing the truth about things. And truth is reality given to knowing through thinking. This whole process gets started by seeing, by the eyes being opened to see. And what is seen starts from seeing (and knowing and thinking) what is good to the human—namely what is good for the surviving, nourishing, and flourishing of life—and that is, obviously, food. What is seen in observing, knowing, and thinking is what makes for "delight" to the human. That means not just food that satisfies, but food that tastes flavorful, food that is delightful to eat. That means knowing not just anything, but things that are beautiful to behold, things not only useful but also enjoyable to the human. That means not any kind of knowing, but knowing that yields understanding; that means not any kind of thinking but rational and practical thinking. That means not any kind of truth about things as they are, but imaginative truth, not just truth about things as they already are, but truth about what they can yet be, about new things, about new possibilities, truth about the future that can become. This truth of the not-yet can only be imaginatively seen or visioned. Food that is "good" for the human, would God withhold this from the human? After all, permission to eat of the fruit of the trees in the garden has already been commanded. It would be palpably odd if God took back his command! Beauty that is a delight to the eyes? It would be odd to deny the eyes this delight. Did not Ralph Waldo Emerson say the classic word about this: "If eyes were made for seeing/Then Beauty is its own excuse for being" ("The Rhodora")? After all, God created a garden of beauty and put the human there to enjoy it.

But the prohibition deals only with the fruit of this one tree? To eat of the fruit of this one tree is to become wise, knowing good and evil (3:5). This human possibility opened by the eating of this one fruit was not revealed by God. What was commanded by God is only the prohibition about eating and its ultimate consequence. The command did not include the possibilities opened to the human by the act of eating. These possibilities were revealed to the human by the serpent.

One may surmise that God did not tell the woman the full truth about the eating of this one fruit, only the final result which is death. God told only half of the full truth. Why? Is it because he leaves this to the human to discover and delight in the discovery? It is the serpent that tells the full truth: He assumes the prohibition is already known by the woman, but he also tells the good consequence of eating the fruit. This puts the human in a dilemma: Whose authority will she obey? God's word comes to the woman as command but does not tell the whole truth, thus, requiring the response of trust in God and obedience to what is so far commanded by him. The serpent's word tells the "whole truth" not as a command, but as a straightforward appeal to the best interest of the human, which is to know. Which is better for the human: to know or to trust? Which yields certainty? The appeal is left to the woman to heed or not. The word of the serpent is prohibitive and permissive. The serpent reverses the structure and direction of the word of God. God's word is permissive and prohibitive. The serpent reverses this. The serpent's word is prohibitive and permissive: "You shall not die." This is prohibitive in the sense that it prevents the consequence of eating. "But if you eat, you will gain this." This is permissive because the eating is what brings about benefits, not the horror of dying. The woman saw the tree and the eating of its fruit in this way: "the tree was to be desired to make one wise" (3:6). It may be asked, is wisdom bad? Is desiring it wrong? Is being wise not good for the human? After all, wisdom is of God. Would he withhold sharing it with the human? Would he not rather share it as a gift and a benefit, as he did with Solomon, for example? Is not the possession of the wisdom ingredient essential to the dignity of being human? Is it really the case that God prevents the acquisition of this human good? Since God did not disclose it to the woman, to which in God's command do they belong, to permission or prohibition?

What we have done so far is to describe both the structure and dynamics of temptation to which the human is vulnerable as a condition of his existence and life. We have seen that the structure is dialogic because it is religaric. There are agent-partners involved: the serpent, the human, and in the background, God. The agent partners are also engaged. The agent partners actively engaged are the serpent and the woman, with both God and the human male silent. The serpent and the woman carry a conversation. They give and take opinions, deliberately discussing and interpreting the subject at hand, namely, God's word of command. One may presume that the woman was also thinking what to do by weighing the pros and cons of a possible choice. In short, the dialogic structure and dynamics are relational! This relational structure and dynamics underlie and condition temptation and the vulnerability of the human to it. Now we ask in pursuit of our claim that it is the Spirit that secularizes: what is the role of the Spirit in temptation as a dialogical engagement and so as a relational reality?

We have claimed that creation—an activity of God as Spirit and Word—is the combining of the possible and the non-possible, resulting in creaturely reality as the intertwining, co-inhering, and interfacing of being and nonbeing in existence, of life and nonlife in being alive. Creation is establishing secular reality.

We have seen that creation is also God's word of command that both permits and prohibits. This command is the charter of human freedom that is exercised between permission and prohibition as ultimate options and parameters. It is this command that structures creation with a moral order and so makes freedom and its exercise a moral reality. This command is what gives secular reality its moral quality.

We have also tried to show that the exercise of freedom is not merely a matter of choosing what to do or not to do—between permission and prohibition—but more important, it is a decision of to be or not to be, to be alive or to die. This decision is not merely moral. It goes deeper than this because it determines not merely well-being, not merely moral quality, but destiny itself. It determines destiny because it is not only an existential decision entailing life or death, being or nonbeing, but it places one under the gaze of God's judgment. God's judgment is what finally decides destiny! That judgment does not come only at the end of things and their times. It is an ongoing judging gaze (Gen. 3:8-24). From this we may conclude that secularity as an ongoing process is continuously and inescapably under the judging gaze of God the Spirit simply because it takes place within the bond of the *religare* who is the Spirit himself. Is it too far-fetched to conclude that the vulnerability of freedom to temptation is a work of the Spirit? Does not the Spirit test? Was not Jesus led to the wilderness by the Spirit to be tested? (Matt. 4:1-11).

Is not testing a crisis, in the sense that it is a critical point or situation at which life or death are put on the chopping block of freedom? Is not temptation a form of testing freedom by giving freedom the choice as to how it is to be exercised or wielded and for what? Where shall the ax of freedom fall as it swings, on permission or prohibition? Or on neither, but inescapably on both, giving rise to the knowledge of good and evil, of what is both permitted and prohibited? We may ask at this point whether temptation is good or bad. Perhaps these categories, if understood as moral, do not apply at this primal level that universally underlies and conditions humans in their decision-making. Morality presupposes this primal level and so is conditioned by them. We have seen that human freedom is what makes the human vulnerable to temptation that is in creation. The categories of good and bad or right and wrong apply only when freedom is exercised between permission and prohibition in terms of a concrete deed that is the proper object of moral and legal judgment. What does the woman do in exercise of her freedom? We shall know this as the woman makes her choice!

And she makes her fateful choice that decisively affects human well- being, morality, existentiality, and destiny! And since she is generic woman, together with the generic man, both representing the human universally, how and what she chooses pictures the conditions presuppositional to all human decisions made under the test of temptation. It is to be noted first of all that her choice was engagingly accompanied by the senses. She has heard the opinion of the serpent about the command. She has seen the tree and its fruit. She has touched the fruit when she took it with her hands. Most likely, she also smelled the fruit as she touched and took it. And then she finally tasted it as she ate it!

Is it not universally the case that the process of acquiring human knowledge is initiated sensibly? From there it can progress into new forms, such as concepts, images, abstractions, theories, and so on. The reason for this is the fact that the senses are part of the human body, and it is through the body that the human is connected necessarily to the rest of earthly, natural, and human reality. The senses are the windows of the body to the world. They are also the most direct and immediate point of entry of the world into the human self. This connection is not passive; it is rather interactive. The world is there to be sensed, and it yields itself to sensing. The human sensing is focused and deliberate. It sees the fruit for food, thus meeting a universal human need, it looks at the tree and what it beholds is delightful, thus meeting a universal need for enjoyment. And because the tree bears fruit for food and is delightful to behold, she appreciates it as desirable for becoming wise, thus meeting a universal human need for value and its appreciation. And wisdom is the goal of sensing, knowing, desiring, and deliberating. Is it too far from the truth to infer that this process of deliberation accompanied the action of the woman in taking the fruit and eating it? And we may ask, does not the same process in varying degrees accompany universally the crisis of being tempted?

But now the acquisition of wisdom does not consist merely in sensible experience, in deliberate thought, and in the appreciation of value. The second thing to be noted is this: All this must lead to a decision to act and to act out the decision. Thought must translate into deed. Thinking must lead into doing. It is by doing the thought that things are changed, including the agent of thought and deed. Without the deed that alters the way things are wisdom is not complete. The one who knows rightly, values appropriately, and acts out the good, and so makes a difference for good in the way things are is wise, ideally. But if one is to know rightly, one must also know what is wrong and false; if one is to appreciate value, one must also know what is worthless; and if one is to do the good, does doing it not also include the bad? And in all cases one must ideally avoid the wrong, and if possible one must also never go for the worthless; and one must overcome the bad with the good. And so to be wise is "to know good and evil." One cannot know and do the one without the other. This is fatefully the human condition that makes for wisdom. But now the question may be raised: Can the human existentially separate the good from the evil and the evil from the good? Can the human undo this co-inhering of the good and the bad in a human way and deal appropriately with the one as with the other?

One cannot even distinguish in thought the one without the other. Even in thought they co-inhere. This is even more so in act. One cannot existentially separate them and deal with them separately. Acknowledging this human condition as universal and inevitable is what appears to make for wisdom. Should this kind of wisdom be denied then to the human since there is no other human wisdom available under human conditions? This is the wisdom that the woman unknowingly desired. And it is what she got. Since she shared the fruit with her partner, primal man, and he ate the same fruit, he thereby shared in what she got. This sharing of this wisdom is a universal reality in which all of us are involved. It is what we get inevitably. Is there another wisdom that can be made available to the human?

The third thing to be noted is this: The situation is far more serious than merely knowing, appreciating, and acting. The woman took the fruit and ate it. Eating is taking something into oneself and processed by the self to become part of itself. What is eaten may appear as food but in the processing may not be food. It may in fact be poison and it may cause death, not the survival of life. The effect of poisoning may be instant, or it may be not. The final result may take some time to happen, but it will occur. But the point is that ingesting something severely affects the one doing it. If real food for the body is eaten, it sustains and keeps the body alive and healthy. But any food eaten includes in it that which is processed by the body as not food for it. That which is not food is part of the food that has to be eaten or ingested. One cannot eat the food without it. Only in the processing by the body, that is, by experiencing, is it distinguished from real food. Wisdom is eating the food that includes what is not food. Is this not the same as knowing good and evil? But to be wise is to be changed by experience from not being wise to being wise. And that means both in knowing and doing and therefore in experiencing and living, one must carry the burden of both good and evil in life. There is no truth without falsehood, no right without wrong, no good without bad, no joy without pain, no achievement without struggle, no life without death. And that is the dignity and burden of being human! Is this good or bad? It cannot be or but both, and so the categories of either good or bad objectively do not apply. One can make a proper judgment of this human wisdom if it can be compared to another wisdom that is also available for the human taking but was not availed of by the human. Is there such a wisdom? More of this below.

In what way were the woman and the man changed? The text says flatly: "the eyes of both were opened." (3:7). This is a most radical and fateful change. This did not mean that the woman and the man did not see before their eyes were both opened. Their seeing then was unknowing, their "seeing" then was made from their "being one flesh" (2:24). They co-inhered each other. Their relation of immediacy and mutuality was unbroken. While they were of different gender, their difference contributed to their mutuality and is the reason for their being one. They saw things from the same point of view and with the same interest and motivation. The woman without any hesitation gave the fruit to the man and the man took and ate it without any question whatever. There was a direct and mutual sharing arising from their intimate and co-inhering togetherness.

The same may be said of the relation of the human with other forms of life in the garden of creation. The serpent, though "wild" and "crafty," and the curious woman could dialogue with each other and exchange ideas about a most important subject, namely, the word of God, freely and without intimidation. The woman had to make up her mind and decide freely, and she did. But now all this has changed by an act, a deed, which is also an event! A point of view that consists only of ideas, opinions, and theories that are not enacted vis-à-vis things, situations, relations, and people are not capable of altering the way things are. But word united with deed activates a power that alters a life-world and changes the way reality is seen. This is the fourth thing to be noted: It is this seeing from being changed by one's action upon the way things are, and thus see things as changed, that constitutes primal change. The eyes of the woman and man were opened. They were changed by their act upon the tree and its fruit. And so their relation to creation—their situation in creation—has changed. From being changed in a situation that they changed by their deed, their way of seeing is also now changed. They now see themselves as changed and reality as changed because their way of seeing has changed.

They now see knowingly. And this is different from seeing unknowingly. To see knowingly is to observe. To observe is to put a distance between the observer and the observed, between the knower and the object of knowing. Thus to know is to turn what is to be known into an object of knowing. To know is to objectify. This objectifying, this making of distance so that a thing stands over against an observer, breaks the primal relation between woman and man, between female and male. They now see each other from the perspective of distance and from being over against the other, rather than from being one in togetherness. They now objectify each other, respectively. They now see each other's nakedness, and "they knew they were naked." Whereas, before they were not ashamed (2:25). Now, however, they are ashamed in their nakedness. Why? This is a fifth point to be noted: To be seen as naked without deliberately exposing oneself as naked, and know that one is being seen as naked, deliberately from a distance by one observing, causes shame to the one being seen in one's nakedness. This is the case for both man and woman. To know oneself as being seen nakedly by an observer from his point of view somehow renders the seeing defiling on the one being seen. It defiles nakedness. It renders one unclean and feeling deeply embarrassed. This feeling of being defiled into shame precipitated by being seen naked from a distance by an observer and the feeling that one comes to know about it appears to be a universal response. Even in the age of pornography, which is seeing nakedness objectively, this sense of shame has not disappeared.

One possible reason for this is the fact that a human person resists being "objectified," that is, turned into an object. It is inherent in a human person, male or female, to resist being made into an object, to be "thingified." When someone is turned into an object or thing by knowing it objectively, that is, in its nakedness, one can make use of it for one's purposes. The person can be turned into a tool of another and be fitted into systems of power. To know is to gain mastery over what one knows. And that mastery is motivated by one's own interest and purpose. Once the one being mastered comes to know he is being mastered and made into a tool, his sense of dignity and honor evokes a sense of shame and provokes resistance. And alternatively, once the master is exposed in his mastering activity he also becomes shameful and provokes resistance to this exposure. The good of one resists the evil of the other; the evil of one resists the good of the other. And so good and evil resist each other. Is this not the knowledge of good and evil? Is not this the primal human condition?

The primal reaction to this mutual sense of shame that eventuates into mutual resistance and so into conflict is to hide it through means humanly available: "fig leaves" sewn together for human covering. But to cover the truth is to turn it into a lie and the lie is what is brought into the open. The truth turned into a lie by covering and hiding it; and the lie exposed openly as the truth, is this not knowledge of good and evil? This tragic situation was poignantly expressed by Paul out of his own personal experience: "I can will what is right, but I cannot do it. For I do not do the good I want but the evil that I do not want is what I do. . . .

Wretched man that I am! Who will rescue me from this body of death?" (Rom. 7:18, 24).

We have been discussing human wisdom as the knowledge of good and evil. We have claimed that this is a universal condition. It is thus presupposed by every human thought and action. For this reason, human thought and action always have some good and some bad in them and the one cannot be had without the other. We have also claimed that the moral categories "good" or "bad" cannot be applied upon this condition because there is "good" in the "bad" and there is "bad" in the "good." But the deeper question is this: Is the knowledge of good and evil as the human condition good or bad? To answer this larger and more serious question, we need to discuss what is meant by the "bad" and the connection between good and bad—signified by the conjunction "and"—in this formulation.

So far, we have sketchily pointed to the "good" in this formulation as that good which has been seen, judged, and declared "good" by God himself. We have done this in chapter 2 above and have given a summary in the introduction to this chapter. Now, we have to ask the question, What is the "evil" entailed by the knowledge of good and evil? The first point to be made in answering this question is that what is evil can only be known in the light of the good and the knowledge of it. Second, since it is God who is solely the judge of the good and the good is the good of his creation, only God can judge the bad and the bad in his creation. It is only and solely God who is judge of the good and so he is solely the judge of the bad in the light of the good and the good in his creation. Only God can judge evil as evil and declare it so. Third, this also means that only God can distinguish and separate good from evil, and they are distinct and separate in his sight. And fourth, only he can break the conjunction of good and evil in the human condition and deal with each, respectively, in the way he sees appropriate.

So now we have to consider God as Judge. This is another turn on the part of God in self-constituting himself as God for and of his creation. His turn to be Judge follows upon—not temporally, but in order and dignity—his turn as creator. His "first" turn is as creator. Now he turns himself as Judge of what has happened to his creation. He is the creator of creation as good. He is Judge of what happened to the good of his creation. To put it tersely: God is creator of the good; he is judge of the evil. He judges the evil that happened in the light of the good he has created.

What has been said seems so obvious that it is not necessary to say it. But it has to be said because if we do not follow the order and dignity in God's turning to self-constitute himself as God of his creation and its Judge, we trap ourselves in the dilemma of theodicy: how to justify God as good in the face of the fact of evil. If God is good, why is there evil? If God is powerful, why can't he eliminate evil?

So the fact of evil falsifies the belief in God as good and powerful. The theodicy issue presupposes that it is the human that judges the evil and he judges the evil in the light of his own good! And so it is the human who is also the judge of his good as created, which he did not create! The theodicy issue reflects and articulates precisely the human condition of the knowledge of good and evil, and it cannot be solved from within and out of this condition because it is this condition itself that has to be dealt with. Ironically, the logic of the theodicy issue shows this up in that it leaves the fact of evil intact, but falsifies and eliminates the belief in the good and the power that can deal with evil! On this issue, atheism is likely to gain the upper hand because it has the facts on its side. Theism is pushed to a corner to defend and justify its belief in a good and almighty God!

What then is the "evil" entailed in the human condition of knowing good and evil? For a clue to an answer we have to look at the way God responded to the eating of the fruit by the woman and the man (Gen. 3:8-24). In doing this, we must not forget that we are dealing with the primal issue of causal origin (etiology) told narratively and not historically (more of this below). The response is set in a context somewhat similar to a court proceeding and is told in a story form. The trial process may be divided into six parts. First is the accusation or charge (Gen. 3:8-11). Next is the inquest (3:11b). Next comes the defense (3:12-13). Then follows the judgment (3:14, 16, 17). Next comes the sentencing (3:14b, 16, 17), and finally the execution of the sentence (3:22-24). One may note that the whole trial proceeding is carried out by one agent, namely, God. In a more sophisticated and modern legally sophisticated court proceeding, the stages in and parts of the trial process are carried out by separate agents: an accuser, an accused, a prosecutor, a defense advocate, a judge, a jury, and an executioner. But all these are rolled into one trial process carried by one agent, God: He is judge of every part of the process and of the process as a whole. This may be justified by the fact that what is being considered here is not an ordinary offense, but an offense considered as sin. This kind of offense is committed against God, his creation, and his commandment. Therefore, only he may try it and judge it and execute the judgment. No one else can or has the right to.

The accuser is not directly named. But it is impliedly clear that it is God, and the charge is specified in the form of a question: "Have you eaten from the tree of which I commanded you not to eat?" (3:11b). The charge is a violation of God's command. The accused are, of course, the man and the woman. They are the respondents to the charge. The word *you* in verse 11 refers to the man and complicitly to the woman. The purpose of the inquest is to establish the facts of the case, namely, what the charge is, whether it happened or not, who committed it, and the circumstances surrounding the case. All these were established by the positive admission of the respondents in answer to the questions of inquest (3:9, 11). They were in God's garden, they could sense God's presence and movement in the garden, they knew the command, they disobeyed the command. The inquest also was the opportunity for the respondents to defend themselves. No one accused must be judged without due process, which includes the right to defend oneself. The respondents were given the opportunity to defend themselves. But their defense is not a denial of the charge of which they stand accused. Their defense is giving a reason for what they did, and the reason given is by way of blaming the other: the man blaming the woman, the woman blaming the serpent. Did the serpent blame God for creating it as serpent? In short, while they admit the fact of the charge, they refused to accept responsibility for it! This is a classic instance of defense by justification and passing on responsibility to another. One can follow the logic of this defense by putting a blame on being created out of the Nothing, out of the lifeless dust, by blaming creation as including the possibility of temptation, by blaming the freedom given the human by making it vulnerable to temptation (the permission), and by blaming the limit put upon the exercise of this freedom (the prohibition). Ultimately then, it is God who is to blame for all this mess. By the logic of this defense, it is God who stands accused and should be held responsible! Apparently, this kind of defense is not given any merit by the Judge and rightly so because it is patently without merit! By their own admission and by the kind of defense that they put up, the accused stand guilty as charged. And the Judge simply acknowledged this. This kind of judgment is palpably just because it is a simple acknowledgment of the truth of the charge as verified by admission of the facts of the case. Its defense is without merit, and is obviously a violation of the law that applies to it!

But still one must ask what exactly is wrong, and in this case, we can use the word *sinful*, with what the woman and the man did, which they admitted but wrongly defended. It appears that they mistrusted God, and doubted his word, and ignored its authority, and dared to probe it. They trusted instead the serpent and its word that cast doubt on the word of God. They followed the authority of the serpent. The offense committed by the man and woman was a confounding combination of mistrusting God, doubting his word, ignoring his authority, and miscalculating the force of God's command and daring to probe it. Aggravating this is the unacknowledged inner movement of curiosity to test the word of God against the word of the serpent. It is all this that led to the act of disobedience that necessarily put the woman and the man under God's judgment. It is a done deed that is judged as sinful! It is obvious that committing a sin is a very complicated matter. It is not easy to sort out the elements and dynamics involved. Could the sinner do this sorting out?

My reading of the judgment rendered by God is that it confirms the human condition of knowing good and evil (Gen. 3:22). It also confirms the manner in which this condition is known and its effect in human activity. The "knowing" that is confirmed by the judgment is a knowing by actual experience. It is not merely a knowing notionally but practically and when combined together it is a knowing experientially that effects change in both the agent and his situation. It is now possible for the human to master God's creation and alter it or aspects of it to suit his own purposes.

Added to this judgment is the sentencing. One aspect of the sentence is a "curse" pronounced by God upon the serpent (3:14-15), and upon the "ground" (3:17). It is to be noted that the "curse" is not pronounced upon the woman or the man. Moreover, the blessing of giving birth in participation of God's creative activity in perpetuating, nourishing, and flourishing life is not removed. It stays. What is added to it is the increase of the pain that accompanies childbearing (3:16). The pain is already there, but it is made more painful and yet the woman still desires her man from whom the pain originated and consents to being ruled by him. The vocation of the man to till the soil and make it produce the food needed to sustain life is also not taken away. Only it is now made more difficult both by adding "toil" to "till," and by making the soil grow not only plants for food but plants not for eating like thorns and thistles (3:17-19). The ground ceases to be a garden but becomes a field cultivated by human toil in order to produce. And finally, the fact of death is simply confirmed as an aspect of creaturely existence and the gift of life: since the human is formed out the dust and is given the life appropriate to it, the human shall return to dust. Dying becomes a part of creaturely life.

The intriguing question that bears asking is, should the sentence be treated morally or legally or both, so that it is to be regarded as "punishment"—which is the way it has been treated in the history of Christian doctrine? Is it possible to construe the texts on sentencing in a way different from understanding them as punishment? Since the texts are etiological and thus seek to provide some primordial explanation to the negative elements in existence and life in a universal way, they can be in interpreted as confirming the truth and dignity and burden of being wise, of knowing good and evil, and of being responsible for it. It is the primordial that is pre-moral and pre-legal, and thus conditions the rise of the moral and the legal.

This is the reason why the good and the evil are inextricably combined and judgments based on the moral and the legal as yet do not apply. What the sentencing is about is that it triggers human participation in the creative struggle to be in the face of the inescapable threat of nonbeing and in the inner drive to stay alive in the face of the threat of nonlife, death, and extinction. Put in another way, the sentencing activates in consciousness the insidious and parasitical penetration of nonbeing into being, thus making being and existence deeply anxious about their survival. The sentencing sensitizes the deep concern and primal feeling for life and its value to the inroads of nonlife such as primordial needs, weaknesses, frustrations, failures, and helplessness that sap the strength to live. Creaturely existence and life are a combining of being and nonbeing, of life and nonlife. This primordial combining is an activity of God the Spirit in creation. As Paul puts it, the God of Scripture in whom we believe is the God who gives life to the dead and calls into being the things that are not (Rom. 4:17). This combining has been breached by the human act of doubt, mistrust, self-assertion, and disobedience. But the breach did not cancel or destroy it. Because it is a primordial relation, it could only be distorted but not broken. The sentencing is the effect of the distorting breach. As a result the combining has become unstable and volatile and so it is always critical. The "and" in the formulation "good and evil" is not a substantive but a conjunctive relation. It is the situation of freedom. The exercise of freedom within and upon this relation makes it capable of being distorted. Relations can and are distorted by freedom and its exercise. It is freedom that breaches and so distorts relation. But since freedom cannot break the relation, and the relation continues to be valid and enforced in a distorted form, freedom suffers the distortion by both bearing it and being responsible for it. And so the freedom to be and to be alive in this distorted relation becomes a constant struggle against primordial threats against it: pain, toil, disease, suffering, aging, and dying. This is what the sentencing is all about! This is the burden and dignity of being made wise.

But bearing this burden in the dignity of freedom still takes place within a valid and continuing relation. Although the "and" in the formula of "good and evil" is relationally distorted, it is still conjunctive. It is still valid and effective creatively because God the Spirit continues to affirm and enforce it. The struggle for existence and life as participative in the creative activity of God is affirmed and protected by the continuing validity and effectivity of this primordial combining. Because of it, the man and woman receive garments of skin custom-tailored by God to protect them against climate change. Does this gift of protective garments license the human to kill and skin fur-bearing animals for luxury clothing? The blessing to multiply and fill the earth continues to generate new life—note the many genealogies in Genesis and in the Gospels! And the multiplying is not only filling the earth but is overfilling it now! Because the blessing has not been withdrawn and remains valid, is that a reason for abusing it and turning it into a curse or a nightmare? The vocation to subdue the earth by tilling and keeping has not been revoked. Bread continues to be produced and made available but no more in a garden of abundance, but in a "field" of scarcity. Because resources are scarce, is that the reason why their distribution is made unequal so that some have more than enough, and others have less than enough? These are perennial problems that being primordially wise—knowing good and evil—must continue to face, even now! Facing them and living with them, let alone solving them, is the responsibility of being wise. Might we not call this secular wisdom? Is it any different from the this-worldly wisdom we all engage in, then and now? Is not this wisdom sought, gained, applied, successfully or not, within the aegis of the *religare* of the Spirit? Secular wisdom is still spiritual wisdom because it is the Spirit that makes it wisdom of and for this world and so it is this-worldly.

We now return to the execution part of the trial proceedings. The first thing that we notice is that it is God who also executes the judgment and the sentence. Since it is God who executes, the execution can only take place within the *religare*, the bonding of the Spirit. The next thing that we must notice is that God confirms what has happened to the human: "Man has become like one of us, knowing good and evil" (3:22). How may we understand this text? One must be careful in interpreting it. One may begin by differentiating what may be clear and not clear. What seems clear, from what has been said so far, is that the human has come to know good and evil, not just notionally but experientially. God does not know evil experientially because he has not done it. We cannot also say he knows it notionally because God knows as he, as God, can only know. We do not know God's knowing. He knows in his own way as God, which is not our way. Our knowing is sensibly, notionally, practically, and experientially—by sensing, thinking and doing—and therefore, experientially. What God knows is the good that he does, and he does it by creating it. It is the good of his creativity, and the good of his creation. Apart from his creating it, that good does not exist. We cannot and do not create that good. Our being good at all is part of being created good. But our being created in existence and life is mixed together with being and nonbeing, with life and nonlife. And since the mixing or combining relation has been distorted by the exercise of freedom, we cannot know good in itself but good for us in distortion. And so what we know is distorted *good* that is both good and evil. God does not know good in the way we know it. He knows it as God because he does it as God. His knowing and doing is of him as God. That is of the nature of his self-constitution as God. It is therefore humanly impossible to know and do and judge as God.

So what is the meaning of "like one of us?" This is the unclear part in the text. Perhaps we can gain some clarity by considering the meaning of "like." This word indicates only similarity not identity; like is not the same. The human is "like" God in the sense that he can know and do. But he is not God and so his knowing and doing is not the same as God's knowing and doing. But because this human knowing and doing is "like," and like only, that of God, it can be a source of temptation. That temptation is the possibility that the likeness can be transformed into identity. The human may become so ambitious as to be tempted to, and regard what he knows and does as precisely the knowing and doing of God. Interestingly, this very likelihood is what God foresees to happen: "and now, he [the human] might reach out his hand and take also from the tree of life, and eat, and live forever" (3:22b).

The possibilities open to freedom under the "permission" of the "command" are enormous. The wisdom of knowing good and evil in the world cover a wide range of opportunities awaiting not only exploration but realization and achievement. But the creativity of freedom may not be content with this. Freedom has the capacity to transcend its own achievements and reach out for more. And the "more" to which it may reach out may not be within the possibilities of permission but beyond them toward what is "prohibited." To transcend limits is constitutive of freedom and limits are a challenge to this transcendence. Moreover, the motivation to know what is yet unknown is of the nature of curiosity. And curiosity is ingredient to the search for wisdom. Even Mephistopheles is willing to make a pact with the devil to satisfy his curiosity (Goethe in *Faust*). So freedom has both the capacity and the motivation to transcend, especially the limits that are put to it!

But there is one limit that freedom persistently wants to transcend, namely, the limit put to life, and that limit is death. It is not surprising that there are a variety of notions in various cultures about transcending this limit, notions such as union with the One, reincarnation, nirvana, immortality, resurrection, eternal life. These notions testify to the human curiosity about what lies beyond death. They also speak of the human drive to overcome the limit of death. And the fact that what lies beyond the limit of death can at least be imagined and desired is a beckoning to freedom to reach out, and if that entails invading the realm of God, why not? Is freedom reduced to what it can only do within the parameters of permission? What is to prevent it from crossing the boundary between permission and prohibition?

The primeval narrative testifies to God's determination to guard his Godself. He cannot and will not tolerate a human invasion into his holiness. He sets up a roadblock to prevent the human from reaching out his hand to grab God's secret of life beyond death. He sets up a cherubim security guard with an AK-47, with authority to kill anyone who seeks entry! God will remain alone as God. He won't tolerate anyone who would even claim any likeness to him. There should never ever be one like him. To make that point and punctuate it with eternity, he drives the human out of the garden and banishes him into where?

He sends the human away from the garden back to "the ground from which he was taken" to till it (3:23). He sends the human back to earth to practice the earthly this-worldly wisdom of knowing good and evil. God is affirming that this this-worldly wisdom is what is fit for creaturely existence and life. If this is what sending the human back to earth means, then what can we say of God doing this? Is it too far out from the truth to say that God is a secularizing God? And since God does this within the ambit of the *religare* of the Spirit, is he not thereby infusing this secularizing activity with a spiritual quality and value? The secular is the sphere in which the Spirit is actively but imperceptively present to invest it with the creaturely, the human!

It now appears from what has been said, assuming that it is not far from the true meaning of the texts, that the sending of the human back to earth to live and cultivate a properly secular life has a twofold purpose: to protect the holiness and otherness of Godself, and to affirm the creaturely this-worldly existence and life of the human. Realizing this twofold purpose primordially within a religaric relationship in the Spirit is primevally the task of God. The task is carried out by God's secularizing activity. In the light of this, it might be honestly asked, Where in this reading is "the Fall" as understood in Christian doctrine?

Is it not the case that Christian doctrine traditionally assumes that the primeval narrative in Genesis 3 is historically true? It assumes that the characters in the story are historical agents, that the plot of the story actually happened, and so the critical events in the story are historical. And since the story is told narratively, it entails both temporal and spatial sequences. Temporally, the story tells of a "before" and an "after," and there is a point of time between the "before" and the "after." This is an event-point that divides time into before and after. The condition of existence and life in this "before" is the historical paradisal state of creation, and the status of man and woman in that state of life is that of original perfection and righteousness. The condition of existence and life in the "after" is that of the fallen state of creation and the status of man and woman in that state of life is that of being in original sin and unrighteousness. Both conditions are historical. The point of change from paradisal state to sinful state is historically "the Fall." That critical event/point is the "sin" of the first woman and man, together with

God's "punishment" of that first and original sin and God's sending them out of the garden of Eden. Spatially, the first man and woman were in the garden and were sent out by God. This point between before and after and between in and out is the historical location of "the Fall," and the Fall is the original sin done by the historical man and woman and God's actual banishing of the first man and woman out of the garden as punishment for their sin.

It may be suggested that the texts on "the Fall" could be read another way. This other way is also suggested by the texts themselves. This other way of reading includes the following. First, the texts might be regarded as primeval story. As primeval they do not deal with history but prehistory, and as such they underlie history and are presupposed by history. For that reason they are universal and have an etiological dimension: They condition history.

Second, this prehistory can only be told narratively, that is to say, as story, not history. And so the story is primeval story, not primeval history. As primeval story told narratively, it necessarily entails characters, agents, and events and a story line. But these are generic, representative, and meant to be universal, and so presuppositional to history. The man and woman are generic; they represent humankind. What they did represents human activity universally. The events constitute conditions that influence universally historical events. The time and space entailed in the story are pre-beginning time and space. They point to a "time" before time and a "space" before space. The paradisal state represents the goodness of creation universally in which all participate. The fallen state represents the sin and evil universally as a condition of human existence and life. The "event" of the Fall represents the sin and evil that is universal in human existence and life. Thus the historical state of life is both good and evil. The whole story is a story "before" history. Read in this way, one cannot pinpoint a historical event in historical time and historical space that is a historical deed done by a historical first man and woman that can be said to be a historical "Fall."

If by "Fall" we then mean that the human knowledge of good and evil is the knowledge of the good of creation mixed with the knowledge of its distortion by the human and is the universal condition in which the human experiences and deals with reality as secular, and so is inevitable but not necessary, then there could be some sense in the language of "the Fall." If that is meant by this language, then is it too far from the truth to say that "the Fall" is a secularizing "event/process" that presuppositionally and universally makes for the integrity, dignity, and value of creaturely, this- worldly, earthly existence and life? This condition cannot be said, properly speaking, as either good or bad. These terms, as said above, do not apply if they are understood as historically moral or legal language. The condition is rather good and evil and it is what gives rise historically to objective "good" or "evil" as moral or legal categories.

"The Fall" as effected by God as Judge is the primordial spiritual process by which God the Spirit protects Godself and his holiness; it is also the means by which he imperceptively but effectively establishes creaturely secular reality as bound to the *religare*. Apart from this binding bond the secular cannot be truly secular. As truly secular it can only be good and evil. It cannot be objectively and wholly good; it cannot also be objectively and wholly evil. It could not be either one of these but each entails the other. It is God the Spirit who still dwells in the midst of the this-worldly and secular reality to keep it as it truly is and to prevent it from becoming something else. It is the Spirit who truly and effectively secularizes.

CHAPTER VI

Covenant and Judgment

1. *Religare* and Covenant

In this chapter we continue discussing the theme of divine judgment on sin and evil within the structure and dynamics of God's special relation with Israel, and through Israel with all of humanity. In doing this we are simply considering the critical placing of Genesis 12:1-3 in the canon. This text is placed between the emergence of the nations from the sons of Noah and the creation of a new people, Israel, out of Abraham and Sarah. The emergence of the nations out of Noah is covered by the covenant of God with Noah and his offspring, a covenant that includes all creation (Gen. 9–10). God established this covenant as "everlasting" (Gen. 9:12, 16). In calling and covenanting with Abraham, God intended to make him and his descendant into a nation, Israel, a blessing to all the peoples of the earth (Gen. 12:1-3; 15:18; 17:1-8). Thus the covenant of God with Abraham is a promise of blessing not only to Abraham and his descendants but to all humanity.

Following this lead given by the critical placing of Genesis 12:1-3 in the canon, it would seem appropriate to consider God's covenanting activity with Israel in relation to God's bonding relationship with creation, which we have called the *religare*. The theological claim we are making is that God's covenanting activity with Israel is a special instance of his religaric activity with all of creation. God's covenanting activity with Israel presupposes and models historically God's religaric bonding with creation and humanity. In making this claim, we are seeking to establish the theological context in which sin takes place and the norms in which it is seen and evaluated as sin.

It may be recalled that God's religaric bonding relation with creation is a free decisive turn in God's self-constitution to be creator. This turn is signified by the agency of both his Spirit and his Word. God the Spirit creates the possible from the non-possible, and this includes the possibilities of something from Nothing, being from nonbeing, existence from non- existence, life from nonlife, the human from the nonhuman, community from noncommunity, cosmos from chaos. These possibilities are made actual by God speaking: God said, let there be . . . and it was so. What came to be by the Spirit through the Word is seen and declared "good" by God. The "good" is everything that he has made and sustains by his presence, power, and blessing. God's turning to create through his Spirit and Word as self-constituting himself as creator is his primal religaric bonding relation and activity with his creation. This religaric relation is rooted in God. It is thus presuppositional to all that happens in creation—natural, human, historical, and cultural. The human cannot undo or break this religaric relation. Only God can break it, if he would. But the human can distort it from his side of the relationship by his freedom, gifted him by God, through its exercise of making a choice. This is a choice not merely to act in a particular way, but to be in a specific way, for which being and doing and living the human is responsible!

This breaching and distorting of the religaric relation does not undo the "good" of God's creation and blessing. It remains a continuing and valid part of the "good and evil" that the human comes to know. He cannot undo that good because he did not make it; it is God who created it. In distorting it and living in its distorted relation, he turns the "good" into a "judge," a measuring rod. This is God's way of protecting the good that he is as creator and the good that he does, namely his creating and his creation. To live under judgment by a valid good that one cannot undo and be free from is to suffer. To live and know good and evil, with the good exposing the invalidity and untruth of the evil, and the evil unable to extricate itself from this exposure because it cannot be "evil" without the good exposing it, is indeed to suffer. To suffer is to live in a contradiction that need not be, but in fact is, and cannot be free from by one's act of freedom, and yet still be responsible for it, that is a tragic condition! Suffering is evil because it is a deprivation of being (Augustine) and a weakening of the will to live.

But the inner aim and intentional drive of "the good" is not only to sustain being and life but to make them delightful and enjoyable. This is the enduring purpose of God's religaric relationship. The continuing and persistent activity of God in this bonding is to affirm existence and sustain life by overcoming evil with good (Rom. 12:9, 21). And so the purpose of exposure (judgment) is to strengthen the will to be and to live by holding fast to the good in order to overcome evil with good. To protect, uphold, and to activate the good of being and life is and always will be the inner drive of God's religaric relationship! And this he does unceasingly and persistently by his Spirit and his Word! He is being faithful to his self-constitution as creator and to his religaric relation to his creation. God's self-protection of his Godself has a secularizing effect upon his creation. He makes creation be exactly what it is and should be, namely, other than him and therefore earthly, this-worldly and so secular. He does this by being true to himself and by being faithful to his religaric relationship. This actively keeping by God of the line of otherness between himself and his creation by being in the midst of it within his religaric relation to his creation is God's activity of judging. It is part of his creative activity, and he does it through his Spirit. Secularization is God's spiritual way of keeping his creation distinct from him as creation, and so makes creation as secular the sphere of the natural, the human, the historical, and the cultural.

God's covenanting with his people may be construed theologically as a historical expression and modeling of his primordial religaric relationship with his creation. This covenanting activity with a particular people whom he elects from the nations is a new expression of his self-constituting turn to be creator. This time it is a turn to be the God of a people and for this people to be his people. In this way he lends palpable historical reality to his primordial religarizing relationship. One may interpret this covenanting with a particular people as having a twofold purpose. One is to express concretely in historical form his primordial religarizing relationship. And the other, related to this, is to provide a historical model in his relationship with the nations, and thus with all humanity. God's covenanting relationship with Israel is the way he also seeks to relate with all of humanity. Though particular and concrete, it intends to be universal. God's primordial religaric relating is thus given both a particular and universal dimension. God's turn in his self-constitution as creator is thus characterized as primordial, historical, and universal.

To be sure, historically speaking, the notion and practice of covenant- making are not unknown to Israel during its formative period. It was common practice among rulers or kings to establish a suzerainty treaty with peoples they conquered into making them their vassals. Israel was itself a vassal several times, to Egypt, Assyria, and Babylon. The structure of these treaties more or less included the following elements: (a) a preamble, which names the victorious king who initiates the making of the treaty; (b) a prologue, which mentions the benevolence of the king and his actions that benefit the vassal; (c) stipulations, which detail the conditions and obligations the king imposes on the vassals; (d) the expectation of the king that the people shall respond in gratitude and obedience; and finally, (e) the vassal's response ratifying the treaty with the promise of submitting to the rule of the king and obeying the conditions of the treaty.

That Israel was aware of this treaty-making practice may be gleaned from the structure of the Decalogue, which somewhat parallels the suzerainty treaty. But of course the content of the Decalogue and the dynamics it entails are quite different from those in suzerainty treaties. The Exodus version of the forging of the covenant of God the Lord with Israel in Sinai is given in chapters 19–20. The covenant was initiated by God the Lord dialogically with the people through Moses the mediator. In 19:3-4 it is clear that it is God the Lord who is initiating the covenant, but in 20:2 this is explicitly stated by God naming himself: "I am the Lord your God." This is the preamble of the covenant. In 19:4, God the Lord mentions what he did to the Egyptians and how he rescued them from bondage: "and how I bore you on eagles' wings and brought you to myself." This is repeated in 20:2. This is the prologue in the covenant. In 19:5 what is merely stated as "if you obey my voice and keep my covenant" is spelled out as stipulations or commands in 20:3-18. These are the Ten Commandments given apodictically, with God's expectation that they will be obeyed by the people. In return for the people's obedience, they will become to God his own "treasured possession from out of all the peoples as a priestly kingdom and a holy nation" (Exod. 19:5). While these words may be interpreted as setting forth the "vassal" status of Israel, on the contrary, they in fact elevate Israel into a special relation to God the Lord as his people, his treasured possession among all the peoples of the earth. The ratification of the covenant and its terms by the people is given in 19:8: "Everything that the Lord has spoken we will do." With this promise to keep the covenant and its stipulation, the people thereby are consecrated to God, that is, set apart from among all the peoples to belong to God as his people (19:19ff.).

While there is some similarity between the covenant and suzerainty agreements, there are, however, fundamental and vast differences. The Sinai covenant is between two unequal parties: God the Lord is not human (Hosea 11:9); he self-constitutes himself (Exod. 3:14). And Israel is a people. The parties belong to different orders of reality. This is not the case with suzerainty treaties in which the parties are both human. Despite this structure of otherness, the covenant is initiated and established dialogically. The bonding established in the covenant is dialogical in its dynamics. The unequal parties are mutually responsive and interactive, entailing possible change in the attitude and behavior of the parties depending on situations and on actions between them. The content of the activity on the part of God the Lord is not of conquest and subjugation but of rescue and liberation unto freedom. There is, moreover, a marked emphasis on what will become of the people as they keep the covenant and obey its terms: They shall become a priestly kingdom and a holy people. They would still remain ordinary human people like all the other nations. But they are given a special vocation and character that elevates them from being vassals to being agents of God's will and witnesses to his living reality.

One may well ask what power is at work in this covenanting activity. What bridges the gap between God and people? What makes this God in his otherness be in the midst of his people? It may not be far from the truth to construe that it is God the Spirit who is at work here. It is the Spirit who is the uniting bond in this covenant relationship. It is the Spirit who makes the relation and its dynamics dialogical and interactive. It is the Spirit who reveals God's will in the form of the Torah and inspires and enables the people to obey in the twists and turns of their historical life. And when they fail in their obedience is it not the Spirit who exposes their disobedience, and as they suffer the consequences of their unfaithfulness inspire them in hope "to cry unto the Lord" for mercy and deliverance out of the steadfast love of the Lord? And if God is persuaded by this cry of his people out of desperation and he responds in mercy, forgiveness, and renewal, is he not thereby being faithful to his resolve to be God for his people? Is this not God reaching out through his Spirit to be with them in their midst? In this covenanting activity of God the Spirit, is it not the case that God remains God in his holiness and the people remain a people other than God, but they nevertheless are a priestly kingdom and a holy nation? Is it not the case that it is the Spirit that both sanctifies and secularizes in the covenant relationship? In that relationship, one cannot be spiritual without being secular; and one cannot be secular without being spiritual: a priestly kingdom and a holy nation. If this is the case, is it too far from the truth to construe that the covenant-making of God is a historical expression and modeling of his primeval religarizing activity? It is a secular embodiment of his religaric activity!

2. Covenant as Criterion for Confession and Judgment

The importance of God's covenanting activity with Israel is in the fact that it provides the theological frame and context for Israel's life and history. This seems already obvious from what has been said so far. But it becomes clearer if seen in the light of a suggestion of Bernhard W. Anderson that each of the historical periods of Israel's history is framed by a covenant with its signs and a name for God.[1] The first period covering creation and primeval history (Gen. 1–11) is framed by

1. See Bernhard W. Anderson, *Contours of Old Testament History* (Minneapolis: Augsburg Press, 1999), 81–86.

the Noahic covenant, with the rainbow as its sign (Gen. 9) and God is named here as Elohim. The second period covers the history of the patriarchs (Gen. 12–50). The covenant with Abraham provides the frame and context for this part of Israel's history (Gen. 12: 1-3; 17:1-8). The sign for this covenant is circumcision (Gen. 17:9-14) and the name for God is El Shaddai. The third period extends from the Exodus up to the establishment of the monarchy (Exodus–Numbers, Joshua, Judges). The theological frame and context of this period is the Mosaic-Sinai covenant (Exod. 19–20). The sign of this covenant is the Sabbath (Exod. 31:12-17), and the name for God is Yahweh (Exod. 3:14). The last period is that of the monarchy until its collapse and termination in the Exile (1 and 2 Samuel; 1 and 2 Kings; 1 and 2 Chronicles). This is framed by the Davidic covenant. Its signs are the monarchical dynasty and the Temple, and the name for God is the Mosaic Yahweh. The book of Deuteronomy is an exposition of the Mosaic- Sinai tradition and so is canonized as a second Law.

The interplay of covenant, sign, and name of God in these historical periods is the theological or faith content of Israel's life and history during these periods. The Noahic covenant is God's pledge that he would never again destroy his creation and the rainbow-sign is a piece of nature to symbolize that pledge. God's name as Elohim stresses God's cosmic power and presence to guarantee his faithfulness to the covenant and to make the sign communicate the covenant and God's presence in it. The covenant with Abraham is God's promise to make a people, provide it with a land of its own, and in and through this people he would bless humankind. The sign of circumcision is a cut of the flesh of a human male from which the seed of life-generation derives. It signifies that Abraham shall become the father of a multitude of people. The name of El Shaddai, the Almighty, stresses God's power to fulfill his promise in the face of odds that seem impossible to overcome. The Mosaic-Sinai covenant is God's resolve to make a people for himself and be the God of this people. The Sabbath sign of this covenant is a piece of time in a piece of space (a shrine) in which God is present to be with his people and to be acknowledged and celebrated in worship by his people. God's name of Yahweh stresses his sovereignty over his people and that, although he makes himself near and available to bless, he is not at their beck and call. It is he who chooses how to be God for his people. The Davidic covenant with its sign of monarchy and Temple—both borrowed from cultures foreign to Israel but incorporated into its life and faith—stresses that leadership for justice and peace and the worship of God go together under the sovereignty of God. In all this, one can discern that the truth and meaning of all this covenanting activity is that God in his Godself as Holy seeks to be with and in the midst of his creation and of humankind: "I am God and no mortal, the Holy One in your midst, and I will not come in wrath" (Hosea 11:9). Anderson uses the above scheme as providing the *Contours of Old Testament Theology*, which is the title of his very helpful book. One can see from the above that the covenant spans nearly the full sweep of Israel's life and history.

It is not our aim in this book to deal in detail with the theological content and dynamics framed by the covenantal perspective.[2] Our aim in this chapter is merely to indicate the basic criterion on the basis of which Israel sees itself as having sinned and confesses its sin, and on which the judgment on that sin is also rendered. The point is to show that the criterion for confessing sin and for judging it is the same for both. If sin is seen and confessed on the basis of one criterion, and the judgment rendered on it is based on another criterion, there could be a basic injustice committed. Scriptures doubtlessly avoid this. Justice is best secured when there is a common criterion for knowing and confessing sin and for judging it as sin. But although the criterion is common for both offender and judge and has to be observed by both, there is room in the criterion for appeal on the part of the offender and some measure of flexibility on the part of the judge rendering judgment in the interest of saving the offender and balancing this with securing justice through law. It has to be shown, however, that the criterion provides justifiably for either case.

An analysis of the various covenants mentioned above may reveal some features that lead to the development of a common criterion for both the confession of sin and its judgment. The features may be classified into two. The one is those features that pertain to God; the other is those features that belong to the human partner. We may deal first with those features that belong to God. For one thing, all the covenants are initiated by God. This may be construed as an expression of his turn to be in religaric relation to his creation and to humankind as creator and savior. Thus, the covenants are grounded in God. For another thing, this grounding in God's turn to be in religaric relation may be seen as an act of free grace that favors and benefits God's partner in the covenant. Furthermore, because the covenants are grounded in God's turn in free grace, the covenants take on the characteristic of "everlasting," which entails unconditionality, universality, and absolute validity. Additionally, the keeping of the covenants is God's way of being faithful to himself as God and of being faithful to his partner as his partner, that is, to Israel.

---

2. For more detailed and comprehensive treatment of Old Testament theology from a covenantal perspective, see Walther Eichrodt, *Theology of the Old Testament*, 2 vols., trans. J. A. Baker (Philadelphia: Westminster, 1967).

Moreover, it is God the Lord who heard the cry of the Hebrew slaves in Egypt and out of a compassionate love he delivered them from bondage and guided their journey through the wilderness by his providential and accompanying presence. *It is solely out of love that he chose this people to be his people.* This people had no merit to deserve this love. Their choice is purely an act of grace on the part of God. There is no explanation or reason for the election of Israel except his love and his faithfulness in keeping the promise he made to the ancestors of Israel (Deut. 7:7-8). Furthermore, to make this people his people, a priestly kingdom and a holy nation, he reveals his will for them. That revelation is the Torah. It is a command to be obeyed. That command presupposes the freedom to obey, and that freedom is a gift already given by their deliverance from bondage. The aim of the command is to form, norm, and motivate the people to be and live as his people. Apart from that command that is both permissive and prohibitive they cannot be his people and he cannot be their God. Finally, for all these reasons, the covenants and their terms are to be taken with absolute seriousness both by God and his covenant partner—by God, because it is his way of constituting himself in religaric relation to creation and humanity and to a particular people—by the human partner, because it is the only way that it is to be sustained as God's people. It is the source and vitality of its life.

The part of the people in the covenant relation is quite simple, though profoundly difficult. It is to acknowledge *this God* who enters into covenant, with all the features mentioned above, with this people for him to be God of this people, and for this people to be his people. Furthermore, in entering into covenant relation with this God by ratifying it, the people commit themselves to stay in it, to keep it faithfully, and to obey all its stipulations. In short, they freely choose to be within, and live in, covenant with this God. And so they are under absolute obligation to obey the command and its statutes. The full and complete keeping of the covenant relation is conditional upon the human partner living up to its obligation to be faithful to it and obey its terms and conditions. It may be safe to assume that God will keep his part in the bargain! But will the human partner do the same? Thus, with the ratification of the covenant relation initiated by God there is in the making a common criterion on the basis of which there can be a determination of a violation that may be acknowledged and confessed and to be judged as such.

It is possible and perhaps wise to put together in a nutshell the elements of a criterion indicated above. Such a criterion in a nutshell has the merit of summarizing the essential features of the covenant relation and at the same time providing a kind of direction that could be useful for a spirituality that secularizes. As indicated earlier, the Decalogue has two parts. The first part, with four injunctions, has to do with God. The second part has to do with injunctions about human relations. The first part is given a terse summary form by the Shema: "Hear, O Israel, The Lord is our God, the Lord alone. You shall love the Lord your God with all your heart, with all your soul, and with all your might" (Deut. 6:4-5). The second part, which has to do with life in community, is given a terse formulation by Amos: "Let justice roll down like waters, and righteousness like an ever-flowing stream" (5:24), or Micah: "He has told you, O mortal, what is good; and what does the Lord require of you but to do justice, and to love kindness, and to walk humbly with your God" (6:8). As is well known, Jesus put the two parts of the Decalogue into two commandments. The first great commandment is the Shema, and Jesus quotes it (Mark 12:29; Matt. 22:24-40; Luke 10:25-28). The second part of the Decalogue is tersely put by Jesus in a one-liner: "Love your neighbor as yourself" (Mark 12:31; Matt. 22:39; Luke 10:27). In the Matthean version, Jesus adds: "On these two commandments hang all the Law and the Prophets" (Matt. 22:40). Although these statements emphasize the human obligation to obey the commandments as tersely stated, I hope I am correct in assuming that all these statements presuppose the covenant relation and its validity. If this is anywhere near the truth, we can then use the covenant relation and the summary of its requirements as the structure of both confession and judgment. What follows seeks to carry out this theological claim or point of view.

How does this criterion function? In a dialogic relationship, which the covenant relation is, when some kind of an offense by either partner is committed, the one offended is the one who makes a complaint. The reason for this is simply the fact that he has been offended and knows it. He may not yet know what "law" has been violated; only that he/she has been offended. The one who committed the offense may also not know that he has committed something that offended the other party in the relationship. The offense takes place within a relationship, and so the offense does something to the relationship, and the relationship "senses" that something has gone wrong with it. It would seem then that an offense does something wrong to the relationship by offending a partner in the relationship. An offense is a relational deed that does something wrong to both relationship and a party in the relationship. And since the offender is in the relation and his deed is a relational deed, his status in the relation is thus called into question.

If this analysis is anywhere near the truth, it is the covenant/dialogic relation that is the first and primary casualty or "victim" of any offense within it. The reason is that the offended party is in relation; he/she can only be offended in the relationship. The offender is also in relation to the other party. What he does that offends takes place within the relationship and is "offensive" only within the relationship.

It may not be known to both offended and offender that it is their relation with each other that is deeply felt as having been "breached," that something has done wrong to it. The inner and depth-drive of any profoundly meaningful relationship is to correct itself, to restore itself, to remove the offending deed, and to reconcile the parties in the relationship. This inner drive to correct itself is also done by the relationship and within it. It mobilizes its resources to deal with what has breached it, and to control the damage that the breach is likely to bring about. And if it succeeds in dealing with the breach, the result is not merely restorative but constructive or transformative because the effect is to change both the offended and the offender and the relationship is deepened, enriched, and strengthened.

What happens when a relational deed breaches the dialogic/covenanting relationship is that the dynamics of the relationship are turned into a law court in which the offended contends with the offender. This is precisely what happened to the covenant relationship between God and Israel. Here the offended one, God the Lord, brings a complaint, a suit, a charge, or an indictment against his own people (Hosea 4:1-3; 12:2; Mic. 6:1-7; Isa. 3:13-15). It is the offended that makes a complaint, or to use religious terms, it is the one sinned against that brings an indictment against the sinner. Sin is a term properly used when the one offended is God. Sin is a breach of the covenant relation by offending God who is in covenant relation. The offender is a "sinner" because he/she is in covenant relation and the offending deed is a relational deed.

In Jeremiah 2:13, God the Lord through the prophet brings a charge to his people, thus: "For my people have committed two evils: they have forsaken me, the fountain of living water, and dug out cisterns for themselves, cracked cisterns that can hold no water." The "people" that committed the "evils" are "my people," the people Israel with whom he is in covenant. The "me" who is "forsaken" is the God in covenant. The offending deed, being "forsaken, is a covenant deed. It is what breaches the covenant relation.

In Hosea 4:1-19, it is God the Lord in covenant with his people who brings an "indictment" against them. The covenant relation is here portrayed as the husband-wife relationship. The husband, God the Lord, has been "forsaken" by his wife who whores. The whoring wife refers to the "inhabitants of the land" who are the covenant people. God the Lord is forsaken in that "there is no faithfulness or loyalty and no knowledge of God in the land" (4:1). The dynamics of the pattern is the same: It is a relational drama. The same is true in Micah 6:1-7 and in Isaiah 3:13-15. Sin is a relational offense against the God who is in relation with his people who in turn are in relation with him as their God. Sin is a deed of "forsaking," of "unfaithfulness," of "disloyalty," of "no knowledge" of God; all are relational categories!

Who is this God who has been "forsaken"? Of course, there is no doubt that it is the God who made a covenant of promise with Abraham, the God of the Fathers. He is the God who heard "the cry" of his people, the cry for deliverance out of bondage in Egypt. He is the God who revealed himself to Moses to deliver his people from Pharaoh and led them through the wilderness, and at Mount Sinai entered into covenant with them and gave them the Torah. He helped them take possession of the land promised to Abraham by routing out their enemies. This God is holy; there is none like him. It is he who self-constitutes himself and is not dependent on anything but himself. He guards and protects his Godself, his holiness, and his glory. And yet he self-constitutes himself to be God of a people and be with and for this people and make them into a people to bless them and make them an agent of his purposes—a priestly kingdom and a holy nation. It is this God who is faithful in steadfast love to the covenant he made with his people who has been forsaken by his own people (Jer. 2:4-8).

And how was he forsaken? Part of the covenant agreement is that the people shall have no other god but Yahweh, and him alone shall they celebrate in worship. This is a command given the people as expressing God's will for them and is a condition that they should fulfill if they are to be his people. If they observe this command and remain faithful in covenant with God, they shall live long in the land given them and they shall enjoy the produce of the land and they shall live not merely by surviving but prosperously and in peace. The source and joy of their life as a people are no other than in being in covenant with this God to whom they shall be faithful and loyal by obeying his command to have no other God but him and him alone. But if the people disobey this command and are unfaithful to the covenant, and so dishonor the God of the covenant and make him a laughingstock among the nations, this God will vindicate his name and his honor and protect his Godself by sanctioning his people and blighting the land so that it will not yield its produce. And so there shall be famine all over the land.

3. Yahweh or Baal?

The question may be asked, If the God of the covenant is so good and so faithful to the covenant and so generous to his people, and if the penalty for forsaking him is severely hurtful and even destructive of life and of the land that sustains it, why would the people forsake him and go after other gods and follow their ways? What made the other gods so attractive that the people would abandon their covenant God in favor of these other gods, and risk the severe sanctions that this disloyalty may entail? Here the people of the covenant are confronted with the same problem that the primordial couple faced in the garden of Eden. There the primordial woman and man were, as it were, given a choice between the word of God and word of the serpent about eating the fruit of the tree of the knowledge of good and evil. Here the choice appears to be between the command of God the Lord not to have any God but Yahweh and of going after other gods besides Yahweh.

The command itself indicates the options: "the Lord you shall fear; him you shall serve, and by his name alone you shall swear. Do not follow other gods, any of the gods of the peoples who are all around you" (Deut. 6:13-14). Clearly then there are other gods besides Yahweh. These other gods are the gods of the people around them. One of these gods is Baal, the god of the Canaanites whose land the Israelites were to take and with whom they shall live. Clearly then there is a choice between Yahweh and Baal. It is also implicitly clear that the Israelites can make a choice. They have the freedom to do so. That freedom has come to them as a gift of their deliverance from bondage in Egypt. It is now a right that belongs to them as a liberated people. It is also their right to exercise it. Freedom is nothing as a right if it is not exercised. It can be exercised by making a choice between real options. The options are not merely in terms of acting in a specific way but of being, and of living, in a particular way under the sovereignty of a deity! And so the choice of a god to follow is to commit one's being and life to such a deity. It is to be "yoked" to such a god (Num. 25:3).

It is apparent from the records that the Israelites, when they began to settle in the land promised them by Yahweh, and which Yahweh helped them to possess, chose Baal as their god and chose to follow in his ways. They have thus forsaken Yahweh, God the Lord. This was a fateful choice with dire consequences. Why would the people of the covenant do this?

To see the importance of this choice, one must understand the situation of the Israelites as they settled in a land that they had to protect against peoples and kingdoms that want to take it away from them. When they entered this land and began to settle it, they had just come from a semi-nomadic form of life in the desert wilderness. There, their existence and life was precarious, constantly threatened by famine and thirst in a desert land that could not yield food to eat and water to drink. They depended solely on manna provided by Yahweh on a daily basis. They could not gather this manna to store. They depended on water to drink from what could be extracted from a rock that only a "miracle" could crack so that water would spring forth from it. They were on a journey to freedom-land to be far away from slavery-land, and so they could not yet settle and be secure until they took possession of the Promised Land! What feelings and psychic state might this situation have produced among the people? Their survival was at stake! Would they not have become profoundly anxious about surviving? Would they not have sought ways to secure their being and life both as individuals and as a people and make their living a little less precarious and anxious?

Even as they entered the Promised Land, Moses had already told them what to expect: "When the Lord your God has brought you into the land that he swore to your ancestors, to Abraham, to Isaac, and to Jacob, to give you, a land with fine, large cities that you did not build, houses filled with all sorts of goods that you did not fill, hewn cisterns that you did not hew, vineyards and olive groves that you did not plant—and when you have eaten your fill, take care that you do not forget the Lord, who brought you out of the land of Egypt, out of the house of slavery" (Deut. 6:10-12). What would the covenant people have felt in their guts and bones upon seeing this land? A settled life in large and fine cities! A fertile land that can be cultured to make it yield all the produce that would make life free from the threat of hunger and thirst, a life that makes for security and delight. Houses filled with "all sorts of goods" that make living convenient and comfortable. There is a technology, agricultural and urban, that is already developed and in full use to make all this possible. And it was not developed and put in place by the Israelites. All they need to do is to learn it from the people who invented it and use it effectively to their full advantage!

Would they not have seen all this in the way the primordial woman saw the tree of the knowledge of good and evil in the garden? "The tree was good for food, and that it was a delight to the eyes, and that the tree was to be desired to make one wise" (Gen. 3:6). Would not the Israelites have seen the Canaanite way of life a stark contrast from life in the wilderness, something more superior, more secure, and more comfortable than what they were used to in the wilderness? Would they not have been tempted? Would not the dynamics between trust and distrust, curiosity and doubt, wisdom and ignorance, played on the Israelites as they did on the primordial woman? Would not the primordial forces of being and nonbeing, of existence and nonexistence of life and nonlife come into the imbalance of anxiety? Were they not under the same human condition as represented primordially by the woman and her husband? Would they not have done as the primordial woman did: "she took of its fruit and ate; and she also gave some to her husband, who was with her, and he ate" (Gen. 3:6). The Israelites did: they partook ("ate") of the Canaanite way of life and had their fill (Deut. 6:11).

There is a difference, however, between Israel and the primordial woman and man. Israel has already made a commitment to this one God and to worship and serve him, and none other. The primordial woman and man only represented the universal human condition. Once a people makes a commitment to a god, she is "yoked" inescapably to such a god. To change one's god in favor of another was unheard of in those days. It would be shocking to all the nations. God the Lord incredibly asks Israel: "Has a nation changed its gods, even though they are no gods? But my people have changed their glory for something that does not profit. Be appalled, O heavens, at this, be shocked, be utterly desolate, says the Lord" (Jer. 2:11-12). This incredible and unheard of deed meant to God that Israel was stepping out of the covenant relation and was forsaking the God of the covenant. It meant to God that the benefits of his grace—all that he is and has as God that he is prepared to give to his people—are being exchanged for the benefits of another god that is no god. The freedom they gained by being liberated from slavery by Yahweh is now being exchanged for a "yoke," for another way of life which is in fact another form of slavery. It meant also that the people are exempting themselves from obedience to the Torah and its statutes. They are now under obligation to fulfill the demands of the new god they now serve.

Who is this god for whom the people are exchanging and abandoning Yahweh? There are several root meanings associated with the term "Baal." It could mean "locality." The term thus appears with the names of places such as "Baal of Peor" (Num. 25:3, 5; Deut. 4:3). It could mean "owner," "lord," "master." Baal can also mean a "sphere of interest or function" such as "Lord of the covenant" (see Judg. 8:33; 9:4). Baal may become a deity when the people who worship him have taken possession of a place or a land and have settled in it. But most important is that Baal is associated with the phenomenon of fertility. And fertility is most closely associated with the fertility of the land. Baal is the owner, master, lord of agriculture, and of the fertility of the land. Peoples depend upon the fertility of the land for the provision of food to sustain life. But fertility is not only associated with the land but also with sexuality that generates life and perpetuates the race. Baal is the owner, master, and lord of fertility both of the land and of the human. He is celebrated as god of fertility in cult rituals and cult festivals (Jer. 19:4-5). The animal that best symbolizes fertility is the bull. The celebration of sexual fertility (sexual prostitution) is common in Baal temples. Moreover, since water is necessary for the soil to yield its produce, and water comes as rain upon the land, and the coming of rain is associated with storm and thunder, Baal is also featured as the storm-god. It is he who has tamed the unruly waters and made them serve the fertility of land and life. It is he who conquers drought and sterility and so of famine and barrenness and death. His enemy is Mot, who is the god of drought, sterility, and death. Baal has defeated Mot by his constant triumph in reviving the fertility of the earth in both the land and the human spheres with the arrival of spring, summer, and winter.

What could all these have signified to the Israelites? Baal as the god of fertility is the absolutely sure provider of food, water, sex, life, the security of land and of settled life, and the tools and technologies necessary for doing all these and enjoying them in spite of periodic threats or occasional difficulties. If one were coming from life in the desert where life is so precarious because there are no secure means and provisions to ensure its survival, and suddenly comes upon "land flowing with milk and honey" (Exod. 3:8), with the conviction that this is the Promised Land, what would one do? On a deeper level, if one comes upon a force for good, a god who is able to neutralize and render powerless the forces of hunger, thirst, sterility, destruction, and death, would not one convert to the worship and celebration of such a god? If there is a godly force that is able to make being prevail over nonbeing, of existence over nonexistence, of life over nonlife, of delight over suffering, would not one ally himself with such a godly force by worshiping and obeying it? After all food, water, fertility, and security of land and life are all secular goods that are absolutely necessary to survival in all its dimensions. And is it not the case that then, as well as now, all humanity is dominantly occupied in the production, marketing, and consumption of these secular goods? Although these are the terms we use to characterize our predominantly human concern, are they not in fact a substitute for the more comprehensive and deeper term "fertility"? And if so, is it not the case that indeed fertility is our god? Has not the god or goddess fertility spawned a whole culture and civilization and a way of life that is called modern and/or postmodern? Is this not the result of what Scripture says "following after other gods"?

It is not only the Baalism of Canaan that constituted the other gods to which the Israelites turned. Israel on many occasions became a vassal of the great countries that surrounded her: Egypt, Assyria, Babylon, Greece, Rome. She had no choice but to include the gods of these empires, together with their cults, in the worship activities of Israel. An example is King Ahaz going to Damascus to pay homage to the King of Assyria, Tiglath-pileser, his overlord. There he saw an altar of an Assyrian temple. He sent "a model of the altar" to the priest Uriah and ordered him to make an exact replica of it and place it in the Temple in Jerusalem. When King Ahaz returned to Jerusalem he "drew near to the altar, went up on it, and offered his burnt offering and his grain offering, poured his drink offering, and dashed the blood of his offerings of well-being against the altar" of the Assyrian god (2 Kings 16:10-13). To make room for the new altar of the foreign god in the Temple, he had to transfer the "bronze altar" of Israel's God to another place in the Temple. He made renovations in the Temple to provide worship space for the Assyrian god and ordered Uriah the priest and the people to observe the cult of the Assyrian god (2 Kings 16:14-18). Another example is the accommodation made by King Manasseh to pagan practices. Of him it is written:

> He did what was evil in the sight of the LORD, following the abominable practices of the nations that the LORD drove out before the people of Israel. For he rebuilt the high places that his father Hezekiah had destroyed; he erected altars for Baal, made a sacred pole, as King Ahab of Israel had done, worshiped all the host of heaven, and served them. He built altars in the house of the LORD, of which the LORD had said, "In Jerusalem I will put my name." He built altars for all the host of heaven in the two courts of the house of the Lord. He made his son pass through fire; he practiced soothsaying and augury, and dealt with mediums and with wizards. He did much evil in the sight of the LORD, provoking him to anger. The carved image of Asherah that he had made he set in the house of which the LORD said to David and to his son Solomon, "In this house, and in Jerusalem, which I have chosen out of all the tribes of Israel, I will put my name forever. (2 Kings 21:2-7)

The result of this mixing together of various religious cults—that of Yahweh, that of Baal and his partner, Asherah, and that of the gods of the overlords of Israel—is an amalgam of various religious practices, of many other gods besides Yahweh (2 Kings 17:33-34).

But what if the gods—the fertility gods, the economic/industrial/ commercial/ consumption gods, and the ideologies that go with them—were tied up completely with the functions they do and the values they provide and the way of life they glorify? They cannot function at all as a measuring rod to determine in life and reality what should go on, and what should not. Everything is "baalized," that is, localized under a local owner and lord and operator competing with other "baals." What if religions relativize one another and so are pluralized? All are gods, and there is no God above the gods? Is this situation not the same as described by the ending verse of the book of Judges: "In those days there was no king in Israel; all the people did what was right in their own eyes" (Judg. 21:25)? To paraphrase Dostoyevsky, if God is dead and there are only local gods each operating in its own sphere of interest, then everything is permitted. Everything is up for grabs.

What happens then to the secular goods that are absolutely necessary for the nourishing, flourishing, and the enjoyment of life if they are pursued outside of the covenant and its mechanism of judgment that we have summarily described above? Don't they become mere idols? Are not idols secular goods pursued in and for themselves outside of the covenant relationship and its criterion of judgment? Outside of the covenant relationship, they become simply secularistic goods, and their pursuit as a way of life is no more than a secularistic style of life. Secularism as a style of life is the modern version of ancient Baalism. In this lifestyle, the blessings of secular goods become merits deserved by the exercise of human creativity. They are goods made by human hands, which is precisely the definition of idol in Scriptures (Ps. 115; Jer. 10:1-8); they are merely human creations, not gifts of God's blessing.

When human creativity is exercised in cooperation with natural fecundity, it is no more than a merely natural force governed by the laws of natural and human behavior. And so secular goods are no more than material and human goods made available by a merely scientific and technological culture. A merely naturalistic, humanistic, and scientific culture is no more than an idol-worshiping culture! It has transformed the relative into an absolute; the finite into the infinite, the proximate into the ultimate! This is idolatry! Does this mean that the goods yielded by nature, the human, and of the sciences cannot be pursued within the covenant horizon of the Spirit? Of course not! They are in fact secular goods of the Spirit! (Jer. 10:12-13; 14:22). But a culture that is merely secularistic breeds a mind-set and an ethos that are not far from cynicism, or agnosticism, or atheism. The reason for this is the fact that nothing more and better transcends what has been achieved by such a secularistic culture. There is no longer "beyond in the midst."[3] Secularization as a process of pursuing and transcending the best that can be attained has ceased! Reality is reduced to what has been achieved and all that is to be done is to improve what has been achieved within the narrow parameters of the secularistic box! Secularity has become secularism! Idols have become idolatry! The relative has been turned into an absolute!

4. Prophetic Judgment

What happens then to the second part of the Decalogue, the vision of social justice and the special concern for the poor: the orphan, the widow, the stranger, the invalid, the marginalized; what has been called "the preferential option for the poor?" What has happened to the prophetic mandate to "let justice roll down like waters, and righteousness like an ever-flowing stream" (Amos 5:24)? The covenant relation is both a comprehensive and an inclusive relationship. It is comprehensive in that it brings God as God into involvement with Israel and its life, and it incorporates Israel into the loving concern of God. God and Israel are brought together into relationship. It is inclusive in that within this relationship, the worship of God shapes and norms Israel's life in community. Worship of God entails necessarily justice in the community. And justice in the community is grounded in

3. Dietrich Bonhoeffer (letter to Eberhard Bethge, April 30, 1944), *Letters and Papers from Prison* (New York: Macmillan, 1971).

and motivated by the worship of God. The co-inhering of one in the other is what makes for righteousness. It is what constitutes shalom! This co-inhering of one in the other and the other in the one, and thus making for shalom, can only happen in and through the Spirit. The Spirit is the religaric/covenant bond of God and his people. The harmony between God and people in the Spirit is righteousness. Justice in the community is achieved when the people behave in themselves and in relation to one another on the basis of the harmony between them and God in the Spirit, which is righteousness. Thus, justice is righteousness and righteousness is justice.

But since Israel has stepped out of the covenant relation and is now yoked to gods other than Yahweh, this means for Israel that it has rejected the "teaching" and is no longer duty-bound to obey the Torah and its statutes (cf. Amos 2:4). It is now free to decide for itself what good makes for community life. This means following invariably the ways of Baalism where there is no one way that is standard for, and is the measure of, all the other ways. There is no transcendent criterion of judgment in Baalism since Baal is identified with its processes, its functions, and its goods. This relativism in which all is relative opens the floodgates of competing for the goods of fertility. And that inevitably means that there will be those who have more than enough, and those who have less than enough. And those who have more than enough want to have more and more. There is no limit to this drive to have more. And those who do not have enough do not have the power to overcome their weakness and poverty because what little they have is taken away from them by those who have more and so they are rendered more powerless and poor. The irony is that there is no way to determine what is enough. This is the perennial problem of justice. When the system as such is inherently unjust, the products of fertility accrue to those who can exploit for themselves the injustice of the system. They need not blame themselves, for they are not responsible for the power structure of the system and the way it operates. There is no overarching standard to judge what is blameworthy or not. Moreover, they are blind to the injustice of the system because they participate in it and benefit from it, and would not want to change it. And if they would change it, what alternative is there to afford them a choice when all the people around have the same system and do what the system offers them!

Earlier it was noted that since it is Yahweh, God the Lord, who has been offended deeply by being "forsaken" by his people whom he loves, he now brings a suit against his people. In Micah, God has a "controversy" with his people and he asks his people "to plead their case" before him (Mic. 6:1-2). In Jeremiah the language used is even stronger: "I accuse you, says the Lord, and I accuse your children's children" (Jer. 2:9). The one accused is not only the people but also their leaders: the king, the elders, the priests, the prophets, the religious cult, and their entire inter- relationship and behavior. It is their entire life-history that is being called into question. The effect of God's bringing a charge against his people is to turn the covenant relation into a law court. And since the life-history of Israel is in terms of the covenant, that history is now weighed and judged in the light of the covenant.

One can take a step further with this claim. Not only Israel's history, but all human history is lived in the religaric/covenant bond. It is therefore to be weighed, evaluated, and judged in the light of the bond, which is the Spirit. The primordial religaric bond and its historical expression, the covenant relationship, are now turned into a law court and bring all humankind into its jurisdiction. The accuser is God the Lord and the respondent is humankind and its history! What a radical twist in relationship! What a reversal of fortune! And what would the judgment be? The "mercy seat" is turned into a court of law where the judgment is rendered on the basis of law and not on mercy?

In this court, the advocate of God, the one who prosecutes his case against the people is the prophet. And the one who pleads the case of the people before God is also the prophet (1 Sam. 12:19, 23; 15:11; 2 Kings. 19:1ff.; Jer. 7:16; 42:2). The prophet's advocacy is double-edged: He is advocate on behalf of God, and he is advocate on behalf of the people. In effect, the prophet plays the role of a mediator. But he is a mediator independent of the official mediator, namely, the priesthood. For the priesthood as an institution is part of the people who are brought to court. The independent prophet mediates God to the people and the people to God. He is both with God and with God's people. It is this being "with" both God and people in their covenant relationship that makes him a prophet. And all three, the accuser, the accused, and the advocate/mediator appeal to one standard, namely, the covenant relation and its terms. But the judge in this court is none other than the initiator, the sustainer, and upholder of the covenant, the one who has been steadfastly faithful to the covenant. And so the court is not just a law court where strict observance of the law without exception is the rule, but a covenant court where love takes precedence over law and is to be expressed through it. What sort of judgment would such a judge render in his own covenant court? As in all courts where judgment is to be rendered, there are four elements that come into play: the facts of the case, the law that applies, the interpretation of the law by the judge, and the whole purpose of the court system. A fifth element is added by Israel's faith that overarches all: the covenant as a religaric relationship as the context of law!

The prophet plays the central role in this justice system. Why? There are several reasons. For one thing, the prophet is said to be privy to the working of God's heart and mind. God reveals his secrets to his prophets: "Surely the Lord God does nothing, without revealing his secret to his servants the prophets" (Amos 5:7). The prophet is one authorized to stand "in the Council of the Lord so as to see and to hear his word . . . [and] give heed to his word so as to proclaim it" (Jer. 23:18). For another thing, the prophet is an astute and keen observer of human relations, institutions, and behavior. His perceptions are of what people do and what they do to one another and how they are affected by what they do. He sees not only the big decisions done by important people but also what little people do, and that includes the trivialities of daily life (Jer. 5:1-5). History consists of what big people and little people do that significantly affect their lives individually and corporately in their religaric/covenantal relationship with God the Lord.

But the prophet sees human experience not as a philosopher who treats human history as data to reflect on and draw general conclusions about reality, both human and nonhuman. He sees human behavior and its institutions not as a social scientist who treats them as data for drawing conclusions that explain why and how humans behave in the way they do. Nor does the prophet see human relations and behavior as a moralist who evaluates what people do in terms of what humans decide as rationally or legally right or wrong, good or bad. The fact of the matter is that the prophet not only sees human relations, human behavior, human institutions, and human experience as such but also the perspectives and the standards in the light of which they are humanly perceived and evaluated. He evaluates and judges all the perspectives and norms—whether philosophical, scientific, moral, or legal—by which human relations, behavior, and experience are assessed! The reason the prophet does this is the fact that he knows the heart of God as it beats in the religaric/covenant relation and brings this insight to bear in seeing and judging the way the covenant partner behaves. It is God's faithfulness to his covenant with his people that is the standard and norm for evaluating and assessing all human relations, institutions, behavior, experience, and their norms and standards. What he sees of the human situation in the light of God's faithfulness to the covenant is the truth of the human condition. All other truth claims are relativized by God's judgment of the truth.

Moreover, the prophet is authorized and empowered by God the Spirit to speak the truth as God perceives it in the light of the covenant relationship. And if the judgment is contrary to human standards and human behavior, he is not afraid to speak the truth as God's word, even when his message has to do with impending danger such as the devastation of Jerusalem, "the city of God," the fall of the nation to an enemy invader (such as Assyria or Babylon), the collapse of the royal dynasty and the destruction of the Temple and its cult, the failure of the land to yield its produce and thus bring about famine across the land, or finally, the exile of the cream of the people to a foreign land. Such a message of doom upon the land is of course unwelcome to the people and its leaders. The message is in fact rejected by leaders and people. The life of the prophet is threatened with danger because he is the prophet of doom. Jeremiah was publicly persecuted and put in prison and he curses the day he was born (Jer. 19–20). Amos was forbidden to further prophesy in Bethel in the north of Israel and was asked to return to the land of Judah and there to do his work as a shepherd (Amos 7:10-15). But no danger, no matter how seriously it threatened the prophet's life and ministry, could intimidate him and prevent him from speaking the Word of God in spite of the fact that this word was rejected by leaders and people. The priest Amaziah, who was in charge of the shrine at Bethel, accused Amos before King Jeroboam of Israel of conspiring against the king with a message that "the land is not able to bear" and Amos was told to go back to where he came from in Judah. To which Amos replied: "I am no prophet, nor a prophet's son; but I am a herdsman, a dresser of sycamore trees, and the Lord took me from following the flock, and the Lord said to me, 'Go, prophesy to my people Israel'" (Amos 7:10-15). This call meant that Amos was to abandon his home, his family, his livelihood, his familiar life-world—everything else he was doing, and related to—and must now devote his life to a new vocation: to serve the Lord as his prophet, to speak the word of doom to God's people!

The call of Amos as a prophet may have ended upon his return to his home, and so his call may not have been lifelong and permanent. But the case of Jeremiah indicates that not only his speaking but his living, his suffering, his whole life was incorporated into his vocation as a prophet of the Lord. Not only what he said but his whole life became his ministry as a prophet. From this, Gerhard Von Rad concludes rightly:

> There was more to being a prophet than mere speaking . . . Not only the prophet's lips but also his whole being were absorbed in the service of prophecy. Consequently, when the prophet's life entered the vale of deep suffering and abandonment by God, this became a unique kind of witness-bearing. Yet even this does not mean that in narrative portions of Jeremiah the account of the prophet's life is given for its own sake. It is given because in his case his life has been absorbed into his vocation itself.[4]

4. Gerhard Von Rad, *The Message of the Prophets* (San Francisco: Harper and Row, 1967), 18, 42. On the theme of God's pathos in Hebrew prophecy, see Abraham J. Herchel, *The Prophets*, vol. 1. (New York: Harper and Row, 1962).

Von Rad takes this insight deeper. Following his analysis of a prophet's visions and being addressed by God, the prophet "became in a strange way detached from himself and his own personal likes and dislikes, and was drawn into the emotions of the deity himself. It was not only the knowledge of God's designs in history that was communicated to him but also the feelings of God's heart, wrath, love, sorrow, revulsion, and even doubt as to what to do or how to do it. Something of Yahweh's own emotion passed over into the prophet's and filled it to the bursting point."

Although the prophet was of the conviction that God has directly called him to his vocation, he responded out of a religious, social, and cultural tradition that nurtured and formed his religious sensibilities.[5] Moreover, his message was partly shaped by, and called forth, by historical events or conditions obtained at the time. And, finally, although he styled himself as bearer of the word of God, that word was couched and communicated by his own thinking and speaking. The prophet's word is spoken humanly to a specific human situation.

And so the prophet's witness truly reveals the mind and heart of God. He does this because he stands within the bond of God and his people. And that bond is none other than God the Spirit. Von Rad observes, however, that in the ninth century B.C.E., with prophets such as Elijah and Elisha, the presence of "the Spirit of Yahweh was absolutely constitutive" of being a prophet. But with the eighth- and seventh-century prophets, beginning with Amos, the role of the Spirit in prophecy recedes into the background and hiddenness. These prophets did not see themselves as the bearers of the Spirit but saw themselves as bearers of the Word.

This may be correct historically. But theologically it falls short of the whole truth. Von Rad himself notes that the call of God directly addressed to the prophet makes the prophet see visions and hear voices that the prophets each attribute as directly coming from God and addressed personally to him. Moreover, the call has the effect of raising the consciousness of the prophet by intensifying the senses in ways not normally experienced in ordinary life. The prophet experiences a stretching of the self in the depth and breadth of consciousness. When added to this the fact noted earlier that somehow some of God's pathos is passed on to, and expressed by, the suffering of the prophet, are not all these indicative that the prophet is taken by the Spirit into the bond between God and his people, which bond the Spirit is? And the reason the prophet bears the Word is because he is in the Spirit and the power of the Word he speaks is none other than the power of the

5. See Bernhard W. Anderson, *Contours of Old Testament Theology* (Minneapolis: Augsburg, 1999), 128–34, 181–92, 224–36; Walter Brueggemann, 623–30; Von Rad, ibid., 15–76.

Spirit. If the prophet is bearer of the Word in the Spirit, is not Spirit then constitutive of prophecy?

5. The Judgment of God

So now we ask, What did the prophet see in God's people and what is the judgment that he spoke? We cannot pursue here in detail what the prophet saw and the nuances of the people's judgment on what they saw. We cannot do more than sketch out the basic lines of their perception and the evaluation they made. We shall combine perception and evaluation in our use of the term "judgment." Perception here would refer to the salient facts of the situation, and evaluation would denote the law or norm that applies and its interpretation. We will deal with the consequences of the judgment in due course. This is our way of framing the structure of the covenant court of Yahweh that we suggested earlier.

The first major judgment, namely, the forsaking of Yahweh by turning to, and being yoked with, other gods has already been noted. This is basic to the whole situation under consideration, and it has profound and far- reaching consequences. For the time being, we shall leave the matter as it now stands and return to it in more detail below.

The next prophetic judgment is that since there is now a breach in the covenant relation caused by Israel's pursuit of other gods, Israel failed to realize the other six provisions of the Torah dealing with the vision of justice in community life. Because the right relation between God and his people no longer prevails, there is no righteousness anymore. The relation has been distorted. An unrighteous, distorted relation between God and people breeds corruption, injustice, and violence among the people and in the land. This verdict may be detailed in a number of ways. Hosea's judgment is that unfaithfulness to the covenant and lack of knowledge of God, results in corruption, crime, and violence among the people in the land.

> Hear the word of the LORD, O people of Israel; for the LORD has an indictment against the inhabitants of the land. There is no faithfulness or loyalty, and no knowledge of God in the land. Swearing, lying, and murder, and stealing and adultery break out; bloodshed follows bloodshed. Therefore the land mourns, and all who live in it languish; together with the wild animals and the birds of the air, even the fish of the sea are perishing. (Hosea 4:1-3)

As Israel became a nation-state with the monarchy as its political center, it persistently pursued the goods that made for the governing of the state. In general, these were three, as indicated negatively by Jeremiah—wisdom, power, and wealth: "Thus says the Lord: Do not let the wise boast in their wisdom, do not let the mighty boast in their might, do not let the wealthy boast in their wealth" (Jer. 9:23). All three are of course required in running a state. Wisdom is enlightened leadership in governance, power is military strength to secure the state, wealth is economic prosperity that provides basic services and life necessities. But since their pursuit has been detached from their covenantal moorings and are now sought within the parameters of the yoke of other gods, their dynamic interplay in community life inevitably leads to an unwelcome result, namely, injustice, corruption, and violence.

The interplay of these goods of governance in community life resulting in injustice may be seen in several of the prophets. Two examples may suffice. One drawn from the Assyrian practice:

> For he says: "By the strength of my hand I have done it, and by my wisdom, for I have understanding; I have removed the boundaries of peoples, and have plundered their treasures; like a bull I have brought down those who sat on thrones. My hand has found, like a nest, the wealth of the people; and as one gathers eggs that have been forsaken, so I have gathered all the earth; and there was none that moved a wing, or opened its mouth, or chirped." (Isa. 10:13-14)

In this text, the Assyrian king declares with unbridled pride that all he has accomplished as a king and ruler is by his might, his wisdom, and the wealth he has plundered from the peoples he conquered. By the way he has manipulated all these resources of might, wisdom, and wealth in his clever hands he has succeeded in conquering, plundering, and reducing all peoples to his imperial rule! And who are the victims? Are they simply reeds cut down to death by his sword? Or are they people alive with feelings and purposes?

The other example is from the way Israel is governed by its own leaders. Is it any different from the Assyrian style? Amos declares the manner in these terms:

> Hear this, you that trample on the needy, and bring to ruin the poor of the land, saying, "When will the new moon be over so that we may sell grain; and the sabbath, so that we may offer wheat for sale? We will make the ephah small and the shekel great, and practice deceit with false balances, buying the poor for silver and the needy for a pair of sandals, and selling the sweepings of the wheat." (Amos 8:4-6; cf. 2:6-8, 6:4-7; Isa. 1:21-23; Jer. 6:13; 8:10-11; Hab. 2:16, 9, 11-12; etc.)

Trampling the poor is an exercise of power, but it also requires wisdom to justify it, and its aim is to acquire wealth. Deciding what goods to buy and sell and when and with whom aims at gaining wealth and this requires wisdom and the use of power. The wise and the mighty are also usually the wealthy because they have the means to acquire it. The interplay of these goods for governing as they are pursued in themselves results also in the emergence of their opposite: power gives rise to dependence and so produces weakness, wisdom protects itself by denying knowledge to others and so produces ignorance, and wealth accumulates by depriving others of it and so produces poverty. But the weak, the ignorant, the poor are people. They are persons who are not abstract concepts or statistical figures. They are also entitled to "life, liberty, and the pursuit of happiness." They are the orphan, the widow, the stranger, the disabled and invalid, the marginalized, and the disenfranchised. They have become victims and so they hurt, they suffer; they are oppressed, stunted, and dehumanized. They are victimized not merely by the powerful, the wise, and the wealthy on a personal basis, and by unfavorable circumstances not of their own making but also in a systematic, institutional, and oppressive way by the manner wisdom, power, and wealth are socially organized. Moreover, the perpetrators of injustice are not aware of the gravity of what they are doing because they are only pursuing values that are necessary for community life in a social system they presuppose. Don't the weak also want power? Don't the ignorant also desire wisdom? Don't the poor also seek wealth? Everyone wants the same things for himself under the same yoke of the other gods. Since all have been formed and normed by a culture of injustice, they are blind to it and could not and would not accept the prophet's verdict that there is no justice, no righteousness, no *shalom*, in the land. And this could only lead inevitably to disaster and ruin, of which the people were forewarned by the prophet in no uncertain terms!

Another prophetic verdict that can be said, following what is said above, is that the goods of governance that have been pursued are sought apart from, and in opposition to, other values stipulated in the covenant relationship. In the same text in Jeremiah where we read the pursuit of the values of wisdom, power, and wealth, we read the following: "Let those who boast boast in this, that they understand and know me, that I am the LORD; I act with steadfast love, justice, and righteousness in the earth, for in these things I delight, says the LORD (Jer. 9:24; cf. Isa. 1:16-1; Hosea 4:1). To know God the Lord is to know him as Lord of heaven and earth, the creator God (Jer. 10), and thus to trust him for being, existence, life, and all that nourishes and flourishes life, and to participate in his creative activity. To know him is to know him as the covenanting God who chose Israel to be his people, liberated her from bondage, led her through the wilderness on eagle's wings, and brought her to the Promised Land, gave her the law to form and norm her as his people, and pledged to her that he shall be her God. To know him is to know that all his acts are acts of steadfast love and justice and righteousness in the earth for the good of the people. It is in this knowledge and practice that the Lord delights. But Israel is no longer faithful to the Lord and so what delights the Lord no longer delights her also.

But this knowledge is for the people. It is for their benefit as a people. The knowledge of God as creator is what founds the earth and blesses it with fertility. It is this blessing of fertility that makes the land produce what nourishes and flourishes life and endows it with self-creative and self-perpetuative capacities. The knowledge of God as the Lord of Israel is he who created Israel as a people from being no people, and not just a people like other peoples, but a priestly kingdom and a holy nation, God's own treasured possession. It is this God who heard their cry in Egypt and acted out of love to free them from slavery and led them through the wilderness and brought them to the Promised Land. It is this God who allowed them to have a king and a royal dynasty to govern them in justice and righteousness and in prosperity. It is this God who is specially concerned for the rights and welfare of the poor, the widow, the orphan, the stranger. All these God did and continues to do in faithfulness to the covenant. And all this activity is for the earth as earth, for the people as people, for community life as a community of people, for the world as world, for all humanity as humanity. All this aims at establishing the integrity and value of the secular as secular.

This knowledge of God, however, has not been taught to the people by the official teachers, namely, the priests, the prophets, and the elders (Jer. 23:13-17). They were supposed to do this faithfully from generation to generation (Gen. 18:18-19; Deut. 6:20-25). And since the people were deprived of this knowledge, they "forgot" the Lord, their God. They forgot whose they were as a people. Instead, they were taught the ways of the gods they were serving and it is this that formed and normed their lives! As a result they lived their lives outside of the covenant. The values they sought from the other gods they served became worthless idols for them, "cracked cisterns that hold no water" (Jer. 2:13). They became like the idols they worshiped. They were deprived of the knowledge of the benefits of God being their God, of God being for them in their earthly, worldly, secular life. Without the presence of the Spirit in the midst of their secular life, their life in the world became secularistic! The secular became separate from and oppositional to the spiritual.

The most profound injustice is to regard God's covenant and his acts of faithfulness to it as anti-earthly, anti-worldly, anti-human, anti-community, and anti-life! The gravity of injustice is that it is directed against the covenant and against the God of the covenant who has turned himself out of grace as God to be the God of the covenant people. This injustice is unrighteousness in its profoundest depth. This separation and opposition between the spiritual and the secular, between the sacred and the profane, between state values and practices and religious values and practices is the most profound injustice there is! It is unrighteousness of the most basic order. It is denial of the presence and work of the Spirit in creation, in humanity, and in the world. It is denial of the possibility that spirituality can and does secularize! Can God overlook this injustice? What is the point of sending the prophets to pronounce the verdict of guilty upon Israel, upon humanity in which injustice still prevails even now? But Israel is not by any means off the hook yet. There is another set of facts in Israel that is seen by the prophets on which they pronounced the verdict of guilty.

This has to do with religion as the practice of faith. We have claimed that religion points to and celebrates in practice the primordial bond between God and his creation and is historically expressed paradigmatically in God's covenant with his people. That primordial bond is precisely God the Spirit. He is the bond between God turning himself to be God for his people and the people being turned to God to be his people, a priestly people and a holy nation. He is the bond that unites the two parts of the Decalogue: the love of God and the love of the neighbor. In this bond, God remains God in his holiness and creation and the people remain creaturely and therefore secular. It is the Spirit that makes God dwell in the midst of and among his people. It is also the same Spirit who inspires the people to celebrate God's presence in their midst by responding in trust expressed in worship, praise, gratitude, a narrative confession of God's story with his people, and obedience to his will as enshrined in the Torah. These acts of trust or faith signify the self-offering of God's people in homage to God and for the extirpation of sin so that the people may be at one with God (atonement) and so remain in covenant with him. What the people offer to God such as animal offering and harvest offering and thanksgiving offering have a vicarious meaning: In and through them the people offer themselves in homage to God and in gratitude for his merciful benefits. The specific forms and ways through human practice to celebrate and express the primordial bond and covenant together form institutionally what is called religion. Faith is the substance of religion and religion is the practice of faith. Theologically, this is the ideal relationship between faith and its practice. When it is realized, righteousness and justice prevail. The religaric/covenant relationship is fulfilled; humanity is blessed with life and all its delights.

What the prophets saw, however, is not the execution of the religaric/covenant relationship in its form and substance. What they perceived was its breakdown and its distortion. The people broke up the unity of the covenant relationship and detached the second half of the Decalogue from its moorings in the first half. The practice of governance and the ordering of community life were pursued as human construct apart from and independent of God the Spirit. This meant forsaking the God of the covenant and rejecting his will.

Instead of participating in working out God's design for the good of the people, the people themselves decided what is good for themselves and to do this good by themselves and for themselves through the means they themselves could devise, such as wisdom, power, and riches and their interplay in human hands. Perhaps without their being aware of it, they were asserting human autonomy and its creativity over against the God of the covenant. Tacitly and implicitly the people were invoking and practicing what today is the mantra of modern humanism: One can be "good without God,"[6] or one can "love one's neighbor without God." The result of all this is that human goods which in themselves are necessary and legitimate were turned into idols and the pursuit of them idolatrous! The pursuit of justice resulted in injustice, the pursuit of wisdom in leadership became manipulative and oppressive, the pursuit of power turned into violence, and the pursuit of wealth was done through corruption and greed.

In our terms today, the pursuit of what is properly and validly secular has become secularistic by sacralizing it, by hallowing it with the aura of the sacred that it does not deserve and is contrary to its proper character and integrity. Sacralization is the pursuit of turning the secular into the sacred and investing it with the spurious dignity of an idol. There does not seem to be an end to this pursuit as it continues until today!

We have already seen the prophetic judgment on this practice, which is nothing less that the practice of injustice. But this did not stop it; it only exposed it. Judgment is the exposure of what is wrong or false, which on the surface appears right or true. With the exposure was the plaintive appeal of the prophet for the people to amend their ways and return to the God of the covenant (cf. Isa. 1:16-20). Instead, the people ironically persisted in their evil ways.

> When Israel was a child, I loved him, and out of Egypt I called my son. *The more I called them, the more they went from me*; they kept sacrificing to the Baals, and offering incense to idols. Yet it was I who taught Ephraim to walk, I took them up in my arms; but they did not know that I healed them. I led them with cords of human kindness, with bands of love. I was to them like those who lift infants to their cheeks, I bent down to them and fed them. (Hosea 11:1-4, emphasis added)

---

6. Greg M. Epstein, *Good Without God* (New York: Harper Collins, 2009).

Instead of returning to God the Lord, they went farther away from him. Why? Jeremiah's answer: "The heart is devious above all else; it is perverse—who can understand it? I the Lord test the mind and search the heart, to give to all according to their ways" (Jer. 17:9-10). It appears that even the Lord does not understand the human heart and its ways. All that he can do is to judge what the heart does and not why it does what it does!

But at least we can learn some lessons. It is possible—and it has happened—that religion as a form of practice can be detached from its moorings in faith and in the religaric/covenant relation. It can distinguish itself from faith and launch out into a career of its own. It will then look after its own survival and flourishing and will inevitably serve its own self-interest. It becomes an institution in itself for itself, and so it is no more than any other institution of society. It can and does become a power structure in itself. Like all other power structures that serve their own interest, it also becomes an idol and the pursuit of it idolatry.

We have up to this point noted ways in which the institutional practice of religion has been severely perverted. The first is that it has been detached from the religaric/covenant bond by the people being yoked with other gods of human making, thus distorting its relationship to the God of the covenant. The second is that institutional religion has lost its power as a motivational force for the just ordering of community life. Instead of grounding justice in the soil of Yahweh's steadfast love and trust in it, institutional religion has delivered it to human construction and so it ironically promoted injustice, corruption, and violence. The third is that since religion has become an official institution, it became a power structure in itself and thus is concerned about its own survival and the promotion of its own interest. All these are a prostitution of the functions of religion as the form of the substance of faith and the religaric/covenant bond.

But there is a fourth perversion of official institutional religion that is as bad as the others that we must note. It is the use of official religion to sanctify the human condition and its social ordering by being invoked as cover for its evil ways and providing it with a false sense of security against threats of disaster. This is clearly evident in Jeremiah's sermon on the Temple (Jer. 7:1-15; cf. 23:9-40). There is no doubt that the Temple is the center of official religion. It is located in Jerusalem, "the city of David," and also "the city of God." It represented God's eternal promise of a royal dynasty. Temple and royal dynasty are the surety against destruction (Pss. 2:4-11; 72:8-14; 89:19-37; 132:11-18). What is practiced in the Temple and what it represented have the aura of sanctity and permanence. But precisely for this, what is done there by the people and its leaders can be invoked as guarantee for the security of the people against the threat of disaster. The people and its leaders trusted in the practice of the cult of the Temple when in fact their ways were evil (Jer. 7:1-11). This is the depth into which official religion can sink into perversion: as a cover up for sin, as protection against disaster, and as guarantee of personal and national security. Religion itself can be used to pervert relations and distort values, sanctifying evil as good, wrong as right, false as true. The religious leaders themselves participate in this perversion (Jer. 23:13-17, 26; Hosea 4:4-6; 8:11-13; 9:7b). When there is no ultimate norm or standard to judge between the one and the other since official religion has been detached from its anchor in the covenant relationship, has not religion itself become an idol and its practice idolatry? For the prophets, the people and their idolatry have become a "burden of the Lord" (Isa. 1:14; Jer. 23:33ff.). And as a "burden" should it not be "cast off"?

It is no wonder then that the prophet's outrage in denouncing the Temple and its cult appears as an abrupt and unwelcome intrusion into the people's practice of it. The following texts lay out clearly and unmistakably the judgment of the prophets.

> I hate, I despise your festivals, and I take no delight in your solemn assemblies. Even though you offer me your burnt offerings and grain offerings, I will not accept them; and the offerings of well-being of your fatted animals I will not look upon. Take away from me the noise of your songs; I will not listen to the melody of your harps. (Amos 5:21-23)

> Hear the word of the Lord, you rulers of Sodom! Listen to the teaching of our God, you people of Gomorrah! What to me is the multitude of your sacrifices? says the LORD; I have had enough of burnt offerings of rams and the fat of fed beasts; I do not delight in the blood of bulls, or of lambs, or of goats. When you come to appear before me, who asked this from your hand? Trample my courts no more; bringing offering is futile; incense is an abomination to me. New moon and sabbath and calling of convocation—I cannot endure solemn assemblies with iniquity. Your new moons and your appointed festivals my soul hates; they have become a burden to me, I am weary of bearing them. When you stretch out your hands, I will hide my eyes from you; even though you make many prayers, I will not listen; your hands are full of blood. (Isa. 1:11-15)

Does this prophetic judgment of official religion in all its distorted functions mean the rejection of the practice of faith in celebration of the religaric/covenant bond? There have been opinions along this line. But this does not appear to be the case. There are several reasons for asserting that this prophetic denunciation may in fact be understood as a reaffirmation and reassertion of the validity of the religaric/

covenant relation. For one thing, it is this relationship and its requirements that are used as criteria for exposing the idolatry, injustice, and the false sense of security that forsaking God the Lord and being yoked with other gods have entailed. For another thing, it is the religaric/covenant relationship that is used as a basis of the prophetic appeal for the people to amend their ways and return to Yahweh, God the Lord.

> Wash yourselves; make yourself clean; remove the evil of your doings from before my eyes; cease to do evil, learn to do good; seek justice, rescue the oppressed, defend the orphan, plead for the widow. Come now, let us argue it out, says the Lord: though your sins are like scarlet, they shall be like snow; through they are red like crimson, they shall become like wool. If you are willing and obedient, you shall eat the good of the land; but if you refuse and rebel, you shall be devoured by the sword (Isa. 1:16-20)

> The word that came to Jeremiah from the Lord: Stand in the gate of the Lord's house, and proclaim there this word, and say, hear the word of the Lord, all you people of Judah, you that enter these gates to worship the Lord. Thus says the Lord of hosts, the God of Israel: Amend your ways and your doings, and let me dwell with you in this place. Do not trust in these deceptive words: "This is the temple of the Lord, the temple of the Lord, the temple of the Lord." For if you truly amend your ways and your doings, if you truly act justly one with another, if you do not oppress the alien, the orphan, and the widow, shed innocent blood in this place, and if or you do not go after other gods to your own hurt, then I will dwell with you in this place, in the land that I gave of old to your ancestors forever and ever. Here you are, trusting in deceptive words to no avail. Will you steal, murder, commit adultery, swear falsely, make offerings to Baal, and go after other gods that you have not known, and then come and stand before me in this house, which is called by my name, and say, "We are safe!"—only to go on doing all these abominations? Has this house, which is called by my name, become a den of robbers in your sight? You know, I too am watching, says the Lord. (Jer. 7:1-11; cf. 4:14)

> Seek good and not evil, that you may live; and so the Lord, the God of hosts, will be with you, just as you have said. Hate evil and love good, and establish justice in the gate; it may be that the Lord, the God of hosts, will be gracious to the remnant of Joseph. (Amos 5:14-15)

Moreover, alongside the appeal is the warning, also based upon the religaric/covenant relationship, that if the people did not change their ways and return to the Lord, there would be no way to avert the threat of destruction. And if destruction came, as it surely would, it would be the people themselves and their leaders who brought it upon themselves. They would have only themselves to blame: "Have you not brought this upon yourself by forsaking the Lord your God? . . . your wickedness will punish you and your apostasies will convict you . . . your ways and your doings have brought this upon you. This is your doom; how bitter it is" (Jer. 2:17, 19; 4:18).

Finally, it is within the religaric/covenant relationship that Yahweh agonized as to what to do with his people whom he loves. Should he relent in his judgment to cast them off?

> My anguish, my anguish! I writhe in pain! Oh, the walls of my heart! My heart is beating wildly; I cannot keep silent; for I hear the sound of the trumpet . . . . Disaster overtakes disaster, the whole land is laid waste. Suddenly my tents are destroyed, my curtains in a moment. How long must I see the standard, and hear the sound of the trumpet? "For my people are foolish, they do not know me; they are stupid children, they have no understanding. They are skilled in doing evil, but do not know how to do good." . . . For thus says the Lord: The whole land shall be a desolation; yet I will not make a full end. (Jer. 4:19-22, 27)

> "O my people, what have I done to you? In what have I wearied you? Answer me! For I brought you up from the land of Egypt, and redeemed you from the house of slavery; and I sent before you Moses, Aaron, and Miriam. O my people, remember now what King Balak of Moab devised, what Balaam son of Beor answered him, and what happened from Shittim to Gilgal, that you may know the saving acts of the Lord." (Mic. 6:3-5)

It is also the basis for the people's plea for God the Lord to relent in his judgment and save his people:

> When they had finished eating the grass of the land, I said, "O Lord God, forgive, I beg you! How can Jacob stand? He is so small!" The Lord relented concerning this; "It shall not be," said the Lord. This is what the Lord God showed me: the Lord God was calling for a shower of fire, and it devoured the great deep and was eating up the land. Then I said, "O Lord God, cease, I beg you! How can Jacob stand? He is so small!" The Lord relented concerning this; "This also shall not be," said the Lord God. (Amos 7:2-6)

From the above, it is clear that the whole purpose of the judgment, the warning, the appeal, the punishment, the plea for God to relent and save, is to awaken the people to their grievous and tragic situation in the hope that they will amend their ways and return to God the Lord and his religaric/covenant relationship. And he, out of his steadfast love, will relent in kindness and in mercy and forgive! For the people to have the right to appeal and for the possibility that God will relent in kindness out of steadfast love and mercy means that the rule of law need not be administered strictly legally in the sense that there is no "rule" above the rule of law. In specific cases, the rule of law applies generally. But does it also apply to the whole law as a rule? Is there no "judge" or "rule" over the rule of law? And if there is, on what basis or standard does one "judge" the rule of law. Is the judge bound also by the rule of law? God as creator means that he produces (creative) and blesses (distributes his goods). It is this that constitutes righteousness. And so righteousness is first in order and dignity; it is creative and distributive. It is this righteousness that makes for justice. But if something goes wrong with what God creates then justice becomes retributive and punitive! It is God as creator and distributor of justice (righteousness) that stands over justice as retribution.

In constitutional democracies the administration of justice is done on the basis of the constitution as the expressed will of the people, and the will of the people can amend the constitution. It is therefore "the will of the people" that stands over, yet is expressed in, the constitution. In the case of the covenant, which is an agreement between two parties of different orders of being, the Torah expresses the will of God for the people, not the will of the people for God. It is therefore God, the giver of the law, that stands over the rule of law, that is, the administration of law. And he may administer the law, not according to the law, but according to the covenant in faithfulness to it. The covenant is a relationship and this relationship takes precedence over, and keeping it or being loyal to it is the goal of, the duties or requirements that it prescribes (law). If the appeal of the people over a judgment seeks to be faithful to the covenant relation and the possibility of relenting the judgment is meant to sustain or maintain the covenant, may not a covenant response of faithfulness to it take precedence over a legal judgment? What if righteousness as the right covenantal relation goes beyond justice as strict and exact conformity with law as giving everyone his due? In a covenant relation should there not be room for compassion, mercy, forgiveness, and reconciliation that aim at saving a sinner and so maintain righteousness? Where could hope arise—from a covenant of love that saves or from a judgment according to the rule of law that condemns?

The covenant relationship—"I will be your God and you shall be my people"—remains valid. It is used as criterion to restore the people as his people to himself; it is used to remind them that he is their God and none other, who is always present in their midst to bless and benefit them even when judging them. What may we conclude from this theological datum? Is it not to claim that judgment and all that it entails seeks to purify the world, the secular, from its dross of idolatry and secularism, and restore it to its secular integrity and value so that it remains as God's creation and God's world? Thus, it is precisely in this creaturely status and integrity that it is to be appreciated and celebrated. If this claim is not far from the truth, we can make a further claim, namely, that it is the Spirit and life in the Spirit, which is genuine spirituality, that truly secularizes! It is the spiritual that makes the secular truly secular!

From this perspective, what can we make theologically of the contemporary movement that seeks to be spiritual without being religious? There are some distinctions that are entailed by this formulation. For one thing, there is an obvious distinction between "spirituality" and religion. The reference of religion is to its historical, institutional, and confessional practice—to the attitudes, relations, beliefs, practices, duties, rites, festivals, and standards of right and wrong, true and false, and possible and not possible that are enshrined in such religious traditions. Whereas spiritual refers to a faith relation to what may be considered divine or ultimate or "heavenly." Such a divine reference need not be vertical and so it may not be viewed supernaturalistically. But it is, nevertheless, somewhat elusive. It transcends things horizontally and the way they are and so it cannot be fixed and put into a box. It takes the semblance of an "elusive presence" (Terrien). And so it is best expressed as a faith relation rather than a religious tradition.[7]

This distinction includes a polemic on the part of "the spiritual" against the "religious." The spiritual broadens; it leads to wider horizons and manifold possibilities; it celebrates freedom; it puts a premium on free choice and so it feasts on plurality of options. The Spirit transcends and eludes, but it also points, it leads, it inspires and enables. Whereas, traditional religion restricts and constricts, it fixes what is possible and not possible, it limits choice and restricts freedom, and is contented in being in the box of a tradition that shapes and norms. It preserves the sense of transcendence by viewing it vertically and so understanding it as supernaturalistic. It has also lost the sense of an elusive presence in things!

This polemic clearly implies that the spiritual can be separated from the religious, and it can be sought or pursued in a direction apart from or in opposition to the religious. And so there are those who abandon a religious tradition if they had been attached to one. Others still seek the spiritual in the religious by pruning it of its institutional accretions that make it irrelevant to contemporary concerns of overcoming poverty; caring for the environment; seeking a more free, more just, and a more global, more peaceful, a more humane form of social order; a more uniting rather than a dividing style of community life.

---

7. See Harvey Cox, *The Future of Belief* (New York: Harper Collins. 2009).

Religion divides, that has been its history. But does Spirit unite the different and the opposites that are many? Why should we not try it? It could work miracles! And in the process of trying it and giving it room and opportunity to do its work, it might take some more tangible form that we can begin to discern, and learn, and share without fixing it into a box!

But this "spiritual" movement is taking place not only in religion but in some of the more basic aspects of contemporary culture. For example, in philosophy there is a style of thinking that "deconstructs" thoughts that have been fixed into totalizing systems, as in metaphysical systems, political philosophies, economic ideologies, and artistic forms. These totalizing systems have been sacralized by tradition and so they function as modern secularistic idols. They have become the sacred cows of modern culture! They are now being dismantled in order to open them up to new possibilities of meaning by letting reality speak for itself in its own light for today's existential significance.

Moreover, in today's understanding of language, what language says in its *Sitz im Leben* is what reality is. The speakability of reality constitutes its truth as real. That is because thinking is done through language, and language is thought formed in a specific speakable way. And so what thought and language say is what reality is. We exist and have our being in language! We have to learn one another's language in order to exist together. There is not one language. Language can be frozen into a variety of texts—classical, canonical, or scriptural. A text can be anything. But if it requires understanding which is what makes it a text, then it should be pried open right through its multileveled accretions of interpretations and let new meanings arise from its depths that can speak existentially in today's life-world. May we not understand this iconoclastic movement of our time as a continuation of the process of secularization? Today, we are in "the twilight of the gods" (Friedrich Hölderlin) in search of a god or gods that may or may not appear in the midst of where we are! And that continuing search is where we are; it is our spiritual fate.

If this is anywhere near the truth, may we not take this situation as a sign of the Spirit being present in our midst? An aspect of the dynamism of that presence is its iconoclastic work, namely, the shattering of "images" (idols, systems, ideologies, religious traditions) that no longer mediate the "elusive presence" but fix it and confine it in a box. If so, does not this iconoclastic movement have the effect of purifying the dross of secularism (the modern version of Baalism) and letting the genuineness of the secular shine through? Is this not a modern expression of prophetic iconoclasm?

To be sure, the prophetic criticism of institutional religion was given some measure of implementation in the reform movements initiated by some of the kings, notably Hezekiah (715–687 B.C.E) and Josiah (640–609 B.C.E.). Both reforms struck at the religious syncretism prevalent in the land. The syncretism was a religious mix of a diminished Yahwism, the fertility cult of Baalism, and the gods of the empires (Egypt, Assyria, Babylon) that took Israel as vassal. As a vassal, Israel had no choice but to acknowledge the gods and the cults of the empires that subjugated her. The reform movements sought to remove from the land all practices and representations of foreign gods (2 Kings 18:1-8; 22:8-13; 23:4-25). These were regarded as an affront to Yahweh and disobedience to the Torah. The reform aimed at restoring the practice of faith and the exercise of political authority and community leadership to the requirements of the covenant relationship. This reform was nothing less than a thoroughgoing iconoclastic movement in its depth and breadth. It was a classic version of prophetic and political secularization in the covenant relationship.

But even this reform movement with its iconoclastic force was not enough to make Yahweh relent and withdraw his judgment of bringing Judah to destruction. At the end of the story of the reform movement of King Josiah are these words:

> Still the Lord did not turn from the fierceness of his great wrath, by which his anger was kindled against Judah, because of all the provocations with which Manasseh had provoked him. The Lord said, "I will remove Judah also out of my sight, as I have removed Israel; and I will reject this city that I have chosen, Jerusalem, and the house of which I said, My name shall be there." (2 Kings 23:26-27)

The judgment to remove Judah out of the sight of the Lord is fulfilled by king Nebuchadnezzar whom God raised as the "rod of his anger." In three waves of military invasion, Judah was conquered by Babylon and the cream of its citizenry, including its reigning king at the time, were taken into exile in Babylon (2 Kings 25:1-30). With the conquest of Judah and its best citizens taken into exile, the people of God as a nation-state has been destroyed. The pillar institutions of the state—the Temple and its cult, the monarchy and its dynasty, Jerusalem as "the city of God" as the seat of both Temple and monarchy have all been destroyed and the whole land brought into ruin. All this brought unspeakable suffering to the people which they could only express in deep lamentation (see the book of Lamentations). How did the people take this extremely traumatic event? The reform movements aimed only at purifying the faith of its dross of other gods and practices of unfaithfulness and disobedience and this was led by prophet and king. But now more than this, the whole nation and its pillars have been brought to ruin. Judgment struck at the roots of the people's existence and life. Did this also include the complete destruction of the people and of the people's faith in Yahweh? Or did it lead to their renewal? We shall take up the meaning of the Exile and what arose out of it in the next chapter.

To be sure, the God who removed Israel out of his sight is the same God who also removed from his sight and from the face of history the imperial violent powers that destroyed Israel. Assyria, which was raised by God to execute his judgment upon Israel's Northern Kingdom was also eventually made to disappear into the slag heaps of history. Babylon, which was raised as the rod of God's anger to bring Judah to its knees, suffered the same violence and conquest that it inflicted upon Judah under the conquering armies of Cyrus, which also has been consigned to oblivion. Egypt, too, was laid to ruins and ashes. The smaller nations that surrounded Israel and Judah suffered the same judgment (Jer. 50:17-18; chaps. 46–50): God's religaric sovereignty over all nations, though breached and distorted, is never broken and canceled.

But for now, it is perhaps not an exaggeration to say from the above as theological datum that there is abroad in human history a judging and winnowing process expressed partially and obscurely, but yet discernible in terms of insight; an iconoclastic and leveling movement that seeks to restore things in their proper character and order for the purpose of renewing and pushing them into new horizons of possibility that is not only their inner potentiality but an entirely new hope that only God can give them (Jer. 29:11). In terms of our language, we call this a movement of the Spirit that secularizes. May not this winnowing process be illustrated by recent historical movements, such as the collapse of Nazism, of apartheid, of communism, of the Berlin Wall and the end of the Cold War; the current assault on the various "isms" of our time, such as imperialism, sexism, racism, ethnocentrism, and the more recent aspirations to freedom, such as the Arab Spring in the decade of the 2010s? Of course other evils have also reared their ugly heads, such as global terrorism, fundamentalism of various sorts, ethnic cleansing, and the unbridled greed of purveyors of untrammeled capitalism. But who knows? These too will someday reckon with the winnowing of history! After all, is there not in history, on the one hand, "plucking up and a pulling down, a destroying and an overthrowing, and on the other hand, a building up and a planting?" (Jer. 1:10; 31:28). It appears that the one contradicts the other and yet both must be said to be fully truthful. May not both be the work of the Spirit that secularizes?

CHAPTER VII

Renewal: Between Creation and Salvation

In this chapter, we take up the theme of renewal. The treatment of this theme is an aspect of our effort to broaden and deepen our understanding of God the Spirit by exploring the horizons in which he moves and is actively engaged, as indicated in Scripture. One trajectory of his movement is toward the secular. We have been considering God's engagement with the secular in terms of his winnowing activity. The first aspect of judgment that we considered is God setting the limit between himself and humankind and all of creaturely reality. He sets himself apart from creaturely reality and this constitutes his holiness, which is his "essence" as God. At the same time, he affirms creaturely secular existence and life, including human existence and life by awakening the human to the knowledge of both good and evil and giving him the choice between the one and the other. This activity of securing his Godself and at the same time affirming the creaturely reality of the secular constitutes a religaric bonding between God and his creation. That bonding is by and in the Spirit.

The second aspect of judgment that we discussed is the relativization of the secular and its restoration to its proper integrity and dignity. It appears that the career of the secular in history is to absolutize itself into the status and dignity of deity, to make of itself an idol. This movement of absolutizing the relative, of sacralizing the worldly, of divinizing the creaturely, of projecting human achievement into divine status and value, is the essence of idolatry. And it constitutes an assault on the deity of God. In response, judgment is God's way of protecting his deity by desacralizing the secular and restoring it to its creaturely reality and dignity! It is done within the covenant relation and its terms. Precisely because it is done within this relation and in faithfulness to it, judgment does not operate mechanically and inevitably as an impersonal fate. It offers the possibility of "return," of "amendment," and of reform and renewal. And when judgment does come, it is as a verdict pronounced by a judge upon the activity of the accused for which he is responsible under the terms of the covenant relationship. It may be asked, does the verdict of guilty and the sentence it entails destroy the covenant relationship? Does the "plucking up and the tearing down" go as far as destroying the religaric/covenantal relationship? Is there at all a possibility of reaffirming and renewing the reality and dignity of the secular in its creaturely goodness without destroying it? It is theologically appropriate to consider judgment by lodging it between creation and salvation, as the affirmation and renewal of the secular. This is the issue we take up in this chapter.

1. The Possibility of Renewal

Where lies the possibility of renewal? Definitely it cannot come from the one to be renewed. Renewal comes to it, not from it. And so, it can be asked, where does it come from? Can it come from the judge who pronounces the verdict of guilty and does the sentencing and enforces both the verdict and the sentence? Can he change the verdict and still be consistent with, and be faithful to, himself and his office as judge? Can he suspend the terms of the covenant that have been violated and still be faithful to the religaric/ covenant relationship?

There is here, it seems to me, an inner tension within God's self-constitution that we need to discern and appreciate. The tension may be described as follows: On the one hand, God self-constituted himself as creator and in so doing bound himself primordially to his creation. He determined himself to create a people for himself and bound himself to this people, to be their God and they his people, in a covenant relationship on behalf of all the peoples of the earth! In both cases, God acted freely in love and so self-constituted himself as love. On the other hand, the human that God created and the people he created for himself did what was evil in God's sight. What God sees as evil is indeed evil, for he alone is good. What God sees in his creation as good is indeed good. What God sees and declares good is indeed good, for it is he who creates good! But what did God see in his creation that is not good? Genesis 6:5-6 puts it this way: "The LORD saw that the wickedness of humankind was great in the earth, and that every inclination of the thoughts of their hearts was only evil continually. And the Lord was sorry that he had made humankind on the earth, and it grieved him to his heart." The "wickedness" that God saw is further described in vv. 11-12 as "corruption" and "violence": "Now the earth was corrupt in God's sight, and the earth was filled with violence . . . for all flesh had corrupted its ways upon the earth."

And what did God see in the people he called for himself? Isaiah put it in a nutshell in this way:

> Hear, O heavens, and listen, O earth; for the Lord has spoken: I reared children and brought them up, but they have rebelled against me. The ox knows its owner, and the donkey its master's crib; but Israel does not know, my people do not understand. Ah, sinful nation, people laden with iniquity, offspring who do evil, children who deal corruptly, who have forsaken the Lord, who have despised the Holy One of Israel, who are utterly estranged! (Isa. 1:2-4)

God's seeing is at the same time his judging. He cannot unsee what he sees, and he cannot unjudge what he sees. And he cannot undo what he judges because what he judges is not his own doing. Does the judge have a choice but to promulgate the verdict and implement the sentence even when this means a plucking up, a tearing down, and a destroying of what he has called into being?

But it may be asked, does this not precipitate a tension, an agony, an anguish within God between creation in love and destruction in judgment?

We can already discern this tension in God's being "sorry" in creating humankind that did evil in his sight and in "grieving" over his decision to "blot out from the earth the human beings I have created—people together with animals and creeping things and birds of the air, for I am sorry that I have made them . . . I have determined to make an end of all flesh, for the earth is filled with violence because of them, now I am going to destroy them along with the earth" (Gen. 6:7, 13). We also catch a glimpse of the divine anguish in the poignant pathos of the prophets as they agonized over the inevitable tension between God's love for his people and his judgment to punish them for the guilt they have brought upon themselves by their own doing.

> "Your ways and your doings have brought this upon you. This is your doom; how bitter it is! It has reached your very heart." My anguish, my anguish! I writhe in pain! Oh, the walls of my heart! My heart is beating wildly; I cannot keep silent; for I hear the sound of the trumpet, the alarm of war. Disaster overtakes disaster, the whole land is laid waste. Suddenly my tents are destroyed, my curtains in a moment. How long must I see the standard, and

> hear the sound of the trumpet? "For my people are foolish, they do not know me; they are stupid children, they have no understanding. They are skilled in doing evil, but do not know how to do good." (Jer. 4:18-22)

> How can I give you up, Ephraim? How can I hand you over, O Israel? How can I make you like Admah? How can I treat you like Zeboiim? My heart recoils within me; my compassion grows warm and tender. I will not execute my fierce anger; I will not again destroy Ephraim; for I am God and no mortal, the Holy One in your midst, and I will not come in wrath. (Hosea:11:8-9)

This anguish within God borne out of the tension between his creative love and his destructive judgment makes God suffer. In self-constituting himself as creator who loves, he makes a commitment not only to create life but to nourish and flourish it. In creating and calling for himself a people and making a covenant of love with it, he gives them all the gifts that would make the people live in his sight, most of all the gift of his being God for this people. Love creates; it saves; it builds up life and makes it hopeful. But judgment destroys, it kills, it punishes! If we were to apply to God our understanding of suffering as being and living within the contradiction of what need not be and should not be, and could have been avoided, and that in fact is what has happened and now is, together with the pain and hurt this contradiction brings about, then we can feel in our own human way God's pain in suffering. If we as humans suffer for living within the contradiction between what now is and need not have been, but has happened and now is, would not God suffer so much more hurtingly and painfully, given the fact that he is utterly more sensitive to what contradicts his holiness? Is there something more hurtful than the hurt felt by God in judging his people? "For the hurt of my poor people I am hurt, I mourn, and dismay has taken hold of me" (Jer. 8:21).

This tension within God from which he suffers may be seen as that which also gives rise to his plea with his people to return to him and amend their ways. If the people heed his plea, he would relent in his judgment and thus he need not vent the full force of his anger upon his people. Their return to him would ease and perhaps even resolve the tension within himself and so make his suffering cease.

> Come now, let us argue it out, says the LORD: though your sins are like scarlet, they shall be like snow; though they are red like crimson, they shall become like wool. If you are willing and obedient, you shall eat the good of the land; but if you refuse and rebel, you shall be devoured by the sword; for the mouth of the LORD has spoken. (Isa. 1:18-20)

> If you return, O Israel, says the LORD, if you return to me, if you remove your abominations from my presence and do not waver, . . . Amend your ways

> and your doings, and let me dwell with you in this place. . . . For if you truly amend your ways and your doings, if you truly act justly one with another, if you do not oppress the alien, the orphan, and the widow, or shed innocent blood in this place, and if you do not go after other gods to your own hurt, then I will dwell with you in this place, in the land that I gave of old to your ancestors forever and ever. (Jer. 4:1; 7:3, 5-7)

God's anguish and his plea that his people return to him is also, strangely enough, what gives rise to the people to cry to the Lord for him to relent in his devastating judgment. In their worship they celebrate their God as love who is ready to save:

> The LORD is merciful and gracious, slow to anger and abounding in steadfast love. He will not always accuse, nor will he keep his anger forever. He does not deal with us according to our sins, nor repay us according to our iniquities. For as the heavens are high above the earth, so great is his steadfast love toward those who fear him; as far as the east is from the west, so far he removes our transgressions from us. As a father has compassion for his children, so the LORD has compassion for those who fear him. For he knows how we were made; he remembers that we are dust. (Ps. 103:8-14)

The people confess their sin and ask to be saved:

> Have you completely rejected Judah? Does your heart loathe Zion? Why have you struck us down so that there is no healing for us? We look for peace, but find no good; for a time of healing, but there is terror instead. We acknowledge our wickedness, O LORD, the iniquity of our ancestors, for we have sinned against you. Do not spurn us, for your name's sake; do not dishonor your glorious throne; remember and do not break your covenant with us. Heal me, O LORD, and I shall be healed; save me, and I shall be saved; for you are my praise. (Jer. 14:19-21; 17:14)

But did God's people heed his plea? They did not! Did they return to him and amend their ways? They did not! The complaint of God in Hosea is so poignantly true: "The more I called them, the more they went from me" (11:2). Did they act on their own plea for help out of their faith that God acts in mercy and steadfast love? They did not! Jeremiah's observation holds true: "The heart . . . is perverse—who can understand it? I the Lord test the mind and search the heart, to give to all according to their ways, according to the fruit of their doings" (17:9-10).

And so the contradiction between creative and life-giving love and destructive and life-denying judgment remains unresolved both within the heart of God and within the human heart! And so God suffers! And the human suffers! His people suffer! They all—each in their own way—live under contradiction and the pain it generates. They may empathize with one another in their suffering and find comfort in sharing the burden of their suffering. But is this contradiction and suffering the destiny of God as God? Is it also the fate of the human as human and his people as his people?

Is there no way of resolving this contradiction within God, and in the relation between God and his creation, and within creation and human life itself? Are life-giving love and death-dealing judgment equal properties of God running parallel to each other? Is the cycle of what is sown is what is reaped, of deed and consequence, of disobedience and punishment, of justice as retributive, permanent, and unbreakable? Put in other terms, are heaven and hell parallel religious realities, based on retributive justice as reward and punishment, so that some are destined to heaven, and others are consigned to hell, depending on the good or evil that they do, thus making fate the order of the divine-human relationship? Put in today's religious terms, are the sacred and the secular, the spiritual and the material, two parallel orders of reality and ways of life, the one leading to life, the other to death? Moreover, this order is assumed as given and works itself out inexorably in nature and in human life. Therefore, neither God, nor nature, nor the human can resolve the contradiction between them and suffering remains unrelieved with no hope of putting an end to it. If this problem remains unresolved, then Ezekiel's verdict on the situation of Israel and of all humankind would become the inexorable fate of all creaturely reality: "Our bones are dried up, and our hope is lost; we are cut off completely" (Ezek. 37:11).

If this contradiction and the suffering it entails were to be resolved, it would have to be resolved within Godself, and only God can do it since it is a matter having to do with his self-constitution as God. There is some evidence in prophetic faith that witnesses to God's resolving this issue within himself by himself and for himself. It may be worthwhile to take note of the following lines of thought.

For one thing, we find the suggestion in Amos 3:1-2 that judgment is an act of love on the part of God: "You only have I known of all the families of the earth; therefore I will punish you for all your iniquities" (v. 2). God's knowing Israel of all the families of the earth is by creating, saving, electing, and forming Israel as his people. And all this has been done out of his steadfast love. It is the same love that established the covenant between God and his people, and all his activities within that covenant aim to be faithful to it as a covenant of love. It is this faithfulness that makes the covenant relation righteous. If so, then would this not mean that judgment that punishes iniquities is an act of righteous love that aims at being faithful to the covenant relation? And if this were the case indeed, would not judgment as an act of love aim at saving life and giving hope and replenishing the earth with its life-sustaining benefits? Would this not mean that judgment as an act of love, aiming at nourishing and flourishing life with a new future with hope, is only temporary (Isa. 42:14-16). It is not the final word of love on life. It is in fact wedged between creative and redeeming love, between faith in love and faith in hope. Judgment takes place between creation and salvation. It is renewal of creation with the view to salvation. Judgment is the renewal of the secular to make it genuinely secular as a religaric reality.

For another thing, Ezekiel 18:23, 32 and 33:10 suggest that God has no "pleasure in the death of the wicked." In fact, the aim of God's judgment is precisely to plead with Israel to "repent and turn from all your transgressions; otherwise iniquity will be your ruin. Cast away from you all the transgressions that you have committed against me, and get yourselves a new heart and a new spirit! Why will you die, O house of Israel? For I have no pleasure in the death of anyone says the Lord God. Turn, then, and live!" (18:30-33). Judgment is to make Israel "turn and live." That turning which results in life is by the way of renewal, by getting "a new heart and a new Spirit." We will return to this theme of renewal below.

Furthermore, and more profoundly and importantly, if God the Lord were to act at all with respect to Israel's apostasy and deeds of abomination, it would be "for the sake of my holy name" and not for the sake of Israel (Ezek. 36:22, 32; cf. Isa. 43:2-5; 48:9-11). God's name is the name he gave to himself that he revealed to Moses: "I am who I am" (Exod. 3:14). Only he can name himself and so only he can reveal himself as he truly is. His name therefore is his self-constitution and self-identification. Moreover, his name is holy. Only he is God; he is a class by himself; there is none like him. His holiness is what makes him God. And so what he makes of himself as God and reveals of himself as God, that is who he truly is. For God to "act on his behalf" presupposes his freedom to be himself as the God who is holy. His acting on his behalf is to protect that freedom and to assert his sovereignty over anything and everything else.

Additionally, in acting on his own behalf, God is also acting in freedom to be God as he determines himself to be God for his people. What his people do to themselves has nothing to do with what he does to himself to be God for them. His self-constituting of himself is not bound to anything other than to himself and so he is not responsible to anyone but himself, not even to his own people. He does not act "on their behalf." If he does something to them for what they have done to themselves, such as judging and punishing them for what they have done, he is doing it for himself as God to assert himself as God. The purpose of his doing so is quite simply for Israel to know that he is Yahweh: I am Yahweh your God! (Ezek. 6:7, 10, 14; 7:4, 9, 27; etc.). If God judges and punishes them for their wrongdoing in order to renew and save them, such as saving them from their "uncleanliness," which is their ruin, he is simply being himself and being true to himself as God (Ezek. 36:29-32).

Furthermore, he has his own reasons for doing what he does as God. Since the ruin of Israel has become a spectacle among the nations, prompting the nations and their rulers to chuckle derisively and contemptuously about the power of their God (Ezek. 36: 19-20) thus humiliating and "profaning" his name among the nations, he would save Israel in order to vindicate his name. Thus the salvation of Israel is for the vindication of God's name among the nations so that "the nations shall know that I am the Lord" (Ezek. 36: 21-23). But the vindication of God's name is also at the same time the vindication of Israel as God's people, since God's name is tied religarically and covenantally to Israel as his people: "No longer will I let you hear the insults of the nations, no longer shall you bear the disgrace of the peoples; and no longer shall you cause your nation to stumble, says the Lord God" (Ezek. 36:15). This "no longer" is both a change in God and a change in the situation and status of Israel. The one entails the other, and both are an assertion of God's freedom to self-constitute himself as God for his people. "I will be your God" means that what he freely determines himself to be God, that is what he is. What he decides of himself as God for his people, that is what and who he is as God for his people. How he deals with his people is what he is as God to his people. And how he keeps his religaric/covenant relation with them is his business as God!

And what would this mean for the resolution of the tension, even contradiction, between creative and life-giving love and destructive and life-devastating judgment? Ezekiel is suggesting that resolving the conflict is God's business as God who freely decides as to whom he is and how he keeps his commitments. He has decided that judgment takes place within his love as God and is to serve the purposes of himself as a loving God!

He has lodged judgment within his creative and saving love. That is the way he has resolved the contradiction! Love creates. Love judges. Love suffers. Love saves. And all is love, for God deals only in steadfast love. That is the way he determines himself as God, as God for creation, for his people, for humankind, and for us! And are not creation, humankind, his people and the earth they dwell in, and the culture they create, the secular world that we are—is it not to and with this secular world that he bonded himself religarically and covenantally in love? Has he not done this by and through his Spirit so that it is the Spirit that keeps the secular truly and genuinely secular? It is the Spirit that resolves the contradiction between the holy and the secular by making the holy dwell in the midst of the secular, and by making the secular what it truly is as secular precisely by making the secular the dwelling place of the holy! It is the Spirit that secularizes!

There is another line of thought in prophetic faith that suggests a further way of perceiving the way God resolves the tension within himself of creative life-giving love and destructive death-dealing judgment. Deutero-Isaiah develops more profoundly than any prophet before or after him Israel's faith in God as the one and only holy God who freely self- constitutes himself by what he does to himself. There is none like him, either before him, besides him, above him, or after him: "Before me no god was formed nor shall there be any after me. I, I am the Lord, and besides me there is no savior" (43:10-11; cf. 40:5, 18, 25; 42:8; 43:11; 44:6-7; 45:5; etc.). Isaiah believes that God embodies in himself without tension or contradiction all attributes and functions of deity, both in relation to himself, for he self-constitutes himself, and to what is other than himself, for he creates, blesses, judges, redeems, and destines all creation and all his creatures; he is Lord of all! In calling and "anointing" Cyrus, King of Persia, to execute his will to redeem his people from exile (Isa. 45:1-4), God says:

> I am the Lord, and there is no other; besides me there is no god. I arm you, though you do not know me, so that they may know, from the rising of the sun and from the west, that there is no one besides me; I am the Lord, and there is no other. (Isa. 45:5)

Then God goes on to enumerate all that he does as Lord. The logic is, I am the Lord, and this is what I do! "I form light and create darkness, I make weal and create woe; I the Lord do all these things" (Isa. 45:7).

Note the verbs used: form, create, make, do. Those verbs are various ways of setting forth God's creative power. And his creative power is the source of everything: light and darkness, weal and woe, blessing and cursing. There is nothing in creation and what happens in it that is outside his sovereign power: He is Lord! But Isaiah goes even further. The notions of creation and salvation are usually seen as distinct and separate acts of God, each independent of the other. But not so with Isaiah. He views salvation as created by God so that in creating he also saves, and in saving he also creates: "Shower, O heavens, from above, let the skies rain down righteousness; let the earth open, that salvation may spring up, and let it cause righteousness to sprout up also; *I the Lord have created it*" (Isa. 45:8, emphasis added).

Here the words *righteousness* and *salvation* are inclusive of all God's saving activity. In this prophetic text it is said that God created them. *Righteousness and salvation arise because God creates them.* They are implementive and performative expressions of his creative power (cf. 45:12-19).

Moreover, the notion that God creates and saves is mentioned especially in the case of Israel, God's people, in their making, calling, forming, redeeming, and homecoming from exile:

> But now, O Jacob my servant, Israel whom I have chosen! Thus says the LORD who made you, who formed you in the womb and will help you; Do not fear, O Jacob my servant. . . . For I will pour water on the thirsty land, and streams on the dry ground; I will pour my spirit upon your descendants, and my blessing on your offspring . . . Thus says LORD, the King of Israel, and his Redeemer, the LORD of hosts: I am the first and I am the last; besides me there is no god. (Isa. 44:1-3, 6)

Since God judges what he creates, and he saves what he judges, judgment is bracketed by creation and salvation and is lodged between them. Thus judgment becomes a passing episode in God's overall activity (Isa. 54:7). It is not God's final word in his religaric/covenanting activity. Thus, the tension between creation and salvation that arises in judgment is resolved by God within himself.

One must also note that in all this, there is a continuity of God's word and his act: What he says, he does; what he promises, he fulfills—"I have spoken, and I will bring it to pass; I have planned, and I will do it." The power that creates is the same power that saves. The power that makes possible out of the non-possible is the same power that actualizes the possible, and thus creates. The power that judges and prunes what has been created of its idolatry and injustice and violence is the same power that restores and forgives and renews so that creation may move on to fulfill its future with hope! And what power is this that is at work through word and deed and event that creates, judges, redeems, and destines this world—this world of things and people and relations and cultures in their own time and space—this secular world? Is it not God the Spirit that secularizes?

Since only God is Lord and none other and combines in himself all the attributes and functions of deity, he sits in his glory and majesty above the earth and the heavens. He is "the high and lofty one who inhabits eternity, whose name is Holy: I dwell in the high and holy place" (Isa. 57:15).

From that "high and holy place" he surveys all creation from beginning to end and all that is in it in their respective identities, integrities, and worth. And what does he see? He sees the peoples "as grass" whose constancy is like the flower of the field: "The grass withers, the flower fades, when the breath of the LORD blows upon it . . . but the word of our God will stand forever" (Isa. 40:7-8). It is the Spirit that gives life to peoples in their time and place. They live and fade in the power of the Spirit but the word of the Lord that creates them endures forever. He looks at the nations with their kings and their power to govern and make war. He says of them: "Even the nations are like a drop from a bucket, and are accounted as dust on the scales. . . . All the nations are as nothing before him; they are accounted by him as less than nothing and emptiness" (Isa. 40:15, 17). And what about the gods and the idols? They are merely created by human hands (Isa. 40:19-20). And as such, they are powerless, useless, and so are worthless. But what is tragic is that those who make them "delight" in them. They become like the idols of the gods they make. In this they will find out that because they become the idols they make, they are useless, profitless, and worthless (Isa. 44:9-20).

What can we make out of this theologically? In asserting his majesty as Lord and protecting his holiness and spreading out his glory to fill all things, he relativizes all things, puts them in their proper life-forms, and places them in their own life-times and life-spaces. It is God's holiness that relativizes all things and, thus, makes them what they truly are: creaturely secular realities!

But strangely enough in the same text where God asserts the majesty of his holiness in its loftiness, he at the same time speaks of his holiness, that is, he himself as God, as dwelling "with those who are contrite and humble in spirit, to revive the spirit of the humble, and to revive the heart of the contrite" (Isa. 57:15). God the Lord in the majesty of his holiness is in the midst of the humble who gratefully acknowledges that they are creaturely, this-worldly, earthly, and secular. His being God as creator is for the good of the creature. His being judge is for the renewal of the creature. His being redeemer is for the salvation of the creature. His being Lord is for the good of all creation. Nothing in the creature—his being earthly and this-worldly, his being alive in the body of flesh, with all the joys of bodily of life—is outside of his being God for it. The God who is holy and is thus both lofty and lowly is for and is in the midst of the earthly. God is for the secular!

2. The Act of Renewal and Salvation

So far we have considered the notion that judgment generates within God the tension between his creating and life-giving grace and his death-dealing judgment over which he inwardly agonized. That tension has been resolved in the thought of Deutero-Isaiah in favor of renewal and salvation based on God's creative grace, thus lodging judgment between his creative and saving grace and so enclosing judgment within the sovereignty of his religaric/covenanting grace and steadfast love. The enclosure of judgment within God's creating and saving grace transforms judgment into renewal unto salvation. In this section we consider God's action of following through on creating renewal and salvation.

In Isaiah 42:8-9 and 43:19, God the Lord declares that he is about to do "new things," and he tells of them before they happen. The new thing that he is doing is in fact already happening (cf. 48:3-7). It is the homecoming of the exiles decreed by Cyrus of Persia (Ezra 1:1-4) whom the Lord "anointed" to be his "shepherd . . . to carry out all my purposes" (44:28; 45:1ff.). The homecoming as an action of God through a foreign king is a historic turn in the life of Israel as a people. It marks the end of exile and it opens up a new future for Israel. It is the "good tidings" announced by Deutero-Isaiah that brings "comfort" and "hope" to Israel to both the homecoming exiles and those who remained in Judah. Historically, the homecoming is a political event. It is the return of a people to their homeland decreed by a political authority who rose to power through violence and conquest. In that sense, the homecoming is a secular event in world history. But the prophet views it as happening within the much larger horizon of God's creating, judging, and saving activity, as the sovereign Lord of creation, history, and destiny. From this prophetic perspective the homecoming is more than a historical, political, and secular event. So we ask, what implications does the homecoming entail? What is new about it? In answering these questions we will gather together what the prophets have said that in our view spells out the various elements of "the new thing" that God is doing in redeeming Israel. By bringing them together we get to view as a whole all the elements and their relationship to one another.

We must consider the fact that with the exile Israel lost practically everything. It ceased to be a nation politically and was crippled religiously. The monarchy was gone. The Temple and its cult were also gone. Jerusalem as the city of David and the city of God was destroyed. A remnant of the population consisting of the returning exiles and those that remained in Judah were all that was left of its citizenry. Its economy has collapsed. Its faith was in severe crisis. Ezekiel voiced the self-judgment of the people with the tragic statement: Our bones are dried up, and our hope is lost; we are cut off completely (Ezek. 37:11). And so the question of the Lord to Ezekiel is plaintive: "Can these bones live?" The answer of the prophet is, "O Lord GOD, you know" (Ezek. 37:3). Only God knows what has to be done and only he can do it. What is entailed here is nothing less than the reconstitution of Israel as God's people. And only God the Lord can and may do this. All the gifts of blessing were gone: land, the cream of the people, the Temple, the monarchy, the economy are all gone. But is the giver of gifts and his giving of gifts also gone? Fortunately, they are still very much around. What are the gifts that are included in the "new" that God is about to do as a blessing to Israel to reconstitute it as his people? We may note the following salient points.

First, *the homecoming is a new exodus* (Isa. 43:15-21; cf. Ezek. 20:34-37). The language used to describe it appears to be modeled on the language of the old Exodus from Egypt. The homecoming is a liberation from Babylon to the homeland through a journey in the wilderness, and the way is paved by God's guiding hand: "I will make a way in the wilderness and rivers in the desert . . . to give drink to my chosen people" (Isa. 43:19b, 20b; cf. vv.16-17). But the model of Exodus from Egypt is also declared "former" and is to be considered as "the things of old." And for that reason they are no longer to be remembered (43:18; cf. 42:9). The "former things" that are to be forgotten covered all that was already lost in judgment, including the sins that were the root cause of the judgment for which Israel received "double" penalty (Isa. 40:2). It is not only Israel that should now forget the sins of the old order, but even God himself "blots out" Israel's transgressions and he "will not remember [their] sins" (Isa. 43:25). God is doing this for his own sake, in faithfulness to himself as the God who made of himself as God of and for this people. And so the new thing that God is now doing is a new exodus that is a new beginning that practically reconstitutes Israel as God's people.

Second, *God is making a new covenant with Israel.* To be sure, the religaric/covenanting activity of God remains intact, for he has not abrogated it. He has not given Israel, his partner in the covenant, a "bill of divorce" (Isa. 50:1). God has kept his part of the covenant relationship in being faithful to himself. It was Israel that sold herself out of the covenant by her transgressions (Isa. 50:1-2).

So why a "new covenant"? Why is there a need for it? Would it be too far-fetched to suggest that the answer to this question is a new turn in God's self-constitution and self-becoming to be God and to be God of and for his people? Up to this point we have been describing God's turn to be himself by turning to his creation and to his people. It is, as it were, a turning outward, a turning to another. This is what established the religaric/covenant relation. This time the turning is inward, a turning to himself in a further reaffirmative resolve to make of himself fully and deeply God without any reservation, mastering all the resources of his holiness and his love to be truly God in himself for this people. A new covenant means for God deepening and strengthening and reaffirming and recommitting himself as fully God in his religaric/covenanting relationship.

This suggestion may be discerned in the following. First, we have already noted that God in the face of Israel's betrayal will act, if he were to act at all, on his own behalf as God and not on behalf of Israel. It is in being faithful to himself that he acts at all.

Second, we have also pointed to what Isaiah has seen of God as gathering into himself all attributes and functions of deity—as creator, judge, redeemer, and as presence in the midst of his creation and people—and dedicating himself fully in his holiness and love to the well-being and future of his creation, his people, and to all humanity. These two points constitute a self-turning inward in God's continuing self-becoming as God in his religaric/covenanting relationship. This is what constitutes the "new" in the new covenant.

But how did this work out in his covenant with his people? What did God do as a result of this self-turning inward in dealing with his people? In answer to this question I would suggest that it is his blotting out of the transgressions of Israel and his casting them out of his memory so that he no longer remembers them—and thus they no longer exist in the sight of God and on the face of the earth—that is what God did! (Isa. 43:25; Jer. 31:74). This radical deed of God goes beyond the act of a judge. In a law court (Isa. 43:26-28) the judge acknowledges and confirms the facts of the case, and if the facts show wrongdoing, the judge confirms them in his judgment. But that does not undo the act of wrongdoing. It does not blot these facts out of existence on the face of the earth. But God does more than what a judge can do: He blots out from his sight the wrongdoing, and thus it no longer exists because it does not exist anymore in God's sight and in his memory! In priestly language, God the Lord will "sprinkle clean water upon you, and you shall be clean from all your uncleanliness" (Ezek. 36:25). The standard theological term for this most profound act of God is "forgiveness." This is an act, not of a judge, but of a savior. To be saved is to be forgiven, not to be condemned. An example in prophetic faith is vividly and incredibly dramatized both in the prophecy and life of Hosea. He married a whore wife who kept on whoring even while they were married. Did Hosea give her up and consign her to "hell"? That is what a judge can do and do rightly as a judge. But Hosea resolved himself to be faithful to his unfaithful wife by being faithful to their covenant of love and marriage. And so he sought her and found her at the auction block and bought her (redeemed) and took her back as his wife (no "bill of divorce"). That is a deed that blots out and forgets the wrong of unfaithfulness! That is forgiveness that restores and reconciles. It can come only from the inner resources of deity, from the heart of God that is compassionate steadfast love.

We have to ask also what is "new" in the new covenant on the part of Israel as the partner in the covenant. And so we come to a third point, namely, the promise: "*I will put my law within them, and I will write it on their hearts; and I will be their God, and they shall be my people*" (Jer. 31:31-34, emphasis added). This is contrasted with "the covenant that I made with their ancestors when I took them

. . . out of the land of Egypt—a covenant that they broke, though I was their husband" (31:32). Notice that it is the same law, the Torah, that is referred to, both in the old and in the new. Notice also that it is the same essence of the covenant that is operative in both the old and the new: God will be their God and they shall be his people. So then what is new with respect to the law? What is new is that the law will now be within them and will be written on their hearts. In the old covenant, the law came to them, was external to them, and was, as it were, imposed upon them by being a mandate for them to obey. Obedience was a matter of duty to an external legal authority. The law in the old covenant was written on tablets of stone by God and given to the people through Moses. In anger Moses threw the tablets of stone and broke them into pieces upon seeing the people worshiping the calf of Baal and dancing around it (Exod. 32:15-20; cf. Deut. 9:8-17). The cause for the breaking of the tablets of stone on which the law was written was the abomination of worshiping another god and disobeying the way of God. That covenant can thus be "broken" by the unfaithfulness of the people and by the anger of an agent of the law. But this time the law will be written on the heart, and obedience is to come from within. What the people are obeying is not something external to and imposed upon them anymore. It is within then; it is in their hearts. If they break it, they are breaking their heart, they are breaking the law—the inner law—of their own heart. In short, they would be ruining themselves by what they are doing on themselves.

What is "new" about the essence of the covenant? The old covenant was a structure that framed a relation. It is a way to walk on. This is not changed. What is new is knowing it from living in it and by it out of one's inner disposition, decision, and action. It is knowing it from within a living experience of it in which it validates itself precisely by being experienced. It is not merely a way to walk on. That stays. What is new is the walking on it, the actual journeying of life on it as the true way of life. Thus, one comes to know it as a way unmistakably by actually walking one's life on it. If the people depart from this way and choose another way, it is their own way that they walk on, and this way moves away from what leads to life; this way ends in the ruin of life (cf. Ps. 1). Thus, the breaking of the covenant by following another way is in fact a self-breaking, a self-shattering, a ruining of self by self! This vicious cycle of deed and consequence, what you sow is what you reap, of reward and punishment based on one's deed is the course of the old covenant. And so what would be "new" in the new covenant in relation to this retributive order? Strangely enough, the promise of the new covenant ends with God's resolve: "I will forgive their iniquity, and remember their sin no more" (Jer. 31:34). It is forgiveness that breaks the vicious cycle of retributive justice!

What the people will know of this God from their heart is the God who forgives iniquity and remembers sin no more, not the God who requites with impunity mercilessly as a judge any wrongdoing that breaks the law! They will know the God who inwardly turned to himself in a further resolve to be faithful to himself in being faithful to the covenant by mercifully forgiving sin and wrongdoing out of his generous steadfast love! It is God as forgiving and restoring and reconciling savior that "rightwises"—makes "righteous"—the covenant relationship, not the merciless God who retributes as judge!

We come to a fourth factor in the "new" that God is doing. *Jeremiah's view of the new covenant makes of the human heart as a "tablet" on which to write inwardly the Torah of God.* Ezekiel goes further than this: "A new heart I will give you, and a new spirit I will put within you; and I will remove from your body the heart of stone and give you a heart of flesh. I will put my spirit within you, and make you follow my statutes and be careful to observe my ordinances" (Ezek. 36:26-27; cf. 11:19-20). In the view of Ezekiel the heart on which the Torah was written (Jeremiah) has become a "heart of stone," as hard as the tablet of stone on which they were originally written. A heart of stone is a hardened heart. This is a heart that has become inured in disobedience. It has become obstinate in its own sinful way. It has become absolutely insensitive to any plea to change its ways. And so it cannot on its own initiate its own reform and renewal. It has to be removed, excised, and replaced with a new heart, "a heart of flesh." A heart bypass is not good enough. A heart transplant is what the Lord, the Surgeon of Life, will do! He cannot wait for the patient to initiate any move to renew himself, because he can't, given his hardened heart. The surgeon-God has to go ahead and do what needs to be done!

But a hardened heart to become flesh must be made alive. Only the Spirit can make a heart of stone become a heart of flesh by infusing or "breathing" into it its life-giving power. This is vividly pictured in the parable of the valley of dead bones. The Lord asked the prophet: "Can these bones live?" The prophet's answer: "O Lord God, you know." Of course, the prophet does not and cannot know! Then the Lord said, "I will cause breath to enter you, and you shall live. I will lay sinews on you, and will cause flesh to come upon you, and cover you with skin, and put breath in you, and you shall live; and you shall know that I am the LORD." And what God said he will do, he did and it happened (Ezek. 37:1-10). It may be construed that this action of God the Spirit is only a "revival," a renewal by Spirit. It is this, no doubt. But it is more than this: It is a parable of resurrection, of being raised to new life from the grave of death. Thus says the Lord God: "I am going to open your graves, and bring you up from your graves, O my people. I will put my spirit within you, and you shall live, and I will place you on your own soil; then you shall know that I, the Lord, have spoken and will act" (Ezek. 37:12-13). The new covenant then entails for Ezekiel the knowledge of God who gives new life with a new heart by the Spirit who raises the dead from the grave of sin and exile and enables one to follow the way of the Lord as set forth in his covenant and statutes and ordinances. All this is accomplished by the Spirit who comes to and stays within and works from within to inspire, to lead, to enable, and to achieve God's purpose for his people. This can be further illustrated by the oracle in Joel 2:28-31 (which was quoted by Peter in Acts 2:12-21). In this oracle God the Lord says:

> Then afterward I will pour out my spirit on all flesh; your sons and your daughters shall prophesy, your old men shall dream dreams, and your young men shall see visions. Even on the male and female slaves, in those days, . . . I will pour out my spirit. I will show portents in the heavens and on the earth, blood and fire and columns of smoke. The sun shall be turned to darkness, and the moon to blood, before the great and terrible day of the Lord comes. (Joel 2:28-31)

Here the Spirit is poured out upon all flesh. Flesh is dust made alive by the Spirit. It is the bodily form of the human. With the Spirit poured upon it, the human not only comes alive, but he does extraordinary things: children will prophesy; old men shall dream dreams; young men shall see visions. Flesh is stretched out of itself and reaches out to know the Lord who is in the midst of Israel (Joel 2:27).

There is a fifth element to this "new thing" that the Lord is doing. It is this: *as the people are restored to their land and soil, so the land and its soil are restored also to them as the habitat of life.* It will be again a home to them. The soil that has dried up and cannot produce oil and wine and milk will again be made productive so that the people will never again suffer famine and be a beggar for food. They will never again be humiliated by the nations. As a result of prosperity and peace, the people will multiply again and fill the city streets with inhabitants. The city of God, Jerusalem and its walls, will be rebuilt again (Ezek. 36:8-12, 30; cf. Isa. 41:17-19, etc.). All secular activity will be restored, resumed, and pursued for the benefits it will bring to the people (see Isa. 54–55). But it will not be a mere secularity, which would be no more than idolatry. It would be a new secularity within a new spirituality! Nature's fertility and its capacity to sustain life will never again be treated as an idol to be worshiped as in Baalism, but as a blessing from God the creator and savior to be received as a gift for life's nourishing and flourishing. A gift is to be received gratefully. But the giving is to be celebrated joyfully. But more than receiving and celebrating but inclusive of them is the worship and praise of the giver, for without the giver, there is no giving and without giving there is no gift, and without the gift of life by the life-giver life will not be nourished and flourish (Isa. 42:10-13, etc.). The renewing of the earth as a "garden of life," God's own garden (Ezek. 28:13) and so the renewal of all earthly secular activity as blessing, as benefit, is an element of the "new" that God is doing. It is a secularity that is permeated by the Spirit and so is worshipful of God. The secular is spiritual because of its worship of God in the Spirit, and the Spirit secularizes because it makes the secular worship God!

There is a sixth factor in the "new" that God is doing. *It is the promise of a new leadership.* A cause of the waywardness of Israel is the failure of its leadership in teaching, living, and leading. They failed to teach the Torah to the people. They themselves disobeyed the Torah in their lives. They were idolatrous and unjust and violent. And so they failed to lead as shepherds of God's people. This has been the perennial complaint of the prophets against king, priest, prophet, and elders. This complaint is vividly portrayed by Ezekiel:

> The word of the LORD came to me: Mortal, prophesy against the shepherds of Israel: prophesy, and say to them—to the shepherds: Thus says the Lord GOD: Ah, you shepherds of Israel who have been feeding yourselves! Should not shepherds feed the sheep? You eat the fat, you clothe yourselves with the wool, you slaughter the fatlings; but you do not feed the sheep. You have not strengthened the weak, you have not healed the sick, you have not bound up the injured, you have not brought back the strayed, you have not sought the lost, but with force and harshness you have ruled them. So they were scattered, because there was no shepherd; and scattered, they became food for all the wild animals. My sheep were scattered, they wandered over all the mountains and on every high hill; my sheep were scattered over all the face of the earth, with no one to search or seek for them. (Ezek. 34:1-6)

Out of this dismal and tragic failure of leadership in the old covenant, God the Lord has promised that a new leadership will come, modeled upon the leadership of David. In Isaiah 9:6-7 the power, authority, character, duties, scope, and length of this leadership are described.

> For a child has been born for us, a son given to us; authority rests upon his shoulders; and he is named Wonderful Counselor, Mighty God, Everlasting Father, Prince of Peace. His authority shall grow continually, and there shall be endless peace for the throne of David and his kingdom. He will establish and uphold it with justice and with righteousness from this time onward and forevermore (Isa. 9:6-7).

And in Isaiah 11:1-5, it is the Spirit of the Lord who does the anointing and resting upon him and so enables him to exercise and accomplish the duties of his leadership:

> A shoot shall come out from the stump of Jesse, and a branch shall grow out of his roots. The Spirit of the Lord shall rest on him, the spirit of wisdom and understanding, the spirit of counsel and might, the spirit of knowledge and the fear of the Lord. His delight shall be in the fear of the Lord. He shall not judge by what his eyes see, or decide by what his ears hear; but with righteousness he shall judge the poor, and decide with equity for the meek of the earth; he shall strike the earth with the rod of his mouth, and with the breath of his lips he shall kill the wicked. Righteousness shall be the belt around his waist, and faithfulness the belt around his loins. (Isa. 11:1-5)

In Isaiah 61:1-2 the leader is "anointed" by the Spirit to empower him to carry out his functions.

> The Spirit of Lord God is upon me, because the Lord has anointed me; he has sent me to bring good news to the oppressed, to bind up the broken-hearted, to proclaim liberty to the captives, and release to the prisoners; to proclaim the year of the Lord's favor, and the day of vengeance of our God; to comfort all who mourn. (Isa. 61:1-2)

In Ezekiel, it is God the Lord himself who will be the leader, the shepherd of his sheep. "I myself will be the shepherd of my sheep, and I will make them lie down, says the Lord God. I will seek the lost, and I will bring back the strayed, and I will bind up the injured, and I will strengthen the weak, but the fat and the strong I will destroy. I will feed them with justice" (Ezek. 34:15-16; cf. vv. 11-14).

Several points are worth noticing in these texts. Leadership is a gift of God to his people. It has many functions aimed at benefiting God's people: securing freedom, ruling justly, caring for the poor and needy, healing the broken-hearted, making the land productive and providing for prosperity, establishing peace and respecting the freedom of the Word of God to be proclaimed and heard, and celebrating the glory of God in worship and praise. Are not these the same services that leadership should attend to, even today? These are all secular activities and done by secular agents, then and now. But they are all done in the power and by the guidance of the Spirit knowingly or unknowingly. It is secular leadership imperceptibly and quietly authorized, inspired, empowered, and led by the Spirit. Truly, secular leadership cannot be other than spiritual. Leadership is a spiritual activity in secular forms and ways.

There is a seventh element in the "new" that God the Lord is doing. *It is the understanding of suffering borne in atoning sacrifice for the salvation of the world. This is Israel's mission of being called and sent to be "light to the nations."* This new understanding of suffering is what shines through in the so-called suffering servant songs in Isaiah (see 42:1-9; 49:1-6; 50:4-11; 52:13; 53:1-12). These texts have put together ideas drawn from the various traditions of Israel's faith into a new synthesis with such original profundity and far-reaching implications hitherto unheard of in Israel's faith traditions and never to be surpassed thereafter! They have also provoked critical controversy among scholars and interpreters, largely centering on the identity of the servant upon whose shoulders the weighty task has fallen.

We do not need to enter this controversy for our purposes in this book. We will simply adhere to the canon and regard Israel as the servant who is viewed both as a community and as an individual. In 42:1-9 the servant is presented by God the Lord as the nation of Israel, as one community. In 49:3 the servant is identified as Israel as a whole. But Israel also speaks as though it were an individual speaking as a whole (49:1-6). In 52:13–53:12 the servant is spoken of as one corporate nation. There are elements in the suffering servant text that belong to the faith traditions of Israel. We may note the following: God has a purpose for Israel, this purpose is connected with the blessing of humankind, and Israel has been chosen to be God's people in covenant with him to fulfill that purpose. In the course of struggling to fulfill that purpose Israel suffers because of its waywardness and is treated as a pariah among the nations. But Israel is made to come home from exile. Its homecoming is part of the "new" that God the Lord is now doing (42:8-9). So what is "new" about all this?

It is possible to locate what is "new" in the relation between the mission of God for Israel and the way it is to be carried out. The servant songs reiterate and reaffirm God's mission of blessing the nations through Israel. God the Lord says to his servant Israel: "It is too light a thing that you should be my servant to raise up the tribes of Jacob and to restore the survivors of Israel; I will give you as a light to the nations" (49:6). In fact, God's covenant with Israel is a covenant for the nations so that as God's people Israel may be "a light to the nations" (42:6). The details of the mission include, liberating the peoples from the prison of their blindness so that they may see what the light reveals, namely, "I am the LORD, that is my name; my glory I give to no other, nor my praise to idols" (42:8). But God's name is the name that "brings forth justice to the nations (42:3-4). This justice is God's righteousness that makes for shalom. It is what makes for right relation and order in creation and in human community. It is what brings fourth peace and prosperity among peoples so that they spontaneously break forth in joyful song and praise of God the creator and redeemer. Justice as righteousness is more than distributive and retributive justice. It is essentially and ultimately redemptive justice. And as such it is salvation. It is the purpose of God that the blessing of salvation is to be extended to all the "coastlands" and "to the end of the earth" (49:1, 6), and indeed, to all creation, for God's sovereignty is over all his works as creator, judge, and redeemer!

The critical question is, how is this mission to the nations to be carried out? How can Israel fulfill this mission to the nations? The fact of the matter is that these nations have given Israel nothing but suffering. It is the gods of these nations that tempted Israel to succumb to idolatry. It is the power play among these nations that made Israel wage war and become a victim of war. It is these nations that did violence upon Israel, destroying it as a nation and carrying off its best citizens into exile! Israel's sin compared with the sin and evil that the nations do among themselves and to Israel does not seem to merit the punishment meted out to it. This historical experience of Israel prompts Job to ask the theodicy question: Why do the righteous suffer and the wicked prosper (Job 21:7-14)? But the theodicy issue is still premised on the view of justice as retributive, as reward and punishment, as deed and consequence, blessing and curse! However, the question of Job is also a questioning of this premise. If the righteous should not suffer for their unrighteousness because they can make a good case for their righteousness, why then should they suffer (see Job's defense of his righteousness in Job 31:1-40; cf. 1:1-5, 8). For what do they suffer then? Is there a purpose for suffering other than bearing it as punishment for the sin one has lived in and done? It is the answer to this profound and poignant question that the "new" in what God is doing is to be found. It is a new understanding of suffering. The suffering of Israel for her sin is also at the same time a suffering for the sin of all. It is a vicarious suffering offered in sacrifice on behalf and for the atonement of the sin of all. This it seems to me is the core message of the suffering servant texts: "Surely he has borne our infirmities and carried our diseases. . . . He was wounded for our transgressions, crushed for our iniquities; upon him was the punishment that made us whole, and by his bruises we are healed. . . . The Lord has laid on him the iniquity of us all. . . . The righteous one, my servant, shall make many righteous, and he shall bear their iniquities" (Isa. 53:4-6, 11b).

Being righteous here is transformed from being right to bearing the wrong of others, from being obedient to being sacrificed for the good of others, from looking after one's own self-interest to serving the best interest of others, from being pure and principled and thus exposed to the danger of being self-righteous, to being responsive to and responsible for others. This is why the servant does not retaliate; this is why he won't lift up his voice in protest (like Jeremiah and Job). He won't break a bruised reed or quench a flickering wick, and yet he will not faint or be crushed until he achieves justice for all (42:1-4). The meaning of the election of Israel is the choice of one on behalf and for the sake of all. The election of Israel from among the many nations to be God's people is on behalf and for the sake of all peoples! This includes the suffering of Israel as vicarious. It is offered by God's will to be a self-offering for the sin of the many so that they may be redeemed and saved! And so if judgment brings about suffering for sin, bearing it on behalf of others for their good makes it redemptive and paves the way for the salvation of all!

Does the Spirit have anything to do with this profound transformation of the understanding of judgment and suffering as redemptive on the way to full salvation of all? Our claim is that it is not at all possible without the Spirit possibilizing and actualizing it. In 42:1 God the Lord said: "I have put my Spirit upon him." This is the same creative Spirit that brought forth creation (42:5). It is the same Spirit who created and formed the Servant "from the womb" (49:1-5). It is to the Servant that "the arm of the Lord [has] been revealed" (53:1). The "arm of the Lord" is none other than the power of God, and the power of God that creates, judges, reveals, and saves is none other than God the Spirit! Yes! The Spirit is deeply involved in the "new" understanding of judgment and suffering as vicarious sacrifice on behalf of and for the sake of the many. It is God the Spirit who makes possibility from non-possibility and who actualizes with the Word what is made possible!

In the light of this, we may want to ask, does the secular suffer? It does because it is creaturely and earthly and of this world. What does it suffer from? It has been judged and winnowed and made to suffer because of the many "isms" that it has spawned in its wake in becoming an idolatry, a secularism, a modern form of Baalism. But must it bear this punishment on behalf of and for the sake of the many, for humankind? My take is that it does. And it can because as a process—a process of secularization that deconstructs and desacralizes and relativizes, it will be purified of its reductionisms and absolutisms and become democratized! This iconoclastic work is the activity of the Spirit. But at the same time, it aims at nothing less than the border-limits and depth-limits of the global world! As the secular process globalizes, it is expanding to the limits of its creaturely, this-worldly, horizons both in depth and in breadth. Only as it is winnowed by suffering does it become a universal good for all. That winnowing for the good of all is an activity of the Spirit in our time!

There is one final thing that is "new" in what God the Lord is doing. *It is the making of "new heavens and a new earth,"* and that includes the making of Jerusalem into a new city and the land of which it is a part (Isa. 65:17-24). Why would this be "new"? It is new in relation to God's covenant with Noah in which he vowed he would never again destroy his creation and all life in it (Gen. 9:1-17). In surveying, as it were, the vastness and depth of redemption, renewal, and salvation that God seeks to bring about in the "new" he is doing, it "occurred" to him that it is not enough to ground his salvation in his creation that to a certain extent and degree has become part of the "former things to be forgotten." Perhaps God was asking himself, why pour new wine into old wineskins? Or sew a new cloth to an old one that has become a piece of rag? Can what is in creation be renewed and saved without renewing and saving all of creation, the heavens and the earth? It appears that God has decided not just to maintain creation as it is, but to remake it into new heavens and a new earth and all that is in it. And so God incredibly makes a new turn in his self-constitution and self-becoming as God. He not only turned outward to relate to his creation, and inward in anguish in judgment, but now he is turning forward, to a new future with a new vision for his creation! He makes a new promise that he alone can fulfill in the new future that he shall yet create. In turning forward to this new future for his creation, he at the same time creates a new future for himself into which he shall become if he is to be the God of this new future for his new creation! The covenant will have to be reworded to fit this new creation! "I will be a new God for this new creation and this new creation shall be mine, my own treasured possession!" I will be God not just for a people but for all peoples, and all peoples shall be my people! I will be God not just of this one land and the life on it, but God of all lands and of all life on it, and all land and all life shall be mine. There shall be a transformation of a magnitude not even seen before:

> The wolf shall live with the lamb, the leopard shall lie down with the kid, the calf and the lion and the fatling together, and a little child shall lead them. The cow and the bear shall graze, their young shall lie down together; and the lion shall eat straw like the ox. The nursing child shall play over the hole of the asp, and the weaned child shall put its hand on the adder's den. They will not hurt or destroy on all my holy mountain; for the earth will be full of the knowledge of the LORD as the waters cover the sea. . . . The wolf and the lamb shall feed together, the lion shall eat straw like the ox; but the serpent – its food shall be dust! They shall not hurt or destroy on all my holy mountain, says the LORD. (Isa. 11:6-9; cf. 65:25)

Can one at this stage catch a glimmering vision of God's future for himself? Is not God's future his vision that he shall be all in all, that is, that God in the fullness of his being—God in himself, God turned toward another, God turned inwardly for the other, and God turned forward in his new creation—shall be all in all that he has created; and alternatively, that all of his creation shall be in him? And that means the religaric/covenanting relationship shall have come full circle and thus be fulfilled to the full! That primordial relationship is nothing less than the bond of the Spirit who is himself that binding bond! It is the Spirit in the fullness of deity that shall be in all and all things in their fullness shall be in the fullness of God.

CHAPTER VIII

Wisdom as a Form of Secularity

1. A New Challenge to Israel's Faith

In the meanwhile, we may well ask, Do the elements that comprise the "new" that God promised to do and is about to do, when taken together as a vision for life, have any bearing on life in the world? Or put in our terms, for secular life? What would life in this world lived in a worldly way look like when it is seen in the light of the promise of the "new"? In seeking an answer to this question, we shall consider certain developments in Israel's postexilic faith that we may reasonably construe as having a bearing on secular knowledge and life. One development is the rise of Wisdom life and thought, with the claim that Wisdom is a form of secular life and knowledge. A second development is the emergence of an apocalyptic perspective, with the claim that life in this secular age has become so desperate in its incapacity to save itself so that only the intervention of God can redeem it. In short, the secular world and its life-form have reached a cul-de-sac and only God may and can save it in fulfillment of his promises. With the apocalyptic perspective, the prophetic "Day of the Lord," with its twofold feature of final judgment and redemption, comes to the fore in intense expectation of its fulfillment. This results, and so we claim, in the radical futurization of this *saeculum*, this time of the world. Or to use a more technical phrase: History is eschatologized; time and history do not only move toward but are met by the future in their end and fulfillment. We shall deal with Wisdom in this chapter and with Apocalyptic in the next.

Before dealing with these developments, it may help our understanding to take note of the historical situation in Israel following the Exile. The economy had been largely devastated. The sources of livelihood had dried up. The land laid fallow. Jobs were scarce. Local leadership was terribly weak. Faith and its spiritual resources were in crisis. The institution of the Temple had collapsed, and although a new Temple was to be built under the leadership of Nehemiah and Ezra, a new Temple institution eventually emerged in the form of postexilic rabbinic Judaism. The monarchy as a political institution had been ruined and Israel became a vassal of a succession of foreign rulers. This political status eventually had the effect of intensifying Israel's awareness that it is a chosen race and this was expressed in a militant nationalism and a deepening of its ethnocentrism, while at the same time it had to come to terms with the impact of the new cultural ethos of Hellenism.

Implicitly, this situation gives rise to the question of how to make sense of it in a way that would enable one to make the best out of it, and thus facilitate the negotiation of life in its daily, worldly concerns, problems, and prospects. After all, life in its everyday forms has to be negotiated regardless of the politics of the historical situation. And it has to be lived out of the resources that are provided by its heritage no matter how scarce and whatever new cultural winds are blowing across the landscape. Tapping these resources in response to the challenge of a changed situation may require developing new forms of piety and of thought and practice that may be necessary in order to survive with dignity. It may not be too far from the truth to claim that the developments mentioned above, as were exilic prophecy, the priestly tradition, and Deuteronomistic piety, are an immediate and responsible response to the postexilic situation of Israel out of the resources of its cultural heritage.

2. Wisdom Is Fear of the Lord

The first claim that we will seek to establish is that the knowledge of good and evil when pursued within the framework of "the fear of the Lord" becomes wisdom of the world. That is to say, Wisdom is a form of genuine secular life and knowledge when sought as beginning in and sustained by the fear of the Lord.

To understand the logic of this claim it might be helpful to recall the origin of wisdom as symbolized in the primordial account in Genesis 2–3. Becoming "wise" is there connected with acquiring the "knowledge of good and evil." This knowledge is the consequence of eating the fruit of the tree of the knowledge of good and evil. This tree is planted by God, together with the tree of life, in the garden of Eden, the garden of Delight, which garden primordially symbolized the goodness of creation. The tree of the knowledge of good and evil is in itself good because it is created by God. However, if one yields to the temptation of eating the fruit by being enticed by the serpent in order to become "wise like God," thus, disobeying God's command not to eat of its fruit, the result is inevitable mortality. The primordial woman saw the "tree was to be desired to make one wise," and so she ate of the fruit and gave some to her husband (Gen. 3:6). The eating of the fruit of the tree was motivated and precipitated by the desire to be "wise like God." God's response to this primal action confirms this desire and its deed but also sees in its movement the possibility of extending its reach to eat of the fruit of the tree of life and thus live forever like God (Gen. 3:22). But God would not let this happen. He did two things to prevent it from happening. First, he threw out the human being from the garden of Eden and returned him to the ground from which he is taken. Second, he placed a "cherubim, and a sword flaming and turning to guard the way to the tree of life," thus preventing the desire to be wise from reaching out to the life of God, which is eternal (Gen. 3:23-24).

The effect of this primordial deed of God is twofold. First, it confines the human to his earthly origin to which he shall return mortally, and make him secure his life by his own ken and toil and its pain from the resources of the earth that he must now till by the sweat of his brow. Second, it prevents the human from participating in the eternity of God, which is an attribute of his self-constitution and self-becoming as holy. There is no way for the human to treat himself as though he were a god. Thus, the "eating" (read: the pursuit) of the fruit of the knowledge of good and evil is confined inescapably to earthly existence and life, with all its worldly and human potential and perils. But this earthly pursuit is now deprived by God of its motive "to be like him," which is idolatrous. Accordingly, the proper domain of the pursuit of the knowledge of good and evil is the earthly, the natural, the human, and the worldly, in their cosmic setting; in a word, the secular realm. Essentially, wisdom is wisdom of and about the world.

Does this casting out of the human from the garden of Eden break the primordial relation between God and his creation, which we have termed the religaric bond or relationship? Absolutely not! When the knowledge of good and evil is pursued by developing the potentialities and possibilities of earthly existence and life and by observing their earthly limit as prescribed by God, then the motive of becoming like God, which seeks to usurp the holiness of God, is set aside and deprived of its tempting and enticing attraction. In its place is put "the fear of the Lord." When the desire to be wise by knowing good and evil is pursued in "the fear of the Lord" and is confined to its proper earthly domain, it becomes genuine secular, this-worldly wisdom. The theological axiom "The fear of the Lord is the beginning of wisdom" provides the ground, frame, substance, and dynamics of the pursuit of wisdom. It is this theological axiom that dominates Wisdom thought and practice (Job 1:1; 28:28; Prov. 1:7; 9:10; 15:33; Eccles. 12:13; Ben Sirach 1:11-28; 19:20). It thereby puts the pursuit of Wisdom within the religaric bond and makes it truly secular.

We cannot here provide a comprehensive and detailed treatment of the full range of Wisdom thought and practice. (The literature on Wisdom has become extensive and specialized, though only recently.) Such a treatment is both beyond my competence and is not the purpose of this section of the book. But we can highlight some of Wisdom's peculiar features, especially those that show their distinctively secular character, but are still consistent with the overall thrust of sapiential thought and practice. In a general sense the axiom "The fear of the Lord is the beginning of wisdom" runs like a red thread that weaves and knits together all the strands of Wisdom. Like the covenant formula and the Torah, it is two pronged. One prong directs attention to the reality of God. The other prong focuses concentration on human life in the everyday world. The issue of what connects the prongs and holds them together is implicit in the axiom, and we shall indicate our take on this issue in due course.

3. Secular Features of Wisdom

But when one examines the axiom more closely, one discovers certain features that are uniquely characteristic of sapiential perspective. To be sure, the phrase "fear of the Lord" means devotion to God. It does not mean being emotionally afraid of and threatened by God, but devoutly orienting all of life in the world toward God. It is the practice of being religious. It is lived-out piety. And so it is a form of spirituality. It assumes a religaric relationship to God, which includes acknowledging the majesty, uniqueness, and perfection of his holiness, trusting him without reservation, obeisance and obedience to him, and staying steadfastly and faithfully in this bonding relation to God. Implicit in this life of devotion to God is without doubt a certain and specific knowledge and understanding of God, which is peculiar to Wisdom and is a defining feature of it.

But this knowledge and understanding of God is a part of Wisdom itself. It is derived from the way Wisdom knows the world and of what it knows of the world. The reason for this is that "fear of the Lord" is not one-sidedly pronged toward God but also toward the world. Included in "fear of the Lord" is the beginning of wisdom; it is the beginning of knowing the world, which knowledge may be summed up as "knowledge of good and evil." Of course, Wisdom does not identify who God is with the world.

But what it knows and understands of God as true and distinctive of God is yielded by Wisdom's intense and critical reflection on everyday life in its various settings, concerns, and forms in the world. The way of Wisdom to God is from bottom up instead of from top down. It is a way of knowing God through the world and of practicing his presence in and for life in the world (Prov. 2:1-6). May not this be called a secular way of approaching God and coming to know and understand him?

To be sure, it is God who ultimately gives Wisdom: "For the LORD gives wisdom; from his mouth come knowledge and understanding" (Prov. 2:6). But he gives it only to those who seek it assiduously and discipline themselves accordingly, who live faithfully by its precepts of righteousness and justice and who thus reject the way of evil and avoid walking in the company of those who walk in the way of darkness, who rejoice in doing evil and delight in the perverseness of evil, whose paths are crooked and who are devious in their ways (Prov. 2:12-15). The fitting conclusion to this disciplined pursuit of Wisdom in the world is an exhortation of Wisdom itself: "Therefore walk in the way of the good, and keep to the paths of the just. For the upright will abide in the land, and the innocent will remain in it; but the way of the wicked will be cut off from the land, and the treacherous will be rooted out of it" (Prov. 2:20-22).

Note that the walking of "the way of the good and keeping to the paths of the just" are done "in the land"; it is the right way of living in the land. If this is the way Wisdom is sought and acquired, then God's giving of it is by meriting it. What God gives as Wisdom is through the world and what one receives as Wisdom is wisdom of the world, and what may be known of God through the world is what Wisdom knows of God. If "the fear of the Lord" as devotion to God is a form of piety turned to the world for life in the world, then is it far from the truth to say that it is a piety, a spirituality, that secularizes?

Another characteristic of wisdom is that it is sought and found in daily life in its various settings with its attendant concerns. For example: family life and the education of the young, the proper use of language, trade and commerce, being poor and being rich, attitudes and values, right behavior in various settings, character and reputation, good governance and the good it brings to land and people, a loose woman and a good wife. In all these situations and concerns the sage clearly compares and contrasts what is wise with folly, the good with the bad, the righteous with the wicked, what builds up with what tears down, what prospers with what ruins, what enhances life and its joys with what makes for its ruin and its sorrow. He uses keen observation and expertly employs rational and critical reflection in seeking understanding and insight into the way things are. He seeks to discern the meaning and purpose of life and its world in his effort to find what would best guide the negotiation of life in a world full of pitfalls, and thus lead it to its well-being and fulfillment. The rewards of wise living that conforms to the way things are include health and long life; wealth and prosperity; honor and fame; a happy family with a good wife and many children; and in the larger community, order, justice, security, peace, and prosperity. And the way wisdom presents its insights for wise living is not by way of command demanding obedience, not by prescription with sanctions that leaves no room for maneuver and choice, not by ideas and theories for contemplation, but by making the options clear and pointing to the likely results of a choice. The responsibility to discern and to decide and to act and to live accordingly is left to the seeker of wise guidance for a life of well-being. Wisdom is pragmatic in aim and practical in means.

What would be the appropriate take on the issues just considered—the search for wisdom in the concerns and prospects of daily life in the world, the various themes that are treated, the method of observation and reflection that is employed, the presentation of insights that challenge the seeker of wisdom to discern and decide and act, the rewards of wise living? Are not these elements of genuine secularity? But there is more that can and must be said. Even more important, we can say that wisdom is the "fear of the Lord." This can be said the other way around. "The fear of the Lord" is wisdom" (Sir. 1–2). It is the practice of devotion to God. While secular in form and pragmatic in operation, it is spiritual in substance. It is not only the thrust of wisdom to discern God's reality in daily life in its setting and concerns, but to "practice the presence of God" even in the most mundane of tasks, such as kitchen activities (Brother Lawrence), in daily life. From the perspective of wisdom, the secular world is not only the horizon in which God is to be sought and found, it is also the arena where his reality, his presence, his blessing are to be lived out faithfully. The secular is not only the vessel of the spiritual, it is realized in it. This is this legacy of wisdom that must be recovered if spirituality is to mean something for life in today's world!

4. Wisdom and the Moral Order

But there is more to wisdom than its patently secular thrust. The fact that there is good and evil in the world and that the way of the good is so much better for the negotiation of life than the way of the wicked and to walk that way is indeed wise living, clearly and unmistakably indicate that reality is morally structured. There is embedded in the way things are an order that guides the dynamism in things and anticipates the likely results of their behavior. This order is what gives a sense of right and wrong in the nature of things. It is a moral order that makes moral sense. Built into this order and its sense is a kind of law that operates by rewarding right behavior and sanctioning wicked activity. What one sows is what one reaps, and most likely the harvest is more than what one has planted. One may sow a wind, but reap a whirlwind! That holds true for both a good and a bad harvest. The moral order works out retributively; it follows necessarily the causal logic of act and consequences: Justice is inexorably retributive. For the most part of history, including the history of wisdom and law, this is the way the shape of justice is seen and how it operates.

It is this moral structure, retributive operation, and moral sense that endow reality with a degree of stability, a measure of reliability and predictability, and some sense of certainty in what to do and what to expect.

One is thus able to negotiate life with some measure of confidence and hope, while at the same time, reckon with chance and change. This view of justice and its retributive order are at the center of things and hold them together in the face of the threat that they might fall apart. This sense of the moral order in the nature of things is elemental to wisdom, for wisdom axiomatically consists in the knowledge of good and evil mediated by experience and gained by observation, reflection, and discernment in the way life is lived in the world. Secularity includes an insight into, a deep sense of, and an inner constraint to conform to, the moral order of things. These features of secularity are an elemental dimension of wisdom. Thus, the piety of wisdom—its fear of the Lord—is inescapably secularizing.

The question may be asked as to how "the sense of the presence of God" (John Baille), the moral order and the sense of it, get embedded in the nature of things and make themselves accessible to human living, knowing, and doing? This question and its answer bring us to another defining characteristic of wisdom, namely, its connection with the theological view of reality as creation and of God as creator. To be sure, the beliefs in God as creator and of reality as creation are not peculiar to wisdom. These beliefs are shared by wisdom with Priestly, Yahwistic, Deuteronomistic, and Prophetic traditions especially in the postexilic situation in which they reached the peak of their development. So what is distinctive about the connection of wisdom with creation? For one thing, wisdom is personified as created by God:

> The Lord created me at the beginning of his work, the first of his acts of long ago. Ages ago I was set up, at the first, before the beginning of the earth. When there were no depths I was brought forth, when there were no springs abounding with water. Before the mountains had been shaped, before the hills, I was brought forth—when he had not yet made earth and fields, or the world's first bit of soil. When he established the heavens, I was there, when

> he drew a circle on the face of the deep, when he made firm the skies above, when he established the fountains of the deep, when he assigned to the sea its limit ,so that the waters might not transgress his command, when he marked out the foundations of the earth, then I was beside him, like a master worker; and I was daily his delight, rejoicing before him always, rejoicing in his inhabited world and delighting in the human race. (Prov. 8:22-31; cf. Sir. 1:9a)

This means that wisdom is framed by the parameters and limits of creation that God the creator himself has determined. Wisdom has the dignity and status of a creature, and thus she shares with all of creation the contingency and dependency upon God of all things created by him. These parameters and limits, however, cannot be crossed by wisdom without consequence. They are guarded by the cherubim of the flaming sword ready to be thrust upon anyone who would transgress the boundary between creator and creation (Gen. 3:22-23). The holiness of God, which is Godself itself, enshrouds the mystery of God even from his creatures and all of his creation. Indeed, to observe this limit, to confine itself within its parameters, and to discern that there is a mystery that cannot be penetrated is itself the better part of wisdom. In short, it is wisdom for wisdom to enjoy its creaturely dignity and status and to exalt in its earthly this-worldly reality.

For another thing, though a creature of God, it is paradoxically by the agency of wisdom that God created the heavens and the earth. Wisdom is the "master worker" through whose skill God the creator crafted and built the heavens and the earth: "The LORD by wisdom founded the earth; by understanding he established the heavens; by his knowledge the deeps broke open, and the clouds drop down the dew" (Prov. 3:19-20; cf. 8:22-31).

Sirach puts it this way: "It is he who created her; he saw her and took her measure; he poured her out upon all his works" (1:9). As created by God and as God's agent in creation, wisdom is thus built and "infused" into the structure, potencies, dynamics, and possibilities of creation. And since what God has created is good and only he creates good, goodness is objective in and spread out across creation. Moreover, the means of pursuing wisdom by human thinking, knowing, deciding, doing, and living are indeed part of wisdom itself and the wise use and practice of them in the pursuit of wisdom are themselves a part of wisdom. Furthermore, since goodness is in creation and can be found in creation, it is what is to be pursued singleheartedly and persistently by wisdom. It is the goodness of creation and in creation that must be mined in specific forms and portions out of the rich mineral goodness of creation. The fact that good is paired with evil, wisdom with folly, right with wrong, justice with wickedness profoundly means that the good is an option for choice; it is to be preferred over what is not good. That choice is left to human freedom to make and so bring it into reality by human action. The dignity of human freedom is precisely the making of this choice. Sirach puts it well:

> I was he who created humankind in the beginning, and he left them in the power of their own free choice. If you choose, you can keep the commandments, and to act faithfully is a matter of your own choice. He has placed before you fire and water; stretch out your hand for whichever you choose. Before each person are life and death, and whichever one chooses will be given. For great is the wisdom of the Lord; he is mighty in power and sees everything; his eyes are on those who fear him, and he knows every human action. He has not commanded anyone to be wicked, and he has not given anyone permission to sin (Sir. 15:14-20)

Wisdom through human activity in realizing the good of creation for human life and its well-being participates in the creative activity of God the creator. The potential for human good in creation which the pursuit and practice of wisdom can realize is enormous in variety and range. It is as wide and manifold as creation itself. No wonder the arena of wisdom is creation itself. Its pursuit is not merely national and confined to a particular culture; it is multicultural and international. It is not merely local, confined to everyday life in the everyday world. It is also at the same time global or universal, for the good it discerns and realizes is also global and universal. It applies anywhere and anytime it fits. Wisdom is both local and global. Its measure, though determined by God the creator, is both the here and now, and the once and for all and always. Wisdom is the wisdom of both the *saecularis* and the *saeculum*. It is secular wisdom; it is the wisdom of the world.

Wisdom in its early provenance includes reference to and to some extent appropriates the wisdom of Egypt and of Mesopotamia. There is hardly any mention of the saving events and the heroes of Hebrew salvation history. The history of salvation seems scarcely known to the sages. No remembrance of deliverance from Egypt, no journey in the wilderness, no Moses and the covenant and the Torah, no Judges, no monarchy, and no prophets. But much later on in Sirach wisdom is indissolubly connected with Israel and the Torah.

> Wisdom praises herself, and tells of her glory in the midst of her people. In the assembly of the Most High she opens her mouth, and in the presence of his hosts she tells of her glory. . . . "Then the Creator of all things gave me a command, and my Creator chose the place for my tent. He said, 'Make your dwelling in Jacob, and in Israel receive your inheritance.' . . . In the holy tent I ministered before him, and so I was established in Zion. Thus in the beloved city he gave me a resting place, and in Jerusalem was my

> domain. . . . All this is the book of the covenant of the Most High God, the law that Moses commanded us as an inheritance for the congregations of Jacob. (Sir. 24:1-2, 8, 10-11, 23; see also chaps. 44–50, which deal with selected heroes of Israel's past and the encomiums showered by wisdom upon them.)

Not only is wisdom connected with Israel's history of salvation but it also reckoned with the ethos of Hellenism as a result of Israel's contact with the culture of Greece as spread out by Alexander the Great and the rulers that succeeded him and divided among themselves the vast empire that he established by military conquest and cultural subjugation (the Wisdom of Solomon). Thus, wisdom makes its inroads into and penetrates the depths of the world's potencies for good in the service of human well-being.

Wisdom as creation and as agent of creation takes us into the issue of the relation of wisdom to the Spirit and Word of God in Genesis 1 as treated in chapter 2 of this book. A few important things are to be noted as in line with the purpose of this book. First, the Spirit and Word are from God and are of God. They are "uncreated." They partake of Godself and are elemental in God's self-becoming in his self-turning to creation. Wisdom does not have this prior order and dignity because she is created by God and thus enjoys the dignity and status of being a creature. Wisdom is encompassed by creaturely parameters and limits that are "marked" by God as creator, and they cannot be crossed by wisdom because by so doing she loses her character and value as wisdom. Moreover, the possibility of wisdom being created out of its non-possibility is the work of the Spirit and its coming to be precisely as wisdom is the work of God's speaking his word of "letting be." Wisdom as being created is thus contingent upon God's Spirit and Word.

But wisdom is said to be the agent of creation. Certainly, this agency cannot be identified with the agency of Spirit and Word, since it is these that created wisdom. In what sense may we then understand the agency of wisdom in creation? Would it be far from the truth to suggest that wisdom is the continuing structure that frames creation and exhibits and expresses the "good" of creation in terms of created being, existence, order, time, space, consciousness, life, the human being as image of God, the blessing of life in its capacity to participate in its self-creativity, and all these together as a whole—as heaven and earth? These forms and aspects of the goodness of creation are revealed by wisdom in their earthly portions and are thus to be sought, found, realized, practiced, and enjoyed in their worldly settings in daily life within the horizon of heaven and earth. If this be true of wisdom, then our theological take on all this is that wisdom is the secular form and agent of Spirit and Word in creation. It is the dynamism of the Spirit and the structure of the Word that are at the heart of secular wisdom. Thus, the substance of the secular is spiritual. One cannot be spiritual without being secular, and one cannot be secular without being spiritual.

The implication of this take or claim for life in today's world are deep and far-reaching. It could mean that all the good in creation that can be known and practiced for the enhancement of life's well-being in all its specific forms—cosmic, natural, human, cultural—could thus be made pleasing to God. Wisdom is spiritual in substance although secular in form. It could mean that nothing so secular and so mundane and so lowly as cooking food and cleaning utensils is not penetrated by and infused with the Spirit. It could mean that nothing so secular and so mundane and so lofty as governing a country or running an industrial empire with all sorts of technologically sophisticated means and highly qualified people with a secular mind-set and a secular scale of values is bereft of the Spirit's dynamism and the Word's actualizing and ordering activity, which are at the heart of worldly wisdom. Creation and its wisdom are within the binding ambit of the religaric bond!

5. The Underside of Wisdom: Job

What we have said about wisdom so far is what is traditionally common to wisdom thought and practice. All of it deals with the positive side—the goodness of creation to be sought and practiced in wisdom. There is, however, a negative side to wisdom. It arises out of its defining character as knowledge of good *and* evil. Reality as experienced and known in wisdom comes in pairs. As put by Sirach: "Like clay in the hand of the potter, to be molded as he pleases, so all are in the hand of their Maker, to be given whatever he decides" (Sir. 33:13-15) and "Good is the opposite of evil, and life the opposite of death; so the sinner is the opposite of the godly. Look at all the works of the Most High; they come in pairs, one the opposite of the other" (Sir. 42:24-25).

To be sure, this piece of Scripture has a positive side, which we have already noted. That reality comes in pairs means it presents options for choice, and so accords human freedom the opportunity to decide and to act, that the good is to be preferred over the wicked because it assures life's well-being, that God is sovereign and he governs justly by rewarding the good and punishing the wicked.

But the text and the point of view it represents have difficulties in dealing with the anomalies of life. For one thing, there is in wisdom a built-in ambiguity in experiencing and knowing reality as both good and evil. One cannot have the good without evil being in it in some measure; and one cannot become wicked without some degree of good being present in one's folly. Although striking a balance between good and evil may be a wise policy behavior, one never knows the right balance and when one side of the scale tips over to the other side. And when the balance is tipped in favor of the wicked side, it may be too late to rectify it. It is in the nature of ambiguity that there is not one and only one view of reality or of only one correct way of dealing with it. And even if a right balance is achieved, it is still composed of both good and evil. And so, one may ask, who can rightfully judge between good or evil when one is unavoidably involved in both? Certainly, not the one who in thought and practice is inevitably involved in both.

Moreover, and more seriously and importantly, if one through the pursuit of wisdom seeks to resolve the ambiguity through to the end by following either the logic of the good and so be purely good, or the logic of evil and so become wholly evil, or of both so that one is both good and evil, one inevitably is brought face to face with the parameters and limits of wisdom that it cannot cross. This effort at resolution will make it crystal clear that one cannot clearly distinguish the one from the other, let alone separate them and accordingly deal with each separately. And if one takes them both together, how can one pass just or correct judgment when both mutually entail and are involved in each other? Furthermore, the cul-de-sac is not a logical dead-end. It is coming face-to-face with limit situations that are existential and not merely logical! The ambiguities point to anomalies and contradictions that are in the nature of things. It would be wise, and so a part of wisdom, to acknowledge them, ask questions about them, and accept the fact that there may not be a way of resolving them from the side of wisdom and its resources.

In what follows, we will deal illustratively with three existential limit life-situations, namely, the experience of human suffering, the fact of death, and the question of the meaning of life.

In the perspective of wisdom, human suffering is grounded in a deeply held theological assumption that human suffering is punishment for sin and wickedness, and a long, fruitful, and prosperous life is a reward for righteous living, that is, fear of God. The way God deals justly is based on the causal logic of act and consequence. Justice is therefore by nature retributive. What a human sows, he reaps. In the book of Job, this view is strongly represented by Job's three friends who visited him to comfort him in his affliction. It is a view gained from both observation and religious experience and therefore unquestionably true. Eliphaz presents this view to Job to persuade him that this understanding of his suffering should bring him comfort:

> "Is not your fear of God your confidence, and the integrity of your ways your hope? Think now, who that was innocent ever perished? Or where were the

upright cut off? As I have seen, those who plow iniquity and sow trouble reap the same. By the breath of God they perish, and by the blast of his anger they are consumed." (Job 4:6-9)

As the dialogue between Job and his friend moves on, Job refuses to be persuaded by this view. He insists on his integrity and asks where he has erred: "Teach me, and I will be silent; make me understand how I have gone wrong" (6:24). Whereupon Eliphaz catalogs a series of wrongdoing and applies them to Job to prove his point that Job's affliction is punishment for his sins:

Is it for your piety that he reproves you, and enters into judgment with you? Is not your wickedness great? There is no end to your iniquities. For you have exacted pledges from your family for no reason, and stripped the naked of their clothing. You have given no water to the weary to drink, and you have withheld bread from the hungry. The powerful possess the land, and the favored live in it. You have sent widows away empty-handed, and the arms of the orphans you have crushed. Therefore snares are around you, and sudden terror overwhelms you, or darkness so that you cannot see; a flood of water covers you. (Job 22:4-11)

But Job denies the allegations of wickedness. He insists on his integrity. Why then is he afflicted? Increasingly Job was realizing that the traditional religious dogma that justice is retributive, that suffering is punishment for sin, does not apply to him because of his innocence, nor does it apply to sinners in their wickedness. The justice of act and consequence is a false religious perspective and Job rejects it as groundless. So now Job states his rejection rhetorically:

Why do the wicked live on, reach old age, and grow mighty in power? Their children are established in their presence, and their offspring before their eyes. Their houses are safe from fear, and no rod of God is upon them. Their bull breeds without fail; their cow calves and never miscarries. They send out their little ones like a flock, and their children dance around. They sing to the tambourine and the lyre, and rejoice to the sound of the pipe. They spend their days in prosperity, and in peace they go down to Sheol. (Job 21:7-13)

Not only do the wicked prosper, but precisely in their prosperity they reject God and claim that their prosperity is their own achievement (21:14-15). And they do all this without being punished (21:17-18, 23-24, 30-31).

Why then is Job being punished for fearing God and keeping his integrity and his avoidance of evil? (Job 1:1). He vehemently insists on his innocence:

"As God lives, who has taken away my right, and the Almighty, who has made my soul bitter, as long as my breath is in me and the Spirit of God is in

> my nostrils, my lips will not speak falsehood, and my tongue will not utter deceit. Far be it from me to say that you are right; until I die I will not put away my integrity from me. I hold fast my righteousness, and will not let it go; my heart does not reproach me for any of my days." (27:2-6)

Since Job rejects the views of his friends and finds no comfort in what they say, he now turns away from them: "How then will you comfort me with empty nothings? There is nothing left of your answers but falsehood" (21:34). His three friends in turn ceased talking to Job "because he was righteous in his own eyes" (32:1). But their point of view is taken up by Elihu, a younger man who now speaks to Job (chaps. 32–37). Elihu repeats to Job in more passionate terms what he already heard from his three friends. Elihu accuses Job of self-conceit, and self-righteousness, and blasphemy:

> "For Job has said, 'I am innocent, and God has taken away my right; in spite of being right I am counted a liar; my wound is incurable, though I am without transgression.' Who is there like Job, who drinks up scoffing like water, who goes in company with evildoers and walks with the wicked? For he has said, 'It profits one nothing to take delight in God'" (34:5-9). For his self-conceit and blasphemy Job has been judged by God rightly by afflicting him and the judgment is retributive justice based on the act-and-consequence logic: "Therefore, hear me you who have sense, far be it from God that he should do wickedness, and from the Almighty that he should do wrong. For according to their deeds he will repay them, and according to their ways he will make it befall them. Of a truth, God will not do wickedly, and the Almighty will not pervert justice. . . . Therefore mortals fear him; he does not regard any who are wise in their own conceit." (34:10-12; 37:24)

Elihu's speech also falls within what Job has rejected as "empty nothings" (21:34).

We must note carefully what Job is rejecting as "falsehood" and "empty nothings." He is not rejecting God as such. What he finds unacceptable is an understanding of God that underpins and supports the idea of God's justice as primarily retributive. This idea of God and its consequent view of justice is well entrenched in religious traditions, not only in Israel and its surrounding cultures but also elsewhere (as in the law of Karma). Job's bold and courageous rejection of it is an instance in the history of religions of iconoclastic movements that shatter religious images, doctrines, and practices that no longer illuminate the depths and complexities of human experience. They no longer serve as resources for negotiating life with some measure of confidence and hope.

Today in our postmodern conditions, we are also rejecting certain ideas about God that are no longer helpful in our efforts to come to terms with the problems and prospects of life that confront us. For example, "the God up there," a supernaturalist God, and its consequent corollary of a God who from time to time intervenes in nature by suspending its laws, or in human affairs by restricting the creativity of freedom, does not seem to ring a bell anymore in today's world. Nor is the idea of a God who created the universe with its own laws and potentialities and then left it to its own devices and the working out of its own destiny, the so-called "God the watchmaker," is also being abandoned. The penchant to make the idea of God explain what in the nature of things cannot be explained by reason or science—the so-called God of the gaps—is no longer rationally tenable. The immutable God who cannot change and is immune to suffering and has no inner sympathy for the messiness of the human condition no longer has any sympathetic appeal to many. A God who makes himself real and worthy of worship by insulting people in their dignity by making them feel like worms and maggots and treating them like beggars of mercy because of their sin and guilt—"a God of hellfire and brimstone"—strikes many as an unworthy deity that has not even a vestige of humanity, let alone humaneness, in him. One may sum up all these rejected ideas of God as anti-earthly, antiworldly, antihuman; in short antisecular. But this does not mean that the idea of God has been abandoned. People still want to be spiritual and at the same time secular without being traditionally religious. What kind of God would sustain and validate such a search for a new spirituality?

At this point the piety of secular wisdom has reached its final limit. It cannot proceed any further. Its pursuit comes to a dead end! This prompts the writer of the book of Job to ask plaintively: "But where shall wisdom be found? . . . Where then does wisdom come from? And where is the place of understanding? It is hidden from the eyes of all living, and concealed from the birds of the air. Abaddon and Death say, 'We have heard a rumor of it with our ears.' God understands the way to it, and he knows its place. For he looks to the ends of the earth, and sees everything under the heavens" (28:12, 20-24). Where is wisdom to be found? It cannot be found anywhere in the world. "It is hidden from the eyes of the living." What is known about it is that it is merely a "rumor" heard from Death and the realm of the dead. It is not a truth to be found in the land of the living. This is rather strange. Is not wisdom the truth of the world gained from actually living in it, experiencing in its day-to-day routine, and reflecting on its problems and prospects? Is not wisdom the crystallization in thought and practice for the well-being of life the insights that one has mined out of the rich ore of human experience? Why is such wisdom nowhere to be found now by a seeker desperately in need of it?

It would seem that the wisdom Job is looking for is not anymore the wisdom of the world. That wisdom as represented by his friends is knowledge of good and evil and holds that the good is rewarded and the evil is punished. That kind of wisdom does not hold true to his experience, for he is righteous and yet he suffers severely while the wicked prosper without impunity. This wisdom has become for Job a conundrum that he wants resolved, but whose resolution cannot be found in the resources provided by the wisdom of the world. The wisdom of the world has its limits and when it reaches those limits it cannot by itself resolve, it looks for a wisdom wiser that its own. Job appears to be seeking for God's wisdom, and God knows this wisdom and he knows the way to it. Indeed, does wisdom have a dimension that is not a part of creation, but is in fact "before" creation? Is not wisdom the agent of creation? If so, then is not wisdom the ground of creation and is indeed presupposed by creation itself? Wisdom in its pre-creation dimension is what limits the wisdom of the world. That dimension is to be found in God at the limit or the boundary between God and his creation. What is that boundary limit? Is it not a mediating limit, an in-between boundary, a bonding limit? May not one construe this bonding limit as the religaric bond? And is it not the Spirit that binds in this bond the force that inspires Job to ask, where is wisdom to be found? That question can only be asked out of the depths of that bond that at the same time shows the boundary between God and his creation.

6. Wisdom and the Search for God

Since God is the source of a wisdom wiser than the wisdom of the world, Job now turns to God and decides to bring his case before him, and make his defense in the hope that God will listen, explain why Job has been made to suffer grievously in spite of his fear of God, his integrity, and his innocence, and finally vindicate him:

> Then Job answered: "Today also my complaint is bitter; his hand is heavy despite my groaning. Oh, that I knew where I might find him, that I might come even to his dwelling! I would lay my case before him, and fill my mouth with arguments. I would learn what he would answer me, and understand what he would say to me. Would he contend with me in the greatness of his power? No; but he would give heed to me. There an upright person could reason with him, and I should be acquitted forever by my judge. (Job 23:1-7)

But will God be found? Will he hear and answer Job? Will God confirm his rejection of his friend's understanding of God and replace its concepts of justice? If that was to happen, what kind of God would he be? How different would he be from the God of his friends?

In turning to God to bring his "bitter complaint" before him, the first thing Job must do is to find God (23:3). Job has just rejected the traditional images and ideas about God espoused by his friends. But does he have a new vision of God that would lead him to where he is and thus find him? But scarcely has he turned in search of God when he is immediately and severely frustrated. The God Job is looking for desperately is nowhere to be found. Can he be found in space? Job complains: "If I go forward, he is not there; or backward, I cannot perceive him; or the left he hides, and I cannot behold him. I turn to the right, but I cannot see him" (23:8-9). Indeed, God cannot be found within space. He is not an object in space. Are not our images and ideas shaped by space? And if God is not space and is beyond space so that he cannot be shaped by space, could space represent him? Is not the reverse the case: that God created space and is no part of it as its creator, that he shaped it, and put its limits to it but is not limited by those limits?

Can God be found in time? Job complains: "Why are times not kept by the Almighty, and why do those who know him never see his days?" (24:1). Indeed, God cannot be found within time. He is not an event within time that happens in time. He is not timed by time. And so if our images and ideas of God are timed by time, they appear and disappear; they occur and pass away. They fleet away with time. How then can they represent what is "before" time and "over" time, and "after" time? Did not God create time by making it begin and so he is not a part of time; he is without beginning? Did he not divide time into night and day, and so is it not he who appoints time for what he makes happen in it? It is not Job or we who make an appointment with him for what we want to happen, and expect him to honor the appointment. God is not at our beck and call.

Will God hear his bitter complaint? His complaint is no longer against his friends, but against God whose "hand" is "heavy" upon him, although he is already "groaning" in pain (23:2). And he is not alone in his misery!

> There are those who snatch the orphan child from the breast, and take as a pledge the infant of the poor. They go about naked, without clothing; though hungry, they carry the sheaves; between their terraces they press out oil; they tread the wine presses, but suffer thirst. From the city the dying groan, and the throat of the wounded cries for help; yet God pays no attention to their prayer. (Job 24:9-12)

So now, not only is God hidden and cannot be found, he is also insensitive and indifferent to human suffering and misery. "God pays no attention to their prayer."

And yet Job believes firmly that he has not done anything to deserve his suffering: "But he knows the way that I take; when he has tested me, I shall come out like gold. My foot has held fast to his steps; I have kept his way and have not turned aside. I have not departed from the commandment of his lips; I have treasured in my bosom the words of his mouth" (23:10-12). So why is he now being punished? God is not only insensitive and indifferent, he is also unjust! Job is afraid to face God because he can do as he pleases (23:13). "I am terrified at his presence; when I consider, I am in dread of him" (23:15). So now God is not only unjust; he can also be a terror. But still fervently believing that God would hear his case, Job even prepared a brief in his defense. He listed all the deeds prohibited by God's commandments and he knows he has not disobeyed them (31:1-40). His conscience is clear. And at the end of his brief as a full account of his life, he put his signature signifying finality to his brief and submitting it for resolution (31:35-37). He believed that in God's court, "an upright person could reason with him, and I should be acquitted forever by my judge" (23:7).

7. Revelation in Dialogue

Lo and behold, God answers Job! (Job 38:1). Before proceeding any further, it would be appropriate here to say that it is not within the competence of the author to give a detailed exegetical exposition of God's answer to Job (chaps. 38–41). But we can suggest some theological reflection on some of the highlights of God's answer. We can begin the reflection by what we think is entailed by God's answering. Is it wrong to surmise that before answering Job, God was in fact already listening in silence to the dramatic dialogue between Job and his friends? Was he not also sympathizing with Job's suffering and misery and listening to his bitter complaint? Did he not realize that the one central subject around which the whole conversation revolved is God himself and the way he governs his creation and deals with the good and evil in it? Did he not take note of the fact that the parties in the dialogue have taken up various positions regarding him and evaluated his ways of dealing with his creatures? Was he not amused by the sort of images and ideas with which the parties in the dialogue represented him to each other? Was he really that sort of God?

Was he really obliged to answer in the first place?

Is it not the case that to give an answer presupposes a question asked? The question may be a specific one to which a specific answer may be given. Or it may be a general question that may require a general but relevant answer. Or it may be a particular question arising from a general condition with a general implication, and the answer could be directed to the particularity of the question but with clear general implications, or the answer could be of a general character with clear specific implications. It not only appears that the question of Job has arisen from his particular experience of personal suffering but also it articulates suffering as a human condition experienced generally. The answer of God addressed to Job does not directly address the particular question raised by Job. However, it sets it in a general context that has clear implications for Job's particular question.

In any case, the point of all this is to argue that asking a question from whatever situation and in whatever form, and giving an answer whether directly addressing the issue at hand or not, presupposes a fundamental relationship between asking a question and giving an answer. The question may be formulated logically and so it may ask for a logical answer, in which case a logical relation is entailed. The question may be about a legal issue requiring a legal answer. The relation is thus a legal one. The question may arise out of a moral problem and the answer may assume that reality may be morally structured and it may therefore be shaped morally. The question may ask about reality and its nature and so the answer may be an ontological one.

But in all this, are not the asking and the answering an exercise in, and an expression of, a *dialogical* relationship? And may not a dialogical relationship rest upon, and is an exercise of, a deeper and more fundamental relationship, which we have referred to as the *religaric* relationship? This more fundamental level would embrace various types of dialogical relations such as those mentioned above, and illustrated by the dialogue between friends, a conversation between equals. The religaric relation would also embrace the covenantal relationship, which could be a relation between unequal parties. We have claimed that in the covenantal relationship God, in his self-creation and self-development as God, has turned to an other—his creation and his people—to be God for this other and for this other to be his! We have claimed further that in the religaric relationship, it is God who has taken the initiative and has established it through his Spirit and Word precisely in the act of creation. The bonding is made by God himself.

Thus, may it not be claimed that God is, as it were, duty bound to answer Job since in doing so he is being faithful to himself as the God for this other and at the same time is fulfilling his commitment to this other. God may not want to step out of this relation, nor would Job. Together they are bound by the religaric relation.

But although the parties in this basic relation are duty bound to ask and answer, the acts of asking and of answering are still a free decision. They are an act of sovereign freedom. They are an act of free initiative. But since the asking and answering are done within the religaric relation, they are not only free but also responsive. The asking expects to be responded to and the answering intends to address the asking.

This means that to ask or to answer has at least two characteristic features. First, to ask arises out of who one is in one's situation of knowing and not knowing. The question indicates where the asking or the answering is coming from. One cannot ask if one does not know in some sense what it does not know yet, but wants to know. But if one already knows, there is no point in asking. Asking arises out of the situation of knowing and not knowing. The philosopher Alfred North Whitehead wisely said: "Not ignorance, but ignorance of ignorance is the death of knowledge." Second, the asking intends to be answered, and is thus directed to a source that can provide an answer to what is sought. That source may also be a part of the question and must also be sought. Both these aspects characterize the asking of Job. The answering has a similar structure. To answer comes from who one is. The answer conveys the identity of the one who answers. The answer is sourced from who one is as the one who answers. The answering is responsive to the one who asks, and the answer addresses what is being asked either directly, or obliquely, or even interrogatively. It seems that this is also the way God answers Job.

8. Revelation by Interrogation

God answers Job. Who is this God who answers Job? The appearance of the divine name, Yahweh, in 38:1 is significant. It does not appear in the dialogues between Job and his friends. There, other names for God are used: "El," "Eloah," "Elohim," and "Shaddai." On the other hand, the name "Yahweh" appears only in the prose narrative in 1:1-2, 13; and in 42:7-17.[1]

What could this possibly mean? In the prose narrative, it is Yahweh who is the sovereign subject of the conversation between Yahweh and Satan, which conversation frames the dialogues. It is Yahweh who made the crucial decisions concerning Job. In the dialogues between Job and his friends, however, Yahweh is made into the object of the conversation, and so a variety of opinions about him occur in the dialogues. May it not be the case that in God's answer to Job, he is as it were retrieving his sovereignty and authority as the sole subject of everything that is, and not the mere object of human opinions? Yahweh is here asserting his selfhood as the one who is as he is: "I AM WHO I AM." It is he who alone determines himself to be and what to become and NOT anyone else! He can put to naught any and all human opinions about him. He can subvert, shatter, and break any and all human images and concepts about him. Only he can and does reveal who he truly

1. See Carol A. Newsom, "Job," *The New Interpreter's Bible* (Nashville: Abingdon Press, 1996), 600.

is! It is also he who may chose how to show himself in answering questions about him.

"The Lord [Yahweh] answered Job out of the whirlwind" (38:1). It is through and out of the whirlwind that God appears and reveals himself to Job. He has chosen this wild phenomenon of nature to reveal himself and respond to Job. But why the whirlwind? In Scripture, storm, fire, and whirlwind are often used as metaphors to symbolize the appearances of the divine (Ps. 18:7-15; Ezek. 1:4; Nah. 1.3; Hab. 3; Zech. 9:14). May it not be the case that these phenomena possess intrinsic properties that aptly fit them for this purpose? The whirlwind or violent storm is strong power. It is also wild. Because it is wild power, it is chaotic. It is ominously presaged and accompanied by thick darkness. It precipitates a deluge of flooding waters or tsunamis. Violent winds and flooding waters overwhelm and destructively sweep away everything along their paths. They cannot be humanly controlled. There is no technology that can tame them. They possess a primal violence of disorder that cannot be humanly transformed into a design of ordered power. There is no latent order in primal chaos!

But now God rides the whirlwind. He controls it and uses it for his purposes. Through it he comes to show himself to Job. What could this possibly mean? Would it be too far from the truth to say that in some sense the whirlwind symbolizes who God is in his majestic sovereign power and his answer to Job comes out of who is in his Godself? God's answer in coming from himself by himself is therefore revelatory of himself. Job has been seeking God and now God comes to him in a way he did not expect. As said earlier, God's coming subverts, shatters, and sweeps away all images, concepts, practices, and representations of himself made of the human by the human. It is God who determines how he reveals and represents himself—through and out of the whirlwind with its darkness and the unruly waters it precipitates! Instead of answering Job directly in declaratory language, he interrogates Job with rhetorical questions that are beyond Job's imagination and reason to answer. The questions also reveal who Job is in God's scheme of things. Instead of locating where God is, it is God who now locates Job and puts him in his rightful place. Instead of bringing a case against God, it is God who now has a case against him: "Who is this that darkens counsel by words without knowledge? Gird up your loins like a man, I will question you and you shall declare to me" (Job. 38:2-3).

The word *counsel* in the text does not mean advice, such as a sage might say to one consulting him about some personal problem. According to Carol A. Newsom the root meaning has to do with "careful thinking and planning and to the capacity to do such planning."[2] "Counsel" therefore is better translated "plan" or "design" so long as these words are not understood passively but actively. Thus "counsel" refers to God's activity of planning and designing the universe and his execution of such a plan or design. The word identifies God as sovereign creator of the whole universe—the heavens and the earth and all that is in them, and describes the universe as his creation and an ongoing work of his. As planning and designing, the word *counsel* also links indissolubly the creator with his creation, inter alia, the creation with its creator. Thus, the word *counsel* refers to the design made in wisdom and embedded in creation and actively operational in it as the work of the creator! Counsel links religarically and primordially creator and creation.

God accuses Job of "darkening" this plan or design of his for creation with words without knowledge. It is for this that Job is called to answer as a man should. He has been dignified by God in creating him in his image and giving him authority to rule over the work of his hands! And so he can if he would. In Job 12:13, Job attributes to God "wisdom and strength; he has counsel and understanding." But in 12:22, the effect of God letting light to shine is only to bring "deep darkness to light." So ironically what the light illumines in creation is the darkness of creation. Light shows darkness more clearly. The darkness of creation that is lighted up is not its mystery and hiddenness but the evil and the injustice in it, such as is exemplified in the personal experience of Job, and about which Job is bitterly complaining and is making a case against God, not only on his behalf but also on behalf of all, both righteous and wicked. Job is also thus questioning the way God governs his creation. His painful experience of evil and injustice clearly shows up God's unjust governing and ordering of things!

Moreover, Job complains that God has not detailed to him what wrong he has done for which he now suffers painfully. He pleads to God: "Teach me, and I will be silent; *make me understand how I have gone wrong*" (6:24, emphasis added). "I will say to God, Do not condemn me; *let me know why you contend against me*" (10:2; 13:20-23, emphasis added). Does not an accused have the right to know what he is being accused of? Of course, he does. That is guaranteed under the religaric covenantal relationship. But Job goes further than this. He already knows that he is righteous and is innocent of any wrongdoing. He has already prejudged his case and he is sure of being acquitted: "But I would speak to the Almighty, and I desire to argue my case with God I have indeed prepared my case; I know that I shall be vindicated" (13:3, 18). Does Job's case have merit? Is it worth a judicial

2. Ibid., 601. Cf. J. Gerald Janzen, "Job," *Interpretation* (Atlanta: John Knox, 1985).

hearing? Does not the case question the judicial system itself as already unjust? Would any answer that may come from it directly addressing the specific case before it be considered as having any judicial merit, coming as it is from a system already prejudged as unjust? What if the case has arisen from, and is stated in, "words without knowledge" as God claims (38:2). The right to file it is not denied; it is affirmed! But the judge could dismiss it as having no merit. And so the judge asks: "who is this that darkens counsel by words without knowledge?"

So now God turns the table against Job. He now makes a case on his own behalf against Job, and he asks Job to answer him as a responsible man should, reckoning with the facts of the case and facing up to a decision about them and its consequences! His interrogation of Job ironically in a rhetorical way lays out the facts about himself as creator who designs his creation in wisdom and his creative power to bring into created reality what he has designed. God undermines the morality of Job's case by showing that there is a pre-moral basis for morality itself over which Job has no control and knowledge. That basis is God's self-constitution of himself as creator and his activity as creator. Morality as the issue of right or wrong of what humans do and so become by their own doing has a deeper basis that is creational. It is this which God now proceeds to make Job understand by the questions he asks of Job, rhetorical questions that Job ironically cannot answer with his own knowledge and understanding, which in God's view are no knowledge and understanding at all!

The first question that God asks is so basic and foundational to all the following questions that he asks: "Where were you when I laid the foundation of the earth?" (38:4ff.). The laying of the foundation means this: What is not and cannot be foundational has become precisely that by making it both possible and actual as foundation. As creational foundation, it is foundational to everything else that is and what it may become! As creational it establishes and comprehends the ontological, the cosmic, the natural, the biological, the human, the cultural and social, including the logical, the legal, and the moral. The measurements and distinctions, limits and borders, dynamics and values, independence and interdependence of all these, their inner complexities and intricate operations, including their potentialities of what they can become, are all part of the creational foundation that God has laid. Was Job there when this foundation was being laid? Of course, he wasn't there. So how could he know? Can Job do this creative act of founding, of making possible what is non-possible, of actualizing what is only possible, of measuring the limits and distinctions of all that is, and establishing their relationships in proper order? Of course not, so how can he know and understand?

The next major question that God asks is about the creativity at work in creation. Has Job become privy to the depth dynamics and processes of creativity that are creationally embedded in living things? God asks Job:

> "Do you know when the mountain goats give birth? Do you observe the calving of the deer? Can you number the months that they fulfill, and do you know the time when they give birth, when they crouch to give birth to their offspring, and are delivered of their young? Their young ones become strong, they grow up in the open; they go forth, and do not return to them." (Job 39:1-4ff.)

Of course Job himself has participated in the generative capacity of life, for he has borne children of his own; he has raised animal life of various sorts; he must have cultivated vineyards that yielded fruits and oil and wine (Job 1:2-3). He must, therefore, have had firsthand knowledge of the self-perpetuating and self-multiplying power of life. However, are these enough bases to question the depth levels and intricate processes of the life-generating, life-giving, and life-nurturing capacity of the earth and of all living things? Does Job know and understand how all this happens? Could he have created life itself and its self-generative capacity? Is not life and its power to multiply given by God as blessing? What is it that generates and nurtures life? Is it the light that shines from God or the darkness upon which the light shines, which darkness cannot overcome? It is of course the light of God overcoming darkness that generates life. If so, why then should Job point an accusing finger at God that by letting light shine, he only intensifies darkness and thereby only increase its power to confuse, obscure, and destroy?

In the third major question that God asked Job to answer, God takes him back to the depth issue of where the primal foundation of creation is laid. Admittedly a foundation is laid on something that is solid, stable, strong enough to carry what is laid on it, and powerful enough to withstand what would shake it or cause it to collapse. There is no question that buildings of any kind have their foundations sunk deep into the earth. But upon which is the earth itself founded? Surely, it is not founded upon itself. But is there something more solid, more stable, more unshakable (even the earth can be shaken by its own quake) than the earth itself upon which it is founded?

God provides the answer to this question since no one else can. God cites two gargantuan creatures. These creatures are named Behemoth (40:15-24) and Leviathan (41:1-34). Why these creatures? What is God's point in citing them in connection with creation?

There are no earlier instances of the appearance of "Behemoth" as a land animal in earlier portions of Scripture.[3] Newsom suggests: "Possibly, it is a creation of the Job poet, who needed a land animal to pair with the sea creature Leviathan, or it may be the poet's rendering of an older tradition otherwise unattested.[4] In any case, it is most likely that it is cited because of its symbolic value. So what does it symbolize? Unlike the animals that Job raised that can be domesticated and thus contribute to human well-being, Behemoth appears to be wild, powerful, unruly, and cannot be tamed. May not these attributes symbolize the wildness, unruliness, unpredictability, and untamability of primal chaos? And yet God made Behemoth out of this chaos: "It is the first of the great acts of God—only its Maker can approach it with the sword" (Job 40:19). But now by God's act of creation Behemoth has come to symbolize the solid, stable, enduring, secure, and strong power upon which the foundation of the earth is laid. It is God's creative act that makes cosmos out of chaos; it is God's creative act upon which the foundation of the earth is laid. And so no one on earth can undo that primal originating act: "Can one take it with hooks or pierce its nose with a snare?" (40:24).

But does that mean that the unruliness and uncertainty of chaos have been completely removed by God's creative and founding act? Is there no measure of these features of chaos remaining in creation? Is not the original untamability of chaos still in creation in some measure or degree? My take on this is that some measure and degree of chaos remain in creation. Creaturely existence is a combination of being and nonbeing, of existence and nonexistence, of order and disorder, of life and death. This combination accounts for the ambiguity, contingency, dependency, and insecurity in creation. The non-possibility in chaos from which the possible may be created remains. And this is simply an absolutely given fact in creation that none on earth and in all creation can undo! Being is always threatened by nonbeing because it is a part of being. Life is always threatened by death and finally succumbs to death because it is a dimension of living itself. Nonbeing and nonlife are incorporated into creation by God's creative act!

But the good news is that God, and only God, can and does make good out of this combination! The possibility of good that God creates comes out of the non-possible in chaos. The fragility of the balance in the combination between the non-possible and the possible and between the possible and the actual in creaturely reality, from which combination arises freedom, accounts also for the vulnerability of creation to temptation and so into being seduced by what could corrupt it.

3. Newsom, "Job," 4:618.

4. Ibid.

The incontrovertible proof that God's creative act transforms chaos into a cosmos and into creaturely existence and life is precisely the fact that Behemoth exists as a creature of God, as the creaturely combining of order and disorder, of cosmos and chaos, of spirit and dust, just like Job is! It seems that it is this ambivalence of the combining of the opposites in creaturely reality that can be tipped into contradiction and distortion by human freedom, and so become the source and cause of human suffering, that Job has failed to realize. It is this ambivalence that could be turned into contradiction and thus lead into suffering that God wants Job to know and understand. Behemoth is the symbol of this creaturely ambivalence: "Look at Behemoth, which I made just as I made you" (40:15).

Like Behemoth and Job, however, the whole earth and all living things in it, in their ambiguity, contingency, dependency, and insecurity, together with their life and its potentialities for its well-being, are in the creative hands of God!

And what about Leviathan, the sea monster? Unlike Behemoth, the earth monster, the name or figure Leviathan appears in mythic traditions in Israelite, Egyptian, and Mesopotamian cultures.[5] These traditions in their own ways associate Leviathan with the waters of chaos. This leads back, in the case of Israel, to the way God has dealt sovereignly with "the waters" in Genesis 1. Chaos is symbolized not only by formlessness, voidness, and darkness but also by the waters of the Deep. The waters are deep, wild, unruly, unstable, untamable, and overwhelming. God dealt with "the waters" in two ways: by putting "a dome in the midst of the waters, and let it separate the waters from the waters." So God "separated the waters that were under the dome from the waters above the dome. And it was so. God called the dome 'Sky'" (Gen. 1:6-7). The next thing that God did about the waters is to " 'Let the waters under the sky be gathered into one place, and let the dry land appear.' And it was so. God called the dry land Earth, and the waters that were gathered together he called Seas. And God saw that it was good" (1:9-10). There is a sequence in this twofold activity: the separation of "waters from the waters" by a dome, and the gathering of the waters under the dome into one place to form the seas, thus making the appearance of dry land. This act of primal ordering by separating the waters and gathering them together into their places by putting "borders" that distinguish them and assign them their appropriate places is foundational to the emergence of seas and earth and "the firmament" and all the myriad and varied forms of life that inhabit them. These "borders" provide appropriate "limits," distinctions, and environments for the various forms of life. These "borders" are both distinct and fluid. They are meant for symbiotic interactions that

5. Ibid., 621.

mutually help and sustain one another, and those that live in them, without neutralizing or abolishing the environmental limits and distinctions.

But the waters have one feature: They can rise up in waves from the depths or pour down in torrents from the heights and overwhelm the earth and all that is in it with uncontrollable and destructive flood (Gen. 7:11ff.). The earth, however, cannot do what the seas can do because it is founded on them by God's creative and ordering activity. "[He] spread out the earth upon the waters" (Ps. 136:6; cf. 104:3). The earth depends on the waters for its moisture and so for its ability to generate, nurture, and develop the life-forms that make it their home.

There is, however, one "border" whose limit, distinction, and separation cannot be crossed over by the waters and the earth and the sky and all the things and forms of life that are in them. That "border" is what God has put in place between him as creator and his creation. However, although there is such a "border," and creation cannot go across it, God can and does cross it for the benefit of his creation, to be God for his creation and for creation to be his! That "border" is the Spirit who differentiates and binds, and penetrates and pervades, imperceptively and quietly but effectively.

And what is the place and role of Leviathan in all this? Leviathan is a creature of God, like Behemoth and like Job, and like all of us. God has placed him as a monster of the sea. That means that he symbolizes that the unruliness of the primal waters has been conquered and calmed by God. They have been rendered safe for the earth to be founded in them. So ships can now go down upon the seas and sail on them; and Leviathan can now sport and play in the sea (Ps. 104:21). But Leviathan remains powerfully elusive. Like Behemoth, he can be hunted, but cannot be hunted down and captured. No human strength, ingenuity, and technology can overcome, capture, and domesticate him. Even the gods are overwhelmed at the sight of him:

> Can you fill its skin with harpoons, or its head with fishing spears? Lay hands on it; think of the battle; you will not do it again! Any hope of capturing it will be disappointed; were not even the gods overwhelmed at the sight of it? No one is so fierce as to dare to stir it up. Who can stand before it? Who can confront it and be safe?—under the whole heaven, who? . . . "On earth it has no equal, a creature without fear. It surveys everything that is lofty; it is king over all that are proud. (Job 41:7-11, 33-34)

What could this possibly mean? Is it too fantastic to suggest that it could mean that although the earthly, the human, and the secular have been given a creaturely environment and home and so are safe and can thrive in it, they should not cross over the waters of the deep in a prideful attempt to penetrate into the mysteries of Godself and his holiness and "be like God"? (Gen. 3:22-24; 11:1-9). Leviathan stands guard over this "border" to bring down the proud that want to cross over. "On earth it has no equal, a creature without fear. It surveys everything that is lofty; it is king over all that are proud" (41:33-34). He represents the elusiveness of this border to earthly, this-worldly, and human exploration! And so the playful presence of Leviathan in the seas serves to confine the earthly, the this-worldly, and the human to the creaturely realm, to creation itself, which is a vast and rich and labyrinthine field for exploring and knowing and enjoying. Creation itself is the arena of wisdom; it is the field-research, the workshop, the laboratory, the classroom, and the lavish feast of wisdom.

And if it can find signs and traces and images of the Creator in it that point to or signify his reality, that is absolutely a good reason to praise and worship him but not to transform the signs, traces, and images into fixed idols of him and mistake them for the true God! But such praise and worship arise only from a life that gratefully values and passionately appreciates living in a creaturely way in a creation in which God is actively at work for the good of his creatures, which good the creature, especially the human, can appropriate for its own good! If so, is it too far-fetched to suggest that indeed that is precisely the practice of a spirituality that truly secularizes? Perhaps Job's reply to his wife as he began to suffer is indeed a genuine practice of this sort of spirituality: "shall we receive the good at the hand of God, and not receive the bad?" (2:9-10). But as his suffering became more intensely and painfully hurting, he seemed to reject the bad and pine only for the good and to complain bitterly of it and go so far as accusing God of unjustly causing it.

We may surmise that this now provides God the occasion for asking Job a fourth question:

> And the LORD said to Job: "Shall a faultfinder contend with the Almighty? Anyone who argues with God must respond." . . . "Will you even put me in the wrong? Will you condemn me that you may be justified?" (40:1-2, 8)

These questions put to Job by God identify Job as a "faultfinder" who is contending with God by putting him in the wrong. By so doing, Job is condemning God and thereby justifying himself as in the right and guiltless. It is as a faultfinder and as a self-justifier that God looks at Job. God identifies Job in this way for raising what in theology is called the question of theodicy. That question, as classically put by Job (21:7ff.) and by Jeremiah before him (Jer. 12:1-4), asks, "Why do the wicked live on, reach old age, and grow mighty in power?" This issue is simplified in theology by being broken up into three major questions. First, if God is loving (as claimed in Scripture and in Christianity) why is wickedness (sin, evil, and innocent suffering) allowed to operate in the world? Second, if God is almighty (again as claimed in Scripture and in Christianity) why does not God remove it? Third, do not the presence, operation, and persistence of wickedness in the world *falsify* belief in a loving and powerful God? The experience of evil, wickedness, and suffering in today's world—its destructive world wars, its nuclear annihilation, its wholesale genocide, its cruel oppression and merciless exploitations in depths and magnitudes never before experienced in all of history—makes the claimed falsification unassailable and incontrovertible. Thus, the rational choice for many is at best agnosticism, and at worst, atheism both theoretical and practical!

But is this the only implied choice? There is no doubt that the theodicy question is a very serious assault on God. But we must note where it is coming from. It comes from human moral experience and this experience is interpreted from the perspective of a moral framework that structures reality. Implicit in it is the poignant plea for the suffering righteous to be vindicated and the prospering wicked to be punished. The question is thus shaped by a view of justice as retributive based on the deed/consequence causal connection. Since the issue is moral, it calls for a judicial resolution based on a specific view of justice. Thus, the theodicy issue does not only raise the question of a loving and almighty God but also of a *just* God. When all three combined are raised in connection with God, they ask about the identity, character, and justice of God. And when the identity, character, and justice of God are raised in connection with God's relation to the world, the issue becomes a problem of God's governance of his creation on the basis of who he is and his character as creator.

But governance is not solely a matter of moral justice. God as creator governs all his creation and distributes his creativity in such a way that all aspects of creaturely existence receive the gifts necessary to their existence, their dignity, their nurture, their development, the purposes for which they are endowed, and their movement to their rightful destiny. Thus, governance is not just moral but in its most basic depth and in its most ultimate reach and in the complexity of its dynamics is *creational*. What is covered by the creational is not just the moral but also the cosmic, the natural, the human, the social, the historical, the cultural, and the eschatological. Governance of creation has to do not only with its parts but with the whole of created reality, with heaven and earth and all that is in them. Creational governance aims at securing, coordinating, promoting the right relations of all the dimensions and levels of created reality. Justice is not just moral but creational. Set in this broad and comprehensive perspective, the complaint of Job, though legitimate and serious, appears as narrow, self-serving, and misleading. It darkens rather than enlightens. It is expressed in words that lack knowledge and understanding!

Moreover, creational governance has to be seen as falling within, and as an active expression of, the religaric/covenantal relation. The reason for this is that God's resolve to be God *of* and *for* an other is what established creation. God's self-constituting himself as creator is what brings creation into being. Seen in the light of this perspective, the theodicy question as raised by Job and Jeremiah does not entail doubting or falsifying the belief in the existence of God, but of attacking his reliability in his governance of creation. In the religaric/covenant relationship God has made promises of well-being for his creation and his people. But in Job's experience God appears that he could not care less in keeping and fulfilling them. God appears unable and unconcerned to govern the world he has created in a morally just way. And so the question of theodicy is a question about the reliability of God, and not about the existence of God. An unreliable God cannot be trusted. A God who breaks his promise has no word of honor and no self-respect; why trust him? In this sense it is a question of the identity and character of God.

If the reliability and credibility of God cannot be reestablished and reaffirmed in the face of the assault on the integrity of God that would abolish the religaric/covenant relationship and all that is entailed by it. That would mean that God has reneged on his self-resolve to be a creator God and that would result in the collapse of creation itself. That is how serious the assault of Job against God is!

Who then can reestablish the integrity of God in its reliability and credibility? Who can steadfastly stand and stay the course of the religaric/covenant relation and keep it going? Who can save creation from collapsing? No one in creation who is a part of creation and is therefore a created reality can do this! Only God who is creator of creation can do this!

9. Creation and the Moral Issue

God indeed has answered Job. He has to. But what is God's answer? Not exactly what Job expected. Instead of vindicating Job in his innocence as he expected, God reaffirmed his self-resolve in self-constituting himself as creator God! He is still sovereignly governing his creation on the basis of the religaric/covenant relation, which includes the moral issue but is not all of it, and appears quite different and less serious than the way Job took it when seen in the larger horizon of creational governance. God is not about to withdraw his Spirit and nullify his

Word in his continuing creative activity. Wisdom as created agency in the making of creation is still embedded in creation and it is processively, quietly, and effectively at work, though hidden to many, but is given to those who diligently seek to know her. All this means that it is God's self-resolve to self-constitute himself as creator that is the unshakable foundation of his reliability and credibility and is the basis of his majestic governance of his creation! It is by being true to himself as creator God that makes him reliable and trustworthy and credible! Is this not the point of all of God's answer to Job in his two speeches? (Job 38–41).

In reestablishing his reliability and credibility in creational governance, God remained true to himself without conceding anything to Job. Although God did not directly answer Job in the way it was put and the premises from which it was asked, God's answer provided Job with a clearer vision and a wider horizon in which to understand the import of his question and to find a more concrete and a more adequate answer to it. The effect of this is that not only did God make his point about himself but also, and equally important, Job saw the point that God was making. In his first answer to God, he saw himself in the light of God's creatorship: "See, I am of small account; what shall I answer you? I lay my hand on my mouth. I have spoken once, and I will not answer; twice, but will proceed no further" (Job 40:4-5). Job has found his true self and place in creation. In his second answer to God as creator and his creational governance Job acknowledged God's almightiness: "I know that you can do all things, and that no purpose of yours can be thwarted" (42:1-2). But although Job has been abased by the majesty and overwhelming power of God the creator, he is nevertheless honored in his humility by God deigning to show himself visibly to Job. Whereas before Job has heard of God only as a *rumor*, hearsay, but now he has been honored with a direct, personal, and revealing experience of God and can now say firsthand: "I had heard of you by the hearing of the ear, *but now my eyes see you*" (42:5, emphasis added). It is the hearsay knowledge of God that led Job to speak unknowingly of God and made him question God in his reliability and credibility. But now that he is honored by God answering him by revealing himself to him, he now relents and recants all that he has said of God unknowingly out of hearsay and finds comfort, pride, and contentment in being a creature of God made of dust and ashes (42:6). Job finally acknowledges God as creator and himself as God's creature in all his earthly, this-worldly, secular reality (his being "dust and ashes"). It is this twin acknowledgment that constitutes a spirituality that secularizes—a spirituality that is secular and a secularity that is spiritual. It is genuine wisdom as fear of the Lord.

Did this mean that the issue of moral justice that Job raised with God is completely ignored and set aside because God did not directly answer it? Absolutely, no! It was not set aside and canceled. It remains an issue, and a perennial one! What God did is to put it in proper perspective to be pursued in the light of that perspective. That perspective is the religaric/covenant relationship. That means Job remains a partner with God in seeking a more enlightened and satisfying solution to the problem of justice in the world. Such a continuing search is, after all, the burden and responsibility of the wisdom of the world. And so it still is until now! Human moral justice in the world as a burden of wisdom is, however, a part and only a part, of a larger vision of justice, namely, creational justice, which is concerned with the "righteousness" of every part, and of the whole, of creation. It is concerned with the right order of all things and all of reality as a whole. This justice has to do with the right relation between God and his creation. And that is God's burden and responsibility. The human in the world has been enlisted by God to be a partner in bearing that burden and in doing what it takes to make a blessing out of the burden. After all, it is for the good and well-being of the human that God has assumed responsibility for realizing this larger vision of creational justice.

Moreover, the human effort to walk the way of righteousness, and thus *be* and *live* righteously in preference over the way of the wicked, is affirmed as humanly right. It is part of the wisdom of the world, and so it is a part of the searching and realizing of the larger vision of justice. The question in the prologue, in which Satan asked God about Job as to whether righteousness is pursued for its own sake, and not for the sake of other ulterior motives and values such as long life and prosperity, is incontrovertibly and positively answered. Job was absolutely in the right in being righteous for the sake of righteousness! But this kind of moral righteousness cannot be used as a means of being right with God and demand being rewarded for it by God. Human righteousness is no substitute for God's righteousness. Not to use it to be right with God is indeed a personal and positive way of partnering with God in the search for the larger righteousness of creational justice! Using personal righteousness as a means of being right with God, together with all its supporting images and concepts of God, is what Job's friends advocated as the way of being righteous with God! God proscribed and rejected this way: "The Lord said to Eliphaz the Temanite, 'My wrath is kindled against you and against your two friends; for you have not spoken of me what is right, as my servant Job'" (42:7, 8). Indeed, Job's complaining bitterly about the absence of moral justice in the world is part of the motivation to seek justice in the world. To complain about its absence in view of the prevalence of injustice is absolutely right and necessary. The courage to do so adamantly and persistently comes from being a partner with God in the religaric/covenant relationship where one has the right to address God in trust or doubt, in praise or lament, in gratitude or complaint, in humble confession and sorrowful repentance, or in song and dance and joyful celebration!

But there is a statement in the epilogue that can be misinterpreted and may negate all that has been said about rejecting the deed/consequence, reward and punishment, causal connection. The statement says: "And the Lord restored the fortunes of Job when he had prayed for his friends; and the Lord gave Job twice as much as he had before" (Job 42:10). God did this after Job prayed for his friends, which is an act that is part of being piously righteous (cf. Job 1:4-5). Does this mean that God's restoring Job's fortune twice as he had before is to be interpreted and understood as reward for his righteousness and piety? Absolutely, not! Rather, it is to read it as meaning that it is God's way of being consistent with his self-resolve to self-constitute himself for the good and benefit of his creation, and for Job particularly. It is a sovereign expression of creational justice that is emphatically graciously distributive and not punitively retributive or meritoriously rewarding. It is by being faithful to himself that he is at the same time graciously faithful to Job because God and Job are bonded together by the religaric/covenant relationship. It is this primal bonding relationship that makes the Spirit secularize, and the secular open to and receptive of the Spirit.

10. Wisdom in Cul-de-sac: Qoheleth

In the light of our purposes in this book, we can only offer some theological reflections on *Qoheleth* (referring to the canonical book Ecclesiastes and its author) in our effort to explore the secularizing thrust of the Spirit which we have tried to do in the previous chapters.[6]

The first observation we offer is the secular framework of Qoheleth. This is indicated by the phrases "under the sun" or "under heaven" on the one hand, and "a time for everything under heaven," on the other hand. The phrase "under the sun" occurs many times in Qoheleth (e.g., 1:3, 9, 14; 2:11, 17, 18, 19, 20, 22; 3:16; 4:1, 3, 7; 5:13, 18; 6:1, 12; 8:9, 15, 17). It signifies the earthiness of creaturely existence and life. Everything that occurs "under the sun," whether natural or human has its own time: "For everything there is a season, and a time for every matter under heaven" (3:1ff.; cf. 7:17; 8:5; 9:12; 10:17). This signifies the temporality of creaturely reality. These two phrases set forth the spatial and temporal

6. For the use of the term *Qoheleth*, see introduction to *Ecclesiastes in The New Oxford Annotated Bible: New Revised Standard Version* (New York: Oxford University Press, 1991), 841. We shall use the term *Qoheleth* or *Teacher* in referring to Ecclesiastes.

horizons of what Qoheleth explores in his search for wisdom. In short, the two phrases together indicate the *saecularis* and the *saeculum* of secular reality. Moreover, the data Qoheleth investigates to find out what he is searching for is everything that happens or is done or known within these parameters. And that includes what happens as nature, what humans do and know, and what God is about or up to in the sphere of his creation. In short, the data that Qoheleth explores in order to find out what he is searching for is secular.

Furthermore, he uses his mind that rationally operates through perception, observation, analysis, reflection, and evaluation. Phrases like "I perceive, "I saw," "I have seen," "I test," "then I considered," "there is nothing better," and "all this I laid to heart, examining it all" appear in Qoheleth's work. One could say that Qoheleth has a secular mind-set that he applied upon secular data that is available in a secular world in his effort to acquire secular wisdom (cf. 1:12-18). For another thing, Qoheleth takes the tradition of wisdom that he has inherited as part of his data and puts it to critical test. After all, he stands in the tradition of wisdom thought and practice and it would not be wise to ignore it. It is of the nature of wisdom to examine critically the gains it has garnered for the benefit of others seeking wisdom. What Qoheleth does is to take the tradition of secular wisdom and put it to a secular test to find out whether there is indeed a secular gain that can be passed on to others in search of wisdom. Finally, it appears that Qoheleth puts his search for wisdom through wisdom as a task given by God to humans under the aegis of "fear of God" (5:7; 8:12; 12:13). The search for and acquisition of wisdom is a human task given by God and so it begins in God and is part of fearing God. This puts Qoheleth's efforts at acquiring wisdom and its values unmistakably and inescapably within the religaric/covenant bond. Qoheleth's findings from his investigation about secular wisdom in a secular world may be at "the far edge of negativity"[7] or what we are calling the "cul-de-sac of wisdom." We must, however, still seek to understand this negative view as falling within, and as a function and value yielded by, the religaric bond, and so it must be affirmed as an aspect of the thrust of the Spirit that secularizes.

The next thing worth noticing theologically is what exactly is Qoheleth looking for in his search for wisdom by means of wisdom as a task given by God. He puts it very succinctly and precisely in 1:3 as a question: "What do people gain from all the toil at which they toil under the sun?" The key word in this text is *gain*, sometimes translated as "profit" or "advantage."

What is it that can be regarded as "gain" or "profit"? Obviously, such a thing would be a good that constitutes the core or substance of wisdom, for that is what

7. Walter Bruggemann, *Theology of the Old Testament* (Minneapolis: Fortress, 1997), 393–98.

people "toil at under the sun" (1:3). And admittedly, it is to be found in what they toil at and by their toiling for it. The "gain" or good that wisdom seeks to find because it is what genuinely makes for wisdom as wisdom is to be found in what people toil at, and in their toiling for it! Both the object of wisdom's search and the way wisdom seeks what it is looking for are constitutive of wisdom itself. The Hebrew word translated as "gain" refers to what "remains" or "survives." I am here following the interpretation of Leo E. Perdue who writes: "Qoheleth is obsessed with discovering something that endures, that would enable one to live beyond the grave at least in human memory. It may well be that *yitron* in Qoheleth suggests not so much the idea of 'profit' or 'advantage' as it does 'continuation' or 'endurance.' Thus he may be asking: 'What continues to endure from the labor at which one toils during life?' "[8]

This quest for what endures and lasts is, strangely enough, declared by Qoheleth as *hebel*. This Hebrew word is translated "vanity" (NRSV), "futility" (REB), or "pointless" (CEB). A repeat of the word is made for strong emphasis: "vanity of vanities (NRSV)" or "futility, utter futility" (REB) or "perfectly pointless" (CEB). Thus, the word *hebel* can mean useless, empty, meaningless, absurd. However, Leo E. Perdue suggests that "the literal meaning of *hebel* is 'breath'." And this implies that *hebel* metaphorically connotes the idea of evanescence and ephemerality (cf. Pss. 39:6, 12; 62:10). According to Perdue, this appears to be the major connotation of the term in Qoheleth (3:19; 6:12; 7:15; 9:9; 11:8).[9] Moreover, the ephemerality of life on earth under the sun is underscored by the phase "a chasing after the wind" that accompanies *hebel*. The Hebrew word for both breath and wind is *ruah,* which connotes "spirit." In Hebrew thought, *ruah* or spirit is that which animates and sustains life. Thus, the statement "all is vanity and a chasing after the wind" can be translated "all is ephemeral and a desire for life's vital spirit."[10] Accordingly, for Qoheleth "everything in human existence: life, experience, activities, events and human thought" must be seen or viewed in the light of breath that fleets and does not last, and yet gives rise to the desire to go after what animates and sustains life and makes it endure and last.

Moreover, the root meaning of the word in Hebrew translated "chasing after" is "to pasture," "to take pleasure in," "to desire." Thus, to desire and to chase after what cannot be caught or pastured—a chasing after the wind—is an act of futility, of absurdity, of pointlessness, of meaninglessness (1:14; 2:11, 17, 26; 4:4, 16; 6:9).

8. Leo E. Perdue, *Wisdom and Creation* (Nashville: Abingdon Press, 1994), 208.

9. Ibid., 206.

10. Ibid., 207.

From his study of the root meanings of the key words in "vanity of vanities, all is vanity and a chasing after the wind," Perdue concludes:

> Hence life is as futile as attempting to shepherd (control, direct, harness) the wind. However, if *re ut* means "desire" and *ruah* is understood to include the God-given breath or spirit that activates and sustains life, we have the fundamental, yet tragic, paradox that resides at the heart of human existence and experience: the ephemeral nature of human existence, contrasted with the innate desire to retain the vital spirit that animates human life.

It is precisely the fact that life vanishes quickly like a shadow that prompts the search for more of it. With this, Qoheleth has taken hold of a searchlight that he now uses to illuminate what humans "toil at" in the hope that they will "gain" some measure of control over the good of which they want more, but is unavoidably elusive and ephemeral.

The next point in Qoheleth that we must therefore consider are the elements of human experience in which traditional wisdom sought the values that would enhance the well-being of life. We cannot and need not make a complete rundown on this, for the list is long. But we can choose some characteristic elements to illustrate what Qoheleth finds with his searchlight.

We may begin with the earthly and temporal frame, the secular parameter, of creaturely existence and life. Qoheleth rightly observes that there is a time for everything under heaven (3:1). His list of times is headed by "a time to be born, and a time to die"—a beginning and ending time. One may extend this to "a generation goes, and a generation comes" (1:4). Time may be measured in terms of birth and death and the succession of life-times and of generations. These beginnings and endings of life and of life-times, of one generation after another, may appear as change, as change of time and time of change. This may be so especially when contrasted with the earth ("under the sun"), which seems to endure and last: "the earth remains forever" (1:4b). On closer look, however, what really happens is a time of repetition and a repetition of time—a repeated cycle of repeated time! This cycle does not change. What has happened before is what will happen again; there is nothing "new" under the sun (1:9). This unending cycle is driven forcefully by a desire for more that is never satisfied and fulfilled and so never comes to an end. This endless cycle of repetition is "wearisome; more that one can express" (1:8).

> A generation goes, and a generation comes, but the earth remains forever. The sun rises and the sun goes down, and hurries to the place where it rises. The wind blows to the south, and goes around to the north; round and round goes the wind, and on its circuits the wind returns. All streams run to the sea, but

> the sea is not full; to the place where the streams flow, there they continue to flow. All things are wearisome; more than one can express; the eye is not satisfied with seeing, or the ear filled with hearing. What has been is what will be, and what has been done is what will be done; there is nothing new under the sun. Is there a thing of which it is said, "See, this is new"? It has already been, in the ages before us. (Eccles. 1:4-10)

The things and events and actions that come to be and pass away in this earthly and temporal framework have their own time in their own space. They have a here and now that is given them and can make their own. And so they fit together, and they are beautiful in their order and fitness. Qoheleth puts it this way: "He has made everything suitable for its time" (3:11). What is more: The human has been given an awareness of timing—"a sense of past and future into their minds" (3:11). And so humans have a deep sense of the beginning, continuing, and ending of things! Their memory, however, cannot go past the beginning and their expectation cannot anticipate the ending. They are trapped in an uncertain present. But with this goes the tragic awareness that humans have no knowledge and control over the beginning, the happening, and the ending of things. What they are aware of is only the cycle of beginning, happening, and ending. The movement of the cycle and the time of the cycle and the time of things in it are in the hand of God. And if one asks what is the point or purpose of this cycle from the one whose hands hold it, does one find an answer that illuminates and satisfies? The only and final answer that is given is, "they cannot find out what God has done from the beginning to the end" (3:11). Add to this tragic sense the forgetfulness and the forgottenness of all things that begin and end in their own here and now and sink into oblivion forever! Only God can remember, but who can penetrate into God's memory? This is the way God made all things:

> I know that whatever God does endures forever, nothing can be added to it, nor anything taken from it; God has done this, so that all should stand in awe before him. That which is, already has been; that which is to be, already is; and God seeks out what has gone by. (Eccles. 3:14-15)

Qoheleth next applies his searchlight to the material goods that humans in wisdom seek to achieve and enjoy with the aim of enhancing the well-being of life. He says to himself, as we do to ourselves, "Come now, I will make a test of pleasure; enjoy yourself . . . I searched with my mind how to cheer my body with wine—my mind still guiding me with wisdom—and how to lay hold on folly, until I might see what was good for mortals to do under heaven during the few days of their life" (2:1, 3). Qoheleth goes on to enumerate all the worldly goods that are traditionally regarded to be the rewards of wisdom, using Solomon, the paragon of wisdom, as his model:

> I made great works; I built houses and planted vineyards for myself; I made myself gardens and parks, and planted in them all kinds of fruit trees. I made myself pools from which to water the forest of growing trees. I bought male and female slaves, and had slaves who were born in my house; I also had great possessions of herds and flocks, more than any who had been before me in Jerusalem. I also gathered for myself silver and gold and the treasure of kings and of the provinces; I got singers, both men and women, and delights of the flesh, and many concubines. So I became great and surpassed all who were before me in Jerusalem; also my wisdom remained with me. (Eccles. 2:4-9)

And what was Qoheleth's evaluation of all these earthly and worldly goods? Of course he cannot say that they did not give him pleasure: "Whatever my eyes desired I did not keep from them; I kept my heart from no pleasure in all my toil, and this was my reward for all my toil." But his final judgment is a negation of the point of view of traditional wisdom: "Then I considered all that my hands had done and the toil I had spent in doing it, and again, all was vanity and a chasing after wind, and there was nothing to be gained under the sun" (Eccles. 2:11).

If Qoheleth were to see the culture of consumption that obsesses us today, which of course we enjoy, would he not render the same judgment? "All this is vanity and a chasing after wind."

Another human concern at which humans toil is the issue of justice. This is a problem that preoccupies all traditions of Israel's faith, including wisdom. It is a perennial issue for humans! But when Qoheleth seeks to find it in the world, what does he find? He says: "I saw under the sun that in the place of justice, wickedness was there, and in the place of righteousness, wickedness was there as well" (3:16). Of course, God is also interested to see to it that justice and righteousness prevail in the world, for he continues to function as judge: "I said in my heart, God will judge the righteous and the wicked, for he has appointed a time for every matter, and for every work" (3:17; cf. 8:12). But the fact of the matter is that the judgment and sentence against the evil of injustice and wickedness are often delayed, and because justice is delayed humans go on in their spree to do evil: "Because sentence against an evil deed is not executed speedily, the human heart is fully set to do evil" (8:11). Moreover, it is also the case that the righteous are treated as wicked, and the wicked are treated as righteous: "There is a vanity that takes place on earth, that there are righteous people who are treated according to the conduct of the wicked, and there are wicked people who are treated according to the conduct of the righteous. "I said that this also is vanity" (8:14; cf. 7:15). If so, and this seems incontrovertible, what happens then to the view of justice as retributive? This view of justice is itself injustice in that it is belied by the way things are and by human behavior and experience and does not provide a solution to the injustice in reality but only exacerbates it. And so like Job, Qoheleth rejects this view of justice. But while Job rejects it with lament and protest, Qoheleth simply accepts it acquiescently as a matter of fact: "If you see in a province the oppression of the poor and the violation of justice and right, do not be amazed at the matter" for it has become part of the established system (5:8). And if that is the way things are, nothing that one can do about it can make a difference. One simply folds his hands and let matters be as they are. The status quo is the established reality. The prophetic passion for reform is absent in Qoheleth! There is no future that promises hope and beckons change for the better.

Another human practice upon which Qoheleth focused his searchlight is Temple worship. This pious activity is premised upon the promise of God that his presence is there in the Temple for him to hear the prayers of his people and respond to their petitions (1 Kings 8:27-53). But Qoheleth qualifies this belief with a more fundamental one: "God is in heaven, and you upon earth" (5:2; 8:27). There is a border-limit between heaven and earth, between creator and creature, whose gap cannot be crossed by humans. The border-limit is not just a matter of space and distance; it is a unique difference in the order of being: God is creator and the human is a creature. Neither one can be the other. So it is well for the worshiper to be aware and to observe this difference. The way to do that is that in worship, it is better to listen than to offer sacrifice because fools are not kept from doing evil by worship for they do not keep the vow they make when they make a sacrifice for the atonement of their sins (5:1). Qoheleth has seen the wicked "go in and out in the holy place, and were praised in the city where they had done such [wicked] things" (8:10). Moreover, in worship it is also better to be few and choosy in words and not make a vow one cannot keep. But if one makes a vow unthinkingly then one must fulfill it: "When you make a vow to God, do not delay fulfilling it; for he has no pleasure in fools. Fulfill what you vow. It is better that you should not vow than that you should vow and not fulfill it" (5:4-5). It would seem that Qoheleth has no place for praise, gratitude, glorifying God, and exulting in joy by being with him and finding comfort in his presence. His approach to God is characterized by caution and trepidation, rather than by thrilling excitement and heightened expectation. The "joy of salvation" sung by the psalmist does not resound from the heart and lips of worshipers in Qoheleth.

We may consider one other feature of human experience, among still many others, upon which Qoheleth focuses his searchlight, and that is wisdom itself.

There is no doubt in Qoheleth that wisdom is a gift of God to the human. But as a gift, it also becomes a task to be carried out with the best tool that accompanies its giving, namely, the human mind. He used this tool very effectively and successfully: "I applied my mind to know wisdom and to know madness and folly. . . . So I became great and surpassed all who were before me in Jerusalem; also my wisdom remained with me" (1:17; 2:9). He also firmly believed that wisdom is so much better than folly, that righteousness is a good that surpasses wickedness: "wisdom gives strength to the wise more than ten rulers that are in a city" (7:19). Therefore, life achieves its well-being when inspired and guided by the strength of wisdom and righteousness. Moreover, wisdom is an essential aspect of fear of God and thus it is a blessing in and for life that comes from God.

And what is Qoheleth's final evaluation of wisdom? First, as a gift from God, wisdom "is an unhappy business that God has given to human beings to be busy with" (1:13). Moreover, because one must toil for it, the more one has wisdom, the more vexation and trouble go with it: "For in much wisdom is much vexation, and those who increase knowledge increase sorrow" (1:18). Furthermore, wisdom cannot be known and practiced without also knowing and doing folly, and the knowledge and practice of righteousness includes knowing and doing wickedness: "Surely there is no one on earth so righteous as to do good without ever sinning" (7:20). If so, then what difference does wisdom make in the way things are? In the end, Qoheleth comes to the conclusion that not only the "good" that wisdom seeks but also the toiling after such a good is pointless and useless and is a chasing after the wind: "What do mortals get from all the toil and strain with which they toil under the sun? For all their days are full of pain, and their work is a vexation; even at night their minds do not rest. This also is vanity" (2:22-23). All the rewards that come from being wise may not be enjoyed by those who earned them, and they are soon left to those who come after them who may be fools, using and enjoying wisdom and its rewards they have not toiled at and earned (2:18-20).

If all that is gained by wisdom and the toil in securing it, indeed, amounts to nothing, for it is all a pointless chasing after the wind, which no one can control (8:8), then there is no wisdom in pursuing wisdom. The search for wisdom and its gain is in itself folly! All is leveled by the same fate, namely death. Those who have never been born are better off than the living (4:2-3). So "it is better to go to the house of mourning than to go to the house of feasting, for this is the end of everyone, and the living will lay it to heart" (7:2). But this wise thing to do ironically is also pointless and a chasing after the wind. It is the folly of being wise!

So since being wise is in the end folly, what "wise" counsel does Qoheleth recommend to the living while they live the few days of their life? Surely, there must be something that is worth salvaging from this tragic wasteland of slag heaps! The following may be worth mentioning.

First, Qoheleth recommends moderation in behavior, striking a balance between righteousness and wickedness:

> In my vain life I have seen everything; there are righteous people who perish in their righteousness, and there are wicked people who prolong their life in their evildoing. Do not be too righteous, and do not act too wise; why should you destroy yourself? Do not be too wicked, and do not be a fool; why should you die before your time? It is good that you should take hold of the one, without letting go of the other; for the one who fears God shall succeed with both. (Eccles. 7:15-18).

That it is possible to achieve this balancing of moral behavior is indicated in the last verse: "the one who fears God shall succeed with both." The problem, however, is where that balance is and when does one come to know it? And if one achieves it, is that all there is in morality that is acceptable to God? This sort of morality may be okay with culture. There it is called "moral decency" and the one who has it is a decent or civilized person. But is that genuinely "fear of the Lord"?

Second, he recommends that humans should "eat and drink, and find enjoyment in their toil," and in their wealth. Such enjoyment is approved by God and is given by him as the human lot. "There is nothing better for mortals than to eat and drink, and find enjoyment in their toil. This also, I saw, is from the hand of God; for apart from him who can eat or who can have enjoyment?" (2:24-25).

He recommends this as a *carpe diem* and does so six times: 2:24-25; 3:12-13, 22; 5:18-19; 8:15; 9:7-10: To eating, drinking, enjoying one's toil, and wealth is added enjoying life "with the wife whom you love," and presumably with one's family. This secular way of living and enjoying by celebrating secular goods and values is no sin at all for Qoheleth. They are a blessing and benefit from God! And he is right up to a point. Moreover, Qoheleth strongly suggests that when these elements of enjoyment come in their time or occasion, one must seize and enjoy them to the full while they last, for they come only in their own time, like everything else. Their timing is not in human hands but in God's hand. They are to be taken humanly and timely when they are divinely given. So one must make the most out of them when they come. To the youth, Qoheleth suggests that the best time to "remember your creator" is "in the days of your youth, before the days of trouble come, and the years draw near when you will say, 'I have no pleasure in them'" (12:1; cf. 11:9). But of course all this enjoyment does not last; it is also a chasing after the wind.

Third, Qoheleth recommends that humans accept, be happy and contented with their earthly and temporal lot because this is what God has apportioned to then, for "this is our lot . . . whatever God does endures forever; nothing can be added to it, nor anything taken from it" (5:18; 3:14). The "lot" given by God to humans includes the finality of death, which no earthly and temporal creature can avoid and cross over:

> For the fate of humans and the fate of animals is the same; as one dies, so dies the other. They all have the same breath, and humans have no advantage over the animals; for all is vanity. All go to one place; all are from the dust, and all turn to dust again. Who knows whether the human spirit goes upward and the spirit of animals goes downward to the earth? (Eccles. 3:19-21)

Another element included in the earthly and temporal "lot" of all life is that one cannot through wisdom discover the workings of God in his creation:

> I said "I will be wise," but it was far from me. That which is, is far off, and deep, very deep; who can find it out? . . . For every matter has its time and way, although the troubles of mortals lie heavy upon them. Indeed, they do not know what is to be, for who can tell them how it will be? No one has power over the wind to restrain the wind, or power over the day of death; there is no discharge from the battle, nor does wickedness deliver those who practice it. . . . When I applied my mind to know wisdom, and to see the business that is done on earth, how one's eyes see sleep neither day nor night, then I saw all the work of God, that no one can find out what is happening under the sun. However much they may toil in seeking, they will not find it out; even though those who are wise claim to know, they cannot find it out." (7:24; 8:6-8, 16-17)

Qoheleth believes that the reason God has made his workings in creation inscrutable for human wisdom is for humans to stand in awe before him (3:14). So for Qoheleth "lot" is *fate* ordained by God! Not even God can change it. This fate is inscrutable and the God who "fates" it for earthly and temporal existence is even more inscrutable.

One may well ask: Why this inscrutability? Why this hiddenness? Why this setting of border-limits whose walls and gaps no human life and wisdom can ever bridge over and cross? Why this fating of the lot of life and of human wisdom to earthly, temporal, secular, and creaturely reality? Why should response to this inscrutable God be "awe" only and not also joy and praise? One may speculate theologically in answering these questions, while knowing full well that any answer belongs to the folly of wisdom, that is, to the earthly and temporal limitations of human wisdom.

One may cite as a fundamental answer the Yahwistic and prophetic insight that God protects his holiness, his Godself, which is his freedom to self-constitute himself. This prerogative is uniquely his and he will not let any creaturely reality come close to it. But this makes room for the possibility that God may reveal himself out of his mystery in his relation to his creation. That means there is the possibility of knowing him as he is in his revelation of himself. It must be that the truth of knowing God humanly must somehow "correspond" to God's knowing himself divinely in his self-revelation. Wisdom as human knowledge of the world as created may not be God's knowledge of himself as he reveals himself in the world as his creation. The human knowledge of God derived from knowing his world must somehow "correspond" to God's knowledge of himself in his creation, otherwise no human knowledge of God is true of God! This "correspondence" knowledge that makes of truth, is it not an aspect of the religaric relation and a function of the Spirit and Word (cf. Rom. 8:16; 1 Cor. 2:6-14)?

Another answer, and equally basic, is that his creation shall have all the freedom and all the room to be itself as creation, with all its potentialities and its limitations. God gives and respects the right and freedom of creation to be itself and what it may become as God's creation. In so doing God may be said to limit himself to make room, all the room, for his creation to be and to become. He has honored the human with the freedom and authority to exercise "dominion" over the work of his hands as a way of imaging him in his creation (Gen. 1:26; Ps. 8:5-8). This royal task given to the human has all of creation as creaturely reality to explore, to know, to develop, to participate in its creativity, to protect, to enjoy to the limits of its possibilities as a creaturely reality! That is enough of an arena for human wisdom to know and practice what it knows and lives by! That can include cosmic, natural, biological, human, and cultural reality—what we today call "civilization."

But at the same time, God in becoming creator has bound himself in religaric/covenantal relation to all of his creation. Creation itself is the visible sign of that bond. Since creation is through and by the agency of the Spirit, it is the Spirit that is the bond! He is as Spirit with and for and in his creation in such a way—which is his way—of respecting and affirming, his creation to be his creation. Alternatively, the human in being human as such and in carrying out its royal responsibility for creation has the duty within the religaric bond not only in observing the limits but also by being grateful to God for such limits, for these limits define the arena of his royal responsibility! The human is bound to the religaric/covenantal relationship that is the arena of his freedom. And so the limit need not be understood as a fated lot but the "sphere" of responsible freedom! Wisdom literature has the valuable function of pointing to the possibilities and limits of creaturely knowing, doing, and living. This is to be celebrated!

But together with this grateful celebration it also points to the tragic dimension in human creaturely existence and life. This cannot be ignored! The theodicy question of Job and the cul-de-sac negativity of Qoheleth are priceless reminders to human wisdom of this "tragic sense of life" (Miguel de Unamuno). This tragic sense arises from being both a creature honored with the responsibility for, and the benefit of, creation by the creator himself, and of painfully suffering the need to be saved from the evil that has fallen on his creation. Is there an alternative way to that of wisdom in dealing with this tragic situation and the profound need that emerges from it? This alternative way is the subject of the following chapter.

CHAPTER IX

The Secular Dimensions of Israel's Hope I: Apocalyptic Hope

1. Setting Up the Issue

In this chapter I am suggesting that the hope of Israel has a secular dimension that is essential to any genuine secularity. I am proposing that this dimension is a necessary component of the primal religaric/covenantal relationship and should be lifted up and emphasized. The aim of such an emphasis is to show that the long-standing opposition between the spiritual as other-worldly and of the secular as wholly this-worldly in traditional spirituality may be neutralized in some measure. We shall do this by considering theologically two features of Israel's hope, namely, the apocalyptic and the messianic. In this chapter we shall deal with apocalyptic hope, and with messianic hope in the next chapter. This may pave the way for developing a more positive, adequate, and wholesome spirituality that secularizes by the mutual enrichment of the spiritual and the secular. To do this, it might be helpful to review briefly what we have done so far to indicate the secular context in which the hope of Israel arose and also its spiritual continuity within the primal religaric/covenantal relation.

So far we have affirmed the secularization movement in its attempt to be free from the dominance of "the religious" by seeking to establish itself in its identity, integrity, and validity. We have sought to do this *theologically* by considering the biblical witness to God self-constituting himself as creator, and so creating the heavens and the earth and all that is in them as the creaturely other by his Spirit through his Word. He as creator thereby establishes a primal religaric relation between himself and his creation. He also created a people and established a covenant relation with this people so that he shall be their God and they shall be his people as a historical witness to himself among all the peoples or nations of the earth. In this religaric/covenant relation in which he is together with his people, God is thereby in the midst of his creation and all of humanity as creative power, as accompanying presence, and as life-giving and life-flourishing blessing, without diminution to his freedom to self-constitute himself. Thus, he is also in the midst of his creation and his people as a measuring rod and so as judge of human conduct and its consequence both of the natural and the human.

We have also sketched out in brief and bold relief the fascinating drama of interaction between God and his people in terms of historical events, social institutions, and theological interpretation—the so-called history of salvation tradition in biblical scholarship. In this drama, we have tried to discern the trajectory of the Spirit in the way God has remained faithful to himself by being faithful to the religaric/covenant relation vis-à-vis the ambiguous love/hate response of his people, Israel, and of humankind. In this drama, there have been critically significant historical events that were very traumatic to Israel's faith, threatening the viability and trustworthiness of the religaric/covenant relation. They ultimately led to question even the deity and sovereignty of Yahweh! These traumas of Israel's history include the Assyrian destruction of the Northern Kingdom, the disappearance from the face of the earth of the ten tribes of Israel in 722 B.C.E., the fate of being a helpless pawn on the chessboard of the powerful players in the history of the Near East (Assyria, Egypt, Babylon, Persia, Greece, and Rome), and eventually the destruction of Jerusalem, the city of God and the center of the earth, the ruin of the Temple and its worship practices, the demise of the monarchy—all this culminating in the Exile to Babylon in 587 B.C.E The question may be asked, can hope be born out of this hopeless condition? Is there a future with hope at all? It is very important to note that those historical traumas are secular events. They happened in time and space under certain worldly conditions and by various earthly and human agents. But they are seen and understood within the religaric/covenant relation. This secular reality remains within the provenance of the spiritual bond.

Woven into this history as an inner red thread in both its daily run and its critical peaks is what God "saw that the wickedness of humankind was great in the earth, and that every inclination of the thoughts of their hearts was only evil continually" (Gen. 6:5); what Jeremiah discerned: "The heart is devious above all else; it is perverse—who can understand it" (Jer. 17:9); and what Qoheleth found out: "See, this alone I found, that God made human beings straightforward, but they have devised many schemes" (Eccles. 7:29). This inclination to evil, this deviousness of the heart, this devising of schemes to contravene what is straightforward, has been expressed in many concrete ways: by disobedience to the Torah, by seeking after other gods, by injustice and oppression, by religious syncretism, by trusting in geopolitics to ensure security, and so on. All this in the end amounted to mistrusting the God of the religaric/covenant relationship. Again the question may be asked, can hope be born out of mistrust and doubt and disobedience and the irresistible inclination to do what in the end is hopeless? It is equally important to see this inner evil inclination of the human heart express itself in deeds and events that are characteristically secular. They take place in the world and by worldly agents. They still remain within the provenance of the Spirit.

But God in faithfulness to himself and to the primal relationship that he himself established cannot allow the sin and evil and their expression and consequence without being judged for what they truly are, namely as a challenge to his sovereignty and witness to the failure of Israel to live up to its responsibility as partner in the religaric/covenant relationship. Since this is the case, what can prevent God's judgment upon Israel that came through Ezekiel from being carried out? "Then he said to me, 'Mortal, these bones are the whole house of Israel. They say, "Our bones are dried up, and our hope is lost, we are cut off completely"' (Ezek. 37:11). Is this the final end?

The traumas of Israel's history had the effect of forcing its leaders to review its history and rethink its implications for its faith in God and its future in the religaric/covenant relationship. It seems that this review and rethinking resulted in two general results. One result is the Deuteronomistic and prophetic view that the traumas of Israel's history and that of humankind are divine punishment for human sin and evil, but paradoxically with the forward view of possible repentance, return to the Lord, and reform in personal and social behavior, and thus, on to salvation. The other general result is the priestly and prophetic development reaching its highest peak in the faith in the one and only creator God and the affirmation of creation as incontestably God's. Both are affirmations of God's sovereignty in his faithfulness to himself and to his commitment to his people to be their God!

One might say that the concrete effects of these general reaffirmations in Israel's self-understanding are twofold. One is the glowing prophetic promises of salvation that are yet to be fulfilled, which we discussed in chapter 7. Promises yet unfulfilled have the effect of casting doubt in the reliability of the maker of the promises! The search for wisdom in earthly life with the whole of creation as the arena for discerning and practicing wisdom arose also as a response to the traumas. But this search has ended, as we have seen, with the theodicy problem unresolved. Moreover, the cul-de-sac limits of creation and the inscrutability of God make this search for wisdom in creaturely life to be in the end ironically as also folly. And so the whole drift of the discussion, if it is not too far from the truth, ends up with holding on uncertainly to hope in an ironically hopeless world. In a way, one can say that these are the twin characteristic burdens of secularity once it becomes thoroughly secularistic. On the one hand, there is the continuous unflagging effort to improve life and make it flourish with all the resources that natural possibility provides and by all the human capability that can be mustered. On the other hand, this is done with a reductionistic mentality and activity that confine themselves within a cosmically bordered though expanding universe, with its borders expanding with it, that does not permit any effort to transcend it. The problem then is, can there be a decisive breakthrough that would inspire a vision that penetrates and transcends this bordered, though expanding, universe? Can such a vision open up the floodgates of new possibilities that could constitute a "future filled with hope?" This is the problem we seek to address in this chapter.

What we have done in the previous chapters in sketching out the drama of Israel's history and its faith traditions may be regarded by the experts as a caricature. That may be so. But even a caricature may possess a modicum of truth that points to a much larger and richer repository of truth. It is not my intention to deny such a larger and richer truth. But the caricature that has been sketched out here may at least be adequate in indicating the problem we wish to address in terms of theological resources available in apocalypticism and messianism.

2. Apocalypticism as a Literary Genre

I am not an expert in the field of apocalyptic literature. What follows is dependent on scholarly opinion in this field of studies.[1] In this section we make a summary description of the essential features of Apocalypse as a literary genre,

1. Paul D. Hanson, *The Dawn of Apocalyptic*, (Minneapolis: Fortress, 1979); *Old Testament Apocalyptic* (Nashville: Abingdon Press, 1987); John J. Collins, *The Apocalyptic Imagination*, 2nd ed. (Grand Rapid: Eerdmans, 1998); Stephen L. Cook, *Prophecy and Apocalypticism* (Minneapolis: Fortress, 1995); Craig C. Hill, In God's Time (Grand Rapids: Eerdmans, 2002); Mitchell G. Reddish, ed., *Apocalyptic Literature* (Nashville: Abingdon Press, 1990); Frederick J. Murphy, "Introduction to Apocalyptic Literature" in *The New Interpreter's Bible*, vol. 7 (Nashville: Abingdon Press, 1996), 1–6; Daniel L. Smith- Christopher, "The Book of Daniel" in *The New Interpreter's Bible*, vol. 7 (Nashville: Abingdon Press, 1996), 19–152.

and offer some theological reflections using the genre as a basis. We may begin by indicating the meaning of *apocalyptic*. The word combines two words in Greek: *apo*, which is a prefix meaning "from"; the other Greek word is *kalypto*, which means "to cover," "to hide," derived from "to bury." The combination yields the meaning "to uncover," "to reveal" something covered or hidden.[2] This meaning is at the root of the various ways in which the word *apocalypto* is made to apply; for example, generally as in biblical studies and in Christian theology or doctrine. In biblical studies the term *apocalypse* is applied to a body of literature, both canonical and noncanonical, which is distinguished from other canonical writings, such as historical writings, prophetic books, Wisdom Literature, liturgical psalmody, Gospels, Epistles. In Christian theology the doctrine of revelation deals with the knowledge of God as revealed. It will do us well to hold on to this essential meaning of apocalyptic as revelatory, as revelation.

Some scholars find the beginnings of these writings (*proto-apocalyptic*) in pre-exilic, exilic, and postexilic prophecy in the canonical Old Testament. Paul D. Hanson classifies these into three groups.[3] The first two are the Isaiah and Zechariah groups. The Isaiah group includes Isaiah 56–66, written between 538–515 B.C.E., the period covering the edict of Cyrus (538 B.C.E), which allowed the exiled Jews to return home, and Isaiah 24–27, usually designated as "Isaiah Apocalyptic." The Zechariah group includes Zechariah 12–14; Joel 2:28–3:21; Ezekiel 38–39. The second proto-apocalyptic group consist of Zechariah 1–6 and the book of Malachi. The last is the canonical book of Daniel, representing a fully developed apocalyptic genre, especially chapters 7–12. According to John J. Collins, the fully developed apocalyptic writings, which are Jewish in provenance and possess a fully developed worldview and structural framework, would include 1 Enoch, regarded to be the earliest, Daniel, 4 Ezra, 2 Baruch, Testament of Levi, the fragmentary Apocalypse of Zephaniah, some portions of Jubilees, and the Testament of Abraham.[4] Although these writings deal with many themes, they also have a characteristic feature: they point to the future; they are eschatological in orientation. Revelation and eschatology, and between them nature and history, provide the frame that structures the apocalyptic genre.

The historical period during which these writings emerged and were composed is debated among scholars. We will not get involved in this debate. But if

2. See Gerhard Kittel and Gerhard Friederich, eds., *Theological Dictionary of the New Testament*, trans. Geoffrey W. Bromiley (Grand Rapids: Eerdmans, 1985), 405–6).

3. Hanson, *Old Testament Apocalyptic*, 35–38; cf. Reddish, *Apocalyptic Literature*, 29–30.

4. See list prepared by Collins in *Apocalyptic Imagination*, 5; Cook, *Prophecy and Apocalypticism*, 23.

we locate the beginnings of apocalypticism (*proto-apocalyptic*), though still lacking a comprehensive structural framework, in pre-exilic prophecy then we may date the emergence of this genre of literature in the late sixth century B.C.E., as Paul D. Hanson does.[5] Hanson finds some measure of configuration in some elements of the message of post-exilic prophecy, but this is not yet a developed worldview with a more or less structural framework that is peculiar to this genre.[6] The more comprehensive structural framework that developed later and which exhibits a word-view that features revelation and eschatology is represented by the list of John J. Collins mentioned above. If we are interested only in the developed structural framework, then we may locate the genre from 250 B.C.E to 150 C.E, with I Enoch as the earliest.

But we are interested in both the *proto-apocalyptic* in pre-exilic prophecy and in its more developed structural framework. So it seems best to locate the apocalyptic genre as having arisen and developed in various ways from the late sixth century B.C.E to the middle of the second century C.E. This would assume a measure of continuity in the development of the genre from prophecy to apocalyptic Hanson has traced, with special emphasis on the development of prophetic eschatology to apocalyptic eschatology in his book *The Dawn of Apocalyptic*. The "general matrix" (Collins) then would be from the prophetic pre-exilic period up to the dawn of the Christian Era. The sociohistorical and religious milieu in this period vary, and the apocalyptic elements may receive varying emphases.[7] For example, for the prophetic proto-apocalyptic texts the sociopolitical and religious context is the Exile and the postexilic situation in the late sixth century B.C.E, a period characterized by the exilic trauma, return, and restoration. The situation of Daniel 7–12 is the Seleucid period, specifically the rule of Antiochus IV Epiphanes. This would fall in the second century B.C.E, a time of severe persecution and suppression of the Jews and their faith. In the opinion of some scholars, the importance of this period together with the developments in it, such as the rise of second Temple Judaism, the emergence of Wisdom and Apocalyptic literature, the emergence of messianism, the rise of certain sectarian groups like Qumran, Pharisaism, and so forth, is that it provides a sociohistorical and religious transition that underlyingly links the Old and New Testaments.[8] And so in selecting apocalypticism and

5. See Hanson, *Dawn of Apocalyptic*.

6. Hanson, *Old Testament Apocalyptic*, 131–37

7. Collins, 23–37

8. E. P. Sanders, *Paul and Palestinian Judaism* (Minneapolis: Fortress, 1977); N. T. Wright, *The New Testament and the People of God* (Minneapolis: Fortress, 1992); Hanson, *Old Testament Apocalyptic*; Hill, *In God's Time*; Collins, *Apocalyptic Imagination*.

messianism for treatment here, we are dealing with an important and necessary link to the New Testament.

Hanson made an internal analysis of the proto-apocalyptic texts, identifying their distinct characteristics and has come out with a working definition of Old Testament apocalyptic.[9] The same was undertaken by the Society of Biblical Literature Genres Project, which set out the distinctive elements and comprehensive structural frame of Jewish apocalyptic. The results of this were published in 1979.[10] Since it is neither within our competence nor will it serve the purpose of this book, we will not follow in great detail the internal and exegetical analysis of the experts of the apocalyptic writings. We shall, however, be guided in our theological reflections by the essential features of apocalypse that they identify in their definitions.

We shall rely on the definitions of apocalypse given by two experts. Hanson defines apocalyptic literature as follows:

> A group of writings concerned with the renewal of faith and the reordering of life on the basis of a vision of a prototypical heavenly order revealed to a religious community through a seer. The author tends to relativize the significance of existing realities by depicting how they are about to be superseded by God's universal reign in an eschatological event that can neither be hastened nor thwarted by human efforts, but which will unfold, true to an eternal plan, as the result of divine action.[11]

The Society of Biblical Literature offers the following definition: "A genre of revelatory literature with a narrative framework, in which a revelation is mediated by an otherworldly being to a human recipient, disclosing a transcendent reality which is both temporal, insofar as it envisages eschatological salvation, and spatial insofar as it involves another, supernatural world."[12]

We may begin with the narratival form of the genre. Hanson refers to apocalypse literature simply as "a group of writings" so as not to make the genre too restrictive as to exclude other writings that have some features of the apocalyptic genre but don't fully fit into it. He does not specify the literary form of the genre though it is implied. The other definition describes the literary form as narrative. Apocalyptic literature is narratival. It tells what it says in story form. Of course,

---

9. Hanson, *Dawn of Apocalyptic*; Hanson, *Old Testament Apocalyptic*.

10. John J. Collins, ed., *Apocalypse: The Morphology of a Genre*. Semeia 14 (Missoula, MT: Scholars Press, 1979).

11. Hanson, *Old Testament Apocalyptic,* 27–28.

12. See the list in Collins, *Apocalyptic Imagination*, 5; cf. Cook, *Prophecy and Apocalypticism*, 23.

this form is not exclusive to this genre. A person's life can be told as a story. A specific event or happening can be told as a story. The history of a nation or people can be told as a story. The discovery of a scientific fact can be told as a story. Some stories report facts or describe events or unveil discoveries or findings. They direct attention to them because they are of interest to an audience that perceives them as bearing some meaning that is deemed important to them. Stories of this sort are rationally told. The criterion for knowing, telling, and understanding the story and what it tells is rationality.

Some stories, however, do not report or describe a life, an event, or a world that is there! Rather, they create a world of their own by combining facts, experience, and fiction, such as dreams and visions, in a story line that has a plot that includes characters and agents and events in interactive relations. In the process a story creates a world that may be different from that of the audience. Into this new or different story world, the audience is invited to participate. Stories of this sort do not direct attention to the facts reported or described by the story, but to the world that the story creates. The appeal is not to reason but to the imagination. What is conveyed is not merely knowledge of facts and things and events and their meaning, but what is aroused are primarily feelings, attitudes, motivations, elicited or provoked by the impact of the story-world that is created by the story upon an audience into which an audience is invited to enter and participate.

To achieve this purpose, the language employed by apocalypse is not literalistic or referential, but metaphorical, allusive, allegorical, and even mythological. The language is symbolic of hidden and deeper meanings and feelings that are sought to be conveyed. According to Collins, "the language of the apocalypse is not descriptive, referential, newspaper language, but the expressive language of poetry, which uses symbols and imagery to articulate a sense of feeling about the world. . . . Apocalyptic language is commissive in character: it commits us to a view of the world for the sake of the actions and attitudes that are entailed."[13] Moreover, apocalyptic literature addresses traumas of history and anomies of life. As Mitchell G. Reddish succinctly describes this literature: "Apocalyptic literature is crisis literature."[14] Because of this, the language of apocalypse is pastoral in intention: It articulates hope, offers consolation, and undergirds and strengthens courage in a situation of profound distress. We shall say a bit more about these distressful crises below.

13. Collins, *Apocalyptic Imagination*, 282–83.

14. Reddish, *Apocalyptic Literature*, 24.

Apocalyptic language stands between the otherness of creator and that of the creature, between God being for his people as God, and the people being for God as people. It locates itself within the religaric/covenant bond. It can therefore mediate God to his people and the people to God. And since the primal bond is the Spirit, apocalyptic language is Spirit language; it is talk that mediates otherness; it is priestly communication. It is thus the language that is fit for God's self-disclosure. It is the language of revelation.

This brings us to the next characteristic feature of apocalypse mentioned above in the definitions of apocalyptic literature: It is "*revelatory* literature," it "mediates" *revelation*. We may well ask: What is the *medium* though which revelation is mediated? The definition given by the Society of Biblical Literature does not mention it directly but presupposes it. The Hanson definition however specifically mentions the medium as "vision." But visions take the form of dreams. Vision is seeing in dreams! Dream is seeing in visions. This may sound irrational by a mentality shaped by a rational and scientific culture, although it may be given a rational explanation as in Freud and Jung. But as Collins points, "Throughout the ancient world dreams were regarded as an important means of communication between gods and humanity."[15] In apocalypse they are affirmed as vehicles of revelation. The Old Testament, however, has an ambivalent attitude toward them as vehicles of revelation. Collins points out: "Their validity is assumed in Genesis, but questioned by Jeremiah" (23:27-28). Part of the reason for this is that dreams and visions require interpretation for their understanding. But understanding in revelation does come not by divination but by prayer to the one and true God (see Dan. 2:9).

3. Historical Apocalyptic

But how is this "seeing" made possible? The Society of Biblical Literature classifies the vision seeing in dreams into two types of "journey." One type is a "journey" through all of history from beginning to end, seen from a historical vantage point. Examples of this type are *The Animal Apocalypse* (1 Enoch 85-90), *The Apocalypse of Weeks* (1 Enoch 93:1-10; 91:11-17), 4 *Esdras* (2 Esdras 3-14), and *Baruch*. The visionary dreamer in 1 Enoch 87 speaks of heavenly beings taking him by the hand and being "*raised* . . . from the generations of the earth and lifted . . . into a high place. [They] showed me a tower above the earth, and all the hills were lower. And one said to me, 'Remain here until you have seen everything which is coming upon these elephants and camels and asses, and upon the stars,

15. Collins, *Apocalyptic Imagination*, 91.

and upon all bulls' " (1 Enoch 87:3). From this vantage point, instead of the prophetic "thus says the Lord," the visionary dreamer says, "I saw in a vision on my bed" (1 Enoch 85:3), or "I looked with my eyes as I was sleeping, and I saw heaven above" (1 Enoch 86:1), "Daniel had a dream and visions of his head as he lay in bed . . . I, Daniel saw in my vision by night" (Dan. 7:1-2). What the visionary "sees" is "everything which is coming." It is a way of seeing the future of history retroactively, that is, in terms of events that have already taken place. The method is technically called *vaticinium ex eventu*, prophecy after the fact. In this way the whole of history from beginning to end is seen synoptically: "And all the deeds of men in their order were shown to me" (1 Enoch 89:41). The men and their deeds, which constitute history, are seen not only in temporal sequence as in historical periods or epochs but synoptically. Humanity and its deeds, which constitute history, are here seen in the imagery of animals fighting and eating each other.

In the *Apocalypse of Weeks* (1 Enoch 91:12-17; 93:1-10), we find other elements in the overview of history. Again this overview is given in a "heavenly vision," mediated by "the words of holy angels," and its "understanding from the tablets of heaven"—elements that constitute the medium or way of revelation (1 Enoch 93:2). Here all history is divided into ten weeks, each week constituting a period. History is thus periodized but seen in its entirety, and both its periods or epochs and its wholeness are under God's sovereignty and control. He will bring the entire historical process, with all its traumas and anomies, into a conclusion that vindicates him and his people! The first week is one in which "justice and righteousness still lasted" (1 Enoch 93:3). In the second week, "great wickedness will arise" and will continue to intensify and extensify in iniquity, impiety, and apostasy until the seventh week. Alongside the growth of evil and sin there will be a remnant of believers and practitioners of holy and righteous living according to a law for all generations. This remnant is made to see a vision of final judgment that vindicates and punishes. The beginnings of this judgment of vindication of the righteous and the punishment of the wicked take place in the eighth week, and so it is already taking place in some measure. But in the ninth week, "the righteous judgment will be revealed to the whole world, and all the deeds of the impious will vanish from the whole earth; and the world will be written down for destruction, and all men will look to the path of righteousness" (1 Enoch 91:11-15; 93:3-10). In the tenth week, "the great eternal heaven will spring from the midst of the angels. And the first heaven will vanish and pass away, and a new heaven will appear, and all the powers of heaven will shine for ever [with) sevenfold light" (1 Enoch 91:15-17).

What is new and distinctive of apocalypticism in all this? We may note the following:

1. The periodization of history and seeing it in its wholeness from the viewpoint of its end is characteristically apocalyptic.

2. The evaluation of the present age as evil and sinful and currently being judged hiddenly, but eventually and finally to be judged openly, is common in all apocalypse.

3. The coexistence in history of good and evil, of the righteous and the wicked, is not new. As we have seen, the resolution of this profound issue is the burden of Job. It is a characteristic of secular life and history. But in apocalypticism, it receives a resolution in terms of final judgment in accordance with a moral structure (the law) that is valid for all times.

4. The possibility of reform and renewal in personal, community, and national life through return and repentance, and by fulfilling the law and obeying its mandate for justice and righteousness by means of human initiative and effort appear impossible and hopeless in the eyes of the apocalypticist. Instead, only a divine initiative and intervention can do what the human cannot do.

5. Finally, there is envisioned the vanishing away of the first heaven and a new heaven "will appear, and all the powers of heaven will shine forever with sevenfold light. And . . . there will be many weeks without number forever in goodness and righteousness, from then on sin will never be mentioned" (1 Enoch 91:16-17). The appearance of this new heaven is to take place on earth and will renew the earth into what it was in the beginning: God's garden of Eden. The vision of a new heaven and a new earth that historically is only seen as mediated in a dream is indeed revealed as already there from the primal beginning when God created "the heavens and the earth." He has never lost sight of his purpose of binding the heavens and the earth in a religaric/covenant relationship in order to make the "earth as it is in heaven."

The apocalypse that is canonical in the Old Testament is the book of Daniel. It can be classified as a historical apocalypse. It has some distinctive features that can be added to those already noted. There is an obvious difference between the tales told in Daniel 1–6 and the visions reported in Daniel 7–12. The unity of these sections and their dating is a matter of debate among scholars. We shall not get involved in this discussion. We may note, however, that in Daniel 2, Daniel, as an interpreter of dreams, was called upon to describe and interpret the dreams of

King Nebuchadnezzar, when none of the magicians, the enchanters, the sorcerers, or the Chaldeans could name the dream and interpret it. The reason the dream could not be interpreted is that the king refused to tell the dream: "Tell me the dream, and I shall know that you can give me its interpretation" (Dan. 2:9). To this demand of the king, the so-called wise men of the Chaldeans replied: "There is no one on earth who can reveal what the king demands! In fact no king, however great and powerful, has ever asked such a thing of any magician or enchanter or Chaldean. The thing that the King is asking is too difficult, and no one can reveal it to the king except the gods, whose dwelling is not with mortals" (Dan. 2:10-11). For their failure to heed the king's demand because of its impossibility these so-called wise men were about to be executed by decree of the king, including Daniel, a Jew in exile in Babylon from Judah. But Daniel responded to Arioch, the king's executioner as to why the king's decree was so urgent. Arioch explained the matter to him. Whereupon Daniel asked that he be given time and he would interpret the dream. Daniel went home and informed his friends, Hananiah, Mishael, and Azariah, of the king's demand and told them to "seek mercy from the God of heaven" (Dan. 2:18) concerning this mystery, as he himself he would do in prayer. Then the mystery was revealed to Daniel in a vision of the night, and Daniel blessed God of heaven:

> Daniel said: "Blessed be the name of God from age to age, for wisdom and power are his. He changes times and seasons, deposes kings and sets up kings; he gives wisdom to the wise and knowledge to those who have understanding. He reveals deep and hidden things; he knows what is in the darkness, and light dwells with him. To you, O God of my ancestors, I give thanks and praise, for you have given me wisdom and power, and have now revealed to me what we asked of you, for you have revealed to us what the king ordered." (Dan. 2:20-23)

Daniel told Arioch that he would name and interpret the dream of the king and asked that he not "destroy the wise men of Babylon" (Dan. 2:24). Arioch brought Daniel quickly to the king and said to him: "I have found among the exiles from Judah a man who can tell the king the interpretation" (Dan. 2:25). So the king asked Daniel whether he could tell the dream and its interpretation. Daniel answered the king: "No wise men, enchanters, magicians, or diviners can show to the king the mystery that the king is asking, but there is a God in heaven who reveals mysteries, and he has disclosed to King Nebuchadnezzar what will happen at the end of days. Your dream and the visions of your head as you lay in bed were these: To you, O king, as you lay in bed, came thoughts of what would be hereafter, and the revealer of mysteries disclosed to you what is to be. But as for me, this mystery has not been revealed to me because of any wisdom that I have more than any other living being, but in order that the interpretation may be known to the king and that you may understand the thoughts of your mind" (Dan. 2:27-30).

Before proceeding any further, it may be worthwhile to note certain points in what has been said that bear on the claim that the mentality and language of apocalypse is revelatory of mystery. We make notice the following:

1. It is widely believed then that visions and dreams signal the appearance of a mystery.

2. The appearance of the mystery is not upon the initiative or summons of the visioner/dreamer. It comes to the recipient *motto propio*; the recipient cannot prevent its coming when it comes. Its coming disturbs the recipient in his sleep, and evokes anxiety because one does not know what it means.

3. The recipient of the dream or vision believes that the appearance of the mystery bears some significance of curse or blessing upon him, his life, his concerns and responsibilities, in short upon his life-world.

4. But he does not know what this is. And so he seeks to know what it means. The meaning of what is dreamed is part of the mystery; it is known only by the source of the mystery. Only the source of the mystery can disclose what the mystery means to the recipient of the mystery.

5. There are interpreters of dreams and visions. But unless they know the dream or vision they cannot interpret it. The dreamer has to tell his dream, if he can or will, to an interpreter so that the interpreter can tell what it means. The interpreter has techniques—magic, sorcery, divination—that he skillfully uses to interpret the dream or vision. But these are human techniques to probe the meaning of a mystery that comes from "the gods, whose dwelling is not with mortals" (Dan. 2:11). There is therefore no guaranteed certainty that the interpretation given by the so-called wise men is right or true.

6. Only the source of the mystery knows the meaning of the mystery that appears to someone! So Daniel tells the king: "No wise men, enchanters, magicians, or diviners can show to the king the mystery that the king is asking, but there is a God in heaven who reveals mysteries, and he has disclosed to King Nebuchadnezzar what will happen at the end of days. . . . But as for me, this mystery has not been revealed to me because of

any wisdom that I have more than any other living being, but in order that the interpretation may be known to the king and that you may understand the thoughts of your mind" (Dan. 2:27-28, 30).

To sum up: Mystery and its meaning come from God. They bear a significance for the recipient of dreams and visions that is the means or form in which they appear to a recipient. Only God may disclose the meaning of the mystery because only he knows it. He discloses the mystery and its meaning through an interpreter of his own choosing. Only then does a dream or vision become a genuine revelation!

Daniel's answer to the king does not only say that it is God who reveals, it also says what God reveals. And what God reveals is "what will happen at the end of days what is to be" (Dan. 2:28, 29). What God reveals are events that will happen, and they will happen in time. Moreover, they are events that will happen at the "end of days," that is, at the end of a period of time that has characteristic features that makes it somewhat different from other periods of time. It may not be the case that "the end of days" means the end of all days or the end of all time. We again find here the periodization of history and its eschatological orientation.

We now ask, what is it that is revealed? What is the dream and what does it mean? The dream is:

> "You were looking, O King, and lo! there was a great statue. This statue was huge, its brilliance extraordinary; it was standing before you, and its appearance was frightening. The head of that statue was of fine gold, its chest and arms of silver, its middle and thighs of bronze, its legs of iron, its feet partly of iron and partly of clay. As you looked on, a stone was cut out, not by human hands, and it struck the statue on its feet of iron and clay and broke them in pieces. Then the iron, the clay, the bronze, the silver, and the gold, were all broken in pieces and became like the chaff of the summer threshing floors; and the wind carried them away, so that not a trace of them could be found. But the stone that struck the statue became a great mountain and filled the whole earth." (Dan. 2:31-35)

And this is the interpretation:

> "This was the dream: now we will tell the king its interpretation. You, O king, the king of kings—to whom the God of heaven has given the kingdom, the power, the might, and the glory, into whose hand he has given human beings, wherever they live, the wild animals of the field, and the birds of the air, and whom he has established as ruler over them all—you are the head of gold. After you shall arise another kingdom inferior to yours, and yet a third kingdom

> of bronze, which shall rule over the whole earth. And there shall be a fourth kingdom, strong as iron; just as iron crushes and smashes everything, it shall crush and shatter all these. As you saw the feet and toes partly of potter's clay and partly of iron, it shall be a divided kingdom; but some of the strength of iron shall be in it, as you saw the iron mixed with the clay. As the toes of the feet were part iron and part clay, so the kingdom shall be partly strong and partly brittle. As you saw the iron mixed with clay, so will they mix with one another in marriage, but they will not hold together, just as iron does not mix with clay. And in the days of those kings the God of heaven will set up a kingdom that shall never be destroyed, nor shall this kingdom be left to another people. It shall crush all these kingdoms and bring them to an end, and it shall stand forever; just as you saw that a stone was cut from the mountain not by hands, and that it crushed the iron, the bronze, the clay, the silver, and the gold. The great God has informed the king what shall be hereafter. The dream is certain, and its interpretation trustworthy." (Dan. 2:36-45)

We may note a pattern of historical apocalyptic in both dream and interpretation that may further illuminate what is said above about apocalyptic revelation.

1. All history is seen in terms of kings and kingdoms. It is thus characterized by what kings do and how they rule and affect the lives of peoples. History is divided into periods of kingship and dynasties depending on characteristic features provided by the way the king exercises his rule.

2. The power to rule is acquired by military might and is enforced by the same, although its administration may be qualified by wisdom, law, and even benevolence.

3. The power to rule is structured hierarchically. It is organized and exercised from top down. It is effective by being enforced by military might and to the extent that the people obey.

4. Any particular king and his kingdom will last until conquered by another king or military power whose rule in turn will last until conquered by another king or military might, and so the same cycle goes on.

5. One important factor here that may need some emphasizing is the character of the feet of the ruling power. They are made of both iron and clay. The same is true, however, of the feet of the people whom the royal feet step on or trample upon. But iron and clay may mix, but "they will not hold together" (2:43). And so there is division in the kingdom right through from the king down to all levels of the hierarchy and the social fabric to the bottom base, namely, the people. It is this mixture of iron and

clay, of strength and weakness, of truth and falsehood, of righteousness and wickedness, of good and evil, of wisdom and folly that no royal rule can eliminate. It is the Achilles' heel of all political power. It cuts through all dimensions of power—political, military, legal, economic, intellectual, and practical. All history is permeated by it. The ambiguities, tensions, and conflicts it creates cannot be resolved from within it! Any resolution from within history partakes of the same history. And so it may be asked, will it ever be resolved? All that has been said so far is characteristic of secular reality.

6. But paradoxically enough, this reality, so palpably secular in character, is viewed from the perspective of the end. It is seen in all its starkness in the light of revelation; that means in the light of God's judgment and mercy and what he will do about it. Therefore, one can say that this reality is not divorced from the primal religaric relationship. Indeed, its true character as secular is seen and affirmed for what it is in the light of that primal relationship. Its future is also to be seen in the light of the primal relation and that future will also be disclosed by God.

7. We now come to a very critical point, a "tipping point." Alongside and in the same "days of those kings the God of heaven will set up a kingdom" (2:44). This kingdom is initiated by God and established by him and so it is his kingdom. Its coming is the end of all earthly kingdoms established and ruled by earthly rulers and their dynasties: "It shall crush all these kingdoms and bring them to an end" (2:44b). They all will be "broken in pieces and [become] like the chaff of the summer threshing floors; and the wind carried them away, so that not a trace of them could be found" (2:35). Because it is by God's action that this kingdom comes and is established on earth and puts an end to all earthly kingdoms, it "shall never be destroyed, nor shall this kingdom be left to another people . . . and it shall stand forever" (2:44). This coming of the kingdom by God's action is the basis for dividing the "ages" into "the present age" and "the age to come." It is also the basis for the judgment that "this present age" is evil and sinful, and therefore it must be put to its end. It is the source of the expectation that "the age to come" would be so much better than the age that is passing away. The hope that is expressed here is double-edged: There is hope that the present evil age will surely come to its end; and there is the promised hope of the age to come, which ushers in a new order of things!

So far we have been following through a third feature of apocalypse indicated by the two definitions quoted above—"the reordering of life on the basis of a prototypical heavenly order" (Paul Hanson), a "transcendent reality which is both temporal insofar as it envisages eschatological salvation, and spatial insofar as it involves another, supernatural world" (Society of Biblical Literature). There is here an expression of hope in a situation of hopelessness. It may be useful at this point to indicate what the situation is and the hope that is envisaged.

We have described apocalypse as expressing a profound feeling about a particular life-world that is in crisis at a particular historical period. The feeling that is expressed is a hope to which people in crisis are being pastorally urged to commit themselves in spite of a given seemingly hopeless situation. We noted above that apocalyptic language is expressive, pastoral, and commissive. Hope is best expressed, urged, and evoked in the language of visions and dreams that seek to transcend a given hopeless situation. This situation is that of exile. To be in exile is to be forcibly removed from one's own homeland. It is to be made to live in another land, a foreign land, as a captive, marginalized, and oppressed people. It is to be ruled by a political (royal) power that the exiled people cannot overthrow and be freed from. It is to be confined into a kind of ghetto existence where the traditional institutions that bind a people into a community are absent—no city that communes, no Temple that gathers the people in worship, no acknowledged king with commanding and binding authority. To be in exile is to be no people at all in the midst of people who are a people! This is the life-world of being in exile.

In this situation, what realistic hopes may a people dream of and see as a vision, even though in the present situation of exile, such a dream may be "an impossible dream"? Would not such a hope consist of liberation from exile and marginalization, return to one's own homeland, restoration of the institutions that bind the people together, the recovery of economic life by making the land yield its produce, and the rebuilding of national life that would again have its own honored identity among the nations? Would not this vision of hope "relativize" the life-world of exile and consign it to only a period of history in the many cyclic periods of history that have their own here and now, their own limited span of time, their own *saeculum*, or *olam*, or aeon, or age? Would not such a "relativization" include the evaluation that the life-world of exile as evil, made unbearably real by the sin of the people themselves (of iniquity, impiety, and apostasy), be judged as absolutely undesirable and must be made to cease? And would not the relativization and passing away of the life-world of exile happen precisely when the new age that is to come is already seen and felt as now being established, and will hold fast as a steadfast hope? Should not such a steadfast hope be grounded in, and framed and sustained by, faith—faith in the one true God? And is not faith the assured feeling that one knows that what one hopes for will indeed happen because faith is trust in the one who can make the impossible happen by making it humanly possible? And is this not precisely the work of the Spirit—making impossible things happen through inspired human agency? Does not the prophet Joel testify that when the Spirit is poured by God upon all flesh, the certain effect is to dream dreams and see visions (Joel 2:28-29)? And so, is it too far-fetched to say that the secularly palpable hopes of all flesh, as the hopes mentioned above are, which are seen only in dreams and visions in a hopeless situation, are in truth the work of God through his Spirit? Secular hopes are grounded in, and framed and sustained by, the Spirit. It is the Spirit that inspires secular hopes because secularity and its hopes are seen within the religaric bond of the Spirit!

Is it too far from the truth to say that in effect this is the interpretation of Daniel of the life-world of the Exile and its hope that he gave to his fellow exiles by way of interpreting the dream of King Nebuchadnezzar whose reign represents only a period of history? His reign is replaced by Cyrus, king of Persia, who conquered the empire of Babylon in 539 B.C.E. The exiles were allowed to return to their homeland by decree of Cyrus. They became vassals of Persia and were allowed some measure of autonomy. They were even helped by Cyrus to rebuild the Temple, which was completed in 515 B.C.E. under Zerubbabel. The walls of Jerusalem were also rebuilt in 445 B.C.E. under Nehemiah. But even though they were back in their homeland they were still under a foreign ruler and the conditions of life were none too good. They were in some sense still exiles, still marginalized and confined in their own walls within a much larger empire ruled by a foreign king.

The Persian Empire was conquered by Alexander the Great, king of Macedonia, in 334 B.C.E., who captured Jerusalem in 332 B.C.E. Following his death in 323 B.C.E., his vast empire was divided among his four generals. Ptolemy took over Egypt, Seleucus took over Babylon/Syria, Lysimachus took over Asia Minor, and Cassandra took over Macedonia and Greece. And so began what in the history of culture is known as Hellenization, which is the spread of the Greek language, education, culture, and religion, aided by political power and military might. In the milieu of Hellenization, the Jews found it very difficult to maintain their racial, religious, cultural, and national identity. In the face of the onslaught of paganism often enforced by persecution, the Jews sought to assert their identity by dutifully observing Temple worship and the Sabbath, the study of the Torah, circumcision as a badge of racial purity and identity, the food laws, and the festivals, and they forbade intermarriage. It is precisely these marks of racial and cultural identity that were severely threatened by being outlawed. Faced with this continuing threat and the danger of violence, resentment became the attitudinal and emotional characteristic of Jewish relation with its Hellenizing environment. Add to this the internal conflict among the Jews—between those who would accommodate to Hellenism and those who would not, between the north of Judah who were poor and those in the south and in the city who were prosperous and enjoyed a measure of privilege and power, and between sectarian groups who vied as to who among them represented the true Israel! This conflict situation gave rise to a revolutionary spirit among the Jews that pervaded the air, ready to explode into violence, if intolerably provoked.

And so we enter the life-world of Judah during the rule of Antiochus IV Epiphanes (137–149 B.C.E.), the Seleucid king. This is the setting of Daniel 7–12, although the story-line in his visions takes place in Babylon, several centuries earlier. It is likely the aim of the editors of Daniel in telling the story in an ex-eventu manner to emphasize the continuing exile situation and mentality of the Jews—in Babylon in a foreign land, as "slaves in their own homeland" under Persia (Neh. 9:36; cf. Ezra 9:8-9) and the Medes, on to Greece through the Ptolemies and the Seleucids, and thence on to Rome, and into the Middle Ages and into the modern world. Has not this feeling and mind-set of being "in exile" given rise justifiably for sheer survival to a siege-mentality among Jews in the face of the deeply entrenched and sometimes violent anti-Semitism of Middle Eastern and of Western cultures up to contemporary times? And when shall this situation of antagonism and conflict end, may we ask?

In entering the canonically apocalyptic life-world of Daniel 7–12, we are ushered into a somewhat familiar milieu already mapped out by Daniel 2. The apocalyptic structure that we outlined above frames the visions of Daniel and their interpretation. There are, however, a number of distinctive elements in the material of Daniel 7–12 that are worth emphasizing.

For one thing, Daniel is now himself the recipient of visions that need interpretation for understanding, and not merely the interpreter of someone's dreams and visions. This exhibits the character of apocalyptic as revelatory. But why is this changed? When Daniel was called to the court of King Nebuchadnezzar, the atmosphere between Gentile and exiled Jew was still somewhat open and friendly. An exiled Jew was welcome in the court of the king and he could even be appointed a courtier if deserving, while remaining a faithful Jew, as Daniel was!

But now, the historical situation has dramatically changed. In Daniel 2, it is the fate of Nebuchadnezzar and his empire that is the focus of the dream, and it was what Daniel interpreted. Although the future of the Jewish people is connected with Nebuchadnezzar's dream, it was nevertheless safely assured. But now it is the fate of the Jews, his own people, that hangs in the balance at the hands of a tyrannical and cruel king. All indicators point to the threat of destruction. Daniel is rightly concerned deep into his bones about the crisis. His anxiety out of concern for the future of his people is what now gives rise to his visions. He had several of them: 1:102ff.; 8:1-2ff.; 10:2-6ff. The visions had the effect of intensifying Daniel's troubled spirit (7:15; 8:15; 10:7-9), and this led him to seek understanding (8:15-15; 9:3). But the interpretation and understanding of the visions did not come from him, but to him through a heavenly messenger, and angel, especially for Daniel's understanding (7:16ff.; 8:15ff.; 10:10ff.). In Daniel 2 it was Daniel, an exiled Jew, who interpreted King Nebuchadnezzar's dream, although the interpretation was revealed to him. In the case of Daniel's vision, the interpretation was given by angelic messengers whose "word" is God's word. The vision, the interpretation, the messenger are from God; together they constitute revelation.

But what is the revelation about? Is it about God? But why would God reveal himself to himself? God's self-knowledge is transparent to himself. And if what God reveals is from himself, but not to himself, to whom does he reveal it? And why would God be so keen about revealing what he has to reveal to someone other than himself? From what has been said so far, the answer to these questions seems obvious enough. What God reveals is about the world and his dealings with it. What he reveals he discloses to the world. It is made known to the world because it concerns the history, destiny, and meaning of the world. And God is concerned about the world because it is his world. And so revelation is from God to the world about the world and for the world. Revelation is this-worldly. What God knows and reveals about this world is genuine knowledge of the world and so is the truth of this world. Can revelation be any more secular than this? And because it is from God in terms of his perspective, it can only be in his power and light. That means in the Spirit who is the religaric bond! If the world is revealed as this-worldly and secular by God in and through the Spirit, can we say of the Spirit anything less than it is the Spirit that secularizes?

Apocalypse has a penchant for viewing history in periods, and periods in terms of kings and their kingdoms and how they affect peoples. We are not surprised that we find this fully developed in Daniel 7–12. How does history as represented by kings and kingdoms arise? In Daniel 7:2-3, we read: "I , Daniel, saw in my vision by night the four winds of heaven stirring up the great sea, and four great beasts came up out of the sea, different from one another." I take this verse as a reading of Genesis 1:1-2 and applied to history! The "winds of heaven stirring up the great sea" is "a wind from God sweeping over the face of the waters." The "great sea" is the waters of chaos. The "stirring up" is the Spirit creating out of the sea of non-possibility, which is chaos. And what emerges out of this creation out of chaos? The existence of the world and its history represented by kings and kingdoms in their own *saeculum*, their own span of time or *olam*. There is a deep irony that is expressed here, however. Instead of bearing the power of the Spirit to create the good of existence, of order, and of life and its flourishing, the kings and their kingdoms become bearers of the beastly and untamed destructiveness of chaos unleashed by the license of disobedient freedom, which freedom is itself a gift of God: the king "takes action as he pleases" (Neh. 9:24, 37; cf. Esther 1:8; 9:5; Dan. 11:3,16, 36;). And so the rule of kings, as their history shows, is one of destroying, killing, plundering, oppressing, and persecuting, and like beasts of prey, they devour one another. And if they do any building up of good in any form, it is for their own glory, even to the height not only of making themselves gods but above all, gods who speak arrogant words against the one true God (Dan. 11:36). All rulership when done in unbridled power is beastly. Is it any wonder that in the vision of Daniel the metaphor used for kings is "beast"?

But this overview of history is seen in its wild destructiveness only because in Daniel it is directed against his own people. Indeed, it is. But does not ruling power victimize those it rules? And how else do victims view their victimizers except from the underside of things, which is their side? In the history that Daniel sees, his people are in the underside of things; there was no way at all to move even only to the level-side of things, let alone to the overside.

For Daniel, the periods of history as a whole with their characteristic features serve only as background for the one period of history that he singles out as of primary interest to him, and that is the reign of Antiochus IV Epiphanes (175–164 B.C.E.). The reason for his special interest is the fact that Antiochus IV inflicted massive destruction and enormous suffering on the Jewish people in their own homeland more than any ruler before him:

> Then I desired to know the truth concerning the fourth beast, which was different from all the rest, exceedingly terrifying, with its teeth of iron and claws of bronze, and which devoured and broke in pieces, and stamped what was left with his feet . . . the horn that had eyes and a mouth that spoke arrogantly, and that seemed greater than the others. As I looked, this horn made war with the holy ones and was prevailing over them. . . . He shall speak words against the Most High, shall wear out the holy ones of the Most High, and shall attempt to change the sacred seasons and the law; and they shall be given to his power for a time, two times, and half a time (Dan. 7:19, 20b-21; 25)

This language puts into the beauty of poetry the utterly ugly deeds that Antiochus IV violently inflicted upon the Jews during his reign. A more straightforward account in prose is found in 1 and 2 Maccabees. He subjugated Judah and destroyed Jerusalem, killing many of the Jews (1 Macc. 1:20, 30-32). Antiochus IV entered the Temple and ransacked it by stripping it of its liturgical furniture, ornaments, and treasures (1 Macc. 1:21-24). He built a pagan altar, with a statue of Zeus to be worshiped—the so-called "abomination that desolates"—on top of the Jewish one (1 Macc. 1:54). He established a military garrison beside the Temple to oversee and enforce the pagan rites that were decreed to be observed (1 Macc. 1:33, 36). He changed the calendar and so he wrought havoc on the observance of "the sacred seasons and the law." He had a gymnasium built and ran it in the Greek style where the Jewish youth and adults could be educated in the Greek language and culture and thus be Hellenized! In a decree imposing paganism upon his kingdom, he wrote:

> Then the king wrote to his whole kingdom that all should be one people, and that all should give up their particular customs. All the Gentiles accepted the command of the king. Many even from Israel gladly adopted his religion; they sacrificed to idols and profaned the sabbath. And the king sent letters by messengers to Jerusalem and the towns of Judah; he directed them to follow customs strange to the land, to forbid burnt offerings and sacrifices and drink offerings in the sanctuary, to profane sabbaths and festivals, to defile the sanctuary and the priests, to build altars and sacred precincts and shrines for idols, to sacrifice swine and other unclean animals, and to leave their sons uncircumcised. They were to make themselves abominable by everything unclean and profane, so that they would forget the law and change all the ordinances. He added, "And whoever does not obey the command of the king shall die." (1 Macc. 1:41-50 cf. 2 Macc. 6:1-10, emphasis added)

How did the Jews respond to this crisis? There were those among them who connived with the ruling power and succumbed to Hellenization (1 Macc. 1:11-15; cf. Dan. 11:32; 2 Macc. 4:7-17; 1 Enoch 90:6-9). Others rebelled in military violence. The story of the rebellion initiated by Mattathias and pursued vigorously by his son Judas Maccabeus is the classic paragon of Jewish militant resistance (1 Macc. 2-9). Of course, all the Jews lamented the traumatic crisis that had befallen them:

> Israel mourned deeply in every community, rulers and elders groaned, young women and young men became faint, the beauty of the women faded. Every bridegroom took up the lament; she who sat in the bridal chamber was mourning. Even the land trembled for its inhabitants, and all the house of Jacob was clothed with shame. (1 Macc. 1:25-28)

The general reaction was resistance, resentment, and hostility (Dan. 11:32; 1 Macc. 1:62-63). But what was hoped to be gained by these responses? Those who compromised with the Seleucid rule and Hellenization aimed at gaining power and wealth. Those who rebelled violently wanted to rid their homeland of a foreign ruler and sought relief from heavy taxation, restoration of their faith and cultural heritage, the cleansing of the Temple of its abomination, and recovery of their honored named among the nations (1 Macc. 1:27-28, 50-64, 66-68; 3:20-22, 58-60). Those who refused to join in violent rebellion, what were they to do? What action were they to take? It appears that they did two things: First, they would educate their own people with their faith traditions and preserve their cultural identity and this would shape their resistance convictionally; and second, they would be ready to make the ultimate sacrifice on behalf of their faith commitments (Dan. 11:32-35). This, of course, included their agreement with the aims of the rebellion, but not with the method of violence.

It may be appropriate to ask at this point the question, What is the basis or ground of these actions and their aims? Apparently both the accommodation and resistance to Greek rule and paganism had aims and methods of a cultural, secular nature. But is there also an ultimate and overarching vision of hope that is at the core of these secular hopes? This is the question raised by the poignant cry: "For how long?" The cry asks not only for "how long" (time wise) will the desecration of Israel last but also, and more important, what will put the end to it, "For how long is this vision concerning the regular burnt offering, the transgression that makes desolate, and the giving over of the sanctuary and host to be trampled?" (Dan. 8:13).

To answer this question, we return to the visions of Daniel. We may note the following points:

1. The visions concern eschatological hope, a characteristic of apocalyptic. They are about what will take place at the end-time (8:17; 10:14; 12:4, 9, 13). The time line is only temporary. Calculations of its temporal length were made (8:14; 9:24; 12:7, 11).

2. The hope about the end-time is revealed by God and interpreted by his messengers. It is not the sort of hope that humans make for themselves, which they can know and realize. Rather it is the hope of God for his world and his people, which he alone knows and reveals and can make happen. It is God's hope for history and his people that generates its expectation and so makes it into human hope, secular hope.

3. Because it is God's hope for his world and his people that he knows, reveals, and executes, there is a sense of necessity and finality to it:

"What is determined shall be done" (11:36). Although kings "act as they please," and even exalt themselves above the gods, there is nothing that they can do to offset or overcome what has been divinely decided for them and their rule (11:36, 45).

4. What is to happen at the end is judgment justly rendered by the "Ancient One" and his hosts or council, acting as a court (7:9-10, 26). The judgment will be upon kings and their evil rule and also upon the holy ones of God's people. But the verdict differs. For the kings and their evil rule as represented by the "beast," the verdict is destruction: "And as I watched, the beast was put to death, and its body destroyed and given over to be burned with fire. As for the rest of the beasts, their dominion was taken away, but their lives were prolonged for a season and a time" (7:11-12; cf. 7:26; 8:25c). In the end, evil is routed out! But for the holy ones of God's people, the judgment is vindication of their faithfulness and obedience. Salvation is the verdict! So it is judgment that constitutes the tipping point that divides history into "this present evil age" that is passing away, and the beginning of the "age that is to come," which is the age of vindication and salvation.

5. The vision is also of the appearance of "one like a human being coming with the clouds of heaven. And he came to the Ancient One and was presented before him" (7:13). There is a great deal of scholarly debate about the identity of this figure. The issue is the apparent difference between 7:13-14 and 7:22 and 27. In the former, kingship is given to the "one like a human being." Is this an individual of heavenly provenance though with human-like appearance? In the latter, kingship is handed over to the "holy ones of the Most High" (7:18) or "to the people of the holy ones of the Most High" (7:27). Are the holy ones the people of Israel, the holy nation and a kingdom of priests? We need not enter this debate. What we can be sure of is that the Ancient One anoints an agent who brings about the reign of God, which puts an end to the reign of the kingdoms of this world and thus ushers in the age to come for all peoples, nations, and languages: "To him was given dominion and glory and kingship, that all peoples, nations, and languages should serve him. His dominion is an everlasting dominion that shall not pass away, and this kingship is one that shall never be destroyed." (7:14; cf. 7:24). The important point to emphasize here is that the age that is to come will come to this world of earthly kings and peoples and nations and languages. When it comes,

it has the effect of transforming them into serving the new king and his kingdom. And so the new king will have a new kingdom consisting of transformed people in a transformed world of nations, languages, and cultures that worship him and obey him and so live in him. Is not this transforming activity the work of the Spirit that makes this world genuinely secular within the religaric bond?

6. This transformation is to take place at the very point when the world under its evil rulers finds itself in "a time of anguish, such as has never occurred since nations first came into existence" (Dan. 12:1). That time is when the rulers of this age do the utmost worst of evil that they are capable of and can inflict upon their peoples who go into panic because evil shall have increased (12:1, 4). But this "time of anguish" is also the anguish that accompanies the birth of the new age: "But at that time [referring to the "time of anguish"] your people shall be delivered, everyone who is found written in the book" (12:1).

7. But what kind of "deliverance"? It is deliverance by resurrection for final judgment (12:2-3). It is, of course, assumed that this deliverance is God's action of bringing in the age to come. The action is one of "awakening" "many of those who sleep in the dust of the earth" (12:2). This obviously refers to the dead. By God's deliverance they shall awake from the sleep of death. This awakening from the sleep of death is metaphor for resurrection. Is this perhaps the earliest canonical into final judgment: "some to everlasting life, and some to shame and everlasting contempt" (12:2). It is also assumed that the judge here is none other than God, the Ancient One. It is he who decides who goes into "everlasting life" and who goes to "everlasting contempt." It is intriguing to ask here the sense of "everlasting." Is it connected to the reign of God on earth that is "everlasting" or to his "eternity" as God in which there is "no end" to his self-constitution and self-becoming as God? Would not "everlasting" here mean the time he creates for his creation and it will last so long as his self-constitution as creator "lasts"? Life still is and remains created life lived in the time created for it and in the space created for it and in the processes and changes entailed by its creatureliness. And this will "last" for "as long" as God as creator reigns over his creation. And so creaturely life becomes "everlasting" within the religaric relationship the bond of which is the Spirit who is active in imparting the power, presence, and blessing of God upon his creation,

which blessing includes the making of the earth as genuinely earthly and the world as authentically this-worldly!

To sum up, historical apocalyptic futurizes time and eschatologizes history. It opens up heaven for its blessing to come down on earth to be received and known and enjoyed by the people of this world. It points to a judgment that is going on in the world and will have a final denouement in the end. It exhibits a just moral structure and an inner dynamism of goodness that cannot and will not be thwarted by the evil that humans do! It sees a vision of hope that rescues this creaturely world from its destruction and transforms it into the world of God's reign and so makes and preserves it as truly and genuinely his creation. This vision of hope enables people going through a traumatic crisis to stand firm, not to lose heart in the face of evil, find meaning in their suffering, loyal and faithful to their covenant obligations, and stay the course of their commitment to the God who makes them see a vision that promises them a future with hope. This is hope that consoles and comforts and encourages and enlivens life to move on! It is pastoral hope! Apocalypticism expresses all this within the primal bond of the Spirit who creatively secularizes by opening up the future with new and unexpected possibilities!

4. Heavenly Apocalyptic

We now take up the other type of apocalyptic literature classified by the Society of Biblical Literature as containing "otherworldly journeys." This literature is not part of the canon of the Old Testament. We have two reasons for considering it here. First, it enriches our understanding of the apocalyptic perspective because it deals with some themes and materials not covered by the historical apocalyptic. Second, and more important, it provides a likely model that anticipates the only apocalyptic literature in the canon of the New Testament, namely, the Apocalypse of John. The writings in this class of apocalypse include the *Book of the Watchers* (1 Enoch 1–36), the *Similitudes* (or *Parables*) *of Enoch* (1 Enoch 37–71), the *Testament of Abraham*. It is not our purpose to consider all these writings here. What we can do is to sample what is distinctive about them that adds up, together with the features of historical apocalyptic, to a more or less adequate and clearer understanding of the apocalyptic perspective.

We begin by considering a basic difference. Historical apocalyptic sees historical reality from a vantage point within history. That vantage point is the end-time, and historical apocalyptic sees history as assuredly moving toward this end-time. Although it sees history in terms of periods, it ultimately divides history into two times or ages, the present one which is evil, and the future one that is to come to put an end to the present evil age and inaugurate the age of vindication and salvation. In the heavenly apocalyptic, all of reality as creation, and thus encompassing cosmological, natural, and historical reality, is what is revealed, seen, and understood. The vantage point is not within but above and beyond history. That vantage point is "heaven." The visioner in dreams is lifted up from earth to heaven by an angel and given a tour of heaven that reveals to him what is happening and what is to happen on earth and in all creation.

In the *Book of the Watchers*, Enoch claims that his "eyes were opened by the Lord, and he saw a holy vision in the heavens which the angels showed to me. And I heard everything from them, and I understood what I saw, but not for this generation, but for a distant generation which will come" (1 Enoch 1:2; 14:8, 24). In the *Similitudes* (*Parables*) *of Enoch*, Enoch says: "And at that time clouds and a storm-wind carried one off from the face of the earth, and set one down at the end of heaven" and from there he is given a tour of heaven and sees "all the secrets of heaven" (1 Enoch 39:3; 41:1). The "one" referred to is Enoch himself. In the *Testament of Levi:* Levi claims that while asleep, he saw "the heavens opened, and an angel of the Lord said to me, Levi, come in. And I went from the first heaven into the second," and into the seventh, the highest level of heaven, and from that high point he saw all the levels of heaven from top down to the bottom. He saw all that was happening in each level, all the way down to the earth and its abyss (*Testament of Levi*, 2:6-9; 3:1-10). In the *Testament of Abraham*, Abraham makes a final wish before dying: "Yet one request I would make of thee; and now, O sovereign Lord, listen to my prayer. I would, while yet in this body, see the whole earth and all created things, which thou didst establish by a single word. When I have seen these, then will I depart from life without regret" (9:8-10). And so upon instruction by God, the archangel Michael "went down and took Abraham . . . on the cherubim-chariot and lifted him up to the heights of heaven and acted as his guide on the cloud together with sixty angels. And Abraham went upon on the chariot over the entire earth; and Abraham looked out on the world just as it was that day" (9:11-10:1-2).

Before we proceed to mention illustratively what is seen in these heavenly journeys, we may pause here and reflect theologically on the created. The way the creator sees his own creation is what may well be the relation between the historical and heavenly journeys in apocalypse. The historical journey is a very important legacy of biblical faith. It is partly what has given us a historical sense and has been developed and sharpened by the Enlightenment and so has become an essential feature of secularization. Today, it is not only human affairs that is understood historically, but all of reality. The universe and its various dimensions and elements have a history. The earth has a history. Life has a history. Nations and countries have their history. Individual lives have histories. Science has a history. Knowledge has a history. Civilization has a history. Even God may be said to have a history because he is God who self-constitutionally becomes!

Moreover, the fact that things happen in time and are timed and thus have an end gives rise to the question as to what historical episodes and all of history might mean. Seeing things from their end makes us ask the question of their value and meaning. Moreover, if things are seen historically, then it is not enough to understand them merely generically in terms of how they began and with what. That way of seeing things in terms of their beginning and their essential nature, though necessary, is not historically sufficient for human understanding today. One must also understand them in terms of what they have become and so what they are at any given time, and in terms of the processes through which they have become what they are! That means, in terms of their history. And this gives rise to the question of whether there is anything that transcends them. Is there anything beyond their end that transcends their history and their becoming? Put in another way, it does not seem adequate to see history in secularistic terms only. Is there anything that transcends the secular in the light of which one may view the secular and its processes? One must see the secular both in terms of what it is in itself, and what it is in the light of what transcends it. This leads us to consider the relation of the historical and the heavenly apocalyptic.

What we are being told, as it were, by the heavenly apocalyptic is that there is another way of viewing history that complements the other view and so makes it truly secular. It is to view it in the light of what transcends it. What transcends the earth and all creation and their histories is the creator of all creation. He has his own perspective on what has truth, meaning, and value in his creation, and not just the way the world or creation sees its truth and value. Would it be wise to prevent human understanding from going this far? But, it may be asked, is it possible? Can one step outside of history or of creation as such in order to see it as a whole? Is it too far from the truth to suggest that the positive answer to this question is precisely the apocalyptic being "lifted up out of earth into heaven" and given, as it were, a tour of heaven, and thus to see all of creation from the perspective of heaven? Would not such a perspective precisely be the "point" from which God views or sees his creation, and what he sees is exactly the truth of his creation and what is happening in it and to it? Would not such a divine viewing be an expression of the religaric bond between God and his creation, and so is in and through the Spirit? Is not the act of self-transcendence ecstatic, a going beyond self? Does not creation have this self-transcending character also? Does it not also stretch itself ecstatically and reach out into what is beyond itself? If so, does this not happen in the power and by inspiration of the Spirit? And is it not the Spirit who knows what God knows about his creation? If so, is it not then the Spirit who reveals the truth and value and meaning of the secular for human understanding?

What is it of heaven and earth—of all creation—that was shown to the visionary who was lifted up from the earth into heaven and given a tour of it? We may note the following:

First, "tourist" traveled through all seven heavens from the lowest to the highest (*Testament of Levi* 2–5) and through all directions of creation: to north, south, east, and west and saw all the scenes and events taking place—the sources of light and darkness, of storm and thunder, the winds, waters and rivers. He saw how the winds adorn all creation. He saw the "foundations of the earth . . . the cornerstone of the earth . . . and the four winds which support the earth and the firmament of heaven (*Book of the Watchers,* 1 Enoch 17–18; cf. *Similitudes*: 1 Enoch 41, 43). In *Similitudes* 60 the heavenly tourist claims:

> And the other angel spoke to me, [the one] who went with me and showed me what [is] secret, what [is] first and last in heaven, in the heights, and under the dry ground, in the depths, and at the ends of heaven, and at the foundations of heaven, and in the storehouses of the winds, and how the spirits are distributed, and how they are weighed, and how the springs and the winds are counted according to the power of [their] spirit; and the power of the light of the moon . . . and the divisions of the stars according to their names, and [how] all the divisions are made, and the thunder according to the places where it falls; and all the divisions that are made in lightning that it may flash, and its hosts, how they quickly obey. (1 Enoch 60:11-13)

The point of all this is to show that creation is ordered to its last and minutest detail by its creator:

> And I saw the chambers of the sun and the moon, whence they go out and whither they return, and their glorious return, and how one is honored than the other, and their magnificent course, and [how] they do not leave the course, neither adding [anything] to, nor omitting [anything] from their course, and [how] they keep faith with one another, observing [their] oath. (*Similitudes of Enoch*, 1 Enoch 41:5)

In the *Book of the Watchers*, the reader is urged:

> Contemplate all the events in heaven, how the lights in heaven do not change their courses, how each rises and sets in order, each at its proper time, and they do not transgress their law. Consider the earth, and understand from the

> work which is done upon it, from the beginning to the end, that no work of God changes as it becomes manifest. Consider the summer and the winter, how the whole earth is full of water, and clouds and dew and rain rest upon it . . . And understand in respect of everything and perceive how he who lives forever made all these things for you; and (how) his words (are) before him in each succeeding year and all his works serve him and do not change, but as God has decreed, so everything is done. (1 Enoch 2–5)

This ordering of creation and the stability it provides evoking trust and confidence is a source of comfort and hope. Like the creator of Second Isaiah, this apocalyptic vision evokes what the psalmist declares: "God is our refuge and strength, a very present help in trouble. Therefore we will not fear, though the earth should change, though the mountains shake in the heart of the sea; though its waters roar and foam, though the mountains tremble with its tumult" (Ps. 46:1-3).

Second, if creation is so ordered and made stable by God, why is the human being accused of causing disorder in creation? "But you have not persevered, nor observed the law of the Lord. But you have transgressed, and have spoken proud and hard words with your unclean mouth against his majesty. You hard of heart! You will not have peace! And because of this you will curse your days, and the years of your life you will destroy. And the eternal curse will increase, and you will not receive mercy" (*Book of the Watchers*, 1 Enoch 5:4-5).

The *Book of the Watchers* provides an explanation of the origin of evil and sin in chapters 6–16, which is an elaboration of Genesis 6:1-4. The "sons of God" are angels who keep watch over human affairs. But they admired the beauty of the daughters of men, and Semyaza, one of their leaders, led them to take wives from the daughters of men and gave birth to the Nephilim, human giants (1 Enoch 6–7). Another leader, Azazel, "taught men to make swords, and daggers, and shields and breastplates. And he showed them the art of making bracelets, and ornaments, and the art of making up the eyes and of beautifying the eyelids, and the most precious and choice stones, and all kinds and colored dyes." If one were to demythologize these mythic visions, we may likely say that the human is a combination of divine and earthly elements (cf. Gen. 2:7). This combination yields human creative freedom, which makes for the blessing of the self-perpetuation of the human species and its development in the art of being civilized. But this freedom was also misused when it claimed independence for itself, resulting in distrusting and disobeying the creator. This freedom and its abuse is represented by "the giants" of men. These giants are presumably the kings and rulers who are the most evil and inflict cruelty upon humankind. Because of them and their ilk, "the world was changed. And there was great impiety and much fornication, and they went astray, and all their ways became corrupt" (1 Enoch 8:1). And so for the sin and evil in the world, the human is held responsible and he is charged accordingly and therefore he must be tried. This primal combination of order and disorder, of spirit and flesh, of creative freedom and its destructive abuse, of good and evil, of trust and distrust, of wisdom and folly, of righteousness and wickedness, of life and death is an unvoidable characteristic of human earthly and secular life. But at the same time there is a moral structure and a dynamism for good woven into the fabric of human earthly reality. And so there is a quiet ongoing process of judgment in the way things are, and this judgment will be completed and rendered final and executory in a divine court trial at the end-time. This moral framework and dynamism and the ongoing process of judgment that is often imperceptible and hidden is also an essential feature of earthly and secular life. Apocalypticism adds closure and finality to it in a great trial at the end-time.

Third, the heavenly "tourist" saw how this judgment is taken very seriously in heaven. A scene of the divine court dispensing justice is provided in the *Testament of Abraham* 12. A full court is assembled in session: a judge, prosecutor, and defense counsels; a book that records evidence; a pair of weighing scales in which the good and the bad deeds are weighed and the balance determined; the judge renders both verdict and sentence. The passage bears quoting in full:

> Now between the two gates stood a fearsome throne, flashing like fire. On it sat a wondrous man, bright as the sun, like a son of God; and before him stood a table, all of gold and [covered with] the finest linen, [which shone] like crystal. On the table lay a book, six cubits thick and ten cubits broad, and on its right and on its left were standing two angels holding paper and pen and ink. In front of the table sat a brilliant angel holding in his hand a pair of scales. On his left sat a fiery angel, entirely without mercy and relentless, and in his hand he held a trumpet that contained all-devouring fire inside it, as a means of testing sinners. And while the wondrous man who sat on the throne was giving his judgments and sentencing the souls, the two angels on his right and on his left were recording. The [angel] on the right recorded the good deeds, the one on the left the sins. And the angel in front of the table, who held the pair of scales, weighed the souls, and the fiery angel, who held the fire, put the souls to the test. And Abraham asked the Prince Michael, what is it we are looking at? And the Prince replied, what you are seeing, holy Abraham is the judgment and retribution.

An intriguing question to ask at this point: is not this winnowing process the work of the Spirit? Is it not the wind that blows the chaff away, and is not the "wind" a word for the Spirit and its power? And where is the "chaff" to be found? Is it not together with the grain, but is to be separated from the grain and blown away? Is not the secular world precisely grain and chaff together, from which the chaff has to be threshed out, removed, and sent into oblivion so that the grain and the seed of life in it may remain alive and life-giving, life-sustaining, and life-flourishing? Does this not strongly and clearly suggest that there is a way of life that is grain and a way of life that is chaff and that there is a "wind" that winnows in the inner movement of things and events, the final outcome of which is the ultimate vindication of a life of grain and the emptiness and unworthiness of a life of chaff? Do not these two ways of life provide guidance for the exercise of freedom to be which is exercised by the freedom to choose and to act and to become (cf. the *Testament of Abraham* 11:1-18)?

Another intriguing question: in this highest court, is there no room at all for appeal for mercy? In the *Book of the Watchers*, Enoch was requested by the leaders of the Watchers, who led their angel followers into grievous sin, to petition the High Court for "absolution and forbearance." Enoch wrote down the petition but saw "a vision of wrath," which meant that he should reprove the angel-sinners, and this he did. He was, nevertheless, taken up to heaven and brought to the chamber of the High Court and into the very presence of the Supreme Judge. Enoch presented the petition for "absolution and forbearance" and it was heard by the High Court. But the High Court noted that the petition is irregular. Why should Enoch, a son of Adam and of the earth, bring a petition on behalf of angels who are of heaven and heavenly? It should rather be the other way round. So the petition has no legal standing before the High Court (1 Enoch 15:2). Because of this, the High Court denied the petition and the verdict to the petitioners is, "You will not have peace" (1 Enoch 15–16). What is decided in heaven merely confirms what has already taken place on earth. The deed of sin cannot be undone even by the High Court. The sinful deed makes the doer become a sinner; what one becomes by what he does to himself by his freedom to be is exactly what he is before the High Court. And that cannot also be undone. The finality of what is at the end-time is confirmed by the finality of the verdict rendered at the end-time! What is done on earth is, as it were, recorded in heaven as it happened. There is only one version of the record; any other version is a tampered one, and it would be false! Judgment is precisely the sifting of the true from the false, the right from the wrong, the good from the evil! There is no doubt that the record in heaven written and kept by a heavenly scribe is accurate; it need not be sanitized like the record of minutes of meetings on earth (*Testament of Abraham* 12:18-33). Alternatively, the verdict upon the righteous also confirms what they have become and are at the end-time before the High Court. They may have been unrighteous at some time but they have changed as a result of the winnowing process on earth. What they have now become at the end-time is what they are before the High Court and that is confirmed as final by the High Court! The verdict of the High Court at its final session at the end-time is thus final and executory!

However, in the *Testament of Abraham* we find a different picture. Of course, some of the judicial principles mentioned above are also held to apply: "all things in all men are tested by fire and scale" (13:12). It is the Lord who sees to it that "the sins and good deeds of each might be recorded" (13:22). "It is the Lord that sentences" (13:24). But here it is possible to be saved from the verdict of guilty by making atonement for one's sins: "Then said the Lord to Enoch, I shall bid you write the sins of the soul that makes atonement, and it shall enter into life. But if a soul makes no atonement and does not repent, you will find its sins in writing, and (that soul) will be sent off to punishment" (13:26-27). For the souls whose good deeds equal their evil deed, they can be saved if one good deed is added so that the good is more than the bad by at least one (14:4). Forthwith, Abraham, joined by the angel that accompanied him in heaven, made "intercession on this soul's behalf, and God heard them; and when they got up from their prayer, they did not see the soul standing there. And Abraham said to the angel, 'Where is the soul you were keeping in the middle?' And the angel said: It has been saved by your righteous intercession" (14:4-10; cf. *Testament of Levi*, 3:5). On the basis of this instance, Abraham, joined by the angel, besought God to forgive him his sin of seeking the destruction of sinners (10:15-19), and "when they had been praying for a long time, there came a voice from heaven, saying, 'Abraham, Abraham, I have heard your voice and your supplication; and I forgive you [your] sin. And those, whom you imagined I destroyed, I have recalled and in my mercy brought them (back) to life; because for a time I have requited them in judgment. But those whom I destroy while they are alive on earth, I will not requite in death' " (14:15-19). So here the possibility of becoming righteous from being a sinner and thus be saved is conditioned on:

1. repentance of and making atonement for sins done on earth while still alive;
2. intercession by a righteous human being, joined by a watching angel, on behalf of human sinners, not a righteous human on behalf of fallen angels whose sins are committed both in heaven and on earth;
3. both repentance and intercession done in prayer appealing for the mercy of the righteous judge;
4. those whom the judge forgives on earth, he will not requite in death at the end-time;

5. the act of forgiving, which is equally an act of judgment as the act of declaring guilt. Only God can do both as judge;
6. acknowledging that for God to be judge is already mercy and judgment is mercy because it settles controverted issues and puts closure to them. If there were no judge whose order is just creation is returned to chaos!

Related to the judgment that the wicked will be destroyed and sin and evil will be wiped away and assigned to their rightful place, for God has prepared a separate place for each, the righteous and the wicked, is the issue of whether life on earth and the earth itself will be destroyed along with the wicked and wickedness. The association of creaturely and earthly life and its cosmic environment with the disappearance of the wicked and wickedness arises from the apocalyptic belief that final judgment is preceded by the earth being shaken to its foundations, together with the horrible calamities and destructiveness that it brings about, the so-called "messianic horrors." These "horrors" will happen but they will not destroy and wipe out creation. Rather, they are evidence or signs that creation is being renewed and that sin, corruption, and death are being threshed out into oblivion. Creation shall be restored to its blessed fruitfulness and life will again not only be nourished but shall flourish. And together with the righteous, the renewed creation will sing praise and glorify the creator who swore that he will not deal with his creation and with life as he had dealt before in Noah's time (*Similitudes*, 1 Enoch 55:2-3b; cf. *Book of the Watchers,* 1 Enoch 10:18-22; *The Testament of Levi,* 2:11-12). The "messianic horrors" are the birth pangs of the birth of a new creation and a new earth!

What might be our take theologically of creation being turned into a cosmic court in which God as judge renders final judgment upon cosmic and human reality? May we not suggest as being close to the truth that God's turning creation into a cosmic court in which he is the highest judge is an aspect of his self-constitution as God, and that his being judge is a mode of his self-becoming? Is not the turning of creation into a cosmic court also a mode of created reality and is thus rooted in God's own self-constitution and self-becoming as God? Are not this cosmic court and the judgment it renders a form of hope (apocalyptic hope) for Israel and for all creaturely reality? As a court of judgment, it is in fact ultimately a court of grace! Judging is a function of grace! In his cosmic court God freely decides what he does in judgment. It is he who judges what is good or evil, righteous or wicked, true or false. It is he who decides whether to relent in mercy and forgive, or to confirm what cannot be undone. He cannot take back the freedom with which he has gifted the human in creating him, nor can he undo what the human exercise of freedom has done to himself and to his environment. The human is he who has become who he is by his freedom to be. Nor does God remove from his sight the creation that he has created as good; he can only remove the evil that has corrupted it and reaffirm the blessing of the measure of self-creation and self-perpetuation that he has pronounced upon life! The acts of God as judge in his cosmic court are therefore a self-vindication of God as a self-constituting and self-becoming God. In self-vindicating himself he reaffirms the religaric bond in the Spirit and at the same time reaffirms his being God for his creation and his people. And so it is in the self-vindication of God in the religaric bond that the distinct identity and integrity of creaturely reality, which includes the earthly, the human, and the secular as being within and encompassed by the Spirit, are rooted and grounded. God's self-becoming is the soil in which the secular is planted and can be rooted and thrive and can remain genuinely secular!

Earlier we claimed that the historical and the heavenly apocalyptic complement each other. It is not enough to see the historical—and so the secular—by itself, from itself, and for itself. It is also to be seen in the light of what transcends it and to view it not only in its episodic periods but as a historical whole. This is to see it from a heavenly perspective. Alternatively, it is also inappropriate (to say the least) to view the heavenly (read: spiritual) as opposed to the historical-secular. The fact of the matter is that the heavenly is concerned about the historical, it deals with the historical; it is about the historical and for the historical. And so we could rightly say that the spiritual (i.e., the heavenly) is for the secular and the secular (i.e., the historical) is open to and for the spiritual. They do more than complement each other. They in fact interweave and interpenetrate each other so that each is in the other without losing their respective identity and integrity. Is it too outlandish then to suggest that this can happen only within the religaric bond that God established through and in the Spirit when he self-constituted himself as creator? After all, is it not he who created "the heavens *and* the earth"?

There is a very important feature of the apocalyptic in its aspect as a heavenly tour given to the visionary that we did not consider thus far. This is the appearance and role of the Son of Man who is here for the first time identified as Messiah (*Similitudes*, 1 Enoch 69:26-29; 71:14-17; *Testament of Levi*, 2:10; *Testament of Abraham*, 12:2-9). Of course, the "one like a human being" is also mentioned in Daniel (7:13-14). But the status and role of "the Son of Man" as "Messiah" in the noncanonical apocalypse is more complex than in Daniel. We shall consider this issue of "the Son of Man" in the next chapter, which deals with the messianic hope of Israel.

CHAPTER X

The Secular Dimensions of Israel's Hope II: Messianic Hope

1. The Problem

In this chapter we shall deal with messianic hope. It has similarities with apocalyptic hope, but it has some features peculiar to it that need to be lifted up and emphasized. Both are historical in provenance; both are eschatological in orientation; both have a pastoral aim in dealing with crises, and both are expressions of hope, more or less peculiar to Israel. But apocalyptic hope is more general in scope; whereas, messianic hope is more focused on divine rule and leadership, which is not the emphasis of the former. In more contemporary, secular terms, messianic hope is concerned with good governance and wise leadership. Moreover, while apocalyptic hope is an essential background to the New Testament, messianic hope is a central issue in it. It is for these reasons that we are dealing with messianic hope in this chapter in the hope of doing justice to it.

What eventually gave rise to messianic hope in the faith of Israel is the deep tension embedded in the covenant relationship. On the one hand, to be God for his people, God must rule *as* God over his people, for that is what he self-constituted himself to be, God for his people. On the other hand, God's rule *as* God must be expressed in earthly ways and forms over an earthly realm. How is this to be done? How can an earthly people living in an earthly world obey the rule of God who is not earthly and human and whose rule expresses his will as God, even though his will is for the good of his people? The problem is not merely a difference in knowing and doing, but more deeply in orders of being. God and people belong to two different orders of being and modes of existence. God is creator, not creature. God is Spirit, not flesh made alive from dust. God is divine, not human. God's will is his will, not human will. God's will is expressed in terms of *his* own rule, his Torah, not in terms of human ways.

And what aggravates the problem is that God's rule is to be carried out for earthly and human good by means of human ways and earthly resources. Can the human realize in human ways a good for him that he himself has not determined as possible by and for him? To be sure, the people have been gifted with the freedom to obey, but it is human freedom exercised between divine permission and prohibition. Its exercise may go the one way or the other. It may or may not obey. It is distinctively human freedom that is vulnerable to temptation, not divine freedom that is fixated on doing good. Moreover, the will of God has been revealed as Torah for human knowing and doing. Thus, it can be known *trustingly*, but not *certainly*, and trust is knowing by faith, not by certain proof or incontrovertible evidence. Since it can be known, does that mean it can also be done? To do it, however, requires being empowered beyond one's native and developed abilities, and that means being enabled by the Spirit. But the Spirit, although always present, is not at the beck and call of the human. It blows where it wills. And if human freedom is exercised in disobedience, which indeed has happened, it cannot by itself extricate itself from its own act and so it becomes bound to it, and so disobedience becomes the inevitable way of unfreedom! The freedom to obey becomes freedom enslaved to and by disobedience. The root of the problem then is theologically the covenant itself. How can the human freely obey the rule of God whose rule is his as God, and yet is for the good of the earthly human?

The problem becomes impossible of solution when one considers God's ruling over his people in relation to the historical situation of this people. They have just returned from exile. But exile was changed to vassalage—exiles in their own homeland ruled by a foreign king. That situation had hardly changed over many years although the rulers have changed: Persians, then Greeks, and then Romans and thence into diaspora. God's people, over whom he should rule, are in fact already ruled by earthly kings who worship and obey their own gods and defy the God of Israel! Could God's rule displace human rule, which is already in place as kingship? If they were to conceive of God's rule, is there another way of conceiving it other than kingship and kingdom? To be sure, while the Israelites were in the wilderness in their exodus from Egypt, they were given the Torah by which they were to govern themselves as a liberated and free people. All of them—individually and as tribes—were to obey the Torah. If all obeyed as they were enjoined to do, there probably would not have been a need for a king-leader, only a military leader to lead them into a land promised to them, which they would then claim by military conquest and settlement. When they settled the land of promise, they could only protect it and secure their settlement of it by charismatic leaders who emerged when there was a need for it, and whose leadership then ended when no longer needed or when the leader died. But charismatic leadership was not good enough to form them into a people with a distinct identity among the nations of the earth. So, with being free, and having a law for obedience by all, and just beginning to settle in a land after living a tribal nomadic life in the wilderness, the defense of which they must secure, and desiring to be a people in their own right in their own land, would this be the kind of rule that God would exercise over his people? If this were God's rule over his people, then there is no doubt that it was a bad rule, for it ended in chaos: "In those days there was no king in Israel; all the people did what was right in their own eyes" (Judg. 21:25).

And so the people besought Samuel to give them a king. But the people have had no experience of being ruled by a human king. Their experience of rule under Moses as liberator and lawgiver, so far, is *freedom* from slavery under a tyrannically human king, a law to be obeyed by all that envisions a community life ordered by justice and that would unite tribal communities into a people with a distinct identity, a land claimed only by promise as their own but was yet to be fully secured and defended, and the worship of a God whom they believed had claimed them as his own people from all the peoples of the earth and therefore had a right to rule over them and make of them a kingdom of priests and a holy nation. These are values of God's rule for his people. Originally they were intended to be realized by self-rule through obedience by all to the Torah, which is God's will expressed as law. There was no figure of a king in their vision of leadership. They have just come out from the reign of a king of Egypt who had oppressed and enslaved them.

Now, strangely enough, they wanted a king-leader to lead and help them realize these values of divine rule for themselves. It is no surprise then that Yahweh felt rejected when the people asked for a king to rule over them (1 Sam. 8:7-9). Can an earthly king realize the values of divine rule in worldly forms and ways over a creaturely people chosen by God as his own? Yahweh's sense of being rejected indicates a measure of doubt on his part that it could and would be done (1 Sam. 8:18). Although Yahweh felt rejected by this move, he allowed it. This sense of rejection but still allowing it has from the beginning a built-in ambiguity in kingship arising from the ambivalence of Yahweh toward it! (cf. 1 Sam. 8:9

with 8:18). Israel had to be told, however, what a human king was, how he ruled, what he would exact from his people: "Now then, listen to their voice; only—you shall solemnly warn them, and show them the ways of the king who shall reign over them" (1 Sam. 8:9). Already we discern here in palpably historical forms the deep tension theologically embedded in the covenant. This is the problem addressed by messianic hope!

But it is not only the desire to realize the values of divine rule through a human king in an earthly human kingdom that is the problem. There is also the problem internal to the people themselves. While they pledged to live in covenant by obedience to the law, on the whole they did not do so. They disobeyed the law and broke the covenant. They have a long and dramatic love/hate relationship with Yahweh, a history of iniquity, impiety, apostasy, and of penitence on the people's part; and a history of Yahweh's steadfast faithfulness to the covenant, which is the basis of God's judgment of sin and forgiveness upon Israel. The human king is to rule over an unruly people with the aim of achieving divine righteousness in a society that is characterized by injustice! This appears to be the problem addressed in a focused way by messianic hope.

2. The Beginning of a Solution

The tension in the covenant we have described above already shows itself from the very beginning of leadership as kingship. We may note the following:

1. It is the people who wanted a king to rule over them. The reason given is "*our king may govern us* and go out before us and fight our battles" (1 Sam. 8:19, emphasis added). The one and only way they could conceive of leadership was in terms of kingship, which is the normal practice of nations.

2. But they wanted a king to be *given* them (1 Sam. 8:6). Normally, a king initially becomes a king by violence and imposes himself upon a people. He then founds a dynasty, and the succession among his children may not be peaceful either. It could be by means of intrigue and/or murder or war.

3. The people come to a "seer," known as "a man of God" (1 Sam. 9:5-15, esp. vv. 6, 9). A "seer" in those days functioned as judge, priest, and prophet. He mediated between people and God. To come to a seer who would "give" them a king assumes that it is God whom the "seer" represents who is the giver of the king.

4. In short, it is God who chooses the king.

5. God's choice of a king for his people is from among his people, not an angel but a human being. He has no right as a human being to be king; it is God's choosing him that makes him a king. From the beginning, kingship in Israel is an unlikely combination of divine appointment and human consent. This means the king represents the God who appointed him and rules on his behalf by doing what God wills for his people, and so is accountable to this God; and alternatively this God rules indirectly over his people through his chosen king by having his will, his law or Torah, be done by both king and people (1 Sam. 12:14-15).

6. The installation or enthronement of a king is by "anointing," the act of pouring oil over his head. It is understood that the "anointer" is God, and this anointing is God's choice of this man to be king, appointing him as such, conferring on him the authority of king, and empowering him to act as king.

7. But if God chooses and anoints the king, he can also withdraw his choice, disauthorize and disempower the king, and reject him (1 Sam. 15:35; 16:1). He rejected Saul and replaced him with David (1 Sam. 16:1-13). "Then Samuel took the horn of oil, and anointed [David] in the presence of his brothers; and *the spirit of the Lord came mightily upon David from that day forward*" (1 Sam. 16:13, emphasis added). This anointing and the coming of the spirit of the Lord upon a man chosen by God to be king over God's people are the essential elements of messianism. Together with the elements mentioned above, they form the basic pattern or model for messianic hope and messiahship.

To the question of whether a human king can govern God's people in God's name for the good of his people, the answer is yes, provided the conditions mentioned above are met. The text indicating in summary form is:

> But when you saw that King Nahash of the Ammonites came against you, you said to me, "No, but a king shall reign over us," though the Lord your God was your king. See, here is the king whom you have chosen, for whom you have asked; see, the Lord has set a king over you. If you will fear the Lord and serve him and heed his voice and not rebel against the commandment of the Lord, and if both you and the king who reigns over you will follow the Lord your God, it will be well; but if you will not heed the voice of the Lord, but rebel against the commandment of the Lord, then the hand of the Lord will be against you and your king. (1 Sam. 12:12-15)

The key that opens the door of messianic possibility is the statement "the spirit of the Lord came mightily upon David from that day forward" (1 Sam. 16:13). The trajectory of the Spirit without doubt includes its movement toward governance and leadership. It is the Spirit that makes political authority a truly secular activity!

3. Israel's Experience of Kingship

Given this initial pattern to frame the experience of kingship, it may be to the point to ask, what has been the experience of Israel as a kingdom ruled by a king on behalf and for the good of God's people? On the whole, it can be said that it has been an ambiguous one: The good mixed with the bad, and in the end kingship ends in failure and is finally destroyed with and by the Exile. We cannot run through the history of kingship in Israel, as this is not our purpose; but we can cite some examples to illustrate the point. We begin with the experience of Israel with its first two kings, Saul and David. In the experience of kingship between the two, a more stable criteria for kingship later developed in which are rooted the elements of messianism.

We may take Saul, the first king (1020–1000 B.C.). Saul began by doing what at that time was on top of the list of the king's job, namely, defending the people and the land against their enemies (1 Sam. 14:47). In his self-estimate, he had done well with this kingly task. This is a task a king has to achieve. But in the judgment of Yahweh, which was rendered through Samuel, this mission was half-done and so he was not fully successful as king. What is worse is that he used his success to cover up and justify his failure. His defense: "I have obeyed the voice of the Lord, I have gone on the mission on which the Lord sent me, I have brought Agag the king of Amalek, and I have utterly destroyed the Amalekites" (1 Sam. 15:20).

So far so good. Then Saul continues: "But from the spoil the people took sheep and cattle, the best of the things devoted to destruction, to sacrifice to the Lord your God in Gilgal" (1 Sam. 15:21). Why did Saul allow this to happen? His explanation: "Because I feared the people and obeyed their voice" (1 Sam. 15:24). God's judgment upon this deed of King Saul through Samuel is:

> And Samuel said, "Has the Lord as great delight in burnt offering and sacrifices, as in obedience to the voice of the Lord? *Surely, to obey is better than sacrifices, and to heed than the fat of rams. For rebellion is no less a sin than divination, and stubbornness is like iniquity and idolatry.* Because you have rejected the word of the Lord he has also rejected you from being king." (1 Sam. 15:22-23, emphasis added)

We could say that the "transgression" of Samuel is that he was to hear God's voice and obey it fully, and this he did not in two ways: he consulted diviners as to what to do, and he believed in divinization, a pagan practice that is proscribed in Israel's faith; he obeyed the voice of the people and not the voice of God. God told him to destroy the Amalekites and all that they had. This he did not do. Instead he took spoils. He also allowed the people to take the best of the spoil for sacrifice to God. He reasoned that sacrificing to God the best of the spoil is better than fully obeying the Lord's word of command. In this he was using "religion," the essence of which is sacrificial worship, to cover up and justify his disobedience. In all this, Saul's priorities as king overturned the priorities of God!

We have in the example of Saul the beginning of what a king should and should not do. Since a king is chosen, appointed, and anointed by Yahweh, he is to carry out fully the will of Yahweh and be accountable to him alone. Saul was a "religious person," but he did not fully commit himself to Yahweh. In response to Samuel, he used the phrase "your God," implying that there are other gods who may have to be obeyed. He believed in sacrificing to God but also in consulting diviners and in the practice of divinization. He obeyed God's word up to a point and also the voice of the people and the voice of other gods. In the end, he used his "religiosity" to cover up and justify his failure as a king and his disobedience to Yahweh. This is the sin of impiety. And Saul was guilty of it.

In the case of David (1000–961 B.C.), the experience of Israel is different. Here, the good appears to predominate over the bad. Soon after David had routed out the enemies of Israel and both land and people were secure, and the king himself safely and comfortably settled in his "house," he felt he should now build a "house" for God in his city, Jerusalem (2 Sam. 1:1-3). But this is not yet what God wants David to do. Rather, God wants to establish a "house of David." So God by this own initiative established a covenant with David for this purpose. It may not be unsound to construe the elements of this covenant as constituting a sort of program that a king should accomplish as a king. The text as reported in 2 Samuel 7:4-17 bears quoting in full as it is basic to the origin and elements of messianism.

> But that same night the word of the LORD came to Nathan: Go and tell my servant David: Thus says the LORD: Are you the one to build me a house to live in? I have not lived in a house since the day I brought up the people of Israel from Egypt to this day, but I have been moving about in a tent and a tabernacle. Wherever I have moved about among all the people of Israel, did I ever speak a word with any of the tribal leaders of Israel, whom I commanded to shepherd my people Israel, saying, "Why have you not built me a house of cedar? Now therefore thus you shall say to my servant David: Thus says the LORD of

> hosts: I took you from the pasture, from following the sheep to be prince over my people Israel; and I have been with you wherever you went, and have cut off all your enemies from before you; and I will make for you a great name, like the name of the great ones of the earth. And I will appoint a place for my people Israel and will plant them, so that they may live in their own place, and be disturbed no more; and evildoers shall afflict them no more, as formerly, from the time that I appointed judges over my people Israel; and I will give you rest from all your enemies. Moreover the Lord declares to you that the Lord will make you a house. When your days are fulfilled and you lie down with your ancestors, I will raise up your offspring after you, who shall come forth from your body, and I will establish his kingdom. He shall build a house for my name, and I will establish the throne of his kingdom forever. I will be a father to him, and he shall be a son to me. When he commits iniquity, I will punish him with a rod such as mortals use, with blows inflicted by human beings. But I will not take my steadfast love from him, as I took it from Saul, whom I put away from before you. Your house and your kingdom shall be made sure forever before me; your throne shall be established forever. In accordance with all these words and with all this vision, Nathan spoke to David. (2 Sam. 7:4-17; cf. Ps. 89)

The word *house* in this text appears to have not one but several meanings. We may take these various meanings as a clue to the several elements that constitute the royal program of David. In 7:1-2, the "house" refers to *the royal palace*—the king's residence and the seat of royal authority built in a city that David himself conquered from the Jebusites with his own personal army. The city is by right of conquest actually *his* personally, and he named it "the city of David." In verses 5, 6, 7, and 13, "house" means *temple*. Up to now there was no need to build a temple to house the ark of the covenant, for Yahweh has shown himself as accompanying David in all his battles: "I have been with you wherever you went, and have cut off all your enemies from before you." It is precisely Yahweh's constantly accompanying presence that was David's opportunity to consult Yahweh at every significant move he made in all his royal rule. But David did bring the ark of the covenant to his city and housed it in a tent specially built for it. And so Jerusalem, his own city, also became "the city of Yahweh," the seat of God's itinerant presence among his people. From his city that now houses the seat of royal authority and the presence of Yahweh in the midst of his people, David can now not only protect land and people but govern them justly in their own land so that they shall no longer be "disturbed," and "evildoers shall afflict them no more, as formerly, from the time that I appointed judges over my people Israel." The just ordering of the affairs of state and the righteous governance of the people will bring honor, peace, prosperity, and a distinct identity to them and to their king, and ultimately to Yahweh, their God. Although not mentioned in the text, this would merit Israel being called a "house" in itself as in the "house of Israel," namely a people in its own land, in its own right and with its own identity and honored by nations.

There is another meaning of "house." This time it means *dynasty*. (vv. 11, 16, 19, 25, 26, 27, 29) A royal dynasty, of course, is new in the experience of Israel, but not in the practice of the other nations. Israel's tradition of leadership is tribal and charismatic, not royal dynastic. But Israel wanted to be "like" the other nations. And the one reason the people would tolerate a royal dynasty is to perpetuate the just rule of a good king and so provide security, justice, stability, prosperity, and peace to the life of the people, on a long-term basis. Yahweh himself, who appears to have a change of mind in granting the people their desire to be ruled by a king but reserved his right to reject a king and replace him, had extended royal rule into a dynastic line. He made a covenant with David, pledging that the throne of his kingdom shall be forever. In a sense the covenant is a personal matter between Yahweh and David: "I will be a father to him, and he shall be a son to me." But because David's kingly rule appears to express and fulfill God's rule to the utmost that a human can do and so provide a model for others to follow, it is worth extending David's rule into a dynasty!

The covenant with David must not be misunderstood as God's surrender of his prerogative to self-constitute himself and to self-become as a covenanting God. Indeed, it should rather be understood as precisely the free exercise of that prerogative! His becoming "father" to David as his "son" and his blessing upon "the house of David" are in fact a mode of his becoming as God! The relation between father and son is one of steadfast love. Because the relation of love unites two different others and because it is steadfast, it can only last—and last forever. The covenant between Yahweh and David is one of love and it is steadfast from God's side. The time will come when the particular historical form of this covenant with human royal rule may come to an end, and it indeed ended. But the covenant of love with human governance after the model of David will live on as a messianic vision and will take on other salvific ways!

David's rule appears to fulfill what the people expected of a king. Indeed, David succeeded to the best that he could do in achieving the diverse, complicated, and expanding responsibilities of king. The use of the metaphor "house" in a variety of meanings means that David combined all these meanings of "house" and more in his long kingship. To do them well together in a lifetime of royal governance against so many odds tells a lot of this one king. Indeed, David was a gifted man. He was a man of honor expressed in fairness, humility, and penitence; a great military commander, a consummate diplomat; a shrewd politician, a skilled organizer and administrator; a wise judge; a poet and a musician; and a deeply spiritual person—all these rolled into one person. He suffused all his secular activities as king with a piety born out of his deep immersion in the power of God's Spirit that "came mightily upon [him] from that day forward" (1 Sam. 16:13).

But there was also a dark underside to David's rule. To cite only a few flagrant ones: There was the unavoidable use of armed violence in routing out his enemies; there was his lust that drove him to covet somebody else's wife and caused the death of her husband so that he could marry the woman; there was a huge harem of women—some wives, some not—with whom he sired many sons and daughters; there was intrigue and treachery within his household, mostly in connection with succession, which finally erupted in the rebellion of his son Absalom who was killed by one of David's own men in a war that he himself authorized in order to quell the rebellion.

Can success be achieved without struggle and conflict, without the use of violence, and without engaging in intrigue, deception, and treachery? It seems that good is always mixed with evil and evil with good. This seems to be an unavoidable characteristic of secular human leadership whether of the royal or ordinary variety! But is this not also balanced by an inner dynamic that seeks to overcome the evil with the good? Is not the royal rule of David a paradigm of this ongoing dynamics that is being constrained by a messianic vision? Is this not the activity of the Spirit that keeps the secular genuinely secular by keeping it open to the creativity of the Spirit who creates new possibilities out of the non-possible?

We can continue illustrating the legacy of bad royal rule that began with Saul. In the case of Jeroboam II, who reigned from 786–746 B.C.E., Israel successfully defended itself against its enemies and expanded its territories. Israel was at peace and it prospered economically. This is part of what a king should do (2 Kings 14:28-29). But there is an underside to this reign, and this is to be found in the prophecy of Amos (760–750 B.C.E.), which evaluates the king's reign. Amos knew and appreciated the peace and prosperity that prevailed in Israel (Amos 6:1, 4-6). But he saw that this was achieved by deceit, corruption, and injustice.

> Hear this, you that trample on the needy, and bring to ruin the poor of the land, saying, "When will the new moon be over so that we may sell grain; and the sabbath, so that we may offer wheat for sale? We will make the ephah small and the shekel great, and practice deceit with false balances, buying the poor for silver and the needy for a pair of sandals, and selling the sweepings of the wheat." . . . (Amos 8:4-6; cf. 5:10-13 below)

> They hate the one who reproves in the gate, and they abhor the one who speaks the truth. Therefore because you trample on the poor and take from them levies of grain, you have built houses of hewn stone, but you shall not live in them; you have planted pleasant vineyards, but you shall not drink their wine. For I know how many are your transgressions, and how great are your sins—and you who afflict the righteous, who take a bribe, and push aside the needy in the gate. Therefore the prudent will keep silent in such a time; for it is an evil time. (Amos 5:10-13)

And what is worse, worship and sacrifice are substituted for injustice and used to cover it up:

> I hate, I despise your festivals, and I take no delight in your solemn assemblies. Even though you offer me your burnt offerings and grain offerings, I will not accept them; and the offerings of well-being of your fatted animals I will not look upon. Take away from me the noise of your songs; I will not listen to the melody of your harps. But let justice roll down like waters, and righteousness like an ever-flowing stream. (Amos 5:21-24)

Clearly, there was *iniquity* in the midst of security, peace, and prosperity. Iniquity is the sin of injustice, deceit, and oppression and of covering this up with the piety of worship and temple sacrifice!

Another example of a bad rule is the reign of Manasseh (687–642 B.C.E.). In the view of the Deuteronomists, the reign of Manasseh was the worst ever. The historian John Bright notes: "The author of Kings can say no good word of Manasseh, but instead brands him as the worst king ever to sit on David's throne, whose sin was such that it could never be forgiven."[1] The sin of Manasseh was the peak of apostasy in the history of Israel's faith. It is summarized as follows:

> He did what was evil in the sight of the LORD, following the abominable practices of the nations that the Lord drove out before the people of Israel. For he rebuilt the high places that his father Hezekiah had destroyed; he erected altars for Baal, made a sacred pole, as King Ahab of Israel had done, worshiped all the host of heaven and served them. He built altars in the house of the LORD, of which the LORD had said, "In Jerusalem I will put my name." He built altars for all the host of heaven in the two courts of the house of the LORD. He made his son pass through fire; he practiced soothsaying and augury, and dealt with mediums and with wizards. He did much evil in the sight of the LORD, provoking him to anger. The carved image of Asherah that he had

1. John Bright, *A History of Israel* (Philadelphia: Westminster, 1959), 291.

> made he set in the house of which the LORD said to David and to his son Solomon, "In this house, and in Jerusalem, which I have chosen out of all the tribes of Israel, I will put my name forever; I will not cause the feet of Israel to wander any more out of the land that I gave to their ancestors, if only they will be careful to do according to all that I have commanded them, and according to all the law that my servant Moses commanded them." But they did not listen; Manasseh misled them to do more evil than nations had done that the LORD destroyed before the people of Israel. (2 Kings 21:2-9)

One may well ask, reading the last sentence in the text, could a king in covenant with Yahweh lead his people to do the worst evil that its God forbids and despises in a way far more evil than nations have done and for which they were punished? The peak of sin is *apostasy* and *idolatry*. That can happen and it has happened again and again by a king, a president, a leader, a manager, leading his people into ruin by his own wayward seeking after other gods! We may notice that there seems to be a worsening of evil at the hands of royal rule—from impiety to iniquity to apostasy, and into what combines all, namely idolatry. Can this slide into the worst of all evils be arrested at all?

Before answering this question by considering the kings who attempted reform, such as Hezekiah and Josiah, by way of illustration, we may have to deal with the question why would apostasy and idolatry loom so large an issue here as to be considered the peak of evil. Apostasy is publicly forsaking one's god or abandoning one's religious faith. In the case of Israel, this would mean breaking covenant with Yahweh and renouncing obeisance and obedience to Yahweh and the Torah. Idolatry is the worship of other gods, either in replacement of Yahweh or alongside of Yahweh. In the case of Israel, this would mean abandoning its faith in the truth that there is only one true God and is the God above all gods! This would entail obeying the ways of these other gods, either by substituting them to the ways of Yahweh, or by practicing them together with the ways of Yahweh. This would return society to religious and ideological anarchy where everyone does what he considers right or good in his own light in pursuit of his own interest by virtue of the gods he worships! This creates the condition for injustice, deceit, and corruption in social life. One can see that both apostasy and idolatry struck at the very roots of Israel's existence as a nation and its reason for being as the people of God! This would mean that apostasy and idolatry together are also a *political offense* constituting *treason* because they entail a people abandoning their right to be free and independent in their own homeland and being ruled by a king of their own! So all three—apostasy, idolatry, and treason—entailed one another and so are interwoven! Together they open wide the gates to paganism and signal the death knell of monotheism.

But what precipitated this very deplorable condition? It was primarily the situation of vassalage. For a country and its king to be a vassal of another country and its king, one may be conquered by the king and army of the other country, or for the sake of avoiding war and being conquered a king may by treaty agree to be a vassal of another king. To be a vassal meant acknowledging the sovereignty of the conquering king, paying the tribute he exacted, and having its gods worshiped and its religious practices observed because of the belief, prevalent at the time, that the god of the conquering king is stronger than the god of the conquered country and so is worthy of worship! In some instances it also meant the citizens of the vassal country were exiled to other countries and peoples of other countries were brought to the vassal country. This happened to the Northern Kingdom of Israel when it fell to Assyria (722–721 B.C.E.) and to Judah in the south when it fell to Babylon (587) and the best of its citizens were exiled in Babylon. Judah had been a vassal to Assyria, to Babylon, to Persia, to Egypt, to the Greeks, and to the Romans!

What would "reform" mean in this geopolitical situation for Israel? It could mean overthrowing the situation of vassalage by military means. This was not a readily likely option for Israel, until an opportune time appears that could be taken advantage of by Israel's king, such as the death of a king to which Israel was vassal or the weakness of his rule! The vassal could withdraw tribute, but this could be construed as rebellion. And so would refusal to worship the gods of the overlord king and follow their ways. While a military rebellion or withdrawal of tribute would be a too public and blatant act of rebellion, the wiser option would seem to be the strengthening of the national faith of Israel in Yahweh, his covenant and his Torah, which were the foundations of Israel's existence. This would in some measure and degree counter apostasy and idolatry and if quietly done, it might not be construed as rebellion. This would also mean letting justice roll down like waters in their internal life and thus strengthen the moral and social fabric of the people. A religious reform would seem the best option since if successful it would restore Israel to its roots and revitalize its national and social life.

But the political implications of such a religious reform cannot be denied or avoided. The king as a political figure must lead it since he was, in the first place, the lead cause in allowing paganism to be practiced publicly in Israel. As king he could wield royal authority, combined with his own religious conviction—the peak of political will and power—to initiate and sustain reform. And so religious reform could be effected only by political authority. But it risked being unmistakably understood as a component part of rebellion against an overlord. The support of the people of a *royal act* also made it a *populist act* and it could be so understood as a people's rebellion. The prophets active at the time, Isaiah and Micah, supported and provided the core of the reform—a return to primitive Yahwism and to the Davidic model of rulership! And that makes religious reform a challenge to the gods of the overlord! And if the ways of these other gods are already entrenched in the religious and social practices of the people, could they still be excised and extirpated? Would religious reform, even if initiated by royal authority, be carried through to the end and be successful? And if put down by military might by the overlord king, would not the fate of the king and its people be a repeat of the disaster that befell the Northern Kingdom of Israel? The odds against religious reform even when done within the aegis of royal authority seem an impossible possibility.

Defying all odds, Hezekiah marched into the fray with his sword drawn! He was twenty-five years old when he succeeded to the throne vacated by the death of his father, King Ahaz. He reigned for twenty-nine years (2 Kings 18:2; 2 Chron. 29:1). His father, King Ahaz, was a royal leader in introducing Assyrian paganism in Israel, which would corrupt the faith and culture of Yahwisim (2 Kings 16:10-16), as a part of his vassalage to the Assyrian king. He ordered, while still in Damascus, to be constructed right inside the Temple in Jerusalem an altar dedicated to celebrate the cult of Asshur, a god of Assyria, with the same specifications as the altar that Ahaz saw in Damascus when he was summoned to appear before the king of Assyria. Ahaz thus surrendered to Tiglath-pileser, king of Assyria, both the independence of his country and the integrity of the faith of his people.

What Hezekiah did was to reverse all the policies of his father, King Ahaz, concerning the practice of religion by removing all visible signs of paganism in stone, in metal, in cult, and in practice, and presumably also in belief! The contrast between the reign of Ahaz and his son Hezekiah is explicitly drawn in bold relief. Of the reign of Ahaz, it is said:

> Ahaz was twenty years old when he began to reign; he reigned sixteen years in Jerusalem. *He did not do what was right in the sight of the Lord his God, as his ancestor David had done, but he walked in the way of the kings of Israel.* He even made his son pass through fire, according to the abominable practices of the nations whom the Lord drove out before the people of Israel. He sacrificed and made offerings on the high places, on the hills, and under every green tree. (2 Kings 16:2-4 emphasis added)

Of the reign of Hezekiah, it is said:

> In the third year of King Hoshea son of Elah of Israel, Hezekiah son of King Ahaz of Judah began to reign. He was twenty-five years old when he began to reign; he reigned twenty-nine years in Jerusalem. . . . *He did what was right in the sight of the LORD just as his ancestor David had done.* He removed the high places, broke down the pillars, and cut down the sacred pole. He broke in pieces the bronze serpent that Moses had made, for until those days the people of Israel had made offerings to it; it was called Nehushtan. *He trusted in the LORD the God of Israel; so that there was no one like him among all the kings of Judah after him, or among those who were before him. For he held fast to the LORD; he did not depart from following him but kept the commandments that the LORD commanded Moses. The LORD was with him; wherever he went, he prospered.* He rebelled against the king of Assyria and would not serve him. He attacked the Philistines as far as Gaza and its territory, from watchtower to fortified city. (2 Kings 18:1-8, emphasis added)

It may be worthwhile to notice four salient points in these texts. First, note the evaluative statements, which typify the point of view of the Deuteronomistic editors, of the reign of King Ahaz. It is said: "He did not do what was right in the sight of the Lord his God, as his ancestor David has done, but he walked in the way of the kings of Israel" (2 Kings 16:2). In stark contrast, it is said of Hezekiah and his reign: "He did what was right in the sight of the Lord just his ancestor David had done" (2 Kings 18:3). Second, note what the two kings did with respect to the practice of religion. Ahaz practiced paganism and was followed by the people (2 Kings 17:7-18), whereas Hezekiah remained faithful to Yahwism and so was honored as such by his people (2 Kings 20:2-3). Third, the model of royal rule is that of David's. Ahaz did not rule according to the model of David, whereas Hezekiah did faithfully and obediently (cf. 20:5-6, 20). Finally, the act of Yahweh in judging the reign of Ahaz as "not right in his sight," and the reign of Hezekiah as "right in his sight" and following the ways of David, is done "for my own sake and for my servant David" (2 Kings 20:6), for the sake of his freedom to be God and for the sake of the covenant that Yahweh made with David.

When we turn to the reign of Josiah (640–609 B.C.E.), we find the same cycle of evil rule and good rule in the sight of Yahweh. Hezekiah was succeeded by his son, Manasseh, whose rule reaches the peak of paganism in Israel. We have mentioned this above. Manasseh was succeeded by his son Amon (642–640 B.C.E.), who apparently continued the policies of his father. Amon was succeeded by his son Josiah (640–609 B.C.E.). Again, the same divine evaluation: "[Manasseh] did what was evil in the sight of the LORD, following the abominable practices of the nations that the LORD drove out before the people of Israel" (2 Kings 21:2); and of Josiah: "He did what was right in the sight of the LORD, and walked in the way of his father David; he did not turn aside to the right or to the left" (2 Kings 22:2; cf. 23:24-25).

It was in Josiah's reign that the "book of the law" was discovered in the Temple as it was being repaired by Hilkiah, the high priest (2 Kings 22:8-10). Most scholars believe that the "book" written on a scroll is the earliest form of the book of Deuteronomy that is in the canon. After the "book" was read to Josiah he gathered all the elders of Judah and Jerusalem in the Temple, had the "book of law" read in the hearing of the people assembled, and "made a covenant before the LORD, to follow the LORD, keeping his commandments, his decrees, and his statues, with all his heart and all his soul, to perform the words of this covenant that were written in this book. All the people joined in the covenant" (2 Kings 23:3). On the basis of the "book of law" and his covenant to obey what is written in it, Josiah launched a reform so broad, so profound, and so encompassing as to remove every and all signs and vestiges of paganism from Israel's practice of its ancestral faith. The whole of 2 Kings 23 is a report on the reform conducted by Josiah. Some portions of the text may be quoted to indicate some aspects and the scope of the reform.

> The king commanded the high priest Hilkiah, the priests of the second order, and the guardians of the threshold, t*o bring out of the temple of the LORD all the vessels made for Baal, for Asherah, and for all the host of heaven; he burned them outside Jerusalem* in the fields of the Kidron, and carried their ashes to Bethel. *He deposed the idolatrous priests* whom the kings of Judah had ordained to make offerings in the high places at the cities of Judah and around Jerusalem; *those also who made offering to Baal, to the sun, the moon, the constellations, and all the host of the heavens. He brought out the image of Asherah* from the house of the LORD, outside Jerusalem, to the Wadi Kidron, *burned it* at the Wadi Kidron, beat it to dust and threw the dust of it upon the graves of the common people. *He broke down the houses of the male temple prostitutes that were in the house of the LORD*, where the women did weaving for Asherah. *He brought all the priests out of the towns of Judah, and defiled the high places where the priests had made offerings,* from Geba to Beer-sheba; *he broke down the high places of the gates that were at the entrance of the gate of Joshua t*he governor of the city, which were on left at the gate of the city. The priests of the high places, however, did not come up to the altar of the LORD in Jerusalem, but ate unleavened bread among their kindred. *He defiled Topheth, which is in the valley of Ben-hinnom, so that no one would make a son or a daughter pass through fire as an offering to*

> *Molech. He removed the horses that the kings of Judah had dedicated to the sun, at the entrance to the house of the Lord*, by the chamber of the eunuch Nathan-melech, which was in the precincts; then he burned the chariots of the sun with fire. *The altars on the roof of the upper chamber of Ahaz, which the kings of Judah had made, and the altars that Manasseh had made in the two courts of the house of the Lord, he pulled down from there and broke in pieces, and threw the rubble into the Wadi Kidron.* The king defiled the high places that were east of Jerusalem, to the south of the Mount of Destruction, which King Solomon of Israel had built for Astarte the abomination of the Sidonians, for Chemosh the abomination of Moab, and for Milcom the abomination of the Ammonites. He broke the pillars in pieces, cut down the sacred poles, and covered the sites with human bones. . . . *Moreover Josiah put away the mediums, wizards, teraphim, idols, and all the abominations that were seen in the land of Judah and in Jerusalem, so that he established the words of the law that were written in the book that the priest Hilkiah had found in the house of the Lord.* Before him there was no king like him, who turned to the Lord with all his heart, with all his soul, and with all his might, according to all the law of Moses; nor did any like him arise after him. (2 Kings 23:4-14, 24-25, emphasis added)

At the beginning of this section, we staked out the claim that Israel's experience of kingship has been ambiguous and the textual record seems to confirm the claim. But did royal authority exercised at effecting religious reform reverse the slide toward paganism? The answer to this question is more complicated than a simple answer of no.

4. God Himself Shall Be the Good Shepherd

When Josiah was killed in the battle of Meggido by Neco, king of Egypt, his reform was unfortunately discontinued. He was succeeded by Jehoahaz, a younger son of his. The same cycle of bad rule in God's sight is repeated (2 Kings 23:31-32). He was deposed by Neco, king of Egypt, and replaced by Jehoiakim, an older son of Josiah. He continued the bad rule of his younger brother (2 Kings 23:37).

All the kings who succeeded Josiah had come under the interdict: they did what was evil in the eyes of the Lord. (See 2 Kings 23:32 on Jehoahaz [609]; 23:37 on Jehoiakim [609–598], 24:9-15 on Jehoiachin [598–597], who was exiled to Babylon by Nebuchadnezzar; 24:19 and 25:7 on Zedekiah [597–587], who was blinded and carried away to Babylon. Under these kings, one could say that the slide to paganism and the corruption of society continued to worsen to their inevitable end in the fall of Jerusalem, the destruction of Judah, and the trauma of exile.

But alongside this slide, we must not also fail to notice that the winnowing activity of the Spirit through divine judgment is effectively at work. Moreover, the spirit and movement of reform that seemed could not succeed did not die. It lived on in articulate intensity in the word and activity of the prophets of this period just before and during the Exile: Isaiah, Micah, Jeremiah, Ezekiel, Zephaniah, Nahum, and Habakkuk. This activity of prophetic judgment and reform are twin sides of the same coin, namely, the Spirit at work in worldly human affairs in politics, in social relations, and in religious practice.

The first target of judgment and reform appears to be kingly rule, especially the rule of the kings shortly before the Exile, which are mentioned above. The *locus classicus* of this is Ezekiel 34. Here we find the core elements of what constitutes genuine royal leadership and governance. We may take note of some salient points indicated in the text. First, the term "shepherd" as used here is metaphor for king; and "sheep" is metaphor for people. This usage is common among the countries in this period (cf. Jer. 23:3; Pss. 23; 80:1; Mic. 4:6; 7:24,). Second, it is Yahweh who judges the kings who ruled their people badly, and he rejects them and their misrule: "Thus says the Lord God, I am *against the shepherds*; and I will demand my sheep at their hand" (Ezek. 34:10, emphasis added).

Third, God's reason for rejecting the shepherds is that they did not do what they were to do as shepherds:

> "The word of the Lord came to me: Mortal, prophesy against the shepherds of Israel: prophesy, and say to them—to the shepherds: Thus says the Lord God: Ah, you shepherds of Israel who have been feeding yourselves! Should not shepherds feed the sheep? You eat the fat, you clothe yourselves with the wool, you slaughter the fatlings; but you do not feed the sheep. You have not strengthened the weak, you have not healed the sick, you have not bound up the injured, you have not brought back the strayed, you have not sought the lost, but with force and harshness you have ruled them" (Ezek. 34:2b-4).

The consequence of the neglect and failure of the shepherds to do their duty is that the sheep were "scattered, they became food for all the wild animals. My sheep were scattered, they wandered over all the mountains and on every high hill; my sheep were scattered over all the face of the earth, with no one to search or seek for them" (Ezek. 34:6).

Fourth, God resolves to be himself the shepherd of his flock: "I myself will be the shepherd of my sheep" (34:15). And so he does what a shepherd should do:

> For thus says the Lord God: *I myself will search for my sheep*, and will seek them out. As shepherds seek out their flocks when they are among their scat-

> tered sheep, so I will seek out my sheep. *I will rescue them* from all the places to which they have been scattered on a day of clouds and thick darkness. *I will bring them out from the peoples and gather them from the countries*, and will bring them into their own land; and I will feed them on the mountains of Israel, by the watercourses, and in all the inhabited parts of the land. *I will feed them with good pasture*, and the mountain heights of Israel shall be their pasture; there they shall lie down in good grazing land, and they shall feed on rich pasture on the mountains of Israel. *I myself will be the shepherd of my sheep, and I will make them lie down, says the Lord God. I will seek the lost, and I will bring back the strayed, and I will bind up the injured, and I will strengthen the weak, but the fat and the strong I will destroy. I will feed them with justice.* (Ezek. 34:11-16, emphasis added)

Fifth, God's judgment does not fall only on the shepherds but also upon the flock: "I will judge between sheep and sheep" (34:22b.). There are among the flock strong sheep who bully the weak ones: "You pushed with flank and shoulder, and butted at all the weak animals with your horns until you scattered them far and wide" (34:21). He will not only judge between sheep and sheep but also between rams and goats. His judgment is framed as an accusing rhetorical question:

> As for you, my flock, thus says the Lord God: I shall judge between sheep and sheep, between rams and goats: Is it not enough for you to feed on the good pasture, but you must tread down with your feet the rest of your pasture? When you drink of clear water, must you foul the rest with your feet? And must my sheep eat what you have trodden with your feet, and drink what you have fouled with your feet? (Ezek. 34:17-19)

Finally, we must not fail to notice that God's judgment upon shepherds and their flock and his taking over himself of being shepherd of his flock to do for them what a shepherd does are prefaced by the divine oath: "As I live" (as God) followed by the prophetic authority. "Thus says the Lord." The divine oath undergirds the prophetic word with divine authority and force (34:2, 8, 10). This means God is exercising his freedom to self-constitute himself as God for his people by becoming their shepherd, and do for them what a shepherd does!

But then there is a surprising twist to God's resolve to be himself the shepherd of his people. Scarcely has he said that he himself shall be the shepherd of his people than he sets up somebody else over them to shepherd them. And who could this be? No other than "my servant David," and he shall feed them . . . and be their shepherd" (34:23).

Moreover, it is not enough that the flock is looked after and cared for by a good shepherd who is a human "prince among them," but that Yahweh must be known by the flock that he is the Lord who will be their God. Shepherding is precisely God exercising his lordship over his people through his anointed servant whom he has set up as king. The one enduring and final aim of shepherding is for God to be acknowledged and worshiped as the one and only Lord even though he shepherds his people through a human prince! And this is Yahweh's final word in resolving this issue of what and who and why shepherding is all about: "I, the Lord, have spoken" (34:24).

We may ask, does David's view and performance of shepherding match Yahweh's own view and practice of shepherding since he doesn't seem to have any other model of shepherding his people than that of David's? We may consider Psalm 23 in answering this question. Tradition has ascribed to David the authorship of this psalm. We have no reason to doubt this, and so we shall take Psalm 23 as expressing David's vision and program of royal rule over God's people.

We note that the psalmist is a king, anointed by God to rule over his people. The office of a king is representative: It represents God to his people, and it represents the people to their God. What the king says and does and lives for are thereby representative. What he says personally as king represents not only himself as an individual but also at the same time his people. And what he personally says of God is not only for himself, but as king it is also for his people. Taken in this sense, Psalm 23 is a statement of *a* king *as* king of his people and as *God's king* over his people. It is both a personal and communal statement; but more than this, it is also a divine-human statement of royal rule.

This is already obviously unmistakable in the first verse of the psalm: "The Lord is my shepherd, I shall not want" (I shall lack nothing). This is a statement or confession of a king acknowledging that the real shepherd or king is the Lord, Yahweh! And since he is king over a people, his statement is also made on behalf of the people he is shepherding. When the Lord shepherds his people through his earthly-human shepherd who does what a shepherd has to do, the people shall lack nothing! All that they need as a flock, as a people, mentioned in Ezekiel 34, is provided for and fulfilled by the human shepherd! And so when David speaks in this psalm of God's shepherding of his people he does so on behalf of both God and people! The rest of the psalm details the provisions made by a shepherd for his flock, his people!

There are at least eight of these. First, we may note the provision for *food* and *drink,* which are absolutely necessary for surviving, nourishing, and flourishing! "He makes me lie down in green pastures; he leads me beside still waters" (v. 2). Second, the good shepherd "restores my soul" (v. 3). The word *soul* refers to "life" and what makes for life, what animates life and keeps it alive. The vigor of life shall not weaken because it is constantly replenished by its vitality! Life shall remain constantly strong and healthy, able to overcome and heal what may ail it because the balm of healing is itself in the process and vitality of being alive!

Third, the king and his people with him are led in the "right paths" (v. 3). The paths are "right" because they lead straight to "green pastures" and "still waters" and so to healthy, vital living. The "paths" are right because they are the ways by which a shepherd leads his flock so that *all* may have access to, and *all* shall share justly in, the resources of life and its vitality! It is the job of a shepherd to be concerned about the welfare of his people and so he must see to it that his governance justly and caringly provides for all, especially the widow, the orphan, the alien, the disabled, the marginalized, the cast out! This he must do for the sake of him who is the true shepherd whose name (i.e., his character or nature) is precisely to care for those who have been rendered helpless! A good shepherd must never let the helpless become hopeless!

A fourth duty of a good shepherd is to banish fear from his people ("I fear no evil" [v. 4]). There is evil in the world. Its strategy is to strike fear. What delivers fear are the threats to life, and there are many of these. They are drought and famine, disease and disability, conflict and war, injustice and exploitation, deceit and corruption, idolatry and paganism. All of them are "shadows of death" and death is the extinction of life and its consignment to oblivion! In that sense it is evil, and its shadowy forms are also evil. They all are evil because they are a threat to life, and as threat they are a challenge to the life-creating, life-giving, life-nourishing, and life-flourishing power and care of the Good Shepherd! Even when one finds himself walking into this valley of darkness and uncertainty and feels helpless, one should "fear no evil." Why? "For you are with me; your rod and your staff—they comfort me" (v. 4).

A fifth duty of a good shepherd is that he is always *with his flock*; he is with them as one who leads; he leads with his rod and staff to protect, to guide, to keep them together. His being with his flock to lead with his rod and staff are clear signs of his sovereignty and lordship to deal adequately with any eventuality that may bring harm to his flock. The shepherd can be trusted and trusting him is the source of comfort and hope in the face of evil! Trust, comfort, hope, which are often scarce or unavailable in the face of threat, are to replace "fear" when walking into the valley of the shadow of death. They are available and accessible because the good shepherd is simply there for his flock.

There is a sixth good that a good shepherd provides his flock; he hosts a lavish dinner for his flock, even in the presence of the enemies that are a threat to the enjoyment of life! Hosting a dinner is the surest sign of hospitality, and hospitality is *welcoming* unreservedly into the intimacy of one's home friends and even strangers, for no other purpose than fellowship and the sheer enjoyment of one another's company! It is this hospitality dinner that makes the cup of enjoying life an overflowing blessing like the pouring of oil! Hospitality is generosity out of the abundance of grace. It is the practice of the inexhaustibility of grace!

There is a seventh good that is made available to the flock by a shepherd: Because Yahweh, the Lord shepherd, is a caring leader and a hospitable host, namely, the king and his flock are certain that "goodness and mercy shall follow me all the days of my life" (v. 6). Instead of being scattered over mountainous terrain and pursued by, and becoming prey to, wild and predatory animals, it is the protecting, rescuing, reconciling, and gathering "goodness and mercy" of the Good Shepherd that shall constantly pursue them all throughout their life together as a flock! Goodness and mercy are the surrounding and encompassing life-sustaining climate and environment of the flock. They are the soil, milieu, and atmosphere in which life and community can thrive and be fulfilled!

And finally, king and flock "shall dwell in the house of the Lord my whole life long" (v. 6). The "house of the Lord" is of course the Temple. But the Temple is not just a building made by human hands. It is the dwelling place of God's presence in the midst of his people to hear and listen to their cries, their petitions, their prayers, spoken or unspoken. But the Temple is only the localized presence of the omnipresence of God that fills the heavens and the earth! He is present in one place and in all places and so is available anywhere and anytime because his shepherding is over all and in all and through all. And so to be shepherded by the Good Shepherd through his human agent, is as it were, to dwell in God's constant and abiding and caring presence. It is in him as the Good Shepherd that one moves, and lives, and has his being.

If a king were to govern according to what the Good Shepherd does as indicated above, would this not constitute the best practice of human governance? Was it not this that David in his kingship sought to achieve and did achieve, thus providing a paradigm for all royal rule? The confession of absolute trust in the statement "The Lord is my shepherd" is followed by a radical and an all-encompassing claim: "I shall not want." The whole statement with its two sentences actually hides an abyss between the one trusted who is divine, and the one trusting who is human, and claims that are all secular goods for his people requiring divine blessing and provision. What makes this spiritual trusting and secular claiming come together in the midst of an abysmal divide? Is it too far from the truth to say that it is the fulfillment of what is said of the Spirit at the anointing of David as king: "the spirit of the Lord came mightily upon David from that day forward" (1 Sam. 16:13)? The thrust of the Spirit's coming is to unite the trusting in God and the claiming from God of earthly human goods for the people by a human king! The Spirit bridges the abysmal divide between the divine shepherd and the human shepherd both on behalf of God's deity and on behalf of the good of his people. The Spirit is the religaric bond between them.

It seems obvious, from what is said above, that genuine shepherding is certainly a political/secular activity whether by a tribal head, a monarch, a prime minister, or a president or under any form of political authority or ideology. Yet it is within the scope of the activity of the Spirit and is carried out under its authority and judgment. If one can still claim that political activity as a human, worldly task for the good of a people is outside of the Spirit's sphere of authority or influence, then one must be talking of a spirit that is not biblical. If politics under the Spirit is not the practice of a spirituality that secularizes, I would not know what else to call the activity of Spirit in relation to politics.

The above considerations lead us to bring out something else that is in the texts we have been considering, that is the crucial distinction between kingship as an office with essential functions, and an occupant king and the quality of his performance in office. It is unmistakably clear that Yahweh affirms kingship both for himself and for his people through a "prince" of his own choice: *"I myself will be the shepherd of my sheep . . . I will set up over them one shepherd, my servant David, he shall feed them . . . and be their shepherd"* (Ezek. 34:5, 23, emphasis added). Moreover, Yahweh also affirms the kingship of David as a model of best practice in royal governance and so as a paradigm for all royal governance over the "house of Israel." It is through "my servant David" that he is shepherd of his people. But at the same time Yahweh retains his right to reject the performance of some occupants of the royal office, notably kings who had done what was evil in his sight and brought ruin to his people! This means that occupants of the royal office, though anointed and in succession in the royal dynasty, come and go with their performance depending upon the judgment of Yahweh. But the office itself and its status and functions endure both as eschatological vision or promise, and as operational standard of performance! Thus, the search for an occupant of the royal office who will perform according to the model of "my servant David" is launched as a messianic eschatological hope. For a possible answer, we turn to consider the prophetic messianic hope.

5. Prophetic Messianic Hope

In what follows we shall briefly discuss illustratively some prophetic texts that have been regarded as bearing messianic hopes. These are: Isa. 9:6-7; 11:1-9, 61:1-4; Jer. 33:14-17; Ezek. 37:24-28; Mic. 5:2-4. They bear messianic hopes for several reasons:

1. They are a continuation of the establishing and anointing by Yahweh of the royal office through the dynasty of David (2 Sam. 7:11-16; 1 Kings 9:5; Jer. 33:17).

2. They speak to a historical situation in which the people and their current leaders felt helpless and hopeless.

3. They proclaim the emergence of help and hope of rescue, renewal, salvation, and an era of peace and prosperity.

4. And with this the honor and majesty of Yahweh among the nations is vindicated and restored as well as that of Israel as his people.

5. And finally, these hopes have been claimed in the New Testament to have been fulfilled in Jesus as the Messiah. They are described as "prophetic" because their provenance is in prophetic literature by way of contrast to apocalyptic hope, which is found mainly in apocalyptic literature.

We shall not engage in a detailed exegesis of these texts, but we shall point out some essential features that bear on the purpose of this book. First, most of the texts point to the source of the hope in the promise of God in establishing and anointing the royal leadership of David and his dynasty. This underscores the fact that in a situation where help and hope seem impossible and nowhere forthcoming, it is Yahweh, the Lord, who creates the possibility of help and hope! Second, the historical situation to which the word of hope is promised is a real threat to the existence and well-being of God's people. In the case of Isaiah and Micah, it is the Assyrian invasion; in the case of Jeremiah and Ezekiel, it is the Babylonian conquest and Exile. Third, the help and hope will come in the form of the birth of a child (Isa. 9:6; 11:1). The birth of a child is a sure sign that God is acting to bring help and hope to his beleaguered people. "Birth" points to God's creative blessing in generating life. Only God, the creator of life through his Spirit, creates and gives life! But every birth of life is the emergence of "new" life. It is the unmistakable sign that a new situation is being born; it is the herald of the coming of the new! Moreover, there is here an ironic paradox. Help and hope will come in the form of a helpless child in a hopeless situation in the face of a powerful king and his mighty invading army! The power of God at work here is that of a weak child that is the bearer of hope! A mighty king cannot prevent a helpless child from being born!

Fourth, the child is "a shoot [that] shall come out of the stump of Jesse" (Isa. 11:1; cf. 9:6), or as "a branch of the Lord" (Isa. 4:2) or a "righteous Branch" from David (Jer. 23:5). "Branch" is a messianic designation (cf. Ps. 132:17; Hag. 2:20-23; Zech. 3:8). This means that the promised messiah will not only succeed to David's office or throne but shall continue to execute the functions of the office in the model of David's performance. Here office and performance fit snugly together. This lays the basis for trusting in the rule of the successor to David's throne. But, as noted earlier, this can also be dangerous in that it may generate a *false* hope in the people by appealing to it as guaranteed by Yahweh and using this appeal as a cover for the disobedience of the people and the corruption and injustice of its leaders! The help that is to come can only become a messianic hope if it were to be used as help for the people to renew themselves and reform their ways and realize the promise of rescue and salvation, and so bring about a new era of justice, peace, and prosperity!

Fifth, the texts describe the authority, character and qualifications of the messianic bearer of hope. The salient feature that deserves notice here is the fusing of all three—authority, character, and qualification—into one seamless whole in the person of the ruler. If the anointing is understood as the activity of the Spirit, as indeed it should, then it is the Spirit that confers authority, shapes the character, and endows the bearer of hope with the gifts and qualifications of a good shepherd of God's people. Authority, character, and qualifications co-inhere one another and each expresses the others! Moreover, the anointed one is "named Wonderful Counselor, Mighty God, Everlasting Father, Prince of Peace" (Isa. 9:6). These are attributes of deity and they can only become gifts of a human ruler by the activity of the Spirit: "The spirit of the Lord shall rest on him, the spirit of wisdom and understanding, the spirit of counsel and might, the spirit of knowledge and the fear of the Lord. His delight shall be in the fear of the Lord (Isa. 11:2-3).

Moreover, since these features are all fused together into the person of the bearer of messianic hope, he is absolutely worthy of trust without reservation. He can never act out of character, his action can never be incompetent, and his authority can never be ineffective! Furthermore, all these features of authority, character, and qualifications are geared toward executing the tasks placed upon the shoulders of the messianic bearer of hope. And these tasks have a secular orientation, are highly political in their purpose, and require political will for their execution.

Sixth, while these tasks are this-worldly and are political, they are inspired and executed by the Spirit through the human bearer of hope in an earthly, worldly realm. Messianic authority aims at making peace; it establishes and upholds the throne and kingdom of David with justice and righteousness (9:7).

> He shall not judge by what his eyes see, or decide by what his ears hear; but with righteousness he shall judge the poor, and decide with equity for the meek of the earth; he shall strike the earth with the rod of his mouth, and with the breath of his lips he shall kill the wicked. Righteousness shall be the belt around his waist, and faithfulness the belt around his loins. . . . (Isa. 3b-5)
>
> In those days and at that time I will cause a righteous Branch to spring up for David; and he shall execute justice and righteousness in the land. (Jer. 33:15)

This is detailed further in Deutero-Isaiah:

> The spirit of the Lord God is upon me, because the Lord has anointed me; he has sent me to bring good news to the oppressed, to bind up the broken-hearted, to proclaim liberty to the captives, and release to the prisoners; to proclaim the year of the Lord's favor, and the day of vengeance of our God; to comfort all who mourn; to provide for those who mourn in Zion—to give them a garland instead of ashes, the oil of gladness instead of mourning, the mantle of praise instead of a faint spirit. They will be called oaks of righteousness, the planting of the Lord, to display his glory. They shall build up the ancient ruins, they shall raise up the former devastations; they shall repair the ruined cities, the devastations of many generations. (Isa. 61:1-4)

Furthermore, the hope that is borne by the royal messiah includes the gathering of all "the remnants" of Yahweh's people from all the nations of the earth into the "city of David," Jerusalem. The animosity between the North (Ephraim) and the South (Judah) will be banished and the two kingdoms shall again be one.

> On that day the Lord will extend his hand yet a second time to recover the remnant that is left of his people, from Assyria, from Egypt, from Pathros, from Ethiopia, from Elam, from Shinar, from Hamath, and from the coastlands of the sea. He will raise a signal for the nations, and will assemble the outcasts of Israel, and gather the dispersed of Judah from the four corners of the earth. The jealousy of Ephraim shall depart, the hostility of Judah shall be cut off; Ephraim shall not be jealous of Judah, and Judah shall not be hostile towards Ephraim. (Isa. 11:11-13)

A seventh aspect of messianic hope added quite abruptly to the Davidic vision is what one might call "paradise regained." This involves peace within nature and peace between the human and the natural!

> The wolf shall live with the lamb, the leopard shall lie down with the kid, the calf and the lion and the fatling together, and a little child shall lead them. The cow and the bear shall graze, their young shall lie down together; and the lion shall eat straw like the ox. The nursing child shall play over the hole of the asp, and the weaned child shall put its hand on the adder's den. They will not hurt or destroy on all my holy mountain; for the earth will be full of the knowledge of the Lord as the waters cover the sea. (Isa. 11:6-9)

The reason for this cosmic peace is because "the earth will be full of the knowledge of the Lord as the waters cover the sea." What is striking in this verse is that it is "the earth" that will be filled with "knowledge of the Lord." But this can happen only if the earth is open and transparent to the Spirit. Moreover, is it too far from the truth to say that this openness and transparency of earthly, this-worldly reality to the Spirit is precisely what the primal religaric bond is all about? It is the Spirit that makes the secular transparent to it and it is the suffusing and permeating and pervasive presence of the Spirit in the secular that makes the secular truly and genuinely secular. It is the Spirit that secularizes within the religaric bond! But paradoxically enough, that brings secular political authority of whatever form and system under the judgment of the Spirit. The disappearance of the monarchy as a historical political form and system of governance in Israel may be seen in the light of the religaric bond as a judgment of the Spirit and an expression of its winnowing and cleansing power. But that does not mean that the eschatological vision of just rule and wise governance after the model of David, the servant of Yahweh, has died with the monarchy! It lives on as vision and hope and it may take on other historical forms or systems!

The figure of "one like a human being" in Daniel 7:13 is not a historical figure. It is a part of the vision of Daniel about the end when God, "the Ancient One," appears to render final judgment on the kingdoms of this world. It is a literary devise to image God's exercise of his sovereign rule and to vindicate his people who have been severely victimized by earthly rulers. And so God's exercise of his sovereign rule is received by his people. "But the holy ones of the Most High shall receive the kingdom and possess the kingdom forever—forever and ever" (7:18). The final decision of the heavenly court presided over by the Ancient One is "The kingship and dominion and the greatness of the kingdoms under the whole heaven shall be given to the people of the holy ones of the Most High; their kingdom shall be an everlasting kingdom, and all dominions shall serve and obey them" (7:27). Is it too far from the truth to say that the vision of a Davidic kingdom lives on in the vision of God's people receiving God's everlasting kingdom through the "one like a human being"?

6. Hope: Between Promise and Fulfillment

We have now considered various elements that comprise Israel's hope. They are the promises of "the New" (chap. 8), the apocalyptic end to this present evil age and the coming of the age to come (chap. 9), and the hope for a messianic leader after the model of David (chap. 10). All of these have one common thread running through them: they reorient time and history toward the future with hope! That means the *saeculum*, the time of this world, secular time, is futurized; or, in theological terms, it is eschatologized. The reason for this is God's promise to do a new thing, to end the time of evil and usher in the time of the reign of good, to inaugurate the era of freedom, righteousness, and peace through just, wise, and caring governance. The promise radically redirects the movement of time to this new future with hope! How is this done?

On the one hand, the making of the promise of this new future with hope makes time and its stories become "former." They are consigned to the "old," and so, they should be forgotten. That time has no future to it; it holds no promise for the future, and so it cannot offer any hope. On the other hand, the future is heavily loaded with the "new" that God is about to do—a new exodus, a new covenant, a new heart, a new Spirit, a new life, a new leadership, a new way of bearing suffering, a new age with a new reign and governance, a new heaven and a new earth. It is this new future promised by God that offers hope and therefore its fulfillment is to be anticipated. This turning from the old to the new, which is about to happen by God's action and therefore to be anticipated with great expectation, radically futurizes time.

With God shaping the future in terms of concrete promises, the future ceases to be vague, amorphous, and uncertain. A promise shapes the future with concrete possibilities that can be imagined and visualized. The not becomes a not-yet that can be! A promise is always about the future shaped in a specifically concrete content or event that can be anticipated.

But a promise is made in the present. While a promise is always about the future, it is, nevertheless, always made in the present. It's being made in the present marks the time up to the present when the promise is made as "former" and so is consigned to the old that has to be forgotten. It is rendered past. Moreover, the future is promised to the present as a critique of the present. The present, no matter how good or satisfying, is always characterized by conditions that are not to be continued into the future. The "new" that is to happen, however, is not yet in the present and its coming shows the shortcomings, the deprivations, the deficiencies, the distortions of this present. Nevertheless, the new has to come to remake, renew, and recreate the present. A promise makes the future come to the present to reconstitute it by bringing to it new possibilities that cannot come from it, or be generated by it, or by the past.

A promise made in the present about the future that has to become present creates a time bracketed between promise made in the present and its fulfillment in the future—an in-between time, between present and future. But this present is now radically oriented to the future: It does not look back to the past—that has to be forgotten; it does not look to itself as present because its possibilities are now being exhausted, and it is passing out. It has to look to the future and its promise for it to be a living present moving to the not-yet and make it be. Alternatively, the future is not a distant vision that recedes farther away into the horizon, but comes to the present and yields its possibilities for realization through human creativity. It is the future with its promises of new possibilities that come to the present to reconstitute it with new possibilities. The future moves as advent upon the present.

Time between promise and fulfillment has some significant features worthy of notice. It is *departure time*: It is a forgetting of the past and a reaching out in vision and hope to the future and its promise. It is *exodus time*. It evokes the adventure of faith. It is *journeying time*, very often in the wilderness of struggle to find a way where there is none yet, with the cloud of promise as the only guide. Journeying time is adventure time, evoking courage, endurance, and creative effort in a wilderness that has become a desert of dried-up possibilities! It is also a *waiting time* because the fulfillment of a promise is done by the one who made the promise. He decides the time when to fulfill the promise. He chooses the content of fulfillment. He selects the method or way of fulfilling the promise. And he calls and anoints the agent who will carry out the fulfillment. The coming of the future and its fulfillment are a blessing, a gift of benefit, not a reward for merit. Waiting time evokes expectation, anticipation, watchful waiting, without diminishing departure, journey, adventure, struggle and creative work. And finally, it is advent time, which is the arrival of the future and the fulfillment of its promise, by breaking into the present and reconstituting it. The making of the promise, the charting of a way toward its realization, and its eventual fulfillment are wholly the initiative and blessing of grace. And grace evokes gratitude, praise, joy, worship. If one were asked, what is secular time, the *saeculum*? The answer is, it is the time between promise and fulfillment. It is temporal time into which the eternal has come to lure it toward the fulfillment of its hope! That can only be the work of the Spirit.

We may observe that this is not the way we live our time today. It is we who make our own time by creating our own future. It is we who shape and plan our future. We shape the future from the lessons of the past and the trends in the present that we decide have a future. We create our own possibilities from what is possible in us and with us. We determine our own possibility! We organize ourselves and our abilities and expertise and harness our resources and decide the sequence of activities—the division of labor and the assembly line—that eventually produce the good that we had planned to make. We create the tools and chart the ways with which to achieve our planned goals. We are the entrepreneurs and managers and workers of our own destiny! Time is time we schedule for ourselves and for what we do! And here is the rub: We take full credit and pride for it. It is we, humans, who made all this and it constitutes the pride of our dignity! To be sure, the human participates creatively in realizing the promise of the future in temporal time, as clearly indicated in the features of futurized time mentioned above. But it is participation in the creative work of the Spirit who is the creator of time and the possibilities of the future. But in taking time and the possibilities of the future entirely into our own hands, we have done exactly what idol-making is! Idols are made by human hands; they are products of human-making and are given intrinsic and absolute value by their makers by dancing the joy of worship around them. Time created by humans and for humans is idol-time, not secular time! This kind of time does not see the Spirit as creating possibility out of non-possibility. It does not find the Spirit as the inspirer of vision and the enabler of its achievement. It has no sense of gratitude that issues forth in praise and worship. The Holy is not in its midst! Instead, it has sacralized itself and so has taken on the semblance of the sacred! Sacral time is not secular time! Genuinely secular time is time between promise and fulfillment. It is time upon which the future comes with hope. It is time in the Spirit who creates new possibilities that generate hope and thus unleashes and motivates human participation in the creativity of the Spirit.

In this participation in the creativity of the Spirit, can one catch a glimmering vision of God's future for himself? Is not God's future his vision that he as God shall be all in all, that is, that God in the fullness of his being—God in himself, God turned toward another, God turned inwardly for the other, and God turned forward in his new creation—shall be all in all that he has created; and alternatively, that all of his creation the heavens and the earth, the whole universe, shall be in him! And that means the religaric/covenanting relationship shall have come full circle and thus be fulfilled to the full! That primordial relationship is nothing less than the bond of the Spirit who is himself that binding bond! It is the Spirit in the fullness of deity that shall be in all, and all things in their fullness shall be in the fullness of God—the Spirit in the secular, and the secular in the Spirit. Is this not a spirituality that secularizes and a secularity that is genuinely secular?

EPILOGUE

A person on a journey may know where to go and where the journey may end but may not know how to get there. Only as the traveler takes the first step may the next step be known. But there may not yet be a road on which to take the step. The way may have to be hacked and a clearing made to pave a path. The hacking and the paving may not be straight but winding and zigzagging. But one does not clearly see this while one walks the way. He hacks out and paves until he gets to the end of the journey and looks back. Then he discovers how winding the road has been, though it got the traveler where he wanted to go.

In some sense that has been the experience of the author in writing this book. He knew where to go, but not the way. He has had to find his way to where he wanted to go and what steps to take to walk the way. At the end of the first leg of the journey, he may want to look back and see how he got to where he now finds himself. Of course, the Bible may serve as a guide. But Scripture is a labyrinth. One still has to read it and find a way among the ways it maps out. And so it may be helpful both to author and reader to sketch out the trail that has been blazed out and traveled.

We felt the need to discern the wide expanse of the activity of the Spirit to include secularization as part of it, and thus to affirm and promote it in its integrity and value for humankind. We also believe that it is by seeing it in the light of the activity of the Spirit that secularization can be genuine in its truth and worth. We therefore wanted to see both Spirit and secularity in profoundly primal relational terms.

We identified this primal relation as a religaric or bonding one. It is established by God himself in self-constituting himself to become creator through his Spirit and Word. In this way, he affirms and protects his Godself and his otherness. But at the same time he establishes a bond with creation and in and with this bond he affirms, protects, and sustains the integrity and good of his creation.

This primal bond is by creation and so is through and in the Spirit since the Spirit/ Word is God's own self-agency in creation! To see all creation—the heavens and the earth, what we today designate by the term "the universe" and all that there is—including the genuinely secular dimensions of creation as God's creation is to bring them under the sphere and blessing of the Spirit. The genuinely secular aspects of creation include the physical, the earthly, the natural, the biological, the human, the social, the cultural, all that is this-worldly! The Spirit is not any or all of these. The Spirit is God as creative, but all creation is creaturely. And so it is the Spirit that binds God's creativity with the creaturely and the creaturely with God's creativity. The one is neither the other but are held in their mutual otherness together in the Spirit. The Spirit is the bond in which both God and creature come together. It is in the Spirit that the opposites come together. The Spirit is the *coincidentia oppositorum*, to use the phrase of Nicholas of Cusa.

At the heart of the creative activity of God is freedom. God in freedom creates by "letting be." Creation is process, it is letting the non-possible become possible; it is letting the possible become actual; it is letting the actual become what it can yet be. Process is letting be. The creaturely is not a fixed substance entity boxed into itself. It is also in process! This letting be also provides the structure for participation in the creative activity of Spirit. The dynamics of participation is framed by the parameters of permission and prohibition. Freedom in creation, especially its peak in human freedom, is participation in creation within the parameters of permission and prohibition! When something goes wrong with freedom by freedom's own doing and so becomes distorted freedom that results in undesirable and deplorable consequences, God decides to deal with distorted freedom and its bad consequences in his creation. He self-constitutes himself us Judge and develops the criteria of judgment by interacting with a people he calls into existence. With this people he establishes a covenant in which he shall be their God and they shall be his people. The covenant with a people he himself has created is the dramatic historical expression of the cosmic religaric bond. With this covenant, together with the promises and commandments (the Torah) that were given along with it, God establishes the valuable, the moral, the legal, the cultural, and the temporal criteria for his work as Judge over this people and through them over all humankind. God's judgment in creation and in history happens between creation and salvation. He preserves and sustains the good of his creation by removing the distortion through a winnowing process that includes punishment, and at the same time moves the good of his creation to its final fulfillment. God judges creation by saving it for its final destiny. Since secularity is a dimension of God's creation, it falls under God's judgment for its distortions, impiety, iniquity, apostasy, and idolatry, which it is when it becomes secularism. But because God judges it he also wills to save it for fulfilling its destiny in God's vision for all his creation. Judgment is what generates a future with hope!

The rest of the argument of the book is simply following and describing the journey of God with his people in this twisting and winding road in which God and his people interact engagingly, with God affirming his right to self-constitute himself as sovereign and with the people wondering trustingly what their future with hope will be in this dialogic relationship. Thus, the story ends open-endedly, with a promised hope that is yet to be fulfilled! Is this not the way that secularization should be? Must it not remain open-ended to a vision of what it can yet be?

We have so far discussed the height, the depth, the breadth, the quiet internal and effective activity of the Spirit in creation, judgment, in blessing, and in the promise of salvation, all of which have a secular thrust. So in the light of what has been said so far, we may well ask, what then does it mean to practice a spirituality that secularizes? What is suggested in answer to this question will be further developed in the volume dealing with the practice of spirituality after taking into account the New Testament witness.

To be spiritual is to participate actively in the work of the Spirit in the world. There are several elements here that may merit some attention. One element is participation. To participate is to take part in, to be fully involved in, to be intimately engaged in. But participating at the same time presupposes having partaken of, having had the experience of, having been acted upon by! One can only participate in because one has partaken of what one participates in. The word *actively* also needs emphasizing because it proposes a needed corrective to traditional spirituality that has been contemplative rather than performative, interiorizing rather than bodying forth or form-making, ascetical by denying the joys of the body rather than appreciating and enjoying them, mystical by seeking inner unity in depth beyond diverse plurality, rather than discerning the unity of complexity in difference! But of course the most important part of the suggested definition is the work of the Spirit, that which one participates in, that of which one partakes. The assumption is that the Spirit is already at work in its own power in the universe both microcosmically and macrocosmically. His work is quietly, imperceptibly, foundationally, constitutively from within. That is why we cannot deny the contemplative, the interiorizing, and the mystical dimensions. But this needs to be balanced by the emphasis on the movement of the Spirit from the inside to the outward, toward bodying forth, toward forming an other. The Spirit at work means that it is active, and activity has to do with doing, acting, performing, realizing, achieving, accomplishing, producing results. To participate in the working of the

Spirit is to join, by invitation, empowering, and being sustained by, the Spirit to take part in its work.

And what would that mean? It means to be creative, to see possibility in the non-possible; to actualize what is possible. It means to be creative of otherness, to produce what is different and new. It means to create and appreciate the good; the good that consists in being, existence, and order, but also of process, freedom, choice, and becoming. The good is the power to be and to be alive and to become what one can yet be.

The work of the Spirit includes the creation, sustaining, nourishing, and flourishing of life. And so to participate in the work of the Spirit is to take part in the making and the sustaining and fulfilling of life, together with all the conditions that make for life. Thus, to be spiritual is to be life-giving, life-nurturing, and life-saving! But no life is without form and body; it can only be earthly, bodily, and physically. To participate in the work of the spirit includes the forming and sustaining of the earthly, the bodily, the physical, the material, and so the this-worldly. One cannot be spiritual without being secular. But bodily life exists only in community and community requires leadership, order, law, justice, peace, and togetherness. One cannot be spiritual without engaging in what makes for community! Withdrawing from community is a most unspiritual act!

But being, existence, life, freedom, and community are also distorted and corrupted in the world. The Spirit is at work to preserve the good of God's creation by judging sin and evil and executing this activity through a winnowing process that is effectively at work in renewing and restoring things to what they are or should be. Thus, to participate in the work of the Spirit is to take part in this evaluating and winnowing and renewing process! Furthermore, the Spirit is the Spirit of promise that creates a future with hope! The making of hope is the work of the Spirit. To take part in the work of the Spirit is to be hopeful; it is to anticipate a future dawning upon the present, creating for it new possibilities that can be actualized by human participation! And finally, the proper place to practice spirituality is in this world. That means in one's life-world, in the specific milieu in which one lives his life, in one's daily activity of living, in one's own experience of this world. A life-world has an integrity and value that can only be protected and enjoyed *in the Spirit*, in the religaric bond that is precisely the Spirit. A spirituality that secularizes is participating in the coming of God's kingdom and doing his will "on earth as it is heaven."

I would have liked to include a chapter on the secular dimensions of Israel's worship as portrayed in the Psalms. But since this is already dealing with the *practice* of a spirituality that secularizes, and since the Psalms have become essentially a part of Christian worship, I decided to reserve discussing it in the volume dealing with the practice of spirituality that secularizes! It is obvious that my treatment of this kind of spirituality is still incomplete. When we come to the New Testament, which is the subject of the next volume, what we discover there is more radical and far-reaching than we have so far envisioned! Without the New Testament thrust, our treatment of the subject would be at best only a half-truth.

BIBLIOGRAPHY

Alexander, Denis. *Building The Matrix: Science and Faith in the 21st Century.* Oxford: Lion, 2001.

Anderson, Bernhard, W. *Contours of Old Testament Theology.* Minneapolis: Fortress, 1999.

———. *Creation Versus Chaos.* Philadelphia: Fortress, 1987.

Barbour, Ian G. *Nature, Human Nature, and God.* Minneapolis: Fortress, 2002.

Barrow, John D. *The Origin of the Universe.* New York: Harper Collins Basic Books, 1994.

Bass, Diana Butler. *Christianity After Religion.* New York: Harper Collins, 2012.

Best, Steven and Douglas Kellner. *Postmodern Theory.* New York: Guilford, 1991.

———. *The Postmodern Turn.* New York/London: Guilford, 1997.

Bond, H. Lawrence, trans. *Nicolas of Cusa: Selected Spiritual Writings.* New York: Paulist, 1997.

Bonting, Sjoerd L. *Creation and Double Chaos.* Minneapolis: Fortress, 2005.

Bracken, Joseph A. S. U. *The One in the Many: A Contemporary Reconstruction of the God-World Relationship.* Grand Rapids: Eerdmans, 2001.

Bright, John. *A History of Israel.* Philadelphia: Westminster, 1959.

Brueggemann, Walter. *A Commentary on Jeremiah: Exile and Homecoming.* Grand Rapids: Eerdmans, 1998.

———. *Deuteronomy.* Nashville: Abingdon, 2001.

———. *Genesis.* Atlanta: John Knox, 1982.

———. *A Social Reading of the Old Testament.* Edited by Patrick D. Miller. Minneapolis: Fortress, 1994.

———. *Theology of the Old Testament.* Minneapolis: Fortress, 1997.

———. *An Unsetting God.* Minneapolis: Fortress, 2009.

Buber, Martin. *Moses: The Revelation and the Covenant.* New York: Harper and Bros., 1946.

———. *The Eclipse of God.* New York: Harper and Bros., 1952.

———. *The Prophetic Faith.* New York: Harper and Bros., 1949.

Caputo, John D., ed. *Deconstruction in a Nutshell: A Conversation with Jacques Derrida.* New York: Fordham University Press, 1997.

Childs, Brevard S. *The Book of Exodus: A Critical, Theological Commentary.* Philadelphia: Westminster, 1974.

Chown, Marcus. *Afterglow of Creation.* Sausalito, CA: University Science Books, 1996.

Clayton, Philip and Arthur Peacocke, eds. *In Whom We Live and Move and Have Our Being: Pantheistic Reflections on God's Presence in a Scientific World.* Grand Rapids: Eerdmans, 2004.

Cobb, John B., Jr. *Spiritual Bankruptcy: A Prophetic Call to Action.* Nashville: Abingdon, 2010.

Collins, John J. *The Apocalyptic Imagination: An Introduction to Jewish Apocalyptic Literature,* 2nd ed. Grand Rapids: Eerdmans, 1998.

Cook, Stephen L. *Prophecy and Apocalypticism: The Post-Exilic Social Setting.* Minneapolis: Fortress, 1995.

Cox, Harvey. *The Future of Faith.* New York: Harper Collins, 2009.

Crenshaw, James L. *Old Testament Wisdom: An Introduction,* 3rd ed. Louisville: Westminster John Knox, 2010.

Darr, Katheryn Pfisterer, "The Book of Ezekiel." In *The New Interpreter's Bible,* 6:1075–1607. Nashville: Abingdon, 2001.

Davidson, Robert. *The Courage to Doubt.* London: SCM, 1983.

de Duve, Christian. *Life Evolving: Molecules, Mind, and Meaning.* Oxford: Oxford University Press, 2002.

Doran, Robert. "1 and 2 Maccabees." In *The New Interpreter's Bible,* 4:3–299. Nashville: Abingdon, 1996.

Eichrodt, Walther. *Theology of the Old Testament*, vols. 1 and 2. Translated by J. A. Baker. Philadelphia: Westminster, 1967.

Fox, Karen C., *The Big Bang Theory.* New York: John Wiley and Sons, 2002.

Fox, Matthew, and Rupert Sheldrake Rupert. *Natural Grace.* New York: Doubleday, 1997.

Fretheim, Terence E. *God and World in the Old Testament: A Relational Theology of Creation.* Nashville: Abingdon, 2005.

———., "The Book of Genesis." In *The New Interpreter's Bible,* 321–674. Nashville: Abingdon, 1994.

Green, Arthur, ed. *Jewish Spirituality, I: From the Bible Through the Middle Ages.* New York: Crossroad, 1966.

Grenz, Stanley J. *A Primer on Postmodernism.* Grand Rapids: Eerdmans, 1996.

Hanson, Paul D. *Old Testament Apocalyptic.* Nashville: Abingdon, 1987.

———. *The Dawn of Apocalyptic,* rev. ed. Philadelphia: Fortress, 1979.

Haught, John F. *Making Sense of Evolution.* Louisville: Westminster John Knox, 2010.

Hawking, Stephen. *A Brief History of Time.* New York: Bantam Dell, 1988.

Hawking, Stephen and Leonard Mlodinow. *The Grand Design.* New York: Bantam Books, 2010.

Heschel, Abraham J. *The Prophets: An Introduction*, vol. 1. New York: Harper, 1962.

Hick, John. *The Fifth Dimension: An Exploration of the Spiritual Realm.* Oxford: One World, 1999.

Hill, Craig C. *In God's Time: The Bible and the Future.* Grand Rapids: Eerdmans, 2002.

Hogan, Craig J. *The Little Book of the Big Bang.* New York: Springer-Verlag, 1998.

Janzen, J. Gerald. *Job: Interpretation.* Atlanta: John Knox, 1985.

Jones, Cheslyn, Geoffrey Wainwright and Edward Yarnold, S.J., eds. *The Study of Spirituality.* New York: Oxford University Press, 1986.

Kung, Hans. *The Beginning of All Things.* Grand Rapids: Eerdmans, 2007.

Lakeland, Paul. *Postmodernity.* Minneapolis: Fortress, 1997.

Macquarrie, John. *Heidegger and Christianity.* New York: Continuum, 1994.

McGinn, Bernard, John Meyendorf and Jean Leclercq, eds. *Christian Spirituality: Origins to the Twelfth Century.* New York: Crossroad, 1993.

McQuillan, Martin, ed. *Deconstruction: A Reader.* New York: Routledge, 2000.

Miles, Jack. *GOD: A Biography.* New York: Vintage Books, 1995.

Miller, Patrick D. "The Book of Jeremiah." In *The New Interpreter's Bible*, 6:555–926. Abingdon, 2001.

Moltmann, Jürgen. *God for a Secular Society.* Minneapolis: Fortress, 1999.

———. *The Source of Life.* Minneapolis: Fortress, 1997.

———. *The Spirit of Life.* Minneapolis: Fortress, 1992.

Murphy, Frederick J. "Introduction to Apocalyptic Literature." In *The New Interpreter's Bible,* 7:1-16. Nashville, Abingdon, 1996.

Peacocke, Arthur. *Paths from Science Towards God.* Oxford: Oneworld, 2001.

Perdue, Leo G. *Wisdom and Creation: The Theology of Wisdom Literature.* Nashville: Abingdon, 1994.

Peters, Ted. Sin: *Radical Evil in Soul and Society.* Grand Rapids: Eerdmans, 1994.

Peters, Ted and Martinez Hewlett. *Can You Believe in God and Evolution?* Nashville: Abingdon, 2006.

———. *Evolution from Creation to New Creation.* Nashville: Abingdon, 2003.

Peters, Ted and Martinez Hewlett. *Theological and Scientific Commentary on Darwin's Origin of Species*. Nashville: Abingdon, 2008.

Pleins, J. David. *The Social Visions of the Hebrew Bible: A Theological Introduction*. Louisville: Westminster John Knox, 2001.

Polkinghorne, John. *Belief in God in an Age of Science*. New Haven: Yale University Press, 1998.

———. *The Faith of a Physicist*. Princeton, New Jersey: Princeton University Press, 1994.

———. *The God of Hope and the End of the World*. New Haven: Yale University Press, 2002.

———. *Testing Scripture: A Scientist Explores the Bible*. Grand Rapids: Brazos, 2010.

Preuss, Horst Dietrich. *Old Testament Theology*, I–II, Louisville: Westminster John Knox, 1995, 1996.

———.*Old Testament Theology*, 1–2. Translated by D. M. G. Stalker. New York: Harper & Row Publishers, 1962, 1965.

Reddish, Mitchell G., ed. *Apocalyptic Literature: A Reader*. Nashville: Abingdon, 1990.

Ricoeur, Paul. *Figuring the Sacred: Religion, Narrative, and Imagination*. Minneapolis: Fortress, 1995.

———. *The Symbolism of Evil*. Translated from the French by Emerson Buchanan. Boston: Beacon, 1967.

Rolston, Holmes III. *Genes, Genesis and God: Values and Their Origins in Natural and Human History*. Cambridge: Cambridge University Press, 1999.

Rowland, Christopher. *Christian Origins: From Messianic Movement to Christian Religion*. Minneapolis: Augsburg, 1985.

Russel, D. S. *The Method and Message of Jewish Apocalyptic*. London: SCM, 1964.

Safranski; Rudiger. *Martin Heidegger: Between Good and Evil*. Cambridge, MA: Harvard University Press, 1998.

Sanders, E. P. *Paul and Palestinian Judaism*. Minneapolis: Fortress, 1977.

Seitz, Christopher R. "The Book of Isaiah 40-66." In *The New Interpreter's Bible,* 6:309–552. Abingdon, 2001.

Smith-Christopher, Daniel L. "The Book of Daniel." In *The New Interpreter's Bible*, 7:19–152. Nashville: Abingdon, 1996.

Snook, Lee E. *What in the World Is God Doing?* Minneapolis: Fortress, 1999.

Taylor, Charles. *A Secular Age*. Cambridge, MA: The Belknap Press of Harvard University Press, 2007.

———. *Sources of the Self: The Making of Modern Identity*. Cambridge, MA: Harvard University Press, 1989.

Taylor, John V. *The Go-Between God*. London: SCM, 1972.

Tilby, Angela. *Soul: God, Self and the New Cosmology.* New York: Doubleday, 1992.

Tucker, Gene M. "The Book of Isaiah 1-39." In *The New Interpreter's Bible*, 6:27-305. Abingdon, 2001.

Von Rad, Gerhard. *The Message of the Prophets,* San Francisco: Harper & Row, 1965.

Ward, James M. *Thus Says the Lord: The Message of the Prophets.* Nashville: Abingdon, 1991.

Wakefield, Gordon S., ed. *The Westminster Dictionary of Christian Spirituality.* London: SCM, 1983.

Welker, Michael. *God the Spirit.* Minneapolis: Fortress, 1994.

Westermann, Claus. *Isaiah 40-66: A Commentary.* Philadelphia: Westminster, 1969.

———. *Genesis: An Introduction*. Translated by John J. Scullion, S.J. Minneapolis: Fortress, 1992.

———. *Genesis 1-11: A Continental Commentary,* trans. by John J. Scullion, S.J. Minneapolis: Fortress, 1994.

———. *Roots of Wisdom.* Louisville: Westminster John Knox, 1995.

White, Michael and John Gribbin. *Stephen Hawking: A Life in Science.* Penguin, 1992.

Worthing, Mark William. *God, Creation, and Contemporary Physics.* Minneapolis: Fortress, 1996.

Zimmerli, Walther. *Old Testament Theology in Outline.* Translated by David E. Green. Edinburgh: T & T Clark, 1978.

CPSIA information can be obtained at www.ICGtesting.com
Printed in the USA
LVOW01s0030120315

430161LV00003B/3/P

9 781630 888374